P9-BIQ-484

CALIFORNIA
Real Estate Economics

Ignacio Gonzalez, Contributing Editor

Dearborn™
Real Estate Education

President: Dr. Andrew Temte
Chief Learning Officer: Dr. Tim Smaby
Executive Director, Real Estate Education: Melissa Kleeman-Moy
Development Editor: Julia Marti

CALIFORNIA REAL ESTATE ECONOMICS FIFTH EDITION
©2015 Kaplan, Inc.
Published by DF Institute, Inc., d/b/a Dearborn Real Estate Education
332 Front St. S., Suite 501
La Crosse, WI 54601

Printed in the United States of America
ISBN: 978-1-4754-2904-6
PPN: 1523-4107

CONTENTS

INTRODUCTION

From the Gold Rush days of 1849 to the explosive growth of the internet at the beginning of the 21st century, California's economic history has been one of constant change, growth, and prosperity. Originally a sparsely populated western frontier with fewer than 100,000 residents in 1850, California is now an extensively developed region whose population exceeds 38 million and whose economy ranks eighth in the world. California's gross domestic product exceeded the trillion-dollar mark in 1997—the first state to achieve this record. California is also the first state to top $1 trillion in personal income.

California is also a world technological and economic leader and an example of what the future has in store for the rest of the country. It has been the birthplace of many of the world's most significant technological innovations, from the aerospace industry to the personal computer to telecommunications and the internet and beyond. California serves as the model for economic innovation and prosperity.

California leads the nation in the production of fruits and vegetables. The state's most valuable crops—grapes, cotton, flowers, nuts, oranges, and dairy products—also contribute to the largest single share of farm income. The state also produces the major share of U.S. domestic wine. California's farms are highly productive as a result of good soil, a long growing season, and the use of modern agricultural methods. Much of the state's industrial production depends on the processing of farm produce and upon such local resources as petroleum, natural gas, lumber, cement, and sand and gravel.

Since World War II, however, manufacturing, notably of electronic equipment, computers, machinery, transportation equipment, and metal products, has increased enormously. Silicon Valley, located between Palo Alto and San Jose, so-called because it is the nation's leading producer of semiconductors, is also the focus of software development. California continues to be a major center for motion picture, television film, and related entertainment industries, especially in Hollywood.

California, like the rest of the nation in 2008–2009, was in the midst of a severe economic downturn. As a result, California experienced falling home prices and shrinking equity values in its real estate, and growing job losses almost devastated both the U.S. and California economies in 2008. Additionally, consumer and business spending, which is at the very core of the economy, also took a shift downward. The efforts of the U.S. government, including Congress, the Treasury Department, the Federal Reserve, and the White House to stimulate the economy appeared to have done little to excite and stimulate the economy, and, thus, economic output fell significantly in 2008. California experienced the highest unemployment rate (12.2% in August 2009) since 1940. Both the California and U.S. economies did not significantly improve until credit became much more available.

As we moved out of the "Great Recession," the U.S. unemployment rate has remained at 5.8%. U.S. total non-farm jobs rose by 321,000 in November 2014, the biggest increase since January 2012. California's unemployment rate remained unchanged in October 2014, at 7.3%. California's non-farm payroll employment grew by 41,500 jobs in October, higher than the 22,500 monthly average for the first nine months of 2014. Relative to the real estate market, the median sales price of an existing single-family home fell in October 2014 by 2.3% to $450,620. Compared to the prior year, the median price was up by 5.4%.

California's strong entrepreneurial spirit, world class seaports, transportation, and university systems, coupled with an existing high technology base developed in part from the defense industry, have contributed to California's venerable position as a world leader.

For many people, the prospect of reading a book about economic principles is not attractive, even when the focus is on their own industry, or even their own state. *California Real Estate Economics* attempts to address this widespread "econo-phobia" by presenting classic and substantive information in a timely, engaging, and understanding way. If we are to succeed in our professions, we must learn to understand our past and prepare for our future. We need to understand how real estate fits into the overall economy of the state and why it is so important to our economic vitality.

A Look Back at Trends in California

By January 2007, the population had increased to 37.7 million, and by July 2008, California's population had surpassed 38 million, which represented a growth rate of 1.6%, adding 436,000 new residents between July 2007 and July 2008. Since April 2000, the State of California has grown by almost 4.3 million people for an overall growth rate of 12.6%. The state's nine largest counties (Los Angeles, San Diego, Orange, Riverside, San Bernardino, Santa Clara, Alameda, Sacramento, and Contra Costa) each have over one million residents. They are home to 70% of Californians. Placer, Imperial, and Riverside Counties had the largest percentage increases in population, each growing more than 2%.

In 2002, the California Association of REALTORS® noted in its monthly affordability index measures that the percentage of households able to afford a medium priced home in San Francisco was about 16% followed by Contra Costa County at 17%. Overall, the San Francisco Bay Area averaged about 25%, while Los Angeles County came in at 36%. The high cost of housing can be attributed to the economic growth that California enjoyed during the late 1990s and into 2000. During this period, California experienced an increase of 2 million jobs, boosting the economic vitality of the state. With unemployment at the lowest level since the 1960s, wages rose, and poverty fell along with unemployment to a record level of 4.5%. However, housing prices continued to outpace people's income. In 2005, the cost of housing throughout California rose, with the median price of a home being $538,770 in October 2005, while the annual income needed to purchase a median-priced home in California stood at $128,480, based on an average mortgage rate of 6.03%. At the conclusion of 2005, the most affordable region of California was the High Desert region with an affordability index of 25%, and the least affordable region was the Northern Wine Country at 7%. Because of this, only one in four households was able to afford a typical home in California. However, by July 2009, primarily due to the national and state recession, the statewide median price stood at $285,480. The recession resulted in the median price falling from $560,270 in 2007 to $346,750 in 2008, which is a 38.1% decrease.

However, by 2014, California's housing market had vastly improved, and by October 2014, the median price was now at $450,620, a significant improvement from 2008. By the beginning of the final quarter of 2014,

California's unemployment rate was at 7.3%, and non-farm payroll grew by 41,500 jobs in October 2014. Additionally, more than 126,000 building permits were issued in October 2014 for the construction of new single-family homes, and 93,000 were also issued for multi-family units.

Despite recent job growth, home appreciation, and more Californians going back to work, many people are still forced to commute long distances in order to afford their first home. Because of this, urban sprawl has continued to be an issue in all parts of the state. Due to the urban sprawl California has endured, there has been a movement by urban planners, environmentalists, and government to practice smart growth techniques, which, in essence, borrow from European and old world planning by implementing mix-use developments and maximizing the state's resources, including land. The vision is that we in California will be able to live and work in the same community without spending hours commuting and, thus, reducing congestion. With no doubt, this trend or desire will continue to be the paradigm for years to come. In 2015, California also embarked on the first phases of the construction of the State's high-speed rail system that will link the San Francisco Bay Area with Southern California. The initial portions of the route will commence in the Central Valley between Madera and Fresno.

Features

This book was designed to take advantage of a variety of instructional design principles and content features, all of which are intended to make it more accessible to students. Page layouts are clean and easy to read and include generous right margins for note-taking. There are numerous illustrations, and all graphic elements have been designed for the greatest possible clarity. Throughout the book, we have tried to ensure that the language is as clear and direct as it can be.

This book has 17 units. The units are arranged in a logical order, from broadest principles down to specific investment applications.

In addition to this book's innovative content and structure, other features have been included to enhance the learning experience:

Learning Objectives

Learning objectives tell readers what they should get out of each chapter's discussion.

A Closer Look . . .

This feature provides relevant real-world, historical, or background information that helps enhance readers' understanding of sometimes difficult issues.

The Next Step

Sometimes a unit's focus will shift to a different direction. This feature alerts readers to such changes within a unit and provides a preview of the next unit's coverage.

In California

Several units of this book are dedicated to California's unique economy. In more general units, however, information about California is sometimes included. This icon lets readers easily locate California-specific information.

Summary

Each unit includes a comprehensive, highlighted summary of its most important information, provided to both reinforce learning and help make studying and review easier.

Unit Quiz

Each unit ends with a quiz covering its material. The questions have been completely revised to reflect the information covered in a challenging and yet constructive way. An **answer key** is included in the back of the book, including page references for each correct answer.

Appendices

We've included some interesting and valuable material at the end of the book, too:

- Appendix I: California Facts
- Appendix II: California Counties
- Appendix III: Websites

Statistical Information Included From the U.S. Census

This text has included the most current information available, including information released by the U.S. Census Bureau. However, it should be noted that the U.S. Census is completely updated only once every 10 years, with all aspects of the census considered and made available. The Census Bureau makes every effort to periodically update its information; however, not all information may be available. Some information may not be completely available at this time due to timing and release of information. Both the author and the publisher encourage the student/reader to constantly check the U.S. Census Bureau's as well as the California Department of Finance's websites for any changes and updates, as information relative to both economics and real estate is ever-changing.

Our goal throughout this book is to provide you with the most current, complete, and relevant information about basic economic principles and the real estate economy. We've tried to make what can be dry information come alive by showing how economic theory is played out in the real world.

TO THE STUDENT: WHY STUDY REAL ESTATE ECONOMICS?

The fundamental question for you right now is, "Why should *I* study real estate economics?" For real estate professionals, the answer is clear: real estate is a constantly changing market that is formed, defined, and manipulated by economic forces on a local, regional, state, national, and even worldwide level. In a highly competitive environment, the players who understand what the rules are that govern the game, how the rules work, and how they can be manipulated will be the ones who not only survive but prosper. Real estate economics is not a dry, theoretical field of academic study for Nobel laureates only: it's the world in which you work and live.

ABOUT THE AUTHOR

Contributing editor Ignacio Gonzalez is a California-licensed real estate broker, a professional land-use planner, and an adjunct instructor/lecturer and Real Estate Coordinator for Mendocino Community College in Ukiah, California. He has been a real estate educator for over 25 years and currently teaches classes in real estate principles, real estate practices, real estate economics, finance, appraisal, and property management as well as land-use planning and home inspection. In 1999, he was the recipient of the Mendocino College President's Award for Outstanding Faculty. He has also taught real estate courses for Anthony Schools in the San Francisco Bay Area and College of the Redwoods. Gonzalez is also a GRI instructor teaching classes in environmental hazards, land use, and construction throughout California. Mr. Gonzalez is currently a consulting land-use planner to government agencies, providing land-use planning services throughout California. Previously he served as the Planning Director for both Mendocino and Santa Clara counties. In 2012, he was appointed by the Governor as Chairman of the State Mining and Geology Board, where he served until January 2015.

ACKNOWLEDGMENTS

Like a real estate transaction, this textbook is the product of teamwork and cooperation among skilled and knowledgeable individuals. The author, the publisher, instructors, and other professionals have worked together to help make *California Real Estate Economics* the best introductory real estate economics textbook in California. The participation of these professionals and their willingness to share their expertise and experience is greatly appreciated.

For his insightful and detailed review in preparation for this Fifth Edition, we would like to thank Edward M. Cohan, MBA, JD, East Los Angeles College (ELAC).

We would also like to recognize those who helped with previous editions of *California Real Estate Economics*:

Thurza B. Andrew, GRI

Thomas B. Gruenig

Howard E. Harris

Fred L. Martinez

Kartik Subramaniam

Martha R. Williams, JD

INTRODUCTION TO ECONOMIC SYSTEMS AND PRINCIPLES

KEY TERMS

capitalism	expansionism	mixed economies
consumption	feudalism	resources
communism	goods	services
distribution	industrialization	socialism
economics	labor productivity	value
economy	laissez faire	wealth
employment	mercantilism	

LEARNING OBJECTIVES

■ Distinguish among different types of historical and modern economic systems

■ Understand how capitalism evolved into its present form

■ Explain how the U.S. economy operates

WHAT IS AN ECONOMIC SYSTEM?

The Study of Real Estate Economics

Real estate economics analyzes national, regional, statewide, city, and neighborhood trends. This allows us to improve our understanding of the various effects these trends have on the real estate market, both locally and regionally. By studying real estate economics, we gain a better understanding of how a market establishes the price of goods and services and how the distribution of these goods and services in the economy affects the real estate market.

An **economy** is any system designed for the production, **distribution**, and **consumption** of necessary and desired goods and services. **Economics** is the social science that studies, describes, and analyzes that process.

As we'll see later in this unit, there is a wide range of economic systems operating in the world. Regardless of their differences, however, all economic systems share these three basic functions:

- Production

- Distribution

- Consumption

These three words form the basis of all economic systems and are the central focus of the science of economics.

Operation

Economic activities draw on the special capabilities of the human species. The means and arrangements that support the operation of economic systems include:

- *Tool*—Humans are inventive toolmakers and tool users. The creation and use of tools makes the production and distribution of goods and services more efficient.

- *Techniques and knowledge*—Human beings are learners; we learn from experience and develop techniques in response to what we learn; that's how we build bodies of knowledge. The progressive evolution of human knowledge creates both greater efficiencies of production and greater demand for new and better goods and services.

- *Social arrangements*—Humans are social animals. We accomplish tasks by organizing ourselves, by cooperating, by taking on specialized roles, and by acting in accordance with rules that the group has agreed upon.

A CLOSER LOOK   The people of a South Sea Island depend on fish in their diet. The fish are caught in a lagoon using canoes and nets (***tools***). They have developed a method of throwing the nets (***technique***) to ensure the greatest catch. The islanders have accumulated a detailed understanding over many generations (***knowledge***) about which fish are desirable. Traditional social arrangements govern who does the fishing (***roles***) and how the catch is shared by the community (***rules***).

The satisfaction of needs and wants almost always requires more than tools, techniques, knowledge, and social arrangements, however. Human effort is required because most of the things needed and wanted are not immediately at hand and freely available. Planning, cooperation, skill, and effort are required to make any economic system function.

Wealth

In economic terms, the word *wealth* does not refer merely to riches. Rather, wealth is anything that contributes to human comfort and enjoyment. Strictly speaking, wealth can only be obtained through some form of labor and is characterized by being desirable by others. That is, wealth is something that is perceived by others as having value, which is evidenced by being sold or exchanged for other goods or services. Wealth, then, requires a community of at least two people and an object that is owned by one and desired by the other.

Adding Value

Wealth is not limited to what currently exists. Human productive activities can create wealth by adding **value** to existing goods or services. Often a productive process has many steps, and value is added at each step, as illustrated in Figure 1.1.

FIGURE 1.1:   Adding Economic Value

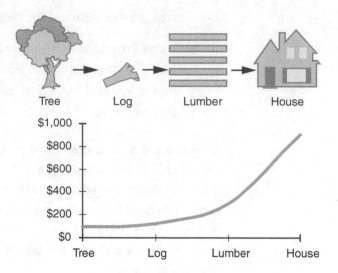

In Figure 1.1, we see how a tree is cut down, the log is cut into lumber, and the lumber is used to build a house. Note how the value of the same material (wood) rises at each stage of the process. After it is cut down, its value increases only slightly. At this point, the wood's value is only *potential value*; it is a raw material waiting to become something else.

Once the log is milled into lumber, however, the value of the wood more than doubles. Once the lumber is assembled into a house, its value skyrockets. We are speaking here, of course, in purely economic terms; the tree may have other value besides economic—it has aesthetic value in its appearance, environmental value in its biological functions, and other intangible values that are real but of less interest to an economist.

Goods and Services

Wealth is used to obtain goods and services. This trading of wealth—whether composed of beads or coins or stock certificates—for goods or services defines economic activity.

The term *goods* usually refers to material things that are perceived to have monetary or exchange value. Here again, as in the case of wealth, perception is everything. Clothing, automobiles, and wheat have economic value only if they are perceived as desirable.

Services, on the other hand, are immaterial. The term *service* refers to activities that are perceived as having monetary or exchange value. Examples of services include legal advice, health care, education, and entertainment. If you are paid a wage, salary, or commission for doing your job, you are receiving money in exchange for your services.

Needs and Desires

The goods and services that are created and distributed through the economy can be classified as those that are necessary for *survival* and those that are desirable for *quality of life*.

Biological Needs   Certain resources are absolutely necessary for human biological survival. These are

- food,

- air,

- water, and

- shelter.

A person who lacks these essential needs for any significant length of time will not survive. They are necessary to life.

Socially Defined Needs   There are other needs, however, that are not vital to an individual's physical survival. Nonetheless, they are still necessary. These are the needs that are dictated by the society in which one lives. Clothing, for example, may not be strictly required for physical survival in some climates, particularly in parts of California. However, social conventions in many societies (including our own) demand that individuals wear clothing when walking around in public places. Failure to comply with such a rule will not be tolerated by the society, so clothing is a socially defined need; while not necessary to biological survival, it is necessary to social survival.

Socially Defined Desires   In any society, but especially in consumer cultures such as our own, individuals may want things that are not necessary to their social or physical survival. This may or may not be a natural human condition. In Western industrial societies, people are taught to desire many of the goods and services they purchase. Through advertising and marketing, consumers are shown how desirable a product is and are encouraged to possess or use it.

Modern industrial economies derive much of their energy from creating and then supplying consumer wants. Throughout the industrialized world, "quality of life" is equated with material prosperity and leisure.

Such a view is not, of course, universal. Throughout history, groups and individuals have rejected materialism and consumer-style culture and have attempted to build simple communities based on ensuring the minimum essentials of life for their members. Such societies, however, have rarely been popular on a mass scale.

Rules

Rules are established principles of behavior. They are guides or regulations agreed upon by groups of individuals among themselves or imposed by an authority. Rules define the rights and responsibilities of people in society. At their best, rules express a social agreement about what is right, what is fair, what is wrong, and what is permitted. Rules also establish mechanisms for their own enforcement.

All economies are governed by rules established and enforced by the society in which they operate. The social rules that govern the functioning of economic systems may be customary and informal, or they may be written into formal law. They may be enforced by individuals, by social pressure, or by the state.

A BRIEF HISTORY OF ECONOMIC SYSTEMS

An **economy** is a system designed for the production, distribution, and consumption of necessary and desired goods and services. Throughout history, a variety of economic systems have been invented, tried, and rejected in favor of new systems. Some have been successful while others have been disastrous failures.

Human history is not a simple timeline. The overview provided here is not intended to be a complete history of the world or even to offer a substantive view of economic history. It is provided, however, to give you some idea of how economic theories and systems have evolved over time, specifically with regard to the U.S. economy.

Hunter-Gatherer Economics

The fossil record shows us that the earliest humans, called hunter-gatherers, lived by hunting and foraging for food. Foraging bands had to cover a wide territory—as much as a 20-mile radius—in order to sustain the small nomadic communities.

Agriculture

A revolutionary development took place between about 10,000 B.C. in the Middle East; some of the nomadic people settled down. Here, people began to develop agricultural technologies to control the production of their food rather than simply gather it. Agriculture requires planting, and planting meant that people stayed in one place, tending crops and, eventually, domesticating animals.

While the hunter-gatherers had congregated in small bands, the agricultural communities tended to be much larger, supported by the surpluses that resulted from controlled food production.

By 4,000 B.C. populous societies with centralized governments had emerged. With a settled life and economic surpluses, complex political structures grew. With the end of subsistence farming, literacy, specialized occupations, art, and architecture flourished.

Trade and Conquest

As agricultural technologies improved and surpluses fed rapidly growing populations, communities found it necessary to expand their geographical boundaries. Exploration gave rise to increased trade with neighboring agrarian cultures.

Economies based on agriculture and trade were easy prey for the armies of a succession of empire-builders, who gained control of large expanses of territory through military force. The empires and expansionist nation-states such as ancient Egypt, Greece, Phoenicia, and Rome served as resource allocators for their neighbors by providing established markets for local natural **resources** like dyes, cedar logs, and shellfish, as well as agricultural products. As the empires grew, the variety of products available rapidly expanded.

Feudalism

Following the collapse of the Western Roman Empire, a complex economic system called **feudalism** developed and flourished. Based on a complex hierarchy of loyalties, services, and land grants originating with the king and supported by a large mass of landless peasantry, feudalism dominated Europe through the end of the 13th century. So deeply did feudalism influence the society and culture of medieval England that modern real property law in both Britain and the United States still reflects much of its terminology and principles (see Figure 1.2).

FIGURE 1.2:   Modern Real Estate's Links to Feudalism

MODERN	FEUDAL
Bundle of Legal Rights	Transfer of land evidenced by the passing of a handful of earth or a bundle of sticks from a tree on the property
Agency	Master-servant relationship, in which servant owed absolute loyalty
Fee Ownership	Feud or fief: an inheritable estate in land held on the condtion that the holder perform some service for the grantor

Rise of the Merchants

As urban culture slowly re-emerged during the late Middle Ages, it was accompanied by a growth in the urban merchant class—a new member of a feudal society formerly composed strictly of the aristocracy, the clergy, and peasants. The new merchant class had little need for the land-based relationships of feudalism and was more interested in maintaining a stable climate in which trade could operate freely. As the strength of the urban merchant class grew, the traditional agrarian feudal hierarchy weakened in the face of this new **mercantilism**.

Exploration and Colonialism

The search for new markets for a growing surplus of goods led to global exploration. The colonial policy was based on creating self-sustaining markets by importing raw materials and valuable resources from the colonies to be converted to finished goods for resale back to the colonies and to other trading partners. As the American Revolution demonstrated, however, there were limits to the colonies' willingness to be exploited without sharing in the economic benefits of international trade.

Adam Smith   Not only was 1776 the year of the American Revolution but it also marked the publication of one of the most influential books in economic history, Adam Smith's *The Wealth of Nations*. Written as a reaction against the dominant economic theory of his time, mercantilism, Smith's book essentially marks the foundation of modern capitalism.

Mercantilism, according to Smith, was flawed in its assumption that a country's wealth was measured by the amount of gold and silver in the government's treasury. Rather, wrote Smith, wealth should be measured by a nation's annual production. Smith's ideal economic system was governed by two forces: the participants' self-interest and the demands of competition. The action of these two forces Smith called "the unseen hand of the market." Smith was convinced that the highest good of both the nation and the individual was best served by permitting the unseen hand to operate freely, with a minimum of intervention by government. This approach, called **laissez faire** or "hands off" economics, assumes that a free marketplace will be self-policing and maximally profitable.

The Industrial Revolution

Between about 1750 and 1850, the adaptation of fossil fuels for industrial use led to a flurry of new mechanical inventions that turned Europe from a collection of farms and small cities into a humming mechanized metropolis. Factory-building surged, and smoke from what the poet William Blake called the "Satanic mills" darkened the skies and rained soot on the cities. This industrialization ushered in a merchant class of factory owners who prospered while the factory workers' quality of life declined. Wages were low as mechanization reduced the number of necessary workers, and conditions in the new factories and factory towns were far from pleasant or healthy.

Political Revolutions

A combination of social and economic factors—the excesses of industrialization, the disparity between owners and workers, and the erosion of monarchies—led to wide-ranging social changes sparked by the Industrial Revolution.

The rise of democracy and the labor movement led to a more equitable allocation of resources among workers, as well as an improvement in working conditions and wages. These reforms were far from universal, however, and in many countries the tensions created by industrialization led to more violent reactions.

Karl Marx   The author of the *Communist Manifesto* (1848) and *Das Kapital* (1867) is another significant figure in economic history. While Adam Smith had prophesied the free-market capitalism that flourished during the

Industrial Revolution, Marx observed the darker side of the reality. Industrialization, according to Marx, exaggerated the normal fluctuations in the economy, creating bigger, more frequent, and for workers, more disastrous depressions. Because wages did not accurately reflect the owners' profits, Marx felt that the surplus value that the workers added to goods was being exploited by the capitalists for their personal profit. Marx's view was not pretty. According to his theory of *dialectical materialism*, capitalism would inevitably create greater and greater burdens for workers until they rose up in revolution, seized the means of production, and ended their exploitation by establishing collective ownership in a socialist society.

Roots of the Modern U.S. Economy

Prior to the colonization of North America by Europeans, the native population of the continent did little to disturb the abundant natural resources that this country possessed. The quantity of resources available for exploitation made for rapid settlement and expansion by Europeans.

The colonial movement was led by England, France, and Spain during the 17th and 18th centuries. Raw materials from this continent were exchanged for finished goods from the occupying nations, in keeping with the prevailing mercantile theory. Cleared fields, villages, and roads soon replaced much of the wilderness. The exploitation of the English colonies by the home government led directly to the American Revolution.

The New Nation   Economic activity had its first restraints under the provisions of the U.S. Constitution, established in 1791. Following the Revolution, the former colonies had remained independent of one another, only loosely tied by the Articles of Confederation. After the enactment of the Constitution, the former colonies were unified with a common currency and without taxes or tariffs between states; a true common market was created.

Certain economic powers were granted to the central government: the regulation of foreign trade and commerce, the printing of money, and the granting of patents and copyrights. A central postal authority ensured continuous and reliable communication.

Divergent Philosophies   The Founding Fathers were, however, not entirely unified in their vision of the new nation. There was considerable disagreement among the ranks of the framers of the Constitution about what form the new society should take. The argument was personified by two divergent points of view:

- *Thomas Jefferson* believed in small farms, an independent press, and a weak decentralized government.

- *Alexander Hamilton* looked toward an industrialized society bolstered by high tariffs and a strong centralized government.

The debate between the Jeffersonians and the Hamiltonians was intense and long-lived. Today, however, it is clear that Hamilton's view, in large part, prevailed.

Expansionism   In the 19th century, land surveys were undertaken to stake out new territories in anticipation of admission of new states when adequate population had settled in the area. An infrastructure of canals, roads, and railroads facilitated the westward transport of goods and people, and the abundance of land lured settlers to seek their fortune beyond the Appalachians. This type of policy, advocating territorial gains, is known as **expansionism**.

The continuing conflict between visions of the nation was played out in the movement west. Many of the pioneers shared the Jeffersonian distaste for large cities and pervasive government regulation of commercial activities. The move west was partly spurred by the settlers' desire for isolation and for a more pure freedom from social and economic constraints on their behavior.

Industrialization   In the 19th century, the United States began to **industrialize**. Cotton from the south was made into finished goods by mills in New England. Iron ore mining began in the 1850s in the Great Lakes area followed at the end of that decade by the discovery of oil in Pennsylvania.

As there was little control of the production, allocation, and distribution of wealth within the country, enterprising individuals were able to seize control of key economic resources. At the top of the pyramid were Andrew Carnegie, who had a stranglehold on the steel industry, John D. Rockefeller in oil, and Leland Stanford in the railroad business. The rise of monopolies spurred greater government regulation of the U.S. economy through enactment of antitrust laws and the breaking up of monopolistic enterprises. The government was concerned that the growing power of the monopolies created a concentration of wealth and influence in a few people and severely hindered competition and a free market.

Labor Movements As was the case throughout the industrialized nations, the rise of factories and industry also spurred the growth of organized labor. The U.S. labor movement grew in visibility and power with establishment of the American Federation of Labor (AFLA) in the 1880s by Samuel Gompers and the Congress of Industrial Organizations (CIO) in the 1930s.

The Great Depression and the New Deal The stock market crash in October 1929 and its aftermath was probably the darkest economic period in U.S. history. Unemployment rose to catastrophic levels, and the nation's social structure was severely tested. Through a series of reforms initiated by the *New Deal* program of President Franklin D. Roosevelt, a variety of new government agencies and programs were established as a means of stabilizing and revitalizing the economy. These included the Federal Deposit Insurance Corporation (FDIC) to regulate savings, the Social Security programs, and the Federal Housing Administration (FHA). The Civilian Conservation Corps and the Public Works Administration were examples of activities undertaken by the government to provide employment in various works projects that are still enjoyed by our citizens today.

The Second World War not only defeated fascism in Europe, it elevated the U.S. economy to a position of preeminent strength in the world. The nation experienced unprecedented prosperity in the years after the war and was lifted out of the lingering effects of the Depression.

Modern Economics

The second half of the 20th century in the United States has been defined by two rival, but related, economic theories: Keynesian and monetarist.

In 1936, the British economist John Maynard Keynes published the *General Theory of Employment, Interest and Money*. Essentially, Keynes rejected the conventional wisdom that full employment was the natural state of a stable economy. Left alone, Keynes wrote, the economy could operate in a stable state that tolerated a significant level of permanent unemployment. Keynes argued in favor of government intervention to stimulate the economy in order to create full employment. This was a radical rejection of traditional capitalist theory. It dominated American economic policy through the 1960s.

The monetarists, on the other hand, continued to advocate an unfettered free market. Led by economists such as Milton Friedman and Arthur Laffer, monetarists contend that the only legitimate role of government is to create and preserve an environment in which a free market can operate with complete freedom. Monetarists, as their name suggests, look to a steadily increasing supply of money as the key to economic stability. They reject any government actions that interfere with the supply of money (such as raising or lowering interest rates to achieve certain social, political, or economic goals). The monetarists and supply-side economists of the 1980s view the free market as the best tool for defining and creating social good.

THE NEXT STEP In this brief historical discussion, we've already alluded to the principal tension underlying economic theory and history: the role of government in defining or controlling the operation of a free market. In the next section, we'll examine the distinction between the two prevailing economic systems in the world today, capitalism and socialism, as they exemplify this tension.

CAPITALISM AND SOCIALISM: THEORY AND PRACTICE

In the modern world, there are a variety of economic systems ranging from simple barter economies, in which goods and services are traded directly, to complex international market economies. They all lie, however, on a broad spectrum between two fundamental economic theories (Figure 1.3):

1. *Pure capitalism:* the complete freedom of individuals to engage in the three essential economic activities without interference from regulatory authorities

2. *Pure socialism:* the ownership, management, and control of all means of production and distribution by the community

FIGURE 1.3:   The Economic Spectrum

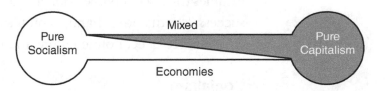

Capitalism

Hand in hand with the industrial revolution, the concept of capitalism took shape. **Capitalism** is a market-driven economic theory fueled by the independent forces of supply and demand (discussed in detail in Unit 2). The major components of this system in its purest form are:

- *private ownership* of the means of production and distribution through which individuals have the right to own, control, and dispose of their property;

- *individual enterprise*, which is the private ownership of the majority of a nation's businesses as well as the private ownership and free control of the resources used to manufacture products;

- *the profit motive*, or the desire for personal gain that inspires individuals to take risks to produce the goods and services desired by the population (this is very characteristic of the California economy where many individuals left their employers in the late 1990s to start their own businesses; any of these individuals ultimately provided consulting services to their former employers);

- *free competition*, which allows buyers and sellers to compete equally and freely among one another to fulfill the needs of the consumer and the producers; and

- *unregulated markets*, or **laissez faire**, which holds that government should not interfere in the economic affairs of a nation.

As we have learned, capitalism's basic philosophy of free and open, unregulated markets was formalized by Adam Smith (a Scottish economics professor) in 1776, in his work, *The Wealth of Nations*. Adam Smith believed the "hands off" approach, or *laissez faire*, would stimulate the production of goods and services without government interference. Capitalism is based on free economic interaction between individuals. The capitalist assumes the *risk* of competition and is entitled to reap the rewards of market success. On the other hand, capitalism can be viewed as "hard-hearted" in its tolerance of economic failure and inequality.

Socialism

To understand **socialism** more clearly, we must understand the roots of socialism. The father of socialism, Karl Marx, wrote *Das Kapital* in 1867, in which he stated that capitalism would fail primarily because capitalists were motivated by profit and would continually pay the labor force low wages in order to attain greater wealth. This, in turn, would thrust workers into abject poverty. Marx further theorized that the impoverished workers would revolt and overthrow the capitalists and seize the wealth on behalf of the workers. Marx believed in a classless society, with the government owning all of the resources and major industries on behalf of the people. Today's modern socialism and even communism have been derived from the writings of Karl Marx.

It should be noted that the development of the socialistic economic system was the direct result of the excess of unregulated capitalism experienced by impoverished and exploited workers during the industrial revolution. In its purest form, socialism is a *command economy* (the market responds to commands from above). Under socialism, the government makes the economic decisions on how and what is to be produced as well as setting the prices for goods and services. This was very true of the former Soviet Union where the state controlled prices. Under socialism, the consumer does not influence the economics of a nation.

The major defining components of socialism are as follows:

- *Public or collective ownership* of the means of production and distribution
- *Regulated enterprise*
- Economic policies reflecting *social/political policies*
- *Economic equality* as a goal
- Resources that are administered and distributed in the *common interest*

Communism

In a strict sense, **communism** is a stage of economic development said to occur when all classes in society have been absorbed into the proletariat. In this society, the state (government) would have withered away and each person would contribute according to ability and receive according to needs. This utopia envisioned by Karl Marx was seen to be the stage of economic development that follows capitalism and socialism.

Mixed Economies

Pure capitalism breeds inequality; pure socialism's equality stifles innovation. What's the answer? The answer, as it has developed in the modern world, is the **mixed economy**—neither socialism nor capitalism but a mix of elements of both. In today's world, there are no pure market economies and no pure command economies.

Look at Figure 1.4. The vertical axis defines a spectrum of government intervention in an economy, from total control to laissez faire. The horizontal axis describes whether the market is based on socialism's policy of protected equality or on capitalist principles of individual responsibility and risk-taking.

FIGURE 1.4:   Modern Real Economic Systems

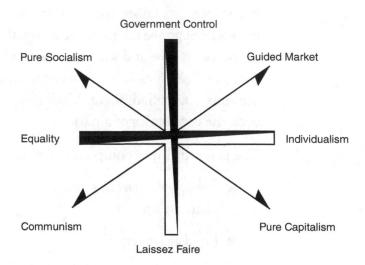

The old Union of Soviet Socialist Republics (USSR) might have been placed in the upper left quadrant, while the U.S. economy placed in the lower right. Note that both of them, being mixed economies, are pulled toward the center rather than toward the extremes of the spectrums. Also, note that communism and capitalism are both on the same end of the government intervention axis. This is because, under the theoretical economic system of communism, there is no government authority; all property is held and administered communally by a wholly self-directed society. In pure capitalism, all property is held by individuals but also in the absence of any government intrusion. This similarity between these two "opposed" economic systems is interesting.

THE NEXT STEP   That completes our overview of economic theory. In the final pages of this unit, we will present a general outline of the U.S. economy as it operates today.

THE U.S. ECONOMY TODAY

By examining the components of production, consumption, employment, and income, we can outline a profile of our national economy.

Note that income can be examined either as national income (employee compensation, proprietors' income, rental income, corporate profits, and net interest) or as personal income (after taxes and including transfer payments such as Social Security and public assistance, as well as wages, dividends, interest, and rents). The first is somewhat analogous to national product, and the second translates more directly into purchasing power.

Employment

As mentioned previously, the U.S. economy has been moving away from manufacturing as it becomes more service oriented. *Service oriented* is best described as an economy that is primarily driven by jobs that provide services to people, such as fast food, cleaning, and other support services.

Productivity is a measure of economic efficiency that shows how effectively economic inputs are converted into output. (Economists view productivity as the ability to produce more with the same or less input.) Relative to the production of goods and services, advances in productivity (such as technological advances) have resulted in a significant increase in national income. The U.S. economy has been able to produce more goods and services over time, not by requiring an increase in labor time, but by making production more efficient. According to the U.S. Bureau of Labor Statistics, output per hour of all persons (**labor productivity**) is the most commonly used productivity measure. Labor is an easily-identified input to virtually every production process. Since our economy is constantly changing, so is our approach to becoming much more productive. For example, many U.S. companies now outsource or offshore much of their production to overseas countries due to lower labor costs. Outsourcing and offshoring have the potential for greater effect on labor productivity at the industry level.

THE NEXT STEP   Now that you have a general idea about the history of economic theory and about what a market economy is, you're ready for more specific economic ideas. In the next unit, we'll look at how the forces of supply and demand interact in a market economy.

SUMMARY

- An **economy** is *any system designed for the production, distribution, and consumption of necessary and desired goods and services.* Economics is the social science that studies, describes, and analyzes that process.

- The word **wealth** describes *anything that contributes to human comfort and enjoyment* that is *perceived by others as having value,* evidenced by being *sold or exchanged for other goods or services.* This *trading of wealth for goods or services* defines economic activity.

- The **goods** and **services** that are created and distributed through the economy can be classified as those that are *necessary for survival* and those that are *desirable for quality of life.*

- Throughout history, a variety of economic systems have been invented, tried, and rejected. Some have been successful, while others have been disastrous failures. Some historical systems include hunter-gatherer, agricultural, feudal, mercantile, colonial, industrial, and monetarist.

- Modern economic systems lie on a spectrum between **capitalism** (a *market-driven* economic theory based on *private ownership* of the means of production and distribution) and **socialism** (a theory that calls for a *command-economy* with *public or collective ownership* of the means of production and distribution). Most world economies are **mixed economies**: a combination of these two theories with one or the other tending to dominate.

REVIEW QUESTIONS

1. What is the definition of *economics?*

2. Define the role of government in both a capitalistic and a socialistic economy.

3. What role does government play in your local real estate market?

4. Have social programs in your area primarily affected real estate in your area?

5. What types of government subsidy programs for the purchase or rent of real estate are in your community?

6. What types of businesses or industries have moved out of your area due to outsourcing or offshoring to other countries, and how has that affected your local economy?

7. What types of businesses has your community been able to attract in recent years, and in what kind of industries are they?

UNIT QUIZ

1. An economy is
   a. the social science that studies, describes, and analyzes any system of production, distribution, and consumption.
   b. any system designed for the production, distribution, and consumption of necessary and desired goods and services.
   c. anything that contributes to human comfort and enjoyment.
   d. any system based on a complex hierarchy of loyalties, services, and property transfers.

2. The trading of wealth for goods or services defines which of the following?
   a. Feudalism
   b. Production cycles
   c. Redistribution of wealth
   d. Economic activity

3. All of the following represent modern real estate's links to feudal economies *EXCEPT*
   a. agency.
   b. fee ownership.
   c. escrow closings.
   d. the bundle of legal rights.

4. Who of the following is considered the founder of modern capitalism?
   a. Karl Marx
   b. Adam Smith
   c. Thomas Jefferson
   d. John Maynard Keynes

5. Productivity is the measure of
   a. economic efficiency.
   b. outsourcing.
   c. offshoring.
   d. service oriented employment.

6.   Which of the following is a market-driven economic theory?
    a.   Socialism
    b.   Communism
    c.   Capitalism
    d.   Command economy

7.   Who of the following argued in favor of free and open, unregulated market economies?
    a.   Karl Marx in *Das Kapital*
    b.   John Maynard Keynes in the *General Theory of Employment, Interest and Money*
    c.   Thomas Jefferson in the *Preamble to the Declaration of Independence*
    d.   Adam Smith in *The Wealth of Nations*

8.   Economic equality is the goal of which type of economic system?
    a.   Capitalism
    b.   Socialism
    c.   Feudalism
    d.   Mercantilism

9.   The dominant economic system in the world today is best characterized as
    a.   capitalist.
    b.   communist.
    c.   laissez faire.
    d.   mixed.

10.   The fastest-growing sector of the U.S. economy is which of the following?
    a.   Goods producing
    b.   Manufacturing
    c.   Service providing
    d.   Real estate

2

SUPPLY AND DEMAND

KEY TERMS

affordability index   inflation   net migration

demand   infrastructure   quantity

demographics   interest rates   supply

diversity   median price   taxation

elasticity   monetary policy   trends

equilibrium   money   uniqueness

government controls   natural increase   value

immobility   net exports

LEARNING OBJECTIVES

■ Distinguish the characteristics of supply and demand

■ Explain the interaction of supply and demand forces in shaping the real estate marketplace

■ Discuss supply and demand curves, and explain how they respond to changing circumstances

SUPPLY AND DEMAND

Supply and demand are the two principal economic forces that drive an open market. *The function of any marketplace is to provide a setting in which supply and demand can operate to establish price.* First, we'll consider supply factors and demand factors separately. (Note that some of the same factors define both forces, although in different ways.) Then we'll look at how they interact to create a dynamic marketplace.

Supply is defined as the quantity of a product or service available at a specified price. Supply is determined by price and the cost to produce the item or service. Supply is also determined by the cost of other goods. **Demand** is defined as the desire for a particular good or service supported by the possession of the necessary means of exchange to affect ownership. **Equilibrium** occurs when the forces that determine the behavior of some variable are in balance and, thus, exert no pressure on the variable to exchange. As an example, equilibrium occurs when there are just as many home buyers as home sellers.

The operation of supply and demand in the market is how prices for goods and services are set. Essentially, when supply increases and demand remains stable, prices go down; when demand increases and supply remains stable, prices go up. Greater supply means producers need to attract more buyers, so they lower prices. Greater demand means producers can raise their prices because eager consumers will compete for the product.

Uniqueness and Immobility

Two characteristics of real estate govern the way the market reacts to the pressures of supply and demand factors: uniqueness and immobility. **Uniqueness**, as we've discussed, means that no two parcels of real estate are ever exactly alike. **Immobility** refers to the fact that real estate cannot be moved to some other location where demand is high. For these reasons, real estate markets are local markets; each geographic area has a different type of real estate and different conditions that drive prices.

Because of real estate's uniqueness and immobility, the market generally adjusts slowly to the forces of supply and demand. Though a home offered for sale can be withdrawn in response to low demand and high supply, it is much more likely that oversupply will result in lower prices. When supply is low, on the other hand, a high demand may not be met immediately because development and construction are lengthy processes. Developers may be wary of responding to a sudden surge in demand by committing to risky construction projects right away. As a result, development tends to occur in uneven spurts of activity that lag behind other economic indicators.

Even when supply and demand can be forecast with some accuracy, natural disasters, such as hurricanes and earthquakes, can disrupt market **trends**. Similarly, sudden changes in financial markets or local events such as plant relocations, civil disturbances, or environmental factors can dramatically disrupt a seemingly stable market.

VALUE

Value is one present worth of all present and future benefits. Because the objective of the owner-occupant is different from that of the investor who seeks a return on investment, the concept of **value** differs among the two groups. An investor would rarely pay as much for an income property as would a person who intends to live in the house. The financial return serves as the principal investor criterion (see Unit 12), while the emotional return is the driving force for most owner-occupants. Factors that must be taken into consideration in determining value include money, inflation, and interest rates.

Money

Like most other products in the United States today, real estate cannot be purchased for a handful of beads, shells, or colorful stones. **Money** is the force that drives the transaction. (Money is discussed in greater detail in Unit 4.) Despite the existence and abundance of cash in our economy, however, credit availability is always a primary concern on the demand side of the real estate marketplace.

Inflation

Providers of credit are as conscious of the impact of inflation as the consumers of real estate. In times of high **inflation** and interest rates, the lending community shifts the risk to the borrower by basing loan products on a variable rate structure. When interest rates are low, consumers will be more likely to demand fixed-rate mortgages. This allows the lender's risk to adjust to the cost of money for mortgage investments.

There is no orderly supply of or demand for real estate funds. Demand for funds may occur when the availability is at its lowest, or there may be little interest in real estate at a time when funds are easily obtained.

Interest Rates

As **interest rates** rise due to restrictions on the overall availability of capital, the affordability index decreases accordingly. The **affordability index** measures the percentage of potential buyers who can afford a **median-priced** home.

The National Association of REALTORS® (NAR) and the California Association of REALTORS® (CAR) carefully follow and chart the affordability of existing single-family homes. Each month, CAR produces the Housing Affordability Index (AFI—also known as the First-time Buyer Housing Affordability Index, or FTB-HAI), which measures the percentage of households that can afford a median-priced home in prevailing market conditions (see Figure 2.1). CAR also reports first-time buyer indexes for regions and select counties within the state. The index is the most fundamental measure of housing well-being for first-time buyers in the state.

FIGURE 2.1:   Historical Affordability Index & Median Price (2000 to 2013)

Year	CA FTB-HAI	Median Price	PITI	Minimum Qualifying Income	Interest Rate
2000 Q1	55	$193,948	$1,365	$40,952	6.83%
2000 Q2	51	$204,085	$1,479	$44,370	7.18%
2000 Q3	50	$210,146	$1,554	$46,610	7.42%
2000 Q4	50	$213,741	$1,567	$47,014	7.32%
2001 Q1	54	$210,630	$1,454	$43,629	6.61%
2001 Q2	55	$220,006	$1,448	$43,441	6.06%
2001 Q3	54	$231,583	$1,488	$44,641	5.79%
2001 Q4	57	$231,880	$1,432	$42,973	5.35%
2002 Q1	54	$251,277	$1,530	$45,889	5.19%
2002 Q2	52	$272,119	$1,611	$48,345	4.89%
2002 Q3	54	$274,635	$1,564	$46,916	4.47%
2002 Q4	53	$282,506	$1,578	$47,334	4.26%
2003 Q1	54	$287,309	$1,559	$46,764	3.96%
2003 Q2	51	$313,327	$1,665	$49,944	3.74%
2003 Q3	49	$329,035	$1,763	$52,877	3.83%
2003 Q4	49	$331,713	$1,778	$53,335	3.83%
2004 Q1	48	$346,554	$1,820	$54,593	3.62%
2004 Q2	41	$392,088	$2,128	$63,854	3.96%
2004 Q3	41	$392,573	$2,167	$65,025	4.14%
2004 Q4	40	$400,214	$2,223	$66,690	4.21%
2005 Q1	38	$411,324	$2,299	$68,962	4.27%
2005 Q2	34	$446,709	$2,510	$75,296	4.33%

Year	CA FTB-HAI	Median Price	PITI	Minimum Qualifying Income	Interest Rate
2005 Q3	32	$462,885	$2,663	$79,899	4.58%
2005 Q4	30	$465,171	$2,820	$84,610	5.15%
2006 Q1	29	$466,489	$2,896	$86,882	5.41%
2006 Q2	26	$481,780	$3,086	$92,592	5.76%
2006 Q3	27	$477,330	$3,059	$91,780	5.76%
2006 Q4	28	$477,220	$3,010	$90,300	5.60%
2007 Q1	29	$478,525	$3,011	$90,332	5.56%
2007 Q2	26	$503,560	$3,193	$95,803	5.64%
2007 Q3	27	$487,970	$3,130	$93,900	5.76%
2007 Q4	35	$418,620	$2,650	$79,500	5.64%
2008 Q1	46	$355,496	$2,168	$65,030	5.21%
2008 Q2	50	$326,450	$2,003	$60,082	5.28%
2008 Q3	55	$290,490	$1,790	$53,700	5.30%
2008 Q4	61	$249,870	$1,530	$45,900	5.22%
2009 Q1	69	$210,490	$1,250	$37,630	4.96%
2009 Q2	67	$224,040	$1,330	$39,910	4.92%
2009 Q3	64	$247,150	$1,450	$43,500	4.79%
2009 Q4	64	$257,970	$1,470	$44,100	4.50%
2010 Q1	67	$244,818	$1,376	$41,274	4.33%
2010 Q2	65	$268,677	$1,476	$44,282	4.09%
2010 Q3	66	$269,360	$1,420	$42,600	3.66%
2010 Q4	68	$257,397	$1,323	$39,679	3.39%
2011 Q1	72	$236,770	$1,210	$36,340	3.35%
2011 Q2	71	$250,620	$1,240	$37,300	3.04%
2011 Q3	71	$249,370	$1,230	$36,920	2.98%
2011 Q4	73	$240,180	$1,180	$35,450	2.95%
2012 Q1	73	$237,310	$1,160	$34,650	2.84%
2012 Q2	69	$268,820	$1,310	$39,170	2.82%
2012 Q3	67	$288,880	$1,390	$41,640	2.71%
2012 Q4	66	$299,490	$1,430	$42,790	2.62%
2013 Q1	62	$297,920	$1,420	$42,730	2.66%

Source: California Association of REALTORS®

Calculating the Housing Affordability Index The following information/assumptions are used to calculate principal, interest, taxes, and insurance (PITI) for the median-priced home, which is the basis of the HAI:

■ Median home price in California

■ Down payment (20%)

■ National average effective mortgage interest rate

■ Monthly property tax (1% of median price divided by 12)

■ Monthly insurance payment (0.38% of median home price divided by 12)

PITI is then divided by 0.3 and multiplied by 12 to calculate the minimum annual income needed to qualify for a loan (assuming PITI can be no more than 30% of a household's income). Assume, for example, that PITI is $2,175. $2,175 × 0.3 = $7,250. $7,250 × 12 = $87,000. In this example, the minimum annual income to qualify for a loan assuming PITI of $2,175 is $87,000.

The minimum income is compared to the income distribution of households in the state. The HAI is the percent of households with incomes greater than or equal to the minimum income.

In November 2014, CAR reported that lower interest rates and minimal home price gains kept California's housing affordability in check in the third quarter of 2014 and even helped improve affordability in some high-cost counties in the San Francisco Bay Area region. The percentage of homebuyers who could afford to purchase a median-priced, existing single-family home in California in the third quarter of 2014 remained unchanged at 30% as in the second quarter of 2014. It was, however, down from 32% in the third quarter of 2013. According to CAR, homebuyers needed to earn a minimum annual income of $94,960 to qualify for the purchase of a $467,700 statewide median-priced single-family home in the third quarter of 2014.

SUPPLY FACTORS

Factors that tend to affect the supply side of the real estate market's supply and demand balance include the *labor force, construction and material costs*, and **government controls** *and financial policies*.

FIGURE 2.2:   Factors Affecting Supply

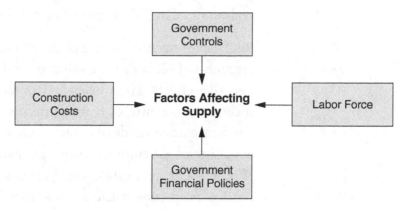

Labor Force and Construction Costs

A shortage of skilled labor or building materials or an increase in the cost of materials can decrease the amount of new construction. High transfer costs (such as taxes) and construction permit fees can also discourage development. Increased construction costs may be passed along to buyers and tenants in the form of higher prices and increased rents, which can further slow the market.

Government Policies

The government's **monetary policy** (discussed in Unit 4) can have a substantial impact on the real estate market. The Federal Reserve Board establishes a discount rate of interest for the money it lends to member commercial banks. That rate has a direct impact on the interest rates the banks, in turn, charge to consumer borrowers. These interest rates play a significant part in people's ability to buy homes. Such government agencies as the Federal Housing Administration (FHA), the Government National Mortgage Association (GNMA), and the Federal Home Loan Mortgage Corporation can affect the amount of money available to lenders. Real estate financing issues are discussed in Unit 11.

Virtually any government action has some effect on the real estate market. For instance, federal environmental regulations may increase or decrease the supply and value of land in a local market. Legislation in California called the Land Conservation Act (a.k.a. the Williamson Act) was passed in 1965 to preserve agricultural and open space land This governmental action has constrained the supply of real estate and has prevented cities, counties, and developers alike from further developing because of the financial incentives extended to landowners and farmers as well as society's desire to preserve open space, both of which have affected the supply side of real estate. The Williamson Act is discussed in more detail in a later unit.

Real estate **taxation** is one of the primary sources of revenue for local governments. Policies on taxation of real estate can have either positive or negative effects. High taxes may deter investors. On the other hand, tax incentives can attract new businesses and industries to areas in desperate need of economic development. Of course, along with these enterprises come increased employment and expanded residential real estate markets. Wisely spent, real estate tax revenues may also contribute to higher values for properties if the local amenities, infrastructure, and schools, for instance, are well funded and of good quality.

$30	30
$35	40
$40	49
$45	57
$50	64

Local governments also can influence supply. Land-use controls, building codes, and zoning ordinances help shape the character of a community and increase real estate values. The dedication of land to such amenities as forest and agricultural preserves, schools, and parks helps shape the character of the market. Zoning and land-use controls are discussed in greater detail in Unit 9.

Monetary vs. Fiscal Policies

Monetary policy is best described as the broad achievement of objects of policy, including stability of employment and prices, economic growth, and balance in external payments through control of the monetary system and operating on monetary magnitudes as the supply of money, the structure of interest rates, and availability of credit. Fiscal policy generally refers to the use of taxation and government expenditures to regulate the level of economic activity. As an example, if unemployment is regarded as excessive, income taxes may be varied to stimulate the level of demand for this purpose. The overall impact on economic activity will depend on the size of the tax cut. Additionally, the use of fiscal policy entails changes in the government's budget including the possibility of deficits.

MEASURING SUPPLY

The easiest way to understand how supply is measured is through an example. Suppose the proprietor of a candle shop is willing to offer a certain number of candles for a certain price. The shopkeeper might produce a supply schedule. A supply schedule is a table of quantities of a given product that sellers are willing to offer at various prices at particular times:

This table simplifies the concept of supply. Relative to real estate, supply is influenced by the following factors:

- Availability of skilled labor

- Availability of construction financing

- Availability of land

- Availability of raw materials

Typically an oversupply of homes or land in a given area will mean lower prices. If there is an undersupply of homes and land, prices will usually rise.

Supply Curve

A supply curve is a distinctive portrait of supply of a particular product or service, indicating the quantity that would be supplied at various prices. When the supply schedule is plotted on a graph with price on the vertical axis (y) and **quantity** on the horizontal axis (x), the line that joins the points slopes upward to the right. This is the characteristic direction of the supply curve (see Figure 2.3).

FIGURE 2.3:   Supply Curve

If the number of products or services offered at each price increases, the whole supply curve shifts to the right (see Figure 2.4). Similarly, if the number decreases, the curve shifts to the left (see Figure 2.5).

Note that the use of the vertical axis for independent variable (price) and horizontal for dependent (demand) is the reverse of most graphs. However, this is the conventional practice for displaying both supply and demand curves.

FIGURE 2.4:   Increased Supply Curve

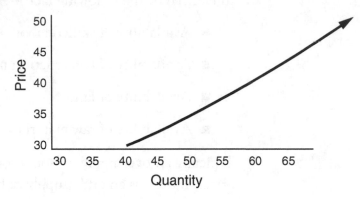

FIGURE 2.5:   Decreased Supply Curve

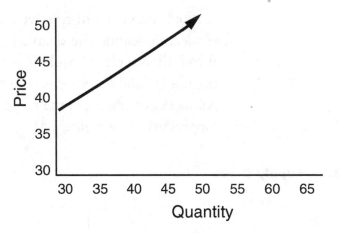

DEMAND FACTORS

Demand refers to the amount of goods or services people are willing and able to buy at a given price. In the real estate market, demand is dependent on a variety of factors, including *affordability*. Unless this factor is present, demand has no way of manifesting itself. Factors that tend to affect the demand side of the real estate market include population, demographics, employment, and wage levels.

FIGURE 2.6:   Factors Affecting Demand

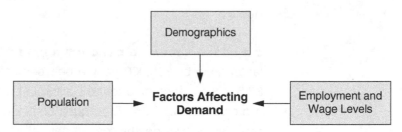

Population

Shelter is a basic human need, so the demand for housing grows with the population. Although the total population of the country continues to rise, the demand for real estate increases faster in some areas than in others. In some locations, however, growth has ceased altogether or the population has declined. This may be due to economic changes (such as plant or military base closings), social concerns (such as the quality of schools or a desire for more open space), or population changes (such as population shifts from colder to warmer climates). The result can be a drop in demand for real estate in one area matched by a correspondingly increased demand elsewhere.

The two basic components of population as a consideration of real estate economics are **net migration** (the number of people coming into an area minus the number of people who leave) and **natural increase** (the number of births minus the number of deaths). This can be measured on a neighborhood, community, state, or national level, depending on the scope of the economic investigation. It is important to remember, however, that although increased population figures may indicate a *potential* demand, they may not reflect *actual* demand. We find that as the population in California increases, existing property owners generally experience and benefit from the concept of "unearned increment," which is an increase in the value of land or any property without expenditure of any kind on the part of the land owner as a result of a general rise in the demand for land.

Demographics

Demographics is the study and description of a population. The population of a community is a major factor in determining the quantity and type of housing in that community. Family size, the ratio of adults to children, the ages of children, the number of retirees, family income, lifestyle, and the growing number of both single-parent and "empty nester" households are all demographic factors that contribute to the amount and type of housing needed.

CALIFORNIA DEMOGRAPHICS IN 2014   California's population grew by 335,000 people between July 1, 2013, and July 1, 2014, to total 38.5 million, according to the California Department of Finance. This represents a growth rate of 0.9%. Birth rates continue to decline, especially the teen birth rate. Births less deaths, called natural increase, remain the primary source of the state's population growth. The natural increase of 243,000 is comprised of 497,000 births less 254,000 deaths. Net migration includes all legal and unauthorized foreign immigrants, residents who left the state to live abroad, and the balance of the hundreds of thousands of people who moved to and from California from within the United States. Net migration added 92,000 persons to California in 2013. Since the natural census on April 1, 2010, California has added 1,245,000 persons. Much of this growth is concentrated in the urban coastal counties, while several inland counties have started to grow again. Smaller counties in more remote areas of California are either still losing population or growing very little.

Quick Demographic Facts

- California has 58 counties ranging in size from Alpine County, with just 1,100 residents, to Los Angeles County, with over 10 million residents.

- The state's nine largest counties are Los Angeles, San Diego, Orange, Riverside, San Bernardino, Santa Clara, Alameda, Sacramento, and Contra Costa. Each has over 1 million residents, and these nine counties contain 70% of California's residents.

- San Benito, Placer, Contra Costa, Riverside, Alameda, and San Joaquin counties had the largest percentage increases in population, each growing by 1.3% or more. Population change ranged from the highest growth rate of 1.4% in San Benito to –0.72% in Modoc County.

- Although natural increase was a significant source of growth in the state, 12 counties experienced natural decrease (more deaths than births during the year): Alameda, Calaveras, Lake, Mariposa, Modoc, Nevada, Plumas, Shasta, Sierra, Siskiyou, Trinity, and Tuolumne.

Employment and Wage Levels

Decisions about whether to buy or rent and how much to spend on housing are closely related to income. When job opportunities are scarce or wage levels low, demand for real estate usually drops. The market might, in fact, be affected drastically by a single major employer moving in or shutting down.

MEASURING DEMAND

The easiest way to understand how demand is measured is through the same example we used for supply. Here, the shopkeeper might produce a demand schedule. A demand schedule is a table of quantities of a given product that are desired at various prices:

Sales Price	Candle Stock
$50	25
$45	29
$40	37
$35	47
$30	65

This table simplifies demand. Relative to real estate, demand is influenced by the following factors:

- Price of real estate

- Demographics, including household composition

- Incomes of consumers

- Availability of mortgage credit

- Consumer's taste or preferences

Demand Curve

A demand curve is a graphic display of demand for a particular product or service. When the candle shop's demand schedule is plotted on a graph with price on the vertical axis (y) and quantity on the horizontal axis (x), the line that joins the points slopes downward to the right. This is the characteristic direction of the demand curve (see Figure 2.7).

Again, note that the use of the vertical axis for independent variable (price) and horizontal for dependent (demand) is the reverse of most graphs. However, this is the conventional practice for displaying both supply and demand curves.

FIGURE 2.7:   Demand Curve

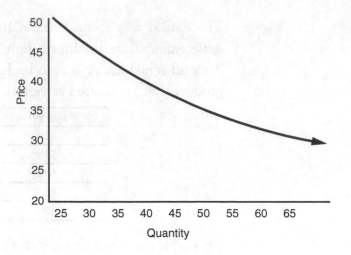

Changes in Income

The curve's slope is determined by the degree to which price affects demand. This reflects the elasticity of demand. When price has a relatively small effect (as with necessities), the curve will be close to vertical. When price has a strong effect on demand (as with luxury items), the line or curve will be closer to horizontal.

If the disposable income of the average household increases, the quantity desired of various products at each price will go up and the demand curve will shift to the right (Figure 2.8). If disposable income decreases, the quantity demanded of various products at each price will go down and the demand curve will shift to the left.

FIGURE 2.8:   Increased Income versus Demand

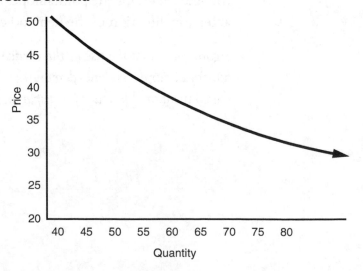

EQUILIBRIUM

The primary objective in any market-driven economy is to reach the stage at which supply and demand are in balance. This is referred to as the point of equilibrium (see Figure 2.9). When a market is in equilibrium, it is balanced; enough product is provided to meet the exact demand for that product and the price is satisfactory to both producers and consumers.

FIGURE 2.9:   Point of Equilibrium

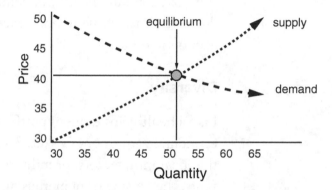

On a supply and demand chart, a line drawn from the point of equilibrium to the vertical (price) axis indicates the equilibrium price. Similarly, a line drawn to the horizontal (supply or demand) axis indicates the equilibrium quantity. Figure 2.9 shows the point of equilibrium for our candle store example. For the shopkeeper, a price of $40 for just over 50 units will achieve an acceptable balance.

A CLOSER LOOK   Here's how one broker describes market forces: "In my 17 years in real estate, I've seen supply and demand in action many times. When a car maker relocated its factory to my region a few years back, hundreds of people wanted to buy the few higher-bracket houses for sale at the time. Those sellers were able to ask what seemed like ridiculously high prices at the time for their properties, and two of my listings actually sold for substantially more than the asking prices! On the other hand, when the naval base closed two years ago and 2,000 civilian jobs were transferred out, it seemed like every other house in town was for sale. The new developments were standing empty, and we were practically giving houses away to the few people who were willing to buy. *That's* supply and demand for you."

LOCAL ECONOMIC STRENGTH

In economics, one must always look at the macro (big picture) issues as well as the micro (localized picture) issues when considering factors that influence demand. International events and local conditions can both have a serious impact on the real estate sector. Some of the macro-factors and micro-factors that may affect the health of the community include **net exports**, population **diversity**, **infrastructure**, and mobility of investment.

Net Exports

If the community produces more than it consumes, it is in an excellent state of economic health. A community that consumes more than it produces (that is, whose imports exceed its exports) is putting itself in a risky economic position.

Diversity

Like a healthy investment portfolio, a healthy economy will not have all its economic eggs in one basket. Towns that exist solely for the employees of the local mill, factory, or military base are extremely vulnerable. In recent years, the closing of numerous military bases across the country sent many local economies into collapse. This was particularly true where the community had become wholly dependent on business generated by the base and had failed to diversify its economy.

Supporting Facilities (Infrastructure)

Community amenities that have a tendency to enhance value include

- *educational opportunities*—public and private schools, colleges, and universities;

- *public transportation*—bus and train transportation within a community and between neighboring communities;

- *streets, highways, and freeways*—well-maintained roads and bridges;

- *utilities*—sufficient water, sewerage, gas, and electricity capacity to meet expanding requirements; and

- *sports, cultural, and recreational facilities*—important for residents as well as for attracting out-of-town visitors for special events.

Diversion of Local Capital to Other Areas (Investment Mobility)

Local investment may be discouraged if rates of return or risk levels are more favorable in other areas. Nations with rising incidents of terrorism and cities with increasing crime rates often suffer when wary investors divert their investments to safer places.

Taxes

As the federal government continues to experiment with capital gains, depreciation, allowable investment expenses, passive income definitions, and other tax policies, demand can be stimulated or stifled in the process. Recent tax laws have sought to encourage home ownership by providing incentives through tax reforms. *Investment property is particularly vulnerable to shifts in tax policy.*

Elasticity

The interrelationship between demand and price is referred to as **elasticity**. Luxury items such as electronics tend to have a high elasticity because demand can increase significantly with a substantial decrease in price. On the other hand, a lowering of the price of necessities, where demand is fairly constant, will produce little increase (other than some possible hoarding). In other words, the demand for many basic products is relatively inelastic.

SUMMARY

■ Prices for goods and services are set by the operation of supply and demand. Essentially, when supply increases and demand remains stable, prices go down; when demand increases and supply remains stable, prices go up.

■ Two characteristics of real estate govern the way the market reacts to the pressures of supply and demand factors: **uniqueness** and **immobility**.

■ Because of real estate's uniqueness and immobility, the *market generally adjusts slowly to the forces of supply and demand.* Even when supply and demand can be forecast with some accuracy, natural disasters, sudden changes in financial markets, or local events such as plant relocations can dramatically disrupt a seemingly stable market.

- Factors that must be taken into consideration in determining **value** include *money*, *interest rates*, and *inflation*.

- Factors affecting **supply** are *labor force*, *construction and material costs*, and *government controls* and *financial policies*.

- Tools that measure supply include *supply schedules* and the *supply curve*.

- Factors affecting **demand** are *population*, *demographics*, and *employment and wage levels*. Demand is dependent on a single general factor, however: *affordability*.

- The *primary objective* of any market-driven economy is to reach *the stage at which supply and demand are in balance*. This is the point of **equilibrium**.

- **Elasticity** refers to the responsiveness of supply or demand to price.

REVIEW QUESTIONS

1. What is the current number of residential listings in your community?

2. What is the time period the average residential listing is on the market in your community? Does it coincide with the state's average? If not, why not?

3. How much has the population in your area/community increased within the last year; five years; ten years?

4. At what point in the last three years did the demand for real estate surpass the supply?

5. With population increases/decreases in your community, how have the educational facilities, such as local schools, been impacted by the demographic changes?

6. Since the end of the recession, how has the number of foreclosures in your community affected the desirability of your community?

UNIT QUIZ

1.   The function of any marketplace is to provide a setting in which supply and demand can operate to establish
     a.   affordability.
     b.   inflation.
     c.   natural increase.
     d.   price.

2.   When supply increases and demand remains stable, which of the following usually takes place?
     a.   Prices go down.
     b.   Prices go up.
     c.   Market equilibrium is achieved.
     d.   Inflation occurs.

3.   Which of the following is *TRUE* of real estate markets?
     a.   They are immune from supply and demand.
     b.   They are primarily local in nature.
     c.   They are national markets.
     d.   They are characterized by uniqueness and mobility.

4.   All of the following are factors that tend to affect the supply side of the market *EXCEPT*
     a.   labor force.
     b.   material costs.
     c.   government financial policies.
     d.   demographics.

5.   On a graph illustrating the supply curve, what characteristic is measured on the y axis?
     a.   Quantity
     b.   Sales
     c.   Price
     d.   Profit

6. The amount of goods and services that people are willing and able to buy at a given price is
    a. value.
    b. demand.
    c. supply.
    d. equilibrium.

7. What is the single most important factor in determining demand in the real estate market?
    a. Population
    b. Demographics
    c. Construction costs
    d. Affordability

8. The number of people coming into an area, minus the number of people who leave, is the way of determining which of the following?
    a. Natural increase
    b. Net migration
    c. Demographics
    d. Local economic strength

9. The characteristic direction of the demand curve is
    a. upward, from right to left.
    b. downward, from left to right.
    c. upward, from left to right.
    d. downward, from right to left.

10. The interrelationship between demand and price is referred to as
    a. elasticity.
    b. equilibrium.
    c. supply.
    d. affordability.

3

ECONOMIC CHANGE ANALYSIS

KEY TERMS

amplitude
business cycles
Consumer Price Index
  (CPI)
contraction
depression
diffusion
Dow-Jones Industrial
  Average
duration
economic trend

economic troughs
expansion
fluctuations
forecasting
gross domestic product
  (GDP)
gross national product
  (GNP)
hidden unemployment
housing starts
indicators

Nasdaq
national income
peak
prosperity
quit rate
recession
recovery
Standard & Poor's 500
  (S&P 500)

LEARNING OBJECTIVES

■ Recognize types of economic trends and fluctuations, and how to use them for decision-making and to generate an economic forecast

■ Describe the components of the business cycle and the cycle's larger implications for the economy as a whole

■ Understand the types of data generated by the CPI, GDP, and stock market indicators

THE INEVITABILITY OF CHANGE

In any vibrant economic system, change is a constant factor. As we've seen in previous units, the forces of supply and demand are constantly adjusting to market conditions. Adam Smith's "unseen hand" of the marketplace does not stay still. In the real estate market, too, the ability of participants to adapt and adjust to change is often what separates success from failure. Much of what defines success in the real estate market is, in fact, the ability to read the early warning signals of change and prepare for coming market shifts. This is the analysis of economic trends.

Trends

An **economic trend** is a change in a market in a consistent direction. A measurement of economic activity over the course of a single day, for instance, would *not* be a trend. A *collection* of such measurements over several days, however, would be more likely to signal a general market direction. If the measurements were consistent over a significant period of time, they would constitute a trend. Economic trends are either *long term* or *short term*. A long-term (or *secular*) trend is made up of short-term changes.

In Figure 3.1, for instance, notice how the long-term trend is made up of somewhat less obvious short-term fluctuations. It's similar to how a newspaper photograph that appears to be a single image is actually made up of hundreds of thousands of tiny dots of ink. Looked at up close, they're only specks; viewed from a distance, they blend together and make more sense.

FIGURE 3.1:   **Economic Changes and Trends**

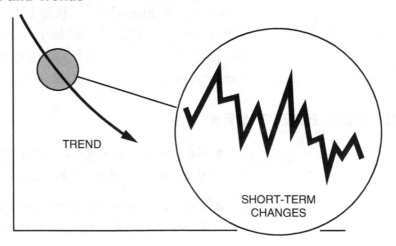

Examples of long-term or secular trends in the United States include

- mechanization of production from the 19th to the 20th centuries; and

- a shift from goods production to a service economy in the second half of the 20th century.

Fluctuations

When levels of economic activity go up and down rather than grow steadily or decline steadily, they are said to *fluctuate*. There are four kinds of **fluctuation**: periodic, irregular, random, and cyclical.

Periodic Fluctuations   Some changes in the market happen regularly. They can be predicted with precision because their pattern has been documented over time. For example, oceanside communities dependent on tourism know very well that the summer's business boom will end abruptly after Labor Day. Similarly, department stores prepare months ahead for the rush of back-to-school and Christmas buying seasons.

Irregular Fluctuations   Other changes are predictable even though they do not occur with any regularity. The effects of certain one-time events on business activity can be forecast because the events are scheduled, and their impact can be estimated based on past experience. For example, a city may never have hosted the Olympic Games before, but the event can be expected to provide a temporary lift to the local economy. Businesses in and around the venue can prepare for a short-term boom, knowing in advance that once the torch is extinguished, the market will return to normal.

Random Fluctuations   Some fluctuations occur as a result of unpredictable events, such as epidemics, wars, international trade embargoes, and crop failures (or unexpected surpluses). A particular product may become unexpectedly popular, causing short-term fluctuations in the market as supply races to catch up with demand. In 1996, for instance, a stuffed toy based on a popular "Sesame Street" character named Elmo became wildly in demand as a Christmas season purchase. Shelf stock was suddenly depleted, and the few dolls available were resold at outrageously high prices for a few weeks. By the time the manufacturer caught up with the heightened demand, however, the frenzy had subsided and the toy became a clearance item.

Cyclical Fluctuations   Experience has shown that the level of overall economic activity and performance rises and falls fairly regularly in a relatively long cycle of several years. However, the same is not true of the economy's periodic behavior. The onset of a periodic rise or fall is influenced by a virtually infinite number of economic and noneconomic factors, alone or in combination, and cannot be predicted. The longer-term fluctuation can be predicted, however, and is known as a business cycle.

Business Cycles

A **business cycle** is characterized by a general, simultaneous expansion or contraction in a number of different economic activities. These broad expansions and contractions reflect the health of the larger market, the region, or the nation as a whole. While the cycles are recurring, they are not periodic; their length, and the direction they take, cannot be predicted with accuracy. The cycles are long term; they vary in duration from one year to a dozen or more.

While the concept of a business cycle is generally used in relation to the larger economy, its phases have applications to each particular business or industry as well. As generally defined, the business cycle contains four components that include (1) contraction, (2) recession, (3) expansion, and (4) peak. Typically it can take several years for the economy to cycle through all four components, but these components can occur on an annual basis for seasonal businesses. Figure 3.2 illustrates a complete business cycle (the area within the dotted box).

FIGURE 3.2:   Business Cycles

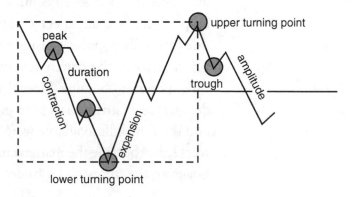

A technical language has evolved to describe phases of and points on the business cycle. The most important terms are defined here.

Peak   The **peak** is the top segment of the cycle, a period during which productivity and employment are higher than the preceding or succeeding period. Many peaks are illustrated in Figure 3.2. Remember, however, that "higher" is a relative term. A peak does not necessarily mean prosperity. In Figure 3.2, if the horizontal line represents the number of people living at poverty level, a peak below that line may be of little comfort.

Upper Turning Point   The upper turning point is the point of the cycle at which contraction of the economy begins. In Figure 3.2, that point is at the upper right-hand corner of the dotted box.

Contraction   The **contraction** is the segment of the curve that reflects a decline in economic activity. In an economic downturn, businesses stop growing. The inflationary tendencies of the peak period can have a dragging effect on sales, and businesses may find themselves with excess capacity in terms of inventory and in their labor. The contraction in Figure 3.2 begins in the upper left and ends at the center of the lower dotted line.

Trough   The trough is the point at which a contraction becomes an expansion. A trough may be the low point of the entire cycle (in which case it is referred to as the lower turning point), or it may simply be another part of an overall trend. During this period, businesses may be reduced for an extended period of time. In a recession, unemployment tends to rise and production declines. During this period, consumers also tend to spend less. For example, a costume shop might not close in April if its owner is confident that the shop can make it to Halloween in that year, but the shop will likely reduce staff and may also reduce hours of operation to curtail costs. In Figure 3.2, there are many troughs.

Lower Turning Point   The lower turning point is the point at which contraction ends and expansion of the economy begins. This point is at the center of the dotted bottom line in Figure 3.2.

Expansion   The **expansion** is the segment of the curve that reflects a rise in economic activity. In Figure 3.2, the portion of the cycle from the lower turning point to the upper right-hand corner is an expansionary period. As an example, in an expansion period, business begins to pick up and consumer confidence grows. The incomes of businesses also rise as does spending. At this point, companies typically expand their operations and their infrastructure. Also during expansion, it may take time for consumers to fully recover the spending habits they had prior to a contraction, and now they are willing to make major purchases. This is where people will tend to purchase appliances, automobiles, or other large-ticket items.

Duration   Usually stated in months, **duration** refers to the length of a contraction, expansion, the period from trough to trough, or the period from peak to peak.

Amplitude   **Amplitude** is a measure of highness and lowness—the difference between trough and peak.

Economic Conditions

The duration and amplitude of phases in the business cycle translate into terms commonly applied to ongoing economic conditions (see Figure 3.3).

FIGURE 3.3:   The Business Cycle and General Economic Conditions

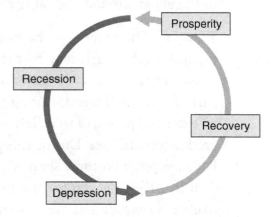

Recession   A **recession** is usually defined as at least *two successive quarters of contraction* characterized by cautious spending, an increase in saving, and a decline in gross domestic product (GDP).

Depression   A **depression** is a period of very low use of productive capacity combined with very high unemployment.

Recovery   **Recovery** is the process of an economy recovering from a depression.

Prosperity   Prosperity is the ideal state of a healthy economy: high employment, productivity, and income combine to create a general sense of stability.

Boom   A period of unusually strong demand for goods and services, accompanied by rapidly rising prices. In a boom time, employment and productivity exceed the stable levels of normal prosperity. The psychological climate of a boom is one of high optimism, often greater than is actually justified. In a sense, a boom represents an economy in a state of intoxication; some innovation or temporary, artificial condition creates the illusion of limitless opportunity for growth. The classic example of a boom is the California Gold Rush of the 1850s. In the space of a few years, whole towns were established, grew, prospered, and were abandoned when the lure of fast wealth proved elusive.

A LOOK BACK IN TIME   The stock market crash of October 19, 1987, did not have the far-reaching effects of its counterpart in 1929. This was, in part, because of the regulatory safeguards created during and after the Great Depression of the 1930s. The Dow fell 508 points in a single day, and many stockholders and traders sustained tremendous losses. Nonetheless, two days after the crash, the stock market enjoyed its fourth-best gain ever. Ten years after the crash of 1987, the stock market was achieving record highs.

However, on October 27, 1997, the market fell more than 554 points in one day. While the 1997 fall was a numerically bigger drop than its 1987 counterpart, and while it certainly caused financial losses and emotional strain, the 1987 crash was still the biggest drop in stock market history: nearly 23%. By contrast, the 1997 crash was only a 7.2% fall. The reason: on August 25, 1987, the market hit an all-time high of 2,722; ten years later, on August 6, trading was almost 8,260. Bigger market, bigger drop, but a smaller percentage of the whole.

Within five years, the stock market again took a nosedive. On October 9, 2002, the Dow Industrials fell 215 points to close at 7,286, the same level as October 1997. The selling that commenced in 2000 took away the blue-chip average of nearly half of the gain posted in the 1990s, which saw a very strong upswing in the market. In 2002, many investors began to feel powerless and worry about the loss of their nest eggs acquired during the 1990s. It appears that October has been a bad month for investors in the stock market.

What Do Business Cycles Mean?

Business cycles describe economic activity in a very broad sense, over a period of time. The cycles themselves are made up of a combination of smaller cycles; changes and circumstances that, viewed together from an informed distance, suggest trends. Just as no single symptom can tell a doctor how healthy the patient is, no single set of data can indicate the level of business activity or condition of the economy. Economists and business people rely on a number of economic "symptoms," called **indicators**, to make informed judgments about the economy's current and prospective condition. Nevertheless, even economists do not always agree on what the figures mean or how they should be interpreted.

Common indicators in use today include quarterly and monthly data on gross domestic product (GDP), employment, income, and spending. The level of activity in the housing construction industry is also a common indicator of overall economic health. An enormous compilation of statistics on the U.S. economy is available from federal government sources, including the Bureau of Economic Analysis, the Bureau of Labor Statistics, the Commerce Department, and the Department of Housing and Urban Development.

Early Warning Indicators

In addition to the formal indicators relied on by economists and the business community, a number of general economic conditions serve as "warning signs" of impending changes.

Employment and Inflation   Abrupt changes in local or national unemployment figures can indicate that the economy is either overactive or stagnant. For instance, full employment in an area raises the possibility of inflation. For an investor, a time of full employment and impending inflation would be a good time for a home purchase with a fixed-rate mortgage. In cooling economies, where purchasers are likely to find bargains, the best bet may be variable rate financing for a short-term hold until the upsurge begins.

Population Shifts   Shifts in population can also serve as stimulators or inhibitors. For example, the departure or arrival of a major employer in the area will have long-term effects on local economies. Many communities have been devastated by the closing of military bases, a result of peacetime economics that removes an enormous employment and consumption factor from the local economy. On the other hand, communities in southern and western states have long been benefiting from the steady emigration of businesses, industries, and jobs from northern and eastern cities.

Saving vs. Spending Savings and consumer expenditures each have widespread economic effects. The savings of investors allow the housing market to expand by making funds available for financial institutions and the secondary mortgage market. Consumer expenditures at a high level, on the other hand, stimulate local retail activity, providing jobs and potential consumers in the local housing market.

Repair vs. Replace The level of activity in remodeling is an indicator that the new housing market is either robust or soft. In any economic downturn, consumers will defer expenditures for "big ticket" items such as houses and vehicles. Accordingly, auto parts and repair businesses flourish as consumers attempt to preserve the family car for a year or so longer. At the same time, manufacturers and dealers of new cars languish. The same attitude prevails in the housing market where the owner of a two-bedroom house who has an expanding family opts to add to the existing residence rather than buy a new, larger home.

A CLOSER LOOK It's important for participants in the real estate market to be able to anticipate and adapt to economic change:

- First, learn to **chart cyclical activity** and recognize the early warning signals. The critical period in the entire cycle is when it is approaching the peak and through the entire contraction period, as this is the time that an investor in real property is most vulnerable to losses.

- Second, **anticipate change** rather than just let it happen. Understanding the mechanics of cyclical activity in the real estate market can be a definite advantage to the investor who, like the stock investor, aims to buy low and sell high.

- Finally, **avoid overextending**. Wise investors with property who can adequately service their debt with either the property's own income stream (income property) or personal income is in a much better position to weather an economic storm than investors who tend to reach out beyond their personal capabilities by overleveraging.

THE NEXT STEP Looking for and describing patterns in past and present economic activity is a natural step to forecasting the future. Toward the end of this book, in Units 13–15, we'll apply the principles of economic forecasting to real estate investment analysis. It's important to have a general understanding of those principles early on, however, to help you analyze the markets, trends, and issues we'll be examining throughout this book.

ECONOMIC FORECASTING

In some ways, we know our future with certainty (the classic inevitables like death and taxes, for example). In most aspects of our lives, however, the future is unknown. There are ways we can, with a reasonable degree of confidence, however, predict and anticipate the probable course of future events. In daily life, this type of clairvoyance is known as "thinking ahead." In economics, it's called **forecasting**.

The Nature of Forecasting

In any modern economy, businesses are constantly engaged in future-oriented decision making. For a business to be successful, it must be able not only to adjust to conditions as they are now but to anticipate conditions as they are likely to be.

Prediction vs. Forecast   The most important quality of a forecast is that it is not a prediction. A prediction asserts that certain events will definitely occur. A forecast, by contrast, is an estimate of future events, stated in terms of probabilities. A meteorologist forecasts the weather, not predicts it.

Implicit vs. Explicit Forecasting   To the extent that decision making is based on assumptions about the future, a business is engaged in implicit forecasting. An example is an automatic assumption that the present growth in demand for a product will continue indefinitely into the future. To the extent that decision making is based on purposely developed and consciously considered estimates about the future, the business is using explicit forecasting.

Uses of Forecasting

Both business and government need a basis for planning their actions. In the business world, a competitive edge goes to firms with the ability to correctly anticipate changes in

- general business *conditions;*
- *demand* for the firm's products or services;
- *labor* costs and needs;
- supply and price of *materials;*

- *production and distribution,* including new technologies and procedures;

- *money supply* and *interest rates;*

- *competitors'* prices, new products, and reactions; and

- *government* policies.

Similarly, the responsibilities of modern governments require massive and accurate economic forecasting on a variety of fronts.

Budget Preparation   Those who prepare federal and state budgets base them on assumptions about tax receipts. Those assumptions, in turn, are based on forecasts of general economic activity in the months ahead.

Business Cycle Crisis Management   Recessions are politically damaging but tolerable. Nevertheless, it has been assumed for the last half century that governments would not permit another deep depression to develop. Governments use forecasting (with varying degrees of success) to contain and manipulate economic contractions once they are under way.

Agricultural Controls and Price Supports   Government controls on production and levels of price support require forecasts of domestic and world production and consumption. Such forecasts also rely on weather forecasts, anticipated natural and social disasters, and political events.

Defense Spending   Budgets for military spending must take account of economic prospects in the nation, especially when an administration's policies call for continued growth in such budgets. Economic conditions in the countries of allies and adversaries also figure into military planning.

Approaches to Forecasting

Forecasting can be based on general patterns (e.g., periodic events, cycle theories) or on specific clues to what is coming next. The most commonly used approach, the use of leading indicators, is an example of the latter.

Data Collection   Like physicians attending to a patient in intensive care, private organizations and government agencies constantly monitor the workings of the U.S. economic system. As discussed previously, huge amounts of data are collected on employment, prices, sales, savings, inventories, and producer and consumer intentions. Each set of data is an indicator of the level of activity in a particular segment of the economy.

Types of Indicators   Experience has shown that various types of data bear different relationships to the economic cycle.

- **Coincident.** Some indicators closely reflect the present state of the economy. These are called coincident indicators.

- **Lagging.** Some indicators trail the business cycle, continuing to rise for several months after a downturn has started. These are termed lagging indicators.

- **Leading.** Leading indicators warn in advance of changes in business activity. These leading indicators are the key to accurate economic forecasting.

Use of Leading Indicators

Leading indicators will start to fall before the business cycle has peaked, and they will start to rise before the trough of a contraction has been reached. Thus, they assist in forecasting the behavior of the economy as a whole.

Major Leading Indicators   The U.S. Department of Commerce publishes a monthly composite index based on 11 economic indicators. The composite index assumes an average 48-month business cycle. The Commerce Department's Bureau of Economic Analysis (BEA) is the primary source of information on economic indicators. Some 300 indicators are studied by the BEA and classified as leading, coincident, or lagging.

Information on economic indicators is available from several sources:

- **Federal government publications and websites**, including the Department of Commerce, the Bureau of Labor Statistics, the Bureau of Economic Analysis, and others.

- **State government publications and websites**

- **News media.** Radio, television, newspapers, and the internet are quick to report changes in the federal government's *Index of Leading Economic Indicators*, as well as other economic activities. More detailed analyses often show up in the weekly news magazines.

Housing Starts as an Economic Indicator Housing starts consist of newly issued building and construction permits for new residential units. The data is derived from surveys of homebuilders nationwide, and the data is released by the U.S. Department of Housing and Urban Development and the U.S. Census Bureau. What is looked at are actual housing starts, building permits, and housing completions. A housing start is defined as beginning the foundation of a home itself. Building permits are counted as of when they are granted. Both building permits and housing starts are shown as a percentage change of the prior month and year-over-year period and divided geographically into four regions: Northeast, Midwest, South, and West.

Housing starts and building permits are considered leading economic indicators, and building permit figures are used to compute the Conference Board's U.S. Leading Index. Construction growth usually picks up at the beginning of the business cycle. Investors and analysts use this data and information to help create estimates for other consumer-based indicators. People who buy new homes will tend to spend money on other consumer goods such as furniture, appliances, lawn and garden supplies, and so forth.

A CLOSER LOOK On February 18, 2015, the U.S. Census Bureau and U. S. Department of Housing and Urban Development released new residential construction statistics for January 2015.

Building Permits. Privately owned housing units authorized by building permits in January were at a seasonally adjusted annual rate of 1,053,000. This is 0.7% (+/–0.6%) below the revised December rate of 1,060,000 but is 8.1% (+/–2.0%) above the January 2014 estimate of 974,000. Single-family authorizations in January were at a rate of 654,000; this is 3.1% (+/–0.9) below the revised December figure of 675,000. Authorization of units in buildings with five units or more were at a rate of 372,000 in January.

Housing Starts. Privately owned housing starts in January were at a seasonally adjusted annual rate of 1,065,000. This is 2.0% (+/–10.4%) below the revised December estimate of 1,087,000 but is 18.7% (+/–14.5%) above the January 2014 rate of 897,000. Single-family housing starts in January were at a rate of 678,000; this is 6.7% (+/–10.6%) below the revised December figure of 727,000. The January rate for units in buildings with five or more units was 381,000.

Housing Completions. Privately owned housing completions in January were at a seasonally adjusted annual rate of 930,000. This is a 1.3% (+/–7.4%) above the revised December estimate of 918,000 and is 9.4% (+/–10.4%) above the January 2014 rate of 850,000. Single-family housing completions in January were at a rate of 649,000; this is 2.3% (+/–7.0%) below the revised December rate of 664,000. The January rate for units in buildings with five units or more was 274,000.

Diffusion Indexes

A **diffusion index** indicates the percentage of items or characteristics in a given population that are rising or falling. This is a broad measure of the direction of change in economic activity.

For example, a report on the percentage of stocks that rose on a given day or over a specified period is a diffusion index. Surveys are often used to generate diffusion indexes. For instance, if 65% of textile manufacturers polled say they intend to employ more workers in the next quarter, the diffusion index is 65.

Diffusion indexes often signal changes in activity before they occur: they are leading indicators. Figure 3.4 shows the percentage of nonfarm industries reporting declining employment during six historical economic contractions. Note that the reports lead the **economic troughs** by several months.

FIGURE 3.4:   Declining Employment Anticipating Economic Troughs

Date of Report	Percentage of Industries	Date of Trough
February 1949	90%	October 1949
September 1957	88%	April 1958
January 1975	90%	March 1975

MAJOR ECONOMIC INDICATORS

Consumer Price Index (CPI)

The **Consumer Price Index (CPI)** is a general average of changes in consumer prices, or the "cost of living," maintained by the Department of Labor's Bureau of Labor Statistics (BLS). Consumer expenditures are categorized as food, housing, and fuel. These major categories are further subdivided into about 400 items (milk, bread, beef; gas, coal, electricity, etc.). These items make up what is called the CPI's *market basket* for comparing the current and base periods. The CPI measures the cost of living for wage-earning, salaried, self-employed, and unemployed urban consumers, representing about 80% of the population. The Consumer Price Index, then, is *a statistical measure of the average change in the prices paid by urban consumers for a fixed market basket of goods and services.*

Calculation of CPI   The CPI is calculated using an index number formula called the *Laspeyres formula.* The Laspeyres formula uses the quantity of goods and services purchased by urban consumers during a specific (base) period as the weight for prices to ensure that the market basket's value is constant. The present weighted cost of the items in the CPI market basket is then compared with the price of the same items during the base period. The current base period is 1982–1984. The Laspeyres formula asks, "What is the value of the base-period market basket in today's prices?" The answer indicates the extent to which the cost of living has risen over time.

The BLS relies on a monthly survey of 7,300 housing units and 22,500 retail and service establishments. Two hundred and six item categories are constructed for 44 different urban areas. A sample of 24,000 families in a point-of-purchase survey tells BLS where the market basket items are being purchased. Twenty percent of the data is revised annually, and the entire sampling of item prices is revised every five years.

Figure 3.5 lists the CPI market basket expenditure categories.

FIGURE 3.5:   **CPI Market Basket Expenditure Categories**

Food	Fuel and Other Utilities	Medical Care
cereals and bakery products	fuel oil and household fuel	medical care commodities
meat, poultry, fish and eggs	gas (piped) and electricity	medical care services
dairy products		professional medical services
fruits and vegetables	**Household Furnishings and**	
sugar and sweets	**Operation**	**Entertainment**
fats and oils	house furnishings	entertainment commodities
nonalcoholic beverages	housekeeping supplies/services	entertainment services
prepared food		
food away from home	**Apparel and Upkeep**	**Other Goods and Services**
alcoholic beverages	men's and boys'	tobacco and smoking products
	women's and girls'	toilet goods and personal
Housing	infants' and toddlers'	care appliances
residential rent	footwear and apparel	personal care services
other rental costs		school books and supplies
owners' equivalent rent	**Transportation**	personal/educational services
household insurance	new cars	
maintenance/repair services	new vehicles	
mainteance/repair commodities	used cars	
	motor fuel	
	gasoline	
	maintenance and repair	
	other private transportation	
	putblic transportation	

Obviously, this calculation is not a simple one. The quality of products changes over time, and other economic and noneconomic factors may be at work, including changes in consumers' shopping habits. Although BLS goes to great lengths to ensure objectivity, interpretation of the raw data depends, in part, on the assumptions, prejudices, and biases of the interpreter. As a result, CPI data is sometimes the subject of controversy. The BLS has responded over the years by building various adjustments into the CPI calculation, including new standards for product quality improvements and for the introduction of new products. A detailed discussion about CPI is provided in Unit 17.

Interpretation   A CPI of 110 means that consumer prices are 110% of what they were in the base year. The *annualized rate* translates a monthly rate of increase into annual terms; a monthly rise of 1% is an annual rise of 12%.

Local CPI

Regions, states, and cities often differ markedly in their CPIs (as anyone can tell you who has moved from a small town to a large city), and CPIs vary over time. For example, in March 1988 the Los Angeles area CPI was 120.6, and the San Francisco area CPI was 119.1. For the same month in 1997, the Los Angeles area CPI was 159.8, and the Bay Area CPI was 159.2. That is, in early 1997 the average cost of the market basket items in San Francisco was $159. Figure 3.6 illustrates the change in California's CPI since 1955. During the recession of 2009, the CPI for the Los Angeles region was 224.5; San Francisco's CPI was 225.8; and the CPI for California as a whole was 225.4. In December 2014, the CPI for the Los Angeles region was 240.4, the San Francisco Bay Area's CPI was 252.2, and the CPI for California as a whole was 246.0. The CPI for the U.S. average city stood at 236.7.

Until the mid-1980s, the California CPI was essentially in line with the national CPI. Since 1985, however, California's CPI has been consistently higher than the national average.

FIGURE 3.6:   A Look Back at California's Entire CPI (1955 to 2014)

California Consumer Price Index (1955–2014)			
All Items (1982–1984=100)			
Year	Month	All Urban Consumers	Urban Wage Earners and Clerical Workers
2014	**Annual**	**246,055**	**238,096**
2014	December	244,812	236,733
2014	October	247,481	240,082
2014	August	247,259	240,289
2014	June	247,228	240,612
2014	April	245,900	239,144
2014	February	244,037	237,021
2013	**Annual**	**241,623**	**234,947**
2013	December	241,526	234,654
2013	October	242,633	235,783
2013	August	241,967	235,196
2013	June	241,926	235,333
2013	April	241,399	234,695
2013	February	241,242	234,887
2012	**Annual**	**238,155**	**231,610**
2012	December	237,705	230,922
2012	October	241,537	235,382
2012	August	239,034	232,427
2012	June	237,781	231,042
2012	April	238,090	231,722
2012	February	235,825	229,430
2011	**Annual**	**232,930**	**226,364**
2011	December	232,985	226,170
2011	October	234,317	227,713
2011	August	233,256	226,427
2011	June	233,285	226,715
2011	April	234,113	228,118
2011	February	230,338	223,663
2010	**Annual**	**226,919**	**219,714**
2010	December	227,487	220,693
2010	October	227,737	220,562
2010	August	227,401	220,109
2010	June	227,113	219,740
2010	April	227,007	219,802
2010	February	225,626	218,299
2009	**Annual**	**224,110**	**216,292**
2009	December	224,349	217,112

California Consumer Price Index (1955–2014)			
All Items (1982–1984=100)			
Year	Month	All Urban Consumers	Urban Wage Earners and Clerical Workers
2009	October	226,035	218,458
2009	August	225.438	217.743
2009	June	224.994	217.322
2009	April	222.896	214.689
2009	February	222.181	214.017
2008	**Annual**	**224.807**	**217.648**
2008	December	219.775	211.519
2008	October	226.572	219.161
2008	August	228.024	220.946
2008	June	228.324	221.798
2008	April	224.323	217.587
2008	February	221.357	214.121
2007	**Annual**	**217.424**	**209.876**
2007	December	219.593	212.559
2007	October	218.959	211.522
2007	August	217.480	209.663
2007	June	217.404	209.859
2007	April	217.704	210.187
2007	February	214.910	206.994
2006	**Annual**	**210.5**	**203.3**
2006	December	211.0	203.4
2006	October	211.8	204.0
2006	August	212.0	205.2
2006	June	210.9	204.2
2006	April	210.5	203.2
2006	February	207.8	200.4
2005	**Annual**	**202.6**	**195.9**
2005	December	204.2	197.1
2005	October	207.1	200.5
2005	August	203.5	197.1
2005	June	201.3	194.6
2005	April	202.0	195.5
2005	February	199.1	192.2
2004	**Annual**	**195.4**	**188.9**
2004	December	197.0	190.5
2004	October	198.0	191.6
2004	August	195.3	188.9

FIGURE 3.6 (continued):   A Look Back at California's Entire CPI (1955 to 2014)

California Consumer Price Index (1955–2014)			
All Items (1982–1984=100)			
Year	Month	All Urban Consumers	Urban Wage Earners and Clerical Workers
2004	April	194.4	187.9
2004	February	193.1	186.4
2003	**Annual**	**190.4**	**183.8**
2003	December	190.1	183.3
2003	October	191.0	184.2
2003	August	190.3	183.9
2003	June	189.9	183.2
2003	April	191.1	184.6
2003	February	190.5	183.7
2002	**Annual**	**186.1**	**179.0**
2002	December	187.2	180.4
2002	October	187.5	180.4
2002	August	186.8	179.6
2002	June	185.9	178.9
2002	April	186.1	178.9
2002	February	184.1	176.9
2001	**Annual**	**181.7**	**174.7**
2001	December	181.8	174.6
2001	October	183.0	175.9
2001	August	182.9	175.7
2001	June	183.2	176.3
2001	April	181.0	174.1
2001	February	179.8	172.8
2000	**Annual**	**174.8**	**168.1**
2000	December	177.3	170.6
2000	October	177.3	170.5
2000	August	175.6	R/168.9
2000	June	R/174.0	167.4
2000	April	173.6	R/167.1
2000	February	R/172.0	165.3
1999	**Annual**	**168.5**	**162.2**
1999	December	170.0	163.8
1999	October	170.2	163.7
1999	August	169.0	162.7
1999	June	167.8	161.6
1999	April	168.8	162.6
1999	February	166.5	160.2

California Consumer Price Index (1955–2014)			
All Items (1982–1984=100)			
Year	Month	All Urban Consumers	Urban Wage Earners and Clerical Workers
1998	**Annual**	**163.7**	**157.6**
1998	December	165.1	159.0
1998	October	164.9	158.6
1998	August	164.3	157.9
1998	June	163.6	157.6
1998	April	163.1	157.0
1998	February	162.1	156.2
1997	**Annual**	**160.5**	**155.0**
1997	December	162.0	156.3
1997	November	161.7	156.0
1997	October	161.9	156.4
1997	September	161.2	155.6
1997	August	160.5	155.0
1997	July	160.2	154.6
1997	June	160.0	154.5
1997	May	160.0	154.6
1997	April	160.2	154.8
1997	March	160.0	154.5
1997	February	159.2	153.8
1997	January	158.8	153.5
1996	**Annual**	**157.1**	**152.0**
1996	December	157.9	152.6
1996	November	158.3	153.0
1996	October	158.6	153.3
1996	September	158.0	152.8
1996	August	157.1	152.0
1996	July	157.4	152.4
1996	June	156.6	151.7
1996	May	157.1	152.3
1996	April	156.9	152.0
1996	March	156.3	151.3
1996	February	155.6	150.6
1996	January	155.2	150.2
1995	**Annual**	**154.0**	**149.1**
1995	December	154.2	149.2
1995	November	154.1	149.2
1995	October	154.7	149.8

FIGURE 3.6 (continued):   A Look Back at California's Entire CPI (1955 to 2014)

| California Consumer Price Index (1955–2014) | | | | California Consumer Price Index (1955–2014) | | | |
| All Items (1982–1984=100) | | | | All Items (1982–1984=100) | | | |
Year	Month	All Urban Consumers	Urban Wage Earners and Clerical Workers	Year	Month	All Urban Consumers	Urban Wage Earners and Clerical Workers
1995	September	154.2	149.3	1992	November	147.3	142.9
1995	August	153.9	149.0	1992	October	147.51	43.0
1995	July	153.9	149.1	1992	September	146.6	142.3
1995	June	154.2	149.4	1992	August	145.9	141.8
1995	May	154.3	149.3	1992	July	145.6	141.5
1995	April	154.1	149.2	1992	June	145.2	141.2
1995	March	153.9	149.0	1992	May	145.1	140.8
1995	February	153.6	148.7	1992	April	144.8	140.6
1995	January	153.4	148.5	1992	March	144.7	140.5
1994	**Annual**	**151.5**	**146.6**	1992	February	144.0	139.7
1994	December	152.5	147.7	1992	January	143.4	139.1
1994	November	152.3	147.4	**1991**	**Annual**	**140.6**	**136.7**
1994	October	152.5	147.5	1991	December	142.4	138.3
1994	September	152.0	147.0	1991	November	142.7	138.5
1994	August	151.5	146.7	1991	October	142.2	138.1
1994	July	151.2	146.3	1991	September	142.0	137.9
1994	June	150.7	145.8	1991	August	141.2	137.1
1994	May	150.8	146.0	1991	July	140.8	136.8
1994	April	151.1	146.1	1991	June	140.1	136.1
1994	March	151.5	146.4	1991	May	139.7	135.8
1994	February	151.1	146.1	1991	April	139.5	135.5
1994	January	151.1	146.1	1991	March	139.0	134.9
1993	**Annual**	**149.4**	**144.7**	1991	February	139.0	135.0
1993	December	150.7	145.9	1991	January	139.3	135.5
1993	November	150.6	145.8	**1990**	**Annual**	**135.01**	**31.5**
1993	October	150.0	145.3	1990	December	138.2	134.6
1993	September	149.4	144.6	1990	November	137.9	134.3
1993	August	149.1	144.4	1990	October	137.7	134.0
1993	July	149.0	144.4	1990	September	136.9	133.1
1993	June	148.9	144.4	1990	August	135.6	132.0
1993	May	149.5	144.8	1990	July	134.9	131.3
1993	April	149.3	144.7	1990	June	134.3	130.8
1993	March	148.9	144.3	1990	May	133.7	130.3
1993	February	148.9	144.3	1990	April	133.4	129.9
1993	January	148.3	143.8	1990	March	133.4	129.9
1992	**Annual**	**145.6**	**141.4**	1990	February	132.5	129.1
1992	December	147.3	142.9	1990	January	131.3	128.0

FIGURE 3.6 (continued):   A Look Back at California's Entire CPI (1955 to 2014)

California Consumer Price Index (1955–2014) All Items (1982–1984=100)			
Year	Month	All Urban Consumers	Urban Wage Earners and Clerical Workers
1989	**Annual**	**128.0**	**124.9**
1989	December	129.9	126.7
1989	November	129.4	126.2
1989	October	129.5	126.4
1989	September	129.4	126.2
1989	August	128.9	125.7
1989	July	128.8	125.7
1989	June	128.2	125.2
1989	May	128.0	125.0
1989	April	126.9	124.0
1989	March	126.4	123.2
1989	February	125.3	122.3
1989	January	124.7	121.6
1988	**Annual**	**121.9**	**118.9**
1988	December	124.0	121.0
1988	November	123.8	120.8
1988	October	123.8	120.9
1988	September	123.3	120.4
1988	August	122.7	119.6
1988	July	122.0	119.0
1988	June	121.7	118.8
1988	May	121.6	118.7
1988	April	120.6	117.8
1988	March	120.4	117.4
1988	February	119.4	116.5
1988	January	119.0	116.2
1987	**Annual**	**116.5**	**113.9**
1987	December	118.4	115.7
1987	November	118.2	115.5
1987	October	118.4	115.7
1987	September	117.8	115.1
1987	August	117.2	114.5
1987	July	116.6	113.9
1987	June	116.3	113.7
1987	May	116.5	113.9
1987	April	115.9	113.3
1987	March	115.2	112.6

California Consumer Price Index (1955–2014) All Items (1982–1984=100)			
Year	Month	All Urban Consumers	Urban Wage Earners and Clerical Workers
1987	February	114.6	112.0
1987	January	113.4	110.8
1986	**Annual**	**112.0**	**109.6**
1986	December	112.7	110.1
1986	October	113.7	111.1
1986	August	112.3	109.8
1986	June	112.2	109.9
1986	April	110.7	108.4
1986	February	110.8	108.7
1985	**Annual**	**108.6**	**106.7**
1985	December	110.4	108.3
1985	October	110.3	108.2
1985	August	109.6	107.6
1985	June	108.4	106.6
1985	April	107.3	105.6
1985	February	106.6	104.9
1984	**Annual**	**103.8**	**102.5**
1984	December	105.7	104.0
1984	October	105.8	103.0
1984	August	104.7	103.8
1984	June	103.6	102.8
1984	April	102.7	101.4
1984	February	101.7	101.3
1983	**Annual**	**98.9**	**99.0**
1983	December	100.7	101.2
1983	October	100.3	100.6
1983	August	99.7	99.3
1983	June	99.1	98.6
1983	April	97.8	97.9
1983	February	96.9	97.7
1982	**Annual**	**97.3**	**98.5**
1982	December	96.2	97.3
1982	October	98.0	99.1
1982	August	98.3	99.4
1982	June	98.5	99.6
1982	April	96.8	98.1
1982	February	96.4	97.7

FIGURE 3.6 (continued): **A Look Back at California's Entire CPI (1955 to 2014)**

California Consumer Price Index (1955–2014) All Items (1982–1984=100)			
Year	Month	All Urban Consumers	Urban Wage Earners and Clerical Workers
1981	**Annual**	**91.4**	**92.7**
1981	December	95.5	96.7
1981	October	95.3	96.5
1981	August	92.9	94.3
1981	June	90.1	91.4
1981	April	89.1	90.5
1981	February	87.3	88.7
1980	**Annual**	**82.4**	**83.6**
1980	December	86.0	87.3
1980	October	84.2	85.3
1980	August	82.8	84.0
1980	June	83.3	84.4
1980	April	81.3	82.5
1980	February	79.5	80.4
1979	**Annual**	**71.3**	**72.1**
1979	December	76.3	77.1
1979	October	74.0	74.9
1979	August	72.6	73.6
1979	June	71.0	71.9
1979	April	69.3	70.0
1979	February	67.4	68.0
1978	**Annual**	**64.4**	**64.7**
1978	December	65.9	66.3
1978	October	66.2	66.5
1978	August	65.5	65.9
1978	June	64.6	64.9
1978	April	63.1	63.3
1978	February	62.0	62.5
1977	**Annual**	**59.5**	**59.9**
1977	December	61.3	61.7
1977	September	60.3	60.7
1977	June	59.5	59.8
1977	March	58.3	58.7
1976	**Annual**	**55.6**	**55.9**
1976	December	57.1	57.5
1976	September	56.4	56.8
1976	June	55.2	55.6

California Consumer Price Index (1955–2014) All Items (1982–1984=100)			
Year	Month	All Urban Consumers	Urban Wage Earners and Clerical Workers
1976	March	54.4	54.8
1975	**Annual**	**52.3**	**52.6**
1975	December	54.2	54.5
1975	September	53.2	53.5
1975	June	52.0	52.4
1975	March	51.2	51.6
1974	**Annual**	**47.4**	**47.7**
1974	December	49.9	50.2
1974	September	48.8	49.1
1974	June	47.1	47.4
1974	March	45.8	46.1
1973	December	44.5	44.8
1973	September	43.8	44.1
1973	June	42.7	43.0
1973	March	42.1	42.4
1972	**Annual**	**40.6**	**40.9**
1972	December	41.3	41.6
1972	September	41.1	41.4
1972	June	40.5	40.7
1972	March	40.2	40.5
1971	**Annual**	**39.3**	**39.6**
1971	December	39.8	40.1
1971	September	39.7	40.0
1971	June	39.4	39.7
1971	March	38.9	39.2
1970	**Annual**	**37.9**	**38.2**
1970	December	38.7	39.0
1970	September	38.4	38.6
1970	June	37.9	38.1
1970	March	37.3	37.6
1969	**Annual**	**36.1**	**36.3**
1969	December	37.0	37.2
1969	September	36.5	36.8
1969	June	36.0	36.3
1969	March	35.7	35.9
1968	**Annual**	**34.4**	**34.6**
1968	December	34.9	35.2

FIGURE 3.6 (continued):   A Look Back at California's Entire CPI (1955 to 2014)

California Consumer Price Index (1955–2014) All Items (1982–1984=100)			
Year	Month	All Urban Consumers	Urban Wage Earners and Clerical Workers
1968	September	34.6	34.8
1968	June	34.3	34.6
1968	March	34.0	34.3
1967	**Annual**	**33.0**	**33.2**
1967	December	33.6	33.9
1967	September	33.4	33.7
1967	June	32.9	33.1
1967	March	32.4	32.7
1966	**Annual**	**32.2**	**32.4**
1966	December	32.6	32.8
1966	September	32.4	32.6
1966	June	32.1	32.4
1966	March	31.9	32.1
1965	**Annual**	**31.5**	**31.7**
1965	December	31.7	31.9
1965	September	31.5	31.8
1965	June	31.6	31.8
1964	**Annual**	**31.0**	**31.0**
1964	December	31.3	31.3
1964	September	30.9	31.0
1964	June	30.9	31.0
1964	March	30.9	30.9
1963	**Annual**	**30.4**	**30.5**
1963	December	30.6	30.7
1963	September	30.5	30.6
1963	June	30.3	30.3
1963	March	30.3	30.4
1962	**Annual**	**29.9**	**30.0**
1962	December	30.1	30.2
1962	September	30.0	30.1
1962	June	30.0	30.1
1962	March	29.7	29.9
1961	**Annual**	**29.5**	**29.6**
1961	December	29.7	29.8
1961	September	29.5	29.6
1961	June	29.4	29.5
1961	March	29.4	29.5

California Consumer Price Index (1955–2014) All Items (1982–1984=100)			
Year	Month	All Urban Consumers	Urban Wage Earners and Clerical Workers
1960	**Annual**	**29.2**	**29.2**
1960	December	29.5	29.5
1960	September	29.2	29.2
1960	June	29.1	29.2
1960	March	29.0	29.0
1959	**Annual**	**28.6**	**28.7**
1959	December	29.0	29.0
1959	September	28.7	28.8
1959	June	28.5	28.6
1959	March	28.4	28.5
1958	**Annual**	**28.1**	**28.2**
1958	December	28.3	28.4
1958	September	28.2	28.4
1958	June	28.1	28.2
1958	March	27.9	28.1
1957	**Annual**	**27.1**	**27.3**
1957	December	27.5	27.6
1957	September	27.3	27.4
1957	June	27.0	27.2
1957	March	26.9	27.1
1956	**Annual**	**26.2**	**26.3**
1956	December	26.8	26.8
1956	September	26.3	26.4
1956	June	26.2	26.3
1956	March	25.9	26.0
1955	**Annual**	**25.7**	**25.9**
1955	December	25.8	25.9
1955	September	25.8	25.9
1955	June	25.7	25.8
1955	March	25.7	25.8

Source: California Department of Industrial Relations (www. dir.ca.gov/OPRL/CPI/EntireCCPI.PDF)

Gross Domestic Product (GDP)

The principal indicator of the total output of goods and services in the United States is the **gross domestic product (GDP)**. This GDP measures the economic effect resulting from the production of wealth by labor and property physically located within the nation's borders. (You will recall from Unit 1 that this is the basis for evaluating wealth proposed by Adam Smith back in 1776.) The GDP is also the standard international measure of economic accounting, so nations share a standard against which to gauge their productivity.

The GDP measures four major components:

1. *Individual consumption*

2. *Investment spending*

3. *Government spending*

4. *Net exports*

Figure 3.7 illustrates how much of the recent U.S. GDP is composed of each factor.

FIGURE 3.7:   Components of Total U.S. GDP (2012–2014)

Gross Domestic Product for the United States Billions of dollars				
	2012 4th Quarter	2013 4th Quarter	2014 3rd Quarter	2014 4th Quarter
Gross domestic product	**16,332.5**	**17,087.3**	**17,599.8**	**17,703.7**
Personal consumption expenditures	**11,222.6**	**11,653.3**	**12,002.0**	**12,120.2**
Goods	3,788.8	3,886.1	4,011.5	4,008.0
Durable goods	1,216.1	1,261.5	1,320.2	1,329.0
Nondurable goods	2,572.8	2,624.6	2,691.3	2,679.0
Services	7,433.8	7,767.2	7,990.4	8,112.3
Gross private domestic investment	**2,481.5**	**2,745.2**	**2,905.1**	**2,943.3**
Fixed investment	2,471.0	2,654.6	2,810.6	2,850.0
Nonresidential	1,998.7	2,118.7	2,244.3	2,272.0
Structures	445.9	481.7	513.3	522.1
Equipment and software	922.8	980.0	1,038.2	1,042.9
Residential	472.3	539.9	566.4	578.0
Change in private inventories	10.4	90.5	94.5	93.3
Net exports of goods and services	**-528.2**	**-462.9**	**-516.5**	**-549.2**
Exports	2,218.5	2,324.6	2,366.5	2,352.3
Goods	1,529.2	1,614.0	1,645.0	1,615.3
Services	689.3	710.7	721.4	737.0
Imports	2,746.7	2,787.5	2,883.0	2,901.5
Goods	2,283.1	2,309.7	2,393.7	2,401.1
Services	436.6	477.8	489.3	500.4
Government consumption expenditures and gross investment	**3,156.6**	**3,142.7**	**3,209.3**	**3,189.3**
Federal	1,269.9	1,216.2	1,241.3	1,216.7
National defense	795.4	757.5	784.0	757.5
Nondefense	474.4	458.7	457.3	459.2
State and local	1,886.8	1,926.5	1,968.0	1,972.6

Source: Bureau of Economic Analysis

Individual Consumption Spending   This section of the GDP is composed of specifically defined elements:

- **Durable goods**—products that are expected to last more than three years, such as cars or major appliances

- **Nondurable goods**—products with a shorter life span, such as clothing or food

- **Services**—activities with a monetary exchange value

Investment Spending The GDP's investment spending measurement includes the following:

- **Nonresidential investments**—expenditures on such capital investments as factories and equipment

- **Residential investments**—single-family and multifamily homes

- Changes in **business inventories**

Government Spending The GDP takes into account the amount of money spent each year by the national government on such things as defense, highways, schools, and social programs.

Net Exports Finally, GDP includes the nation's *net exports*. Net exports is the amount remaining after total imports are deducted from total exports. If a nation has a trade deficit, for instance, that means that it imports more than it exports. A trade deficit will reduce GDP and reflect a less wealthy national economy.

Using GDP By tracking GDP, economists can measure the relative health of a national economy. If the GDP figure for a given year has increased over the previous year, the nation's economy has grown.

Recent Statistics by State According to the Bureau of Economic Analysis, the United States has been undergoing slow but steady growth since 2013.

- Real GDP increased in 49 states in 2013. Leading industry contributors were nondurable goods, manufacturing, real estate (including rental and leasing), agriculture, forestry, fishing, and hunting.

- Nondurable goods manufacturing was the largest contributor to U.S. real GDP by state growth in 2013. This industry was the leading contributor to real GDP growth in 10 states, contributing 2.65% to growth in Louisiana and 1.19% to growth in Texas.

- Real estate was the leading contributor to growth in the New England region and contributed 0.5% or more to growth in North Dakota, Nevada, and Massachusetts.

- Agriculture, forestry, fishing, and hunting contributed to real GDP growth in 49 states and the District of Columbia.

- In North Dakota, the fastest-growing state in 2013, mining contributed 3.61% to the state's 9.7% growth in real GDP.

- In contrast, in 2013, government subtracted from real GDP growth in six of eight BEA regions, 39 states, and the District of Columbia.

- Alaska was the only state where real GDP decreased in 2013, primarily due to the decline in mining.

- Per capita real GDP ranged from a high of $70,113 in Alaska to a low of $32,421 in Mississippi. Per capita real GDP for the United States was $49,155.

Looking at the GNP

The **gross national product (GNP)**, commonly referred to as the **national income**, represents the sum of consumption spending, investments, government expenditures, and imports minus imports, or $C + I + G + X - M = GNP$.

$$GNP = C + I + G + X - M$$

Many of the economic indicators that we use fall into one or more of the categories previously listed, and each one is useful for the information it provides about the overall economy.

In further deriving the GNP, there are three approaches to measuring the money value of the goods and services that become available to a nation from its economic activity. The three approaches include:

- a sum of the incomes derived from economic activity, broadly divided into incomes from profits and incomes from employment;

- a sum of the expenditures with the main distinction between expenditures that add to the capital stock (investment); and

- the sum of the products of various industries of the nation.

These three measures—the income, expenditure, and output (product) approaches—give rise to several different ways of describing the various aggregates employed in compiling the national accounts. The three approaches also give rise to estimates of the GNP, which, once adjusted to take account of capital consumption, provide the measure of national income or net national product. Only the value of final products is included in the GNP. Items produced and used as inputs by other businesses are not included.

Double counting is avoided by considering only the value added at each stage of production. Goods and services produced during the time period are included in the GNP. Goods produced and added to inventory are included in the GNP even though they are not sold during the time period. The GNP is calculated using the market prices of goods and services. Items without market prices are either excluded from the GNP, or a value is given to them.

It should be noted that the GNP is probably **the most** important report during any given quarter. Real or inflation-adjusted, the GNP is the best single measure of U.S. economic output and spending. Data contained in the GNP accounts affect the markets because, from that data, investors, analysts, traders, and economists acquire a comprehensive sense of where the economy is heading. The GNP reports also play a major role in influencing decisions at the highest levels, from Congressional budget staffers and Federal Reserve policy makers to corporate strategic planners. When all is said and done, the GNP is the figure by which the nation keeps score, both domestically and internationally.

Unemployment

The *unemployment rate* is a percentage used to characterize the employment situation in specified areas. Its calculation is simple: the number of unemployed persons divided by the total civilian labor force. The Bureau of Labor Statistics defines an unemployed person as anyone older than 16 who is available to work but who has not worked at a paying job during the past week and who has sought employment at some time during the previous four weeks. "Unemployed persons" also includes people who are waiting to be called back from a layoff or who are waiting to report to a new job sometime in the next 30 days.

FIGURE 3.8:   **U.S. Monthly Unemployment Rates for 2005 Through 2014**

Year	Jan	Feb	Mar	Apr	May	Jun	Jul	Aug	Sep	Oct	Nov	Dec
2005	5.3	5.4	5.2	5.2	5.1	5.0	5.0	4.9	5.0	5.0	5.0	4.9
2006	4.7	4.8	4.7	4.7	4.6	4.6	4.7	4.7	4.5	4.4	4.5	4.4
2007	4.6	4.5	4.4	4.5	4.4	4.6	4.7	4.6	4.7	4.7	4.7	5.0
2008	5.0	4.9	5.1	5.0	5.4	5.6	5.8	6.1	6.1	6.5	6.8	7.3
2009	7.8	8.3	8.7	9.0	9.4	9.5	9.5	9.6	9.8	10.0	9.9	9.9
2010	9.8	9.8	9.9	9.9	9.6	9.4	9.4	9.5	9.5	9.4	9.8	9.3
2011	9.2	9.0	9.0	9.1	9.0	9.1	9.0	9.0	9.0	8.8	8.6	8.5
2012	8.3	8.3	8.2	8.2	8.2	8.2	8.2	8.0	7.8	7.8	7.7	7.9
2013	8.0	7.7	7.5	7.6	7.5	7.5	7.3	7.2	7.2	7.2	7.0	6.7
2014	6.6	6.7	6.6	6.2	6.3	6.1	6.2	6.1	5.9	5.7	5.8	5.6

Source: Bureau of Labor Statistics

The unemployment rate is an important economic indicator, and understanding its significance and movements is very helpful in assessing inflationary pressures. In the second half of 2013, the labor market continued to improve. Payroll employment increased an average of approximately 175,000 per month since June of that year. The unemployment rate declined from 7.7% in June 2013 to 6.6% in January 2014.

Hidden unemployment or disguised unemployment must also be considered when analyzing the true state of unemployment. Because the labor force varies procyclically, it can be argued that the unemployment count or enumeration will understate the true volume of unemployment by excluding discouraged workers who form hidden unemployment. In this view, such workers would otherwise be available for work if they did not regard the search as hopeless. Accordingly, an estimate of the hidden unemployed should be added to the official unemployment figures to obtain a true reading of the labor market slack.

The rates of a variety of alternative measures of labor force underutilization have also improved, according to the BLS. In addition to the unemployed, these measures include those classified as discouraged, other individuals who are out of work and classified as marginally attached to the labor force, and individuals who have a job but would like to work more hours.

Since August 2012, total payroll employment has increased a cumulative 3¼ million, and the unemployment rate has declined 1½ percentage points. Despite recent declines in the unemployment rate, the rate remains well above the estimates of the Federal Open Market Committee (FOMC) of the Federal Reserve long-run sustainable rate of unemployment and well above rates that prevailed prior to the recession. According to the Federal Reserve, there is still concern in looking beyond labor participation. For example, the share of unemployed who have been out of work longer than six months and the percentage of the work force that is working part time but would like to work full time have only modestly declined.

Another area of concern is that the **quit rate** still remains low. The quit rate is an indicator of workers' confidence in the availability of other jobs. The Federal Reserve and the BLS also measure and track the behavior of wages or costs index for private industry workers. This index measures both wages and the cost to employers of providing benefits. Throughout the post-recession recovery, this has remained close to 2%. Similarly, average hourly earnings for all employees have only increased 2% as well. This tells us that gains in compensation have been slow compared to pre-recession days.

A CLOSER LOOK   According to the BLS, the share of long-term unemployed (people who have been looking for work for 27 weeks or longer) reached a record high in 2010. After expanding for three consecutive years, the number of long-term unemployed reached a record high of 6.7 million or 45.1% of the unemployed in the second quarter of 2010. Since then, the number has gradually declined to 2.8 million (or 31.6% of the unemployed) as of the fourth quarter of 2014. The share of the unemployed who were out of work for 52 weeks or longer reached a record high of 31.9% in the second quarter of 2011. The share unemployed for 99 weeks or longer reached a record peak at 15.1% in the fourth quarter of 2011. All of these measures of long-term unemployment have trended down since their respective peaks but remain high by historical standards. Additionally, the BLS also reported that more than one in ten unemployed in 2014 were jobless for 99 weeks or longer, and that men were more likely than women to be unemployed 99 weeks or longer (11.8% versus 10.9%).

The *labor force* is defined as every person older than 16 who is either working at a paying job (full time or part time) or who fits the definition of unemployed. Those not in the labor force include anyone older than 15 who is neither employed nor unemployed and those persons who are retired. The Bureau of Labor Statistics releases unemployment figures every month. Figures are reported for different categories, such as gender, race, ethnicity, and geographic location.

Data   As with the CPI, a sample is used to obtain data. A rotating sample of 50,000 households is contacted each month and asked whether each person worked at all during the week and whether nonworking members have been recently laid off or are looking for work. Of course, if they do not meet those tests, they are considered no longer in the labor force. They are, therefore, not counted as unemployed.

Limitations Because of the limited definitions used in compiling employment statistics, the true extent of joblessness in the economy is very likely higher than the official reported number. For instance, the official employment figures exclude "discouraged workers"—people who have given up hope of finding a job and have stopped actively looking. On the other hand, individuals who are participants in the U.S. "underground economy" of bartered services and undeclared income from cash-paying work may be counted as unemployed, even though they are not. Further, the government unemployment figures may not be giving a truly qualitative reflection of employment conditions. Unemployment figures do not take into consideration people who are working part-time jobs out of desperation, people who have been downsized into part-time status, or the underemployed. Workers are simply counted as employed, whether or not society (or the worker's family) is receiving the full benefit of their skills.

The Stock Market as Indicator

The **Standard & Poor's 500 (S&P 500)** is a stock index compiled by Standard & Poor's, a division of the McGraw-Hill Companies, Inc. Since 1957, the S&P 500 has been made up of stocks from 500 companies selected by Standard & Poor's Index Committee. The index is made up of leading U.S. companies in important industries in various U.S. markets. The index is weighted by the size of the companies and is designed to reflect the composition of the U.S. economy. Other attributes of the companies in the S&P 500 are that their stocks are widely traded and are considered relatively stable. The S&P 500 provides a number of valuable functions for investors and economic observers. Many people who invest in stock diversify their portfolios against company and sectoral risk by buying stock through mutual funds (these are funds that pool investment monies and buy a diverse portfolio of stock). Because investors around the world consider the S&P 500 to be the standard representative of the U.S. market, the quality of stock mutual fund managers can be assessed by comparing the performance of their mutual funds to that of the S&P 500. Finally, the S&P 500 is a component of the Conference Board's Index of Leading Economic Indicators.

The **Dow-Jones Industrial Average** is a measure of the prices that are paid for shares in major industrial corporations in the stock market. The **Nasdaq**, *New York Stock Exchange Index*, and *S&P 500* are similar measures. The Dow-Jones is based on a group of 30 stocks, considered representative of the market as a whole. The Dow-Jones average on a single day says very little; what matters is its direction over a period of time.

The *Nasdaq 100 Index* is commonly relied on as a measure of the stock market and the nation's general economic health. The Nasdaq 100 represents the 100 largest nonfinancial domestic companies listed on the Nasdaq market across industry groups. The *Willshire 5000* index measures the daily performance of the 5,000 largest U.S. companies.

Limitations   Fluctuations in stock prices reflect the expectations of people who trade in stocks. The greater their confidence that business will be good, the more likely they are to buy shares. The more demand for a particular share, the higher its price. When investor confidence in a particular company or in the market as a whole is low, the more likely investors will sell their shares and cause prices to drop.

The stock market has obvious limits resulting from its character as an arbitrarily processed nonrandom sample representing a very specialized part of the economy. The Dow-Jones index is heavily skewed toward blue chip stocks (those that consistently show solid growth and reliable dividends). It does not look at either less successful stocks or the sharply rising glamour stocks associated with a new process or product. Nasdaq is frequently accused of emphasizing high-tech stocks, and the *American Stock Exchange* is thought to be weighted in favor of natural resource companies. As an indicator of economic performance, the stock market offers a wealth of information but significant limitations as well. (Note: In the first quarter of 1998, Nasdaq and the American Stock Exchange entered into merger negotiations. The proposed merger was seen as a move to create more effective competition against the New York Stock Exchange.)

Why Are All Eyes on the Nasdaq?

The Nasdaq Composite Index measures all Nasdaq domestic and international-based common type stocks listed on The Nasdaq Stock Market. Launched in 1971, the Nasdaq Composite Index is a broad-based index. Today, the index includes over 3,000 securities, more than most other stock market indexes. The Nasdaq Composite Index is calculated under a market capitalization weighted methodology index.

FIGURE 3.9:   Top 10 Largest Nasdaq Volume Days (accessed April 2015)

Date	Nasdaq Trading Volume
6/26/2009	5,214,013,855
6/25/2010	5,033,380,789
3/25/2014	4,486,188,694
9/19/2014	4,425,874,101
3/24/2014	4,309,048,275
3/21/2014	4,281,975,528
6/27/2014	4,243,483,489
2/19/2014	4,239,640,335
6/24/2011	4,111,764,592
6/27/2008	4,018,529,536

Eligibility Criteria   To be eligible for inclusion in the Nasdaq Composite Index, the security's U.S. listing must be exclusively on the Nasdaq Stock Market (unless the security was dually listed on another U.S. market prior to January 1, 2004, and has continuously maintained such listing) and have a security type of

- American Depositary Receipts (ADRs),

- common stock,

- limited partnership interests,

- ordinary shares,

- Real Estate Investment Trusts (REITs),

- Shares of Beneficial Interest (SBIs), or

- tracking stocks.

Security types not included in the index are closed-end funds, convertible debentures, exchange traded funds, preferred stocks, rights, warrants, units, and other derivative securities. If at any time a component security no longer meets the eligibility criteria, the security is removed from the Nasdaq Composite Index.

The Market Reacts to Indicators

While it is clearly important to understand what indicators tell us about the economy or inflation, it is also extremely important to recognize that the market's reaction is going to be determined more by how it compares to the market's consensus forecasts than by absolute change in an indicator. For example, let's say that the market believes that the GNP growth for some particular quarter is going to rise only ½ percent. If the Commerce Department data reveal that growth was actually 1%, the fixed-income markets probably will decline because GNP was more rapid than had been expected. The equity markets will probably also decline because the higher-than-anticipated GNP advance reduces the likelihood that the Federal Reserve will ease monetary policy and, hence, interest rates may not decline in the near future.

Generally speaking, the market's short-term reaction is determined by whether a number is higher or lower than expected rather than by the absolute value of the number.

It is also important to understand that an indicator's value is determined to some extent by its release date. Figure 3.10 represents a list of approximate release dates for indicators. The first hard data that we receive each month are car sales, released shortly after the end of each 10-day period. Typically on the first Friday of each month, the employment report is released , which provides us with a complete sense of what occurred in the economy during the prior month.

FIGURE 3.10: Release Dates for Economic Indicators

Report	Release Date
Car Sales	13th, 23rd of same month; 3rd of following month
Purchasing Manager's Report	1st business day of the following month
Employment	1st–7th of following month
Producer Price Index (PPI)	9th–16th of following month
Retail Sales	11th–14th of following month
Industrial Production/Capacity Utilization	14th–17th of following month
Housing Starts/Building Permits	16th–20th of following month
Consumer Price Index (CPI)	15th–21st of following month
Durable Goods Orders	22nd–28th of following month
GNP	21st–30th of following month
Personal Income/Consumer Spending	22nd–31st of following month
New Home Sales	28th–4th for two months prior
Construction Spending	1st business day for two months prior
Factory Orders	30th–6th for two months prior
Business Inventories	13th–17th for two months prior
Merchandise Trade Deficit	15th–17th for two months prior

Exercise in Forecasting

At this point you have a basic understanding of the economy and the driving forces affecting the economy's well-being. Now begin examining the state of the economy by looking at the various "economic indicators" covered in this unit. Record your findings in a manner in which it will be easy for you to retrieve your data. Do this for two months.

During the last week of the term (semester/quarter), report your findings to the class. Now attempt to forecast potential changes in the economy for the upcoming months. Additionally, as you charted the information after the release of each indicator's data, how did the real estate market in your area react? This can be in the form of sales or lack of, mortgage interest rates fluctuating, and so forth.

If you find it helpful, you may also work in groups or teams in which each person is responsible for assembling one's own share of the data to be collected.

Note: An excellent source for leading economic indicators is the *Wall Street Journal* and the various television financial news programs such as those on CNN, Headline News, Money Line, and so forth. When people hear positive statistical information about the markets and employment, they are more apt to look at investment opportunities and, for some, they will choose real estate as an investment. The key indicators to watch as they relate to real estate are employment, new home sales, construction spending and, most important, housing starts/new building permits issued.

THE NEXT STEP In the next unit, we'll devote our full attention to a subject that is of great interest: *money*. In addition to considering the evolution of paper money as a medium of exchange, we'll look at the Federal Reserve System, the money supply, and inflation.

SUMMARY

- An **economic trend** is a *change in a market in a consistent direction, over time*. Trends may be classified as **long term** or **short term**.

- There are four types of economic fluctuations: **periodic** (*predictable and regularly occurring*); **irregular** (*predictable but not regularly occurring*); **random** (*unpredictable and irregular*); and **cyclical** (*predictable and regular over a long period of time*).

- A **business cycle** is characterized by a *general, simultaneous expansion or contraction in a variety of different economic activities*, reflecting the broader economic health of the nation, region, or local market.

Business cycles are *recurring but very long term*. Business cycles are composed of periods of *prosperity*, *recession*, *depression*, and *recovery*.

- **Economic indicators** provide analysts with the data necessary to make informed judgments about the current and future economic health of a market. Indicators may be *coincident*, *lagging*, or *leading*.

- The **Consumer Price Index (CPI)** is a major economic indicator prepared by the *U.S. Department of Labor*. The CPI relies on analysis of the changing prices of a **market basket** of typical consumer items.

- The *principal indicator of the nation's total output of goods and services* is the **gross domestic product (GDP)**. GDP measures *individual consumption, investment spending, government spending*, and *net exports*.

- The **gross national product (GNP)** is a monetary measure of the value of all final goods and services produced in the economy during a year.

- The **unemployment rate** and the **stock market** are two other indicators that provide valuable current information about a local, regional, state, or national economy.

REVIEW QUESTIONS

1. What is a business cycle?

2. How are unemployment rates determined, and what do they mean?

3. What is the difference between the New York Stock Exchange, the American Stock Exchange, and the Nasdaq?

4. What is inflation, and why is everyone afraid of it?

5. What is the most important sector of the economy, and why would it be grouped under the GNP?

6. As a homebuyer seeking financing, which of the leading economic indicators would you give the most weight to and why?

7. Which stock composite index is much more closely related to the real estate industry, including financing activity and REITs?

8. Explain the difference between the GNP and the GDP.

UNIT QUIZ

1.   A market change in a consistent direction over a period of time is referred to as an economic
     a.   expansion.
     b.   fluctuation.
     c.   trend.
     d.   amplitude.

2.   All of the following types of economic fluctuations are predictable *EXCEPT*
     a.   periodic.
     b.   irregular.
     c.   random.
     d.   cyclical.

3.   In a business cycle, the period between two peaks is referred to as
     a.   a contraction.
     b.   a duration.
     c.   an expansion.
     d.   an amplitude.

4.   The point on a business cycle at which a decline in economic activity reaches bottom is referred to as
     a.   the trough.
     b.   the contraction.
     c.   the amplitude.
     d.   the lower turning point.

5.   Two successive quarters of contraction, characterized by cautious spending and increased saving, are referred to as
     a.   a boom.
     b.   a recovery.
     c.   a depression.
     d.   a recession.

6. All of the following terms accurately describe characteristics of an economic forecast *EXCEPT*
   a. prediction.
   b. explicit.
   c. implicit.
   d. estimate.

7. Which of the following major economic indicators uses a "market basket" of consumer goods?
   a. GDP
   b. CPI
   c. BEA
   d. Nasdaq

8. The gross national product is commonly known as
   a. the national income.
   b. the national debt.
   c. the total output of all goods and services produced.
   d. none of these.

9. In a GDP analysis, a refrigerator would be considered which of the following?
   a. Durable goods
   b. Nondurable goods
   c. Investment spending
   d. Household furnishings

10. Which of the following stock market indicators relies on a sample of 100 nonfinancial domestic companies across industry groups?
    a. Dow-Jones
    b. Nasdaq
    c. Willshire
    d. American

MONEY AND
MONETARY POLICY

KEY TERMS

bimetallism	electronic funds	notes
Board of Governors	Federal Reserve (Fed)	quantitative easing
COLAs	Federal Reserve Board	quotas
commodities	fiscal policy	reserve requirements
currency	gold standard	value
deposit money	inflation	
discount rate	money	

LEARNING OBJECTIVES

■ Understand how money evolved as a form of exchange, from simple barter economies to modern electronic funds transfers

■ Explain the structure and importance of the Federal Reserve System in the U.S. economy

■ Define the economic measurement terms M1, M2, M3, and L

■ Describe the role of inflation and the impact of government monetary policies on the real estate market

THE EVOLUTION OF MONEY

Money is any medium of exchange adopted by a society as a means of acquiring goods and services. Money may or may not have any intrinsic value of its own—gold coins, for instance, have an independent value; paper money, which is merely ink and paper, only *represents* value. The value assigned to money is dependent on a variety of political, economic, commercial, and psychological factors.

Figure 4.1 is a timeline highlighting some of the more significant moments in the history of money.

FIGURE 4.1:   Important Moments in Money

c 2500 BC	Banking invented in Mesopotamia
c 1700 BC	Code of Hammurabi includes banking laws
c 1000 BC	Cowrie shells used as money in China
c 500 BC	Gold and silver coins produced in Lydia, Asia Minor
c 400 BC	Silver-coated bronze coins minted in Athens
c 250 BC	Romans circulate silver coins
c 100 BC	Chinese issue leather money
10 AD	Augustus establishes sales, land, and poll taxes
410	Fall of Rome to Visigoths; end of European banking
c 430	Use of coins ends in Britain
c 550	Use of coins resumes in Britain
c 800	China introduces paper money
c 11th–13th Century	Crusades stimulate reemergence of European banking
1156	First foreign-exhange contract (Genoese pounds for Byzantine bezants)
1292	Marco Polo, returning from China, introduces paper money to Europe
1455	China abolishes paper money
1545	In England, King Henry VIII legalizes charging interest on loans
c 1600	Tobacco is legal currency in the Virginia Colony
c 1630	Wampum shells are legal currency in Massachusetts Bay Colony
1661	Bank of Sweden issues first European paper money
1690	Massachusetts Bay Colony issues paper money
1764	Britain forbids use of paper money in American Colonies
1776	Adam Smith praises paper money
1789	U.S. Constitution empowers Congress to issue paper money
1861–1865	U.S. Civil War: Confederate notes become worthless
1900	U.S. adopts the gold standard
1944–1971	Bretton Woods Agreement attempts to standardize international trade
1973	U.S. abandons gold standard
1984	U.S. courts legalize national ATM networks
1992	Maastricht Treaty calls for common European currency by 1999
c 1995	More than 90% of transactions in the U.S. involve electronic transfers
2002	The Euro is adopted by the European Union

Money Through History

Early Barter Economies   In early human commercial transactions, money was not an issue. In a *barter economy,* goods or services are traded directly for other goods or services. A cow, for instance, might be traded for so many bushels of corn, or a cobbler might agree to make a pair of shoes in exchange for a quilt. A barter economy values **commodities** (goods and services) both for their own usefulness and for their potential in exchange.

While often thought of as an ancient relic, barter economies are not confined to prehistory. Even in the modern U.S. economy, barter is alive and well in the *underground economy,* where individuals commonly trade goods and services as a way of avoiding income taxation or of obtaining goods or services they could not otherwise afford.

Primitive Money   There is, obviously, a limit to the number of cattle or bushels of corn a person can reasonably be expected to cart around. Just as our concept of numbers may have arisen out of the convenience of using abstract symbols to represent physical quantities, so too the idea arose over time of using a particular commodity as the basic means of exchange. If a cow, for instance, was worth 17 bushels of corn, then a bead or shell might just as easily *represent* 17 bushels of corn, making the transfer somewhat more convenient. In various parts of the world, the common means of exchange has taken many forms: amber, beads, cowries, eggs, feathers, ivory, jade, leather, nails, quartz, oxen, rice, and salt have all, at one time or another, been somebody's "money."

This system of exchange only works, however, if it is agreed upon by a larger society. Persons who receive the bead or shell only receive **value** for the cow if they can, in turn, exchange the bead or shell for 17 bushels of corn's worth of blankets or chickens or legal advice. The development of money, then, is closely linked to the development of interdependent social structures.

The whole history of money can be viewed as the refinement of this basic abstraction: a monetary unit may represent a certain fixed value in gold or some other standard. That standard has value only because the society agrees that it does. Its value is reflected in what it can buy. A coin may be worth three ounces of gold, and three ounces of gold may buy a dozen cows or 200 bushels of corn, which brings us right back where we started: barter.

Early Civilizations   As society became increasingly urbanized, merchants, writers, and skilled craftsmen played a larger role in the economy. As a result, more sophisticated exchange systems were possible, and metal became a prominent medium of exchange.

Prior to the development of a minting process, metal was measured out by weight. A Greek *drachma* originally represented six obols, and each obol represented a handful of nails. Other currencies today that started out as metal measurements are the English *pound*, Russian *ruble*, and Italian *lira*.

Gold and silver were especially favored as a medium of exchange because they were scarce and durable, and small amounts could command large amounts of goods and services.

Development of Coinage   Due to the inconvenience of measuring out metal for each transaction, coinage appeared as a sort of preweighed medium of exchange in Europe. The first coins were solid precious metals, such as gold or silver; later, less expensive metals, such as bronze or copper, were covered with a thin layer of gold or silver.

In the New World, the Mayas and Aztecs used measured gold dust held in hollow, transparent quills, as well as large sacks of cocoa beans, for money. (The Incas, interestingly, did not develop a monetary system despite their high degree of civilization. This unusual situation may have resulted from the intensity of their centralized state planning.)

Medieval to Early Modern Era   With the fall of the Roman Empire, a general cultural regression occurred, including a return to the use of metal in bulk as a form of payment.

Paper Money   An early form of paper money was developed in China around the ninth century, in large part due to a shortage of copper. Marco Polo reported the innovation to Europeans with the publication of his travel journals in 1295. The new medium of exchange was viewed with suspicion and was slow to catch on among Europeans; paper money was not in general use by merchants until the late 1600s. In the meantime, China had abandoned the use of paper money by the middle of the 15th century.

Goldsmiths' Notes   The use of currency backed by metal started in England in the 1600s when merchants stored their gold with goldsmiths, receiving receipts for their deposit. These receipts, in turn, gained acceptance as a means of exchange as the recipients were confident that they could be redeemed in gold.

Eighteenth and Nineteenth Centuries   Paper money gained acceptance and sophistication during this period, and the banking industry flourished throughout Europe. With this financial boom, however, came confusion. Without a centralized monetary authority, private individuals, companies, and banks of varying reliability issued *fiduciary money*— **notes** promising to pay gold or silver.

The promises associated with fiduciary money were not always kept, however, and trust in paper money was often low. Even in respectable banks, such notes were fractionally rather than fully backed by precious metal. This ordinarily sufficed, as only a few individuals at a time wanted to redeem their notes. Nevertheless, if even a few too many depositors asked for specie (coin), bank resources might be strained and rumors of inadequate reserves to back the issued notes would sweep through the streets. This, in turn, might set off a "run on the bank," in which frantic depositors would close their accounts. Banks often failed, with depositors losing everything. The recurrent pattern of bank failure was a strong argument for the development of central banks.

Central Banks   It soon became apparent that only large, centralized banks, with enormous, reliable reserves of precious metals to back their notes could support smaller banks in times of stress. Initially, the central banks were not always government-owned; eventually, however, they became so. Gradually, central banks became the main issuers of paper money. However, even the central banks did not fully back paper money with gold or silver.

Much of the paper money issued in the 18th and 19th centuries was backed by precious metal (however fractionally or unreliably). Nevertheless, governments could issue paper money or coins whose value was simply decreed. Because another word for an official order or decree is *fiat*, such money is called fiat money.

Paper Money Debate in America   Although paper money had long circulated in some sectors of European commercial life, the widespread use of paper money in America was strongly resisted. A bitter debate between the "paper money men" and the "gold bugs" lasted through most of the 19th century.

If suspicion was aroused by fiduciary money (which at least promised redemption in precious metal), the level of trust in money unsupported by precious metal reserves was intense. The debate in the United States over whether or not to abandon **bimetallism** (the use of gold and silver to back currency) and adopt the international gold standard divided the largely urban, eastern interests who favored the standard from the rural western-ers who opposed it. The **gold standard**, which theoretically limited the amount of money in circulation to the value of gold held in reserve by the issuing government, was adopted in 1900 and remained the basis for valu-ing the U.S. dollar until 1973. In the years between World Wars I and II, most of the world's countries gave up the gold standard.

A CLOSER LOOK   William Jennings Bryan's famous "Cross of Gold" speech, delivered at the Democratic party convention in Chicago on July 8, 1896, is an example of the intensity of feeling created by the gold standard debate:

...We do not come as aggressors. Our war is not a war of conquest; we are fight-ing in the defense of our homes, our families, and posterity. We have petitioned, and our petitions have been scorned . . . we have begged, and they have mocked when our calamity came. We beg no longer; we entreat no more; we petition no more. We defy them. If they dare to come out in the open field and defend the gold standard as a good thing, we will fight them to the uttermost. Having behind us the producing masses of this nation and the world, supported by the commer-cial interests, the laboring interests, and the toilers everywhere, we will answer their demand for a gold standard by saying to them: You will not press down upon the brow of labor this crown of thorns, you shall not crucify mankind upon a cross of gold.

Forms of Modern Money

Money today consists of four main categories:

- **Currency.** Governments issue *legal tender* in paper form to be accept-able in payment of all obligations by law.

- **Coins.** Fractional currency is stamped in metallic form by govern-ments or their central banks. This minting process in the United States is under the authority of the Secretary of the Treasury. The actual metallic value of coins is usually far less than their face value. The difference between the cost of minting and the face value of the coin is called *seigniorage*.

- **Checks.** Although not considered a form of legal tender, checks are a demand to pay upon a depository, which may be backed by government deposit insurance. A check is not reduced to legal tender until such time as the depositing institution pays the item and allows credit for it.

- **Electronic Funds.** The current trend is toward **electronic funds—** fewer checks of the paper variety and more electronic transfers, through the use of debit cards at retail establishments and automatic funds transfer (ATM) transactions. In 1984, a U.S. federal court cleared the way for interstate ATM networks, and by 1995, 90% of the value of all transactions in the United States was transferred electronically. That includes everything from electronic trading of soy bean futures to withdrawing cash from an ATM machine in a convenience store miles from the nearest bank.

Today, more than 200 forms of **currency** are used in the world. Figure 4.2 provides a sample.

FIGURE 4.2:   Some Representative Currencies of the World

Country	Currency	Symbol
Afghanistan	afghani	Af
Venezuela	bolivar	B
Nicaragua	cordoba	C$
Germany	Euro	€
United States	dollar	$
Greece	Euro	€
Portugal	Euro	€
France	Euro	€
Peru	sol	S
Malawi	kwacha	K
Italy	Euro	€
Mozambique	metical	Mt
Bhutan	ngultrum	Nu
Mexico	peso	$
United Kingdom	pound	£
Guatemala	quetzal	Q
Russia	ruble	R
Israel	shekel	IS
Bangladesh	taka	Tk
South Korea	won	W
Japan	yen	¥
Zaire	zaire	Z

U.S. MONETARY POLICY AND THE FEDERAL RESERVE SYSTEM

The traditional, long-term goals of U.S. monetary policy are:

- growth in productive capacity,

- high employment,

- stable prices, and

- stable foreign exchange.

Attaining and maintaining economic conditions that reflect those goals obviously calls for more than a monetary policy; just saying it won't make it so. Productive and organizational efforts in the private sector are required. Private efforts, however, depend on sound and available financial resources and a business climate unmarred by panic and crisis. The *Federal Reserve System* was created with the precise aim of reducing the risk and severity of financial crises.

Stated goals often yield to special circumstances. A stable exchange value for the dollar may be a long-term goal, but the exchange value of the dollar is sometimes allowed to fall in order to encourage foreign purchases of U.S. goods. This way, progress toward a long-term goal is sacrificed in order to address trade deficits.

History of the Federal Reserve System

As we've seen, the need for a strong, reliable central bank was recognized in Europe as early as the 1600s. Americans, however, with their deep cultural distrust of concentrated power and central authority, were slow to accept a central bank. In the 19th century, certain central banking functions were handled by the partly government-owned First and Second Banks of the United States and by the Treasury Department. However, growing demands for agricultural credit in the latter part of the century often outstripped bank reserves and repeated cycles of booms and busts led to financial panic. These crises eventually forced recognition of the desperate need for a central bank in the United States.

Founded by Congress in 1913, the **Federal Reserve** is the central bank of the United States. The *Fed,* as it is known, is responsible for ensuring a sound banking industry and a strong economy. Unlike other nations' unitary central banks, though, the Fed consists of 12 independent regional banks that together process more than a third of the nation's $12 trillion in checks. The Fed's electronic network handles $200 trillion—more than the U.S. gross domestic product. Altogether, there are more than 1,000 state-chartered banks in the Federal Reserve System, representing 11% of all U.S. insured commercial banks and a quarter of U.S. commercial bank assets.

Structure of the Fed

The **Federal Reserve Board** is composed of seven governors appointed by the President and confirmed by the Senate. The governors regulate the entire system and set reserve requirements.

Each of the 12 regional Federal Reserve banks is, in turn, governed by a nine-member board of directors. The regional banks are largely independents. They are responsible for monitoring economic conditions in their regions and for setting regional discount rates (subject to approval by the governors).

The 12 Federal Reserve District banks provide central banking services to the commercial banks in their geographical region. In addition, district banks provide banking services to the U.S. Treasury, clear checks, provide currency, and make loans to member banks in their region. Member banks own stock of the district bank in their region, but the district banks are not profit seeking. Each district bank has nine directors, three each from banking, business, and the public. See Figure 4.3 depicting the location of each of the district banks.

FIGURE 4.3:   Federal Reserve Districts

Source: Federal Reserve Board

Most large banks are members of the Fed, accounting for almost 75% of the commercial banking assets. The intertwining of the commercial banks and the central bank provides a means of central control over the U.S. money supply. Nonmember banks are private-sector commercial banks chartered by state governments, while member banks are chartered by the federal government. A further distinction between member and nonmember banks was blurred by the Depository Institutions Deregulation and Monetary Control Act of 1980. Since the passage of the Act, nonmember as well as member banks are required by federal law to hold reserves against certain types of deposits. Prior to that time, only member banks were subject to the reserve requirements.

The governors and directors form the Federal Open Market Committee (FOMC), the body responsible for making monetary policy. Only 5 of the 12 directors vote (on a revolving basis), although all participate in decision making. The decisions reached by the FOMC have a significant impact on the availability of money and credit in the United States. Figure 4.4 illustrates the structure of the Federal Reserve System, the 12 districts, and the reserve bank cities.

FIGURE 4.4:   The Federal Reserve System

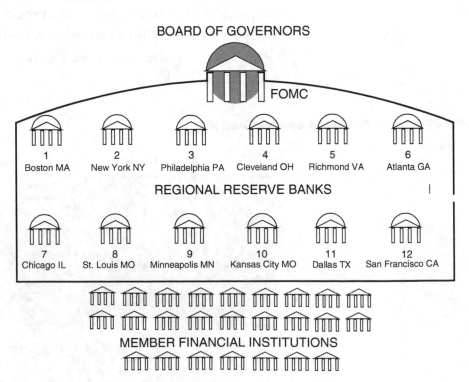

BOARD OF GOVERNORS

FOMC

| 1 | 2 | 3 | 4 | 5 | 6 |
| Boston MA | New York NY | Philadelphia PA | Cleveland OH | Richmond VA | Atlanta GA |

REGIONAL RESERVE BANKS

| 7 | 8 | 9 | 10 | 11 | 12 |
| Chicago IL | St. Louis MO | Minneapolis MN | Kansas City MO | Dallas TX | San Francisco CA |

MEMBER FINANCIAL INSTITUTIONS

Fed's Duties

The Fed's duties fall into four general areas:

1. **Conducting the U.S. monetary policy.** The Fed accomplishes this by influencing the money and credit conditions in the economy. The goal of the policymaking decisions is full employment and stable prices.

2. **Supervising and regulating the banking industry.** The Fed is responsible for ensuring the safety and soundness of the U.S. banking and financial system and for protecting the credit rights of U.S. consumers.

3. **Maintaining the stability of the financial system.** One of the primary reasons the Fed was established was to contain the risks that arise in financial markets and prevent economic crises.

4. **Providing financial services.** The Fed is a "banker's bank," but its services extend to the U.S. government, the public, and to foreign institutions. The Fed is closely involved in operating the U.S. debt payment system.

Just like the rest of us, the Fed looks at leading economic indicators, the inflation rate, the value of the dollar, and the conditions in the financial markets before making policy decisions. These factors are all detailed in the minutes of each FOMC meeting.

If the Fed decides that the economy is growing rapidly and the inflation rate is unacceptably too high, it will move to tighten monetary policy. In the theoretical world, this means that the Fed tries to slow down the growth rate of bank reserves in an effort to moderate growth in the money supply. However, in the real world, typically this process has an immediate effect on short-term interest rates—the federal funds rate in particular. The link between the theoretical and the real-world aspects of the monetary policy, therefore, is interest rates. As interest rates rise and fall, firms and consumers alter their spending plans. Therefore, changes in the monetary policy are transmitted through the economy via changes in interest rates.

Tools of Monetary Policy

The Fed also issues U.S. coins and paper money. While the currency is actually manufactured by the Treasury Department's *Bureau of the Mint* (coins) and the *Bureau of Engraving and Printing* (paper), it is the Fed that distributes the money into circulation through the regional banks and financial institutions. The currency does, in fact, circulate; all U.S. currency eventually returns to the regional banks for inspection. Damaged, worn out, or counterfeit money is destroyed. The rest is put back into circulation.

The Fed adjusts the country's money supply by buying and selling securities and by influencing the amount of money banks have available to lend to businesses and consumers.

A CLOSER LOOK   Quantitative easing is a monetary policy used to stimulate the economy when standard approaches are ineffective. The central banks implement quantitative easing by buying specified amounts of financial assets (e.g., stocks, bonds, savings accounts) from commercial banks and other financial institutions, which raises the prices of those financial assets and lowers their yield, while at the same time increasing the supply of money. Quantitative easing was intended to create more resources for the financial system, giving banks a greater ability to lend money and the public a greater ability to borrow. Historically, traditional tools used by the Fed to lower interest rates became ineffective when rates hovered near zero. Many economists agree that additional monetary easing does not help when there is not a demand to borrow. Additionally, many have argued that conventional monetary policies were deemed largely successful at achieving their domestic goals and were very effective at the time of the greatest financial crisis faced by the United States. Quantitative easing was looked at as an unconventional monetary policy where financial assets were purchased and interest rates were kept low to ensure macroeconomic stability. The major impact or benefit realized on the world resulted in the increased capital flows, especially to emerging markets. With U.S. economic growth rebounding and unemployment falling below 6%, the Fed has ended quantitative easing and has moved to reduce its balance sheet to prerecession levels. The next step is for the Fed to decide when to begin raising interest rates back above the near zero rate.

If the Fed reduces the supply of money, the cost of credit (in the form of interest rates) will rise as a result of the operation of supply and demand. This is a *tight money policy.*

A *loose money policy,* on the other hand, will help stimulate the economy by making credit easier to obtain at lower rates.

These policies can be put into effect through one of three methods:

1. **Reserve Requirements.** All depository institutions are subject to certain requirements regarding the amount of money they must have on reserve. These are called **reserve requirements**. *Reserve funds* cannot be used for lending or investment but must be held to cover depositors' accounts. By raising the reserve requirement, the Fed forces financial institutions to keep back more of their reserves, limiting the amount of money on hand to loan or invest (a tight money policy). The opposite is also true: a lower reserve requirement frees the institutions to lend or invest more money. Only the Board of Governors may change reserve requirements.

2. **Discount Rate.** The Fed sets the interest rate that institutions must pay to borrow money from it. A higher **discount rate** reduces the amount of money institutions are able to borrow and, so, reduces the amount available to them to lend or invest. Because institutions can borrow from other sources, however, this method is not particularly effective in slowing down financial activity. Changes in the discount rate may be made by the regional banks, subject to the approval of the Fed's Board of Governors.

3. **Open Market Operations.** The Fed's buying and selling of government securities, as discussed earlier, is referred to as *open market operations*. Open market operations are undertaken by the FOMC.

The Fed and Politics

A question frequently asked is how it is possible for the Federal Reserve System and the federal government's Administrative Branch to simultaneously pursue conflicting economic policies. The Fed has an unusual degree of political independence. Members of the **Board of Governors** serve 14-year terms, and the terms are staggered such that one expires every 2 years. Thus, a president cannot pack the Board of Governors with "like-minded" supporters. Additionally, the Fed is funded from interest earned on its holdings of U.S. Treasury bonds, so it is not subject to the usual congressional appropriation process.

The Leaders of the Fed

Alan Greenspan   Alan Greenspan was born on March 6, 1926, in New York City. He received a BS in economics (summa cum laude) in 1948, an MA in economics in 1950, and a PhD in economics in 1977, all from New York University. Dr. Greenspan also performed advanced graduate study at Columbia University.

Dr. Greenspan took office June 19, 2004, for a fifth term as Chairman of the Board of Governors of the Federal Reserve System. Dr. Greenspan also served as Chairman of the Federal Open Market Committee, the System's principal monetary policymaking body. He originally took office as Chairman and to fill an unexpired term as a member of the Board on August 11, 1987. Dr. Greenspan was reappointed to the Board to a full 14-year term, which began February 1, 1992, and ended January 31, 2006. He was designated Chairman by Presidents Reagan, G. Bush, Clinton, and G. W. Bush.

Ben Bernanke   Ben Shalom Bernanke was nominated by George W. Bush and sworn into office as the 14th chairman of the Federal Reserve Board, succeeding Alan Greenspan on February 1, 2006.

Bernanke received his undergraduate bachelor's degree in Economics from Harvard University in 1975. He subsequently went on to receive his PhD in Economics from the Massachusetts Institute of Technology (MIT) in 1979. From 1979 to 1985, he taught at Stanford University's School of Business, was a visiting professor at New York University, and went on to become a tenured professor at Princeton University in the Economics Department.

FIGURE 4.5: **The Chairmen of the Federal Reserve**

June 2, 1987	President Reagan nominates Greenspan for chairman of the Federal Reserve Board. Greenspan completes the unfinished term on the Board of Governors for resigning chairman Paul Volcker.
August 11, 1987	Greenspan is sworn in as chairman of the Federal Reserve Board.
July 10, 1991	President George Bush nominates Greenspan for a second term as Fed chairman and for a full 14-year term as a member of the Fed's Board of Governors.
February 27, 1992	The U.S. Senate confirms Greenspan for his second term as Fed chairman and for a full term as member of the Board of Governors. He is sworn in on March 3.
February 22, 1996	President Bill Clinton nominates Greenspan for a third term as Fed chairman.
June 20, 1996	The U.S. Senate confirms Greenspan for his third term as Fed chairman. He begins his term that same day.
December 5, 1996	Greenspan makes a speech in which he refers to "irrational exuberance" in the stock market.
January 4, 2000	President Clinton nominates Greenspan for a fourth term as Fed chairman.
February 3, 2000	The U.S. Senate confirms Greenspan for his fourth term as Fed chairman.
June 20, 2000	Greenspan begins his fourth term as Fed chairman.
May 18, 2004	President George W. Bush nominates Greenspan for a fifth term as Fed chairman.
June 17, 2004	The U.S. Senate confirms Greenspan for his fifth term as Fed chairman. His new term begins on June 19.
October 24, 2005	President George W. Bush nominates Ben Bernanke to succeed Greenspan as Fed chairman. Greenspan issues a statement supporting the nomination.
January 31, 2006	Greenspan's term on the Federal Reserve Board ends.
February 1, 2006	Ben Bernanke began his first term as Federal Reserve Chairman.
February 1, 2010	Ben Bernanke begins his second term as Federal Reserve Chairman.
October 9, 2013	Janet L. Yellen is nominated by President Obama to replace Bernanke.
January 6, 2014	The U.S Senate confirms Yellen for her first term as Federal Reserve Chairman.
February 3, 2014	Yellen was sworn in as the first female Federal Reserve Chairman.

Dr. Bernanke served as a member of the Board of Governors of the Federal Reserve System from 2002 to 2005 and was the Chairman of the President's Council of Economic Advisors from June 2005 to January 2006. On February 1, 2006, he was appointed as a member of the Federal Reserve Board for a 14-year term and to a 4-year term as Chairman of the Federal Reserve. Dr. Bernanke has extensively studied and written on the economic and political causes of the Great Depression. Instead of focusing his writings on the role of the Federal Reserve, he turned his attention on the role of private banks and financial institutions that led to the Depression. He found that the financial disruptions of 1930–1933 reduced the efficiency of the credit allocation process and that the resulting higher cost and reduced availability of credit acted to depress aggregate demand, identifying an effect he termed the *financial acceleration*. He has received numerous awards, including Fellow Economic Society (1997) and distinguished leadership in Government Award, Columbia Business School (2008).

Janet Yellen Janet Louise Yellen was nominated by President Barack Obama and sworn into office as the fifteenth Chair of the Board of Governors of the Federal Reserve System and as the first woman to hold that position, succeeding Ben Bernanke on February 3, 2014. She graduated from Brown University with a degree in economics and subsequently received her PhD in Economics from Yale University. Prior to her appointment as Chair of the Federal Reserve, Dr. Yellen served as vice chair of the Board of Governors of the Federal Reserve, taking office in October 2010, when she simultaneously began a 14-year term as a member of the Board of Governors that will expire on January 31, 2024.

The Role of the Chairman

The Chairman is the public face of the Fed and has many responsibilities. Some of them are included here:

- Testifying twice a year before Congress regarding the Fed's observations and explanations for the current U.S. economy

- Providing recommendations to the Fed regarding interest rates and key policies

- Serving as a member of the Group of Seven, a committee composed of finance ministers and central bankers of the world's largest economies

THE MONEY SUPPLY

Economists agree that the quantity of money in circulation and the rate at which that quantity changes have a significant effect on the U.S. economy. The specific nature of that effect, how it occurs, and how it should be measured, however, are the subjects of extensive theorizing and debate.

For instance, the *Chicago School* economists (so called because its key theorists, such as Milton Friedman, are from the University of Chicago) takes a monetarist position. *Monetarists* believe that money supply is the primary factor in a nation's economy. They pay particular attention to growth rates of money supply.

The monetarist position is that prices change in proportion to changes in money supply. Monetarists see the rate of inflation as closely tied to the rate of increase in money.

While other, nonmonetarist economists accept the influence of the money supply, they are also likely to consider other factors as well.

Measures of Supply

The size of the money supply depends, of course, on how we define what money is. If people are asked how much money they have, the answer does not ordinarily describe their total net worth but the total amount of their cash and bank deposits. This commonplace definition of money is also one of the technical definitions of money. Most economists agree that money consists of things that are spendable: that which directly drives and supports a transaction. This is called the *transactions definition of money*. The Fed uses a transactions definition in measuring the nation's monetary supply.

The Fed's transactions-based measure includes four categories. From most liquid (convertible into cash) to least liquid, they are as follows:

1. **M1.** M1 is the Fed's basic measure of money supply in the nation. M1 includes

   - currency,

   - coins,

   - demand deposits,

   - traveler's checks from nonbank issuers, and

   - other checkable deposits.

2. **M2.** M2 includes the M1 items, plus

   - repurchase agreements issued by commercial banks,

- overnight Eurodollars,
- money market mutual funds,
- money market deposit accounts,
- savings accounts, and
- time deposits less than $100,000.

3. **M3.** M3 includes M2, plus

- institutionally held money market funds,
- term repurchase agreements,
- term Eurodollars, and
- large time deposits.

4. **L.** L equals M3, plus

- Treasury bills,
- commercial papers, and
- liquid assets (such as savings bonds).

Money Supply and Banks

Money consists of currency held by the public and checkable deposits. If you cash a check and receive currency, the amount in deposits goes down, the amount in currency goes up, but the money supply does not change. The total money supply grows when banks make loans. Banks have been creating this kind of money for several centuries.

This kind of money is called **deposit money**. It can be created in amounts substantially greater than the deposits that support it. This is because banking laws permit banks to maintain reserves that represent only a fraction of deposits.

For instance, if the reserve requirement is 10%, then a bank with $1 million in reserves can have deposit liabilities of $10 million. Every new deposit, by adding to the reserves of the bank, permits a multiple of that deposit to be added to deposit liabilities. Remember, the reserve requirements are set by the Board of Governors of the Federal Reserve. The Fed has sole authority over changes in the reserve requirement, which is imposed on commercial banks, savings banks, savings and loan associations, credit unions, U.S. branches and agencies of foreign banks, Edge Corporations, and Agreement Corporations.

A CLOSER LOOK   A small bank operates under a 10% reserve requirement. This bank has $500 in reserves and $4,700 in outstanding loans. These reserves and loans are the bank's assets. The bank's liabilities consist of $200 in capital and $5,000 in deposits. Under the Fed's regulations, the bank's reserves are 10% of its liabilities.

A depositor opens a new account and deposits $50. The bank adds this $50 to both its assets and its liabilities. Now the bank's reserves are $550, and the deposits are $5,050. With the additional deposit, however, the bank now has excess reserves. Reserves are 10.9% of deposits ($550 ÷ $5,050), more than the 10% required.

Under the 10% requirement, $550 in reserves will support $5,500 in deposit liabilities ($550 ÷ 10% = $5,500). So, deposit liabilities can grow by $450, from the present $5,050 to $5,500. This means the $450 can be offered in new loans.

Circulation of Deposit Money

There are about 35,000 depository institutions in the United States. A bank knows that any money it creates will be used to make payments, and those receiving the payments will almost certainly deposit them in one of those other institutions.

When payment checks return to the original bank, they draw on the bank's reserves. To protect those reserves, a bank is likely to originate loans (create money) equal only to the actual amount of excess reserves. The full amount of new money is created as the process is repeated in a number of banks and thrifts. As each institution receives new deposits, it holds a percentage in reserve and originates loans equaling the balance of the new deposit.

As each bank receives payments and makes loans, it holds a percentage in reserve and originates loans equaling the balance. In this way, new money is created as the original loan amount is circulated through the banking system. Figure 4.6 illustrates how this works, with more than $4,000 in new money created by an original loan of $1,000 from Bank A, which is deposited in Bank B, and so on. The example assumes a reserve rate of 10%.

FIGURE 4.6:   Bank Reserves versus Deposits

Bank	Deposit	Reserve	New Loan	Total New Money
A	—	—	$1,000	$1,000
B	$1,000	$100	$900	$1,900
C	$900	$90	$800	$2,700
D	$810	$81	$729	$3,439
E	$729	$73	$656	$4,095

INFLATION

Any rapid growth in the money supply is likely to create inflation unless it is accompanied by a correspondingly rapid increase in goods and services. **Inflation** can be best described as an increase in the money supply relative to the GDP. It is also described as a sustained rise in the general rate of increase in the general price level per unit of time.

Inflation has a number of effects on an economy, but not all of them are negative. Inflation means higher prices, which, in turn, means that consumers have less money to spend. Eroded purchasing power tends to destroy consumer confidence in a country's medium of exchange.

In some developing nations, for instance, skyrocketing inflation rates have rendered the local currency virtually worthless, resulting in thousand-dollar loaves of bread and widespread popular unrest. In Germany between the world wars, inflation was so far out of control that people carried cash with them in baskets and wheelbarrows, only to find that the prices of basic necessities had doubled during the time it took to walk to the store.

Inflation makes lenders wary of fixed-rate yields that erode profits over the long term. On the other hand, inflation is used by real estate investors and other borrowers to pay off yesterday's purchase with today's less expensive money.

Causes of Inflation

Demand   When the money supply grows faster than gross domestic product (GDP, discussed in Unit 3), excess demand pushes up prices. In effect, there are too many dollars chasing too few goods. Easy credit has the same effect on the economy: more money than things to spend it on.

Supply   In modern market economies, government price supports, union contracts, and trade quotas may prevent prices from dropping naturally when supply is in excess. In fact, prices may continue to rise.

- **Labor.** When the supply of labor is in excess, such as in periods of high unemployment, the price of labor (manifested in wages) would naturally be expected to fall: it's basic supply and demand. Wages do not, however, necessarily respond naturally to excess labor. Agreements between workers and employers often provide artificial wage protections that shield workers' income from the effects of actual market conditions.

- **Agriculture.** The agricultural industry in the United States has sufficient political influence to obtain and preserve government subsidies and price supports. As a result, an excess supply of agricultural goods is not necessarily reflected in reduced prices in grocery stores. Instead, surplus agricultural products fill warehouses with unused grains and dairy products. Other segments of the agriculture industry, such as tobacco farmers, are protected by artificial government subsidies from declining demand for their product.

- **Quotas.** Domestic producers often seek protection from foreign competition. One form of protection is the **quota,** which artificially manipulates the market by limiting consumer choice in order to pursue a social policy. Quotas often lead to higher prices.

- **COLAs.** Cost of living adjustments—**COLAs**—built into wage contracts, pensions, and government social programs are designed to protect purchasing power against inflation. Automatically triggered by price rises, however, COLAs encourage prices and income to spiral up together, each driving the other.

Measuring Inflation

Inflation is measured primarily by monitoring changes in wholesale and consumer prices.

In the 20th century, governments found it increasingly necessary to measure and report on inflation rates. Moreover, many private contractual arrangements now depend on price indexes, such as the CPI, discussed in Unit 3.

Indexes are commonly used as a basis for

- early warnings of *business fluctuations* for government policy makers and the business community;

- calculating *price-support programs* and *subsidies;*

- changes in *transfer payments* such as Social Security;

- *wage adjustments* in labor-management contracts; and

- adjustments in *commercial rents.*

IMPACT OF MONETARY POLICY ON REAL ESTATE

Like money itself, real estate is a measure of value. Moreover, **monetary policy** and the real estate industry are inextricably linked to one another. One of the key elements in a decision to purchase or sell real estate is the availability of money. Real estate finance and the volatility of the real estate market are influenced by a variety of monetary pressures.

Monetary Policy

As we've seen, when the Fed makes a policy decision to expand or contract the money supply, the move has a definite impact on the availability of lendable funds. The real estate industry is dependent on the availability of credit, and favorable interest rates tend to increase activity in the real estate market. The general results of a shrinkage of available money and credit are higher interest rates and a reduction in home sales. This is a simple case of supply and demand.

Fiscal Policy

The spending and revenue policies of the federal government—its **fiscal policy**—all play a part in either stimulating or depressing real estate market activity. When the federal government decides to devote greater energies toward increasing home ownership, for instance, through such programs as tax incentives, FHA project financing, and rent subsidies, the real estate market benefits. When the federal government's attention shifts to other issues—jobs creation or foreign policy—real estate receives less of the benefit. (See Unit 2 for a discussion on the differences between monetary and fiscal policies.)

State and Local Governments

State and local government attitudes toward such issues as infrastructure (transportation and utilities services), toxic waste disposal, regulation of financial institutions, and property disclosure laws have a nonfinancial effect on the level of development and resale activity in the real estate market. As the impact of suburban sprawl becomes both more obvious and more unpleasant, many communities are adopting controlled-growth policies. While perhaps improving the quality of life for residents (or at least slowing the decline in quality), such policies diminish supply and create an upward pressure on value of the existing housing stock.

WHAT DETERMINES THE OVERALL LEVEL OF INTEREST RATES?

A person who wishes to borrow money for the purchase of a residence may wish to reference the federal funds rate to determine the cost or the interest rate that she can expect to pay.

Interest is the price of a loan, so it is determined to a large extent by the supply of, and demand for, credit or loanable funds. Many different parties contribute to the supply and demand for credit.

- When you put money into a bank account, you are allowing the bank to lend the funds to someone else. So, through the bank, you are contributing to the supply of credit in the economy.

- When you buy a U.S. Savings Bond, you are lending funds to the U.S. government. Again, you are contributing to the supply of credit.

- On the other hand, when you borrow (to buy a car or by keeping a balance on a credit card account), you are contributing to the demand for credit. Individual savers and borrowers aren't the only ones contributing to the supply of, and the demand for, credit. Business firms and governments in this and foreign counties also affect the demand for, and supply of, credit.

Together, the actions of all of these participants in the credit market determine how high or low interest rates will be.

A CLOSER LOOK   On November 30, 2005, President George W. Bush told the banking industry to stay out of the real estate business by signing the

Transportation, Treasury, and HUD spending bill, banning the Federal Reserve Board/Treasury's ability to allow banks to operate real estate brokerage, leasing, and property management businesses. This continues to keep the banking and real estate industries separate from one another, and this has prevented the creation of large conglomerates. Prior to 2005, many banks had acquired title and escrow companies with the idea of creating a one-stop shop approach to better serve the real estate needs of their clients. The banking industry moved afterwards to introduce the concept of in-house real estate services. This was greatly opposed by the National Association of REALTORS® and is still the case today.

THE NEXT STEP This concludes our general discussion of economic principles and tools. You should have a clearer idea now of how the market economy operates. In the next units, we will apply the theory to the real world as we consider more closely the real estate market and the housing industry in the United States.

SUMMARY

- **Money** is *any medium of exchange* adopted by a society as a *means of acquiring goods and services*. Money may or may not have any *intrinsic* value; the value it represents is assigned to it by its users.

- In a **barter economy**, goods and services are traded directly for other goods and services. Money developed from barter economies as an *abstraction*—a thing that represented something of value. Over time, money came to be seen as having value *independent* of what it represented, evolving into metal coins, paper money, and electronic funds transfers.

- The United States has a two-tiered banking structure consisting of a central banking system and a system of commercial banks.

- The **Federal Reserve**, established by Congress in 1913, is the *central bank of the United States*. It consists of a central board of governors and 12 independent regional banks. Monetary policy is made by the *Federal Open Market Committee*, consisting of the governors and the directors. The Fed is responsible for formulating monetary policy, regulating the banking industry, maintaining financial stability in the U.S. economy, and providing financial services to the federal government.

■ The Fed *manipulates the money supply* through its **reserve requirements** and **discount rate**. **M1** is the Fed's *basic measure of money supply*.

■ **Inflation** is a sustained upward movement of prices on a broad scale. Inflationary pressures may come from many sources.

■ The **real estate industry** and government monetary policy are closely linked. The real estate market is dependent on availability of credit, and favorable interest rate policies tend to increase activity in the real estate market.

■ **Overall level of interest rates** dictate the price of loans and are determined, to a large extent, by the supply and demand for credit or funds available for loans.

REVIEW QUESTIONS

1. What fiscal actions can the government take to control inflation?

2. Why does uncertainty create problems in implementing fiscal actions?

3. What is the role of the Federal Reserve, and how does the Fed affect real estate markets?

4. What is meant when it is said that the Federal Reserve System is "independent"?

5. How does the Federal Reserve transmit policy changes to the economy?

6. Who is currently the Chairman of the Federal Reserve, and which president appointed this individual to the position?

7. What is the role of the Federal Open Market Committee?

8. Who was previously the Chairman of the Federal Reserve Board, and for how long did this individual serve?

9. Who led the Federal Reserve during the longest expansion period in history?

UNIT QUIZ

1. Which of the following *BEST* describes an economy in which goods or services are traded directly for other goods or services?
   a. Feudalism
   b. Fiduciary
   c. Seigniorage
   d. Barter

2. When did the gold standard stop being the basis for valuing the U.S. dollar?
   a. 1896
   b. 1900
   c. 1973
   d. The dollar is still based on the gold standard.

3. All of the following are one of the four main categories of money *EXCEPT*
   a. specie.
   b. currency.
   c. seigniorage.
   d. electronic funds.

4. The central bank of the United States, founded in 1913, is
   a. the Treasury Department.
   b. the First Bank of the United States.
   c. the Bureau of the Mint.
   d. the Federal Reserve.

5. How many governors serve on the Federal Reserve Board, and how are they selected?
   a. Five; appointed by the Secretary of the Treasury
   b. Seven; appointed by the president
   c. Nine; elected by popular vote
   d. Twelve; elected by the FOMC

6. Interest rates and the cost of credit rise as a result of
   a. a tight money policy.
   b. a loose money policy.
   c. an open market operation.
   d. a transactions-based fiscal policy.

7. The Fed's buying and selling of government securities is referred to as
   a. the discount rate.
   b. open market operations.
   c. a loose money policy.
   d. transactional economic policy.

8. All of the following are included in M1 *EXCEPT*
   a. traveler's checks.
   b. currency.
   c. coins.
   d. savings accounts.

9. Money that is "created" by a bank making a loan is referred to as
   a. deposit money.
   b. reserve funds.
   c. M2.
   d. loan money.

10. All of the following contribute to inflationary price increases *EXCEPT*
    a. COLAs built into wage contracts.
    b. price indexes.
    c. agricultural subsidies.
    d. trade quotas.

UNIT FIVE

THE REAL ESTATE MARKET

KEY TERMS

Americans with
  Disabilities Act
  (ADA)
appurtenances
bundle of rights
chattels
compartmentalization
complexity
consumer protection

Dodd-Frank Wall
  Street Reform
  and Consumer
  Protection Act
equal credit
  opportunity
finite
growth control
heterogeneity

improvements
land
market
negotiate
real property
rent control
SAFE Act
topography
transfer

LEARNING OBJECTIVES

■ Define real property in economic terms

■ Describe the unique characteristics of the real estate market

■ Explain the factors that create a dynamic real estate marketplace

THE NATURE OF REAL PROPERTY

Real property is distinguished from personal, movable property, or **chattels**. The term refers to the **bundle of rights** held by a landowner. Those rights affect the land itself, as well as any improvements, appurtenances, or attachments. The bundle of legal rights includes

- *possession* of the property;

- *control* (within the framework of the law);

- *enjoyment* (use of the property in a legal manner);

- *exclusion* (to keep others from using the property); and

- *disposition* (to sell, will, transfer, or otherwise dispose of or encumber the property).

Land

Because of its fixed location, land possesses unique characteristics not normally identified with other assets. Many of these characteristics contribute to the high cost of real property and the major role it plays in the U.S. economic system. In real estate, the term *land* includes the surface and subsurface of a property, as well as the usable air space above it. **Improvements** are anything attached affixed to the land; **appurtenances** are the rights to something outside of the land, which are auxiliary to the rights to the land.

Durability Although it may be altered in shape or form, land is virtually indestructible. Similarly, improvements on the land, such as buildings, walls, fences, and other structures, are designed to last for many years.

Limited Supply The amount of land available on this planet is **finite** (see Figure 5.1). In addition, various local, state, and federal government constraints further limit the supply. Practical considerations (such as climate, geology, and location) further limit the amount of land available for development.

Cost Factors Construction technology did not experience the revolutionary breakthroughs that occurred in other trades during the 20th century. That relative inefficiency has translated into higher costs to improve land. High improvement costs now further translate into a major investment decision for the real property consumer. In turn, that translates into long-term financing to support the purchase.

FIGURE 5.1:   Land Surface of the Earth

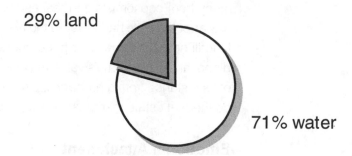

29% land

71% water

Heterogeneity Unlike products of our mechanized society that are produced in a uniform manner, real property has a unique feature: **heterogeneity**—that is, *no two parcels are exactly alike.* Each parcel of real estate is in a different location. Even though two adjacent parcels may contain exactly identical improvements, each location is different in various ways.

- *Topography.* Is the parcel's **topography** relatively level or is it clinging to the side of a mountain? Topographical features can definitely affect value of a property.

- *Proximity.* Is the parcel isolated or is it linked to other improved parcels in a planned pattern of development? Is it a corner or inner lot? Is it near amenities, such as shopping, recreation, and schools?

- *Improvements.* Is there a uniform quality presented by the neighborhood, or is it a patchwork pattern of varying quality and size of improvements?

- *Ingress and Egress.* Is the access a poorly maintained and bumpy dirt road or a well-paved street?

- *Annoyances.* Noxious or offensive activities, such as a factory, landfill site, or heavy traffic near a residential area will usually have a negative effect on a property's value.

- *Panorama.* The view from a property can impact its value. A 3,500-square foot house overlooking the ocean may be far more valuable in the typical consumer's eye than the same size property with a view of a parking lot.

A CLOSER LOOK Environmental issues have a very real impact on the real estate industry. In 1995, a jury awarded $6.7 million to homeowners whose property values had been lowered because of a nearby tire company's negligent operation and maintenance of a dump site. Nearly 2,000 plaintiffs relied on testimony from economists and real estate appraisers to demonstrate how news stories about the site had lowered the market value of their homes. Nationwide, some landfill operators now offer price guarantees to purchasers of homes near waste disposal sites; a home's value may increase by as much as $6,000 for each mile of its distance from a garbage incinerator. (Environmental issues and their impact on the real estate market are discussed in Unit 10.)

Emotional Attachment

Home ownership has a subjective worth to the consumer that is difficult to measure on a dollars and cents basis. Although the normal home purchase might not make economic sense as a commercial investment, the satisfying idea of home ownership enhances a property's value.

Political Implications

The Preamble to the Code of Ethics of the National Association of REALTORS® begins with these words: *"Under all is the land. Upon its wise utilization and widely allocated ownership depend the survival and growth of free institutions and of our civilization . . ."*

As we will see, land ownership has a wide variety of economic impacts. The proper utilization of land as an economically viable vehicle is overseen by government through the planning process as a safeguard against abuses. The political implications of home ownership cannot be overestimated, and the sense of being a home owner often has a significant impact on economic behavior.

CHARACTERISTICS OF THE REAL ESTATE MARKET

The real estate market is not as organized as the stock market or other financial markets. It is a more local market, with inexperienced sellers and buyers assisted by professional real estate agents.

Components of the Marketplace

A **market** is a place where goods can be bought and sold. A market may be a specific location, such as a village square. It may also be a vast, worldwide economic system for moving goods and services around the globe.

The real estate marketplace has its own unique set of ground rules, technical terms, and specialized tasks to address the marketing process.

Complexity   Real estate is not a simple product, and its marketplace reflects this **complexity**. There are many types of real property and an even greater number of financing strategies and valuation requirements. Individual investors have widely different expectations. Tax considerations and unique local conditions also play a significant role.

The complex nature of real estate transactions tends to encourage specialization among its professionals. Some areas of specialization include the following:

- Brokerage

- Finance

- Consulting

- Investments

- Development

- Appraisal

- Escrow

- Title insurance

- Property insurance

- Pest control

- Home inspections

- Law

- Property management

- Environmental assessment

Compartmentalization   Within these broad areas of professional expertise, even further specialization—called **compartmentalization**—is common. For example, a brokerage can specialize in only commercial or industrial properties. An escrow agency may specialize in tax deferred exchanges, or an appraiser may specialize in condemnation work. A property manager may specialize in both residential and commercial projects.

Functions of Components

In order for any economic product or service to be sold, there must be some way to expose it to the marketplace. A wonderful product has little value if no one knows it exists. In the real estate market, each component must perform certain functions to ensure that its products or services are made available to consumers.

Advertise Potential purchasers and renters need to know that a particular property is available. This requires some form of advertisement in the media most likely to reach the desired consumers.

Inform Consumers need specific information in order to make an informed decision. In real estate brokerage, a disclosure statement will be provided for the benefit of brokers and consumers. The federal government requires that mortgage consumers be given particular information about the costs involved in a loan.

Appraise Consumers should be provided with a realistic, impartial estimate of the property's value.

Negotiate The real estate brokerage community serves as a buffer between seller and buyer in price negotiations. Whichever party they represent, brokers help **negotiate** a mutually acceptable agreement.

Arrange Financing There must be a way to provide appropriate financing to meet the needs of the parties. Financing is an integral part of marketing real estate because it can make or break a sale. Lenders screen prospective purchasers for their ability to manage the debt.

Transfer There must be a reliable way of establishing that all legal and financial requirements have been satisfied. Escrow agents and title insurers work as a protective team in the transfer process, preparing the necessary transfer and loan documentation.

Respond to Consumer Demand To meet consumers' needs in housing and other types of property, real estate developers and contractors must provide a product that combines utility, attractiveness, and affordability. A range of external pressures, from escalating costs and consumer expectations to regulatory requirements and investor pressures, often make this a challenging goal.

Manage Risks Business decisions must be made not only on the basis of sound economics but also on the basis of which approach to a project creates the least risk of financial loss, physical damage, or personal injury. In a society in which lawsuits are common, the risk of litigation arising out of any project is a very real one. A variety of insurance options help deflect risk.

Interface   Real estate brokers need to be aware of all the market functions available. This includes financing plans, property insurance requirements, structural pest control requirements, home inspection procedures, comparable sales in the market, and a variety of factors necessary to market the property effectively.

Other practitioners, such as financial consultants, escrow officers, lenders, property managers, appraisers, and title insurers, must apply and coordinate their specialized knowledge at various points in the process.

Market Familiarity   If any of the professionals in the marketplace are unfamiliar with a particular area, they do their customers an injustice by failing to consult with local practitioners. This is especially important in appraisal where detailed knowledge of the area is critical.

EVOLVING ISSUES

Although real estate ownership continues to be a status desired by a majority of consumers, certain issues have evolved that may affect its future investment potential.

Ethnic Mix

The United States is a nation of immigrants, and that characteristic is rapidly growing today. In California, for instance, one quarter of the population is foreign-born, and a fifth of those residents immigrated to the state during the 1990s. At the turn of the 21st century, 40% of the population of California was composed of ethnic minorities. Between 2009 and 2013, the U.S. Census reported that 27% of the state's population was foreign born. This continues to be good news for the real estate industry. In 1996, more than 60% of California's first-time new homebuyers were foreign-born; by 2011, the rate of first-time new homebuyers who were foreign born had risen to 64%.

The U.S. population mix continues to be steadily influenced by migration from Latin America, the Mideast, Europe, and Asia. As immigrant populations continue to be assimilated, one result is a shift in housing needs and expectations. The top ten countries of origin for purchasers of homes in California include Mexico, China, India, Philippines, Dominican Republic, Cuba, Vietnam, South Korea, Columbia, and Haiti.

Architectural Fashions

Residential and commercial architecture and interior and exterior features are influenced by changes in popular taste. For example, sunken living rooms and featureless steel office buildings were once the height of architectural fashion; today, open beamed ceilings, whirlpool tubs, and fanciful postmodern building facades are much more attractive to consumers. A property that is considered out-of-date or old-fashioned cannot command the same price as one that reflects the latest design.

Laws Affecting Real Estate

Consumer Protection Consumer concerns first manifested in Fair Housing in 1968, followed by Title I of the Consumer Credit Protection Act in 1969 (Truth in Lending—Regulation Z). Since then, a series of laws and court opinions have marched steadily toward increased disclosure to protect real estate consumers, particularly purchasers in the single-family residential area (one- to four-family dwellings).

SAFE Mortgage Licensing Act The Secure and Fair Enforcement Mortgage Licensing Act of the Housing and Economic Recovery Act of 2008 was signed into law on July 2008 to enhance **consumer protection** and reduce fraud in mortgage loan originators that meets the minimum requirements of the SAFE Act. The Conference of State Bank Supervisors (CSBS) and the American Association of Residential Mortgage Regulators (AARMR) have created, and will maintain, the National Mortgage Licensing System and Registry (NMLSR) to streamline the licensing process with oversight by HUD.

The NMLSR will be maintained to

- provide uniform license applications and reporting requirements for state licensed loan originators;

- provide a comprehensive licensing and supervisory database;

- aggregate and improve the flow of information to and between regulators;

- provide increased accountability and tracking of loan originators;

- streamline the licensing process and reduce regulatory burden;

- enhance consumer protections and support anti-fraud measures;

- provide consumers with easily accessible information regarding the status of loan originators, including any disciplinary and enforcement actions against loan originators;

- establish a means by which residential mortgage loan originators would, to the greatest extent possible, be required to act in the best interest of the consumer;

- facilitate responsible behavior in the subprime mortgage marketplace and provide comprehensive training and examination requirements related to subprime mortgage lending; and

- facilitate the collection and disbursement of consumer complaints on behalf of state mortgage regulators. (12 CFR 1008.301)

In California there are two state agencies that have oversight authority for the enforcement of the SAFE Act. The agencies are the California Department of Business Oversight and the California Bureau of Real Estate. Each is tasked with specific licensure oversight.

California Department of Business Oversight

- Residential Mortgage Lending Act License

- Residential Mortgage Lending Act License (Branch)

- Finance Lenders Law License

- Finance Lenders Law License (Branch)

- Mortgage Loan Originator License

California Bureau of Real Estate

- Real Estate Broker License Endorsement (Sole Proprietor-Company)

- Real Estate Corporation License Endorsement

- Branch Office License Endorsement

- Real Estate Salesperson License Endorsement

- Real Estate Broker License Endorsement (Individual)[1]

---

1.   State of California, "About Mortgage Loan Originators," Department of Business Oversight, www.dbo.ca.gov/Licensees/Mortgage_Loan_Originators/About.asp (accessed April 2015).

Dodd-Frank Wall Street Reform and Consumer Protection Act (Dodd-Frank Act)   The Dodd-Frank Wall Street Reform and Consumer Protection Act was signed into law in July 2010 and went into effect in January 2014. The act's purpose was to protect consumers and prevent another financial crisis like the United States experienced in 2007–2009.

Regarding real estate, Dodd-Frank changes the way people finance their home purchases. Lenders have more responsibility to determine a borrower's ability to repay the loan. In addition, certain nonqualified loans (e.g., loans with balloon payments, negative amortization loans) have additional requirements for qualification.

Dodd-Frank also created the following:

- Financial Stability Oversight Council. According to the U.S. Department of the Treasury,"…the Council provides, for the first time, comprehensive monitoring of the stability of our nation's financial system. The Council is charged with identifying risks to the financial stability of the United States; promoting market discipline; and responding to emerging risks to the stability of the United States' financial system. The Council consists of 10 voting members and 5 nonvoting members and brings together the expertise of federal financial regulators, state regulators, and an independent insurance expert appointed by the President."[2]

- Consumer Financial Protection Bureau. For more information, visit http://www.consumerfinance.gov/.

Federal Insurance Office. According to the U.S. Department of the Treasury, "The Dodd-Frank Wall Street Reform and Consumer Protection Act established Treasury's Federal Insurance Office (FIO) and vested FIO with the authority to monitor all aspects of the insurance sector, monitor the extent to which traditionally underserved communities and consumers have access to affordable non-health insurance products, and to represent the United States on prudential aspects of international insurance matters, including at the International Association of Insurance Supervisors. In addition, FIO serves as an advisory member of the Financial Stability Oversight Council, assists the Secretary with administration of the Ter-

---

2.   U.S. Department of the Treasury, "Home," Financial Stability Oversight Council, www .treasury.gov/initiatives/fsoc/Pages/home.aspx (accessed April 2015).

rorism Risk Insurance Program, and advises the Secretary on important national and international insurance matters."[3]

Mortgage Disclosure Improvement Act (MDIA)   Since July 30, 2009, if the APR on an initial good-faith estimate is no longer accurate (within a 0.125% range) at close of escrow, a lender must generally provide a residential borrower with a new disclosure and a three-day right to rescind before consummating the loan. This requirement is part of the Mortgage Disclosure Improvement Act implementing new loan procedures to protect borrowers and foster greater transparency in mortgage lending.

Tax Laws   Real property ownership can be stimulated or slowed by federal, state, and local tax policies. For instance, in 1997, President Clinton signed an important and wide-ranging new tax relief bill that included significant reforms designed to encourage home ownership through federal tax policy:

■ Taxpayers who file jointly are entitled to a $500,000 exclusion from capital gains tax for profits on the sale of a principal residence (single-filers are entitled to a $250,000 exclusion).

■ First-time homebuyers may make penalty-free withdrawals of up to $10,000 from their tax-deferred individual retirement fund (IRA).

■ The tax rate on capital gains decreased.

Real estate taxation is one of the primary sources of revenue for local governments. Policies on taxation of real estate can have either positive or negative effects. High taxes may deter investors. On the other hand, tax incentives can attract new businesses and industries. Of course, along with these enterprises also comes increased employment and expanded residential real estate markets.

Equal Credit Opportunity   A commitment to **equal credit opportunity** has made financing available to many who had routinely been rebuffed in the past. Female heads of households, who are increasing in number, have particularly benefited. Households composed of unmarried adult partners of one or both sexes are also commonplace today. All these changes expand the need for housing.

---

3.   U.S. Department of the Treasury, "Home," Federal Insurance Office, www.treasury.gov/initiatives/fio/Pages/default.aspx (accessed April 2015).

Americans with Disabilities Act (ADA)   The **Americans with Disabilities Act (ADA)** has had a significant impact on commercial, nonresidential properties and leasing practices. Any property in which public goods or services are provided must be free of architectural barriers or must accommodate individuals with disabilities so that they can enjoy access to those businesses or services. Disabled tenants of certain residential buildings must be permitted to make reasonable modifications to a property (at their own expense), but a landlord may require that rental premises be restored to their original condition at the end of the lease term.

Rent Control   Several California cities have local ordinances that regulate rent increases, called **rent control** ordinances. Rent control ordinances specify procedures that a landlord must follow before increasing a tenant's rent or that make evicting a tenant more difficult for a landlord. Each community's ordinance is different and varies from community to community.

Some ordinances permit landlords to evict tenants only for "just cause." Under these ordinances, the landlord is required to state and prove a valid reason for terminating a month-to-month tenancy, while other communities do not have this requirement. Some communities have boards with the power to approve or deny rent increases. Other cities' ordinances provide for certain percentage increases in rent each year. Other communities also provide for "vacancy control" in their ordinances, which means that the landlord cannot raise the rent when the tenant leaves the unit. Many such provisions were phased out between January 1, 1996, and January 1, 1999.

With the passage of the Costa-Hawkins Rental Housing Act in 1995 by the State Legislature, when a tenant leaves voluntarily or is evicted for most reasons, the landlord can raise the rent to any amount for the new tenant, whose rents are, therefore, locked into the rent control limits. However, the law specifies that any rental unit built after February 1, 1995, as well as houses and condominiums, are not under rent control restrictions. According to the California Department of Consumer Affairs, properties that receive a certificate of occupancy after February 1, 1995 are exempt from rent control. Additionally, commencing January 1, 1999, tenancies in single-family homes and condominiums are also exempt from rent control if the tenancy began after January 1, 1996. SB505, known as the Ellis Act, was passed by the State Legislature in 1986 that permits owners of rent stabilized properties to opt out of the rental housing business, thus contributing to the depletion of affordable rental housing stock in the state.

Both the Costa-Hawkins Rental Housing Act and the Ellis Act can be seen as really encouraging landlords to promote tenant turnovers, as landlords will receive higher rents from the new tenants. What has ultimately occurred as a result of these laws is that landlords not only receive higher rents, but many landlords are simply selling their "rent-controlled" properties to developers. These properties are subsequently razed and new modern units built in their place and are ultimately rented at market rate, resulting in lower income individuals being displaced who once benefitted from stable rents in a community.

Thus, in reaction to the ever-changing real estate market in California, what has become most common in recent years is "vacancy decontrol," which allows a landlord to re-rent a unit at the community's market rental rate when a tenant moves out voluntarily or when the tenancy is terminated for "just cause." Rent control seems to stymie the local rental markets by providing disincentives for developers to build rental units in those communities where rent control ordinances have been adopted by law makers. Few developers or landlords would want to lock themselves in at a given time period in the market and then later have obstacles to overcome to be able to raise rents. It can also be argued that rent control has significantly impacted the San Francisco Bay Area residential rental markets as the number of required multi-family units are not being built to meet the demands of the market and is leading to a very tight rental market and exorbitant rents.

As an example, in 2015, an average 754 square foot one bedroom/one bath apartment unit in Mountain View, California, located in the heart of Silicon Valley, rents for $3,520/month. An average 1,080 square foot two bedroom/two bath apartment unit rents for $5,031/month. As a comparison just a few miles away to the north in East Palo Alto, which is currently covered by rent control, a 602 square foot one bedroom/two bath apartment unit rents for $1,640/month, while an 849 square foot two bedroom/two bath apartment unit rents for $2,334/month. It could be argued that communities nearby to those that have rent control will also bear the burden of tight real estate rental markets, where no new units are introduced due to rent control, the newer units are constructed in nearby cities, and rents are attributed to the market.

If landlords were not allowed to raise rents freely to keep up with inflation or maximize on their investments, would developers continue to build rental units in communities with rent control ordinances?

Since January 1, 1999, the following communities in California have had rent control ordinances:

- Berkeley
- Beverly Hills
- Campbell
- East Palo Alto
- Fremont
- Gardena
- Glendale
- Hayward
- Los Angeles
- Los Gatos
- Oakland
- Palm Springs
- San Diego
- San Francisco
- San Jose
- San Leandro
- Santa Monica
- Thousand Oaks
- West Hollywood
- Westlake Village

Mobile home parks are a type of affordable housing in California. With pressures to convert such land uses in California for other more profitable uses, many communities still consider preserving such housing to be important. Since November 16, 2007, the following communities in California have had rent control ordinances for mobile home parks:

- Calistoga
- Concord

- Cotati

- Escondido

- Fontana

- Grover Beach

- Malibu

- Milpitas

- Morgan Hill

- Novato

- Pleasanton

- Redlands

- Rohnert

- Santa Cruz County

- San Jose

- San Juan Capistrano

- Santa Rosa

- Sonoma County

- Thousand Oaks

- Union City

- Yucaipa

- Windsor

Growth Control

Growth control—also called growth management—is not a new concept in California. Since the late 1960s, many communities have developed a variety of growth control systems to address various environmental, social, and economic problems. Growth management legislation has been inspired by the costs and revenues associated with development as well as by a desire to protect the aesthetic and environmental quality of community life. Providing adequate water, sewer, and infrastructure—and preserving community identity, such as the "small town, rural character" sought by many leaving the metropolitan areas—are among the many issues growth control seeks to address.

Some communities and cities practice limited growth management or none at all. In recent years attempts to manage growth have been unsuccessful when dealing with traffic congestion, school facilities, water availability, clean air, parks, and related issues encompassing areas beyond city limits. Many who oppose growth management argue that the issue of growth is merely related to being a NIMBY (Not In My Back Yard), as the problems associated with growth are simply passed to the next community—the one with no growth management regulations.

Housing prices in communities with growth control restrictions tend to be significantly higher. The consequence of the law of supply and demand pushes new homebuyers farther and farther from workplaces. As a result of growth management legislation, by the 1980s, development began to spill out of the San Francisco Bay Area and the Los Angeles Basin to nearby counties some hundreds of miles away. Workers were willing to endure long commutes, large expanses of agricultural land began to be developed for housing, and the Central Valley and the Sierra Nevada foothills began to experience unprecedented growth.

Over the years, growth control legislation enacted by California communities has occasionally been challenged in court. In all cases the legislation has been deemed constitutional. One of the most famous cases dealing with growth management is the landmark 1975 *Construction Industry of Sonoma County v. City of Petaluma*. In 1969, Highway 101 was transformed from a two-lane road to a four-lane and six-lane freeway between the Golden Gate Bridge in Marin and Sonoma counties. Petaluma is the southernmost community is Sonoma County and had plenty of rural land for expansion. Petaluma became the most logical residence for commuting homebuyers, and between 1970 and 1971, 50 to 65% more homes were built in Petaluma than had been built prior to the freeway expansion. In response to the rapid development, Petaluma imposed the first growth management restrictions in California, a cap of 500 housing units per year allocated to builders who met certain criteria for aesthetic and public services. When the Construction Industry Association of Sonoma County challenged Petaluma's growth restrictions, the U.S. Ninth Circuit Court of Appeals upheld the city's limit.

Since then, many communities throughout California have adopted similar versions of growth management by restricting the number of permits for new homes issued, while other communities restrict the amount of land to be developed. Other communities restrict commercial development and set ceilings on square footage. Still other communities and cities allow development only if adequate water and infrastructure, such as roads, are available.

It's not just California who employs growth management or growth control through land use practices. In the state of Washington, cities and counties have prepared land use plans similar to California for years. Washington passed the Growth Management Act (GMA) in 1990 in response to the rapid population growth and concerns of suburban sprawl. Washington requires the fastest growing cities and counties to plan extensively in keeping with the growth management goals that include sprawl reduction, concentrated urban growth, affordable housing, economic development, regional transportation, open space and recreation, environmental protection, and permit processing. While growth management in California is handled at the city and county level, by contrast, Washington's Department of Commerce has oversight authority to ensure that comprehensive planning and growth management is conducted and land use plans are prepared in a timely manner, while funding for a variety of local projects can be withheld by the state. Under the Washington GMA, a city would be prohibited from extending utility services (water/sewer) into rural areas. By allowing such services to be extended out into rural areas, this would ultimately lead to suburban sprawl, which the GMA attempts to address.

Cary, North Carolina, is another example of a community that has implemented growth management in response to rapid growth. In the late 1990s, Cary undertook a comprehensive planning effort to examine growth; in January 2000, it adopted its growth management plan. The guiding principles of the growth management plan are five aspects of growth, which include (1) rate and timing, (2) location, (3) amount of density, (4) cost, and (5) quality. The management of growth was very important to Cary because of rapid population growth and its burden on city services. Between 2000 and 2013, the population had increased 53%. Cary's population had doubled every 10 years from 1960 to 2000, growing by more than 90,000 people during a 40-year period. As of 2013, the population of Cary was 144,316. The city's infrastructure and its ability to continue to provide a high level of service was being taxed by the rapid growth. This included streets, sewer, water, and schools. Much of the growth has been attributed to the Research Triangle Park and the Raleigh-Durham International Airport that continues to acts as a major growth engine for the region.

A common approach to managing growth is to limit annual growth to a specified percentage increase in population (usually 1–3%) by placing a cap on the number of building permits that can be issued in any one year. Other communities link their number of permits to be issued more directly to infrastructure availability or to a predetermined period of years within which it desires to reach projected build out (typically 20 to 30 years). Cary chose the latter approach, restricting new residential development based on water availability until expansion of the water treatment plant was completed and also requiring that adequate transportation and school facilities be in place before new development occurs. Other cities employing growth management include Boulder, Colorado, and Hudson, Ohio. These communities limit building permits so their annual population growth does not exceed 1%.

How Growth Is Managed in California

Growth management is achieved through a variety of ways, whether by local municipalities through their legislative bodies (city councils or county board of supervisors) or through voter-initiated processes. Many communities have also accepted the fact that they are unable to continue to grow due to the lack of available resources such as water. This has been quite prevalent during California's prolonged drought. The following is a list of examples of how growth is managed:

- Establishing geographical limits to growth (i.e., urban growth boundaries)
- Zoning for larger lot sizes
- Charging development impact fees
- Public acquisition of development rights
- Adequate infrastructure requirements (sewer, water, roads, etc.)
- Preserving of agricultural lands through annexation policies

- Preferentially assessing agricultural and timber lands (Williamson Act)

- Establishing conservation easements

- Limiting the annual number of building permits for new homes

Who Employs Growth Management in California?

The following communities have enacted an Urban Growth Boundary or Urban Limit Line (including boundaries enacted by voter initiative):

Alameda County	Kerman	San Diego
American Canyon	Kingsburg	San Diego County
Antioch	Livermore	San Jose
Arcata	Livingston	San Juan Bautista
Atascadero	Lompoc	San Luis Obispo
Azuza	Los Gatos	San Luis Obispo
Buellton	Mammoth Lakes	County
Calabasas	Merced	San Mateo County
Chico	Merced County	Sanger
Clearlake	Monte Sereno	Santa Barbara County
Colfax	Monterey County	Santa Clara County
Colusa	Moorpark	Santa Cruz
Contra Costa County	Morgan Hill	Santa Cruz County
Cotati	Morro Bay	Santa Maria
Crescent City	Mountain View	Santa Rosa
Cupertino	Napa	Sebastopol
Danville	Napa County	Sierra County
Del Norte County	Nevada County	Sonoma
Delano	Newman	St. Helena
El Dorado County	Novato	Stockton
Escondido	Palm Desert	Tulare
Exeter	Petaluma	Tulare County
Fairfield	Placerville	Tuolumne County
Farmersville	Pleasanton	Ukiah
Fremont	Point Arena	Vacaville
Gilroy	Porterville	Visalia
Half Moon Bay	Redlands	Watsonville
Hanford	Ripon	Windsor
Hayward	Rohnert Park	Winters
Healdsburg	Sacramento County	Woodland
Hollister	Salinas	Yountville
Humboldt County	San Bernardino County	

THE NEXT STEP This unit has explored real property as a basic commodity, together with those forces that have a tendency to affect its value. Unit 6 will explore the interaction of these forces in the real estate market generally.

SUMMARY

- **Real property** refers to the *bundle of legal rights held by a landowner*. The **bundle of legal rights** includes *possession, control, enjoyment, exclusion*, and *disposition*.

- **Land** is the *property's surface, subsurface*, and *usable air space*. **Improvements** are *anything affixed to the land*. **Appurtenances** are the *rights attached to land ownership*. Although it may be altered in shape or form, land is *virtually indestructible*.

- The amount of land available on this planet is *finite*. In addition, various local, state, and federal government constraints limit the supply. Practical considerations (such as climate, geology, and location) further diminish the amount of land available for development.

- Unlike products of our mechanized society that are produced in a uniform manner, real property has a unique feature: *no two parcels are exactly alike*.

- **Home ownership** has a *subjective worth* to the consumer that is difficult to measure on a dollars-and-cents basis.

- A **market** is a place where goods can be bought and sold. The function of a marketplace is to provide a setting in which supply and demand can interact. The **real estate market** is a *local market* with inexperienced sellers and buyers.

- Real estate is not a simple product, and its marketplace reflects its complexity. Because of this *complexity*, real estate tends to encourage **specialization**.

- In the real estate market, each **component** must perform *certain functions* to ensure that its products or services are made available to consumers. These include *advertising, informing, appraising, negotiating, financing, transferring, responding, managing risk*, and *interfacing*.

- Although real estate ownership continues to be a resource desired by a majority of consumers, certain **issues** have evolved that may *affect* *its future investment potential.* These include *new laws* (consumer protection, equal housing, ADA, and tax reforms) and *changing ethnic mixes.*

REVIEW QUESTIONS

1. What market restrictions are present in your community?

2. How many residential units are currently available in your community, and how does this figure compare with one year ago?

3. What is the home ownership rate in your community?

4. Generally speaking, what are the major factors influencing the real estate market in your area versus other nearby communities?

5. What is your community doing to encourage additional housing units for all population groups?

6. Does your community have growth management controls in place? And, if so, are there any exclusions for affordable housing projects?

7. Does your community employ rent control? If so, how has this constrained the development of new residential development?

8. How many new housing developments have been constructed in your community, and how has that affected the price of existing residential units that may be considered outdated?

UNIT QUIZ

1. All of the following are included in a real property owner's bundle of legal rights *EXCEPT*
   a. possession.
   b. exclusion.
   c. proximity.
   d. disposition.

2. The SAFE Act was designed to
   a. enhance consumer protection.
   b. require states to establish standard licensing standards.
   c. reduce fraud.
   d. all of these.

3. The term *heterogeneity*, when applied to real property, refers to which of the following?
   a. Land is an interchangeable commodity.
   b. Parcels are inextricably linked to one another.
   c. No two parcels are exactly alike.
   d. Adjacent parcels are usually identical.

4. Which of the following correctly describes the real estate market?
   a. Approximately as organized as the stock market and other financial markets
   b. Involved with a simple, homogeneous product
   c. Populated by generalists rather than specialists
   d. A local market with inexperienced buyers and sellers

5. Providing consumers with a realistic, impartial estimate of the value of a specific property is a function of which component of the real estate market?
   a. Negotiation
   b. Appraisal
   c. Advertisement
   d. Risk management

6.   How are single, first-time homebuyers encouraged to enter the housing market by the 1997 tax law changes?
    a.   They may deduct up to $10,000 from their income taxes for the year in which they purchase a home.
    b.   They are entitled to a $250,000 exclusion from their income taxes.
    c.   They may withdraw up to $500,000 from their tax-deferred IRA without penalty.
    d.   They may make a penalty-free withdrawal of up to $10,000 from their tax-deferred IRA for the purchase of a home.

7.   Growth management in California has been primarily inspired by
    a.   developers of land.
    b.   the desire to protect resources.
    c.   the governor.
    d.   schools.

8.   Which of the following is *NOT* true regarding the effect of taxes on the real estate market?
    a.   High tax rates are likely to attract investors.
    b.   Tax incentives may attract new business.
    c.   Real estate taxation is a primary source of local government revenue.
    d.   Low tax rates are likely to encourage development.

9.   What has been the major effect of fair housing laws on the real estate market?
    a.   Fair housing laws have brought a once-vibrant market to a virtual standstill.
    b.   Fair housing laws apply only to multifamily properties and, thus, have had no effect on the single-family residential housing market.
    c.   Fair housing laws have made financing available to many who had been rebuffed in the past, expanding the pool of potential homeowners.
    d.   Fines for violations of fair housing laws are a primary source of revenue for local governments.

10. A residential property that was very fashionable in 1972 is no longer considered very attractive. However, it is in very good shape physically. Based on these facts, which of the following statements is *TRUE*?

    a. Whether or not the property is architecturally fashionable does not affect its value.

    b. The property is likely to command a higher price in the real estate market.

    c. The property is likely to command a lower price in the real estate market.

    d. The property will probably be unsellable if it is considered dated or old-fashioned.

UNIT SIX

THE U.S. HOUSING MARKET

KEY TERMS

balloon frame	housing stock	retail sales
Census Bureau	housing unit	subjectivity
contractor system	HUD	value in context
households	industrialized housing	zoning
housing market	on-site construction	
housing starts	regulations	

LEARNING OBJECTIVES

- Understand the role of residential housing in the U.S. economy and the effect of local business and financial conditions on the market

- Define the various types of housing available

- Explain the characteristics of the housing market and the demographics of U.S. home ownership

RESIDENTIAL CONSTRUCTION

Housing is a major factor in the U.S. economy. The housing industry accounts for about 30% of investment spending and 16% of overall economic activity in the United States.

According to the National Association of Home Builders (NAHB), housing stock in the United States is worth more than $20.7 trillion.

Home buying typically generates a wave of activity as people who purchase homes spend money on improving their homes, which includes buying new appliances, furnishings, and other household items. According to the NAHB, a typical buyer of a single-family residence tends to spend on average $7,400 more on improvements/furnishings than an owner who does not move.

The **housing market** is not only big, it's vitally important. The NAHB tells us that more than 42% of the typical home-owning family's wealth is accounted for by equity in their home—the biggest source of U.S. families' net worth.

For economists, construction spending is an important indication of the nation's overall economic health. The NAHB estimated that out of 8.9 million people working in the construction industry in 2013, close to 3.45 million people worked in residential construction, accounting for 2.4% of the U.S. employed civilian labor force. In 2013, California had the most residential construction workers in the nation, as approximately half a million California residents worked in home building, accounting for 2.9% of the state's employed labor force.

Expenditures on Maintenance and Alteration

Annual spending on housing upkeep and alterations runs into billions of dollars. Because such spending provides jobs for people in many trades and industries, it has meaningful repercussions across the economy.

Evolution of U.S. Housing

Until the early 1800s, most quality residential construction in the United States relied on heavy posts and horizontal timbers, held together with mortise and joints. Those who did the work were craftsmen skilled with the hand tools of the carpenter's trade. Around 1830, however, the invention of the balloon frame revolutionized the industry.

The **balloon frame** is a house built on a shell of light lumber, held together with nails. Heavy posts are not needed. The sheathing on the frame, like the skin of an airplane wing, provides strength. The term *balloon frame* derives from the fact that such light frame homes seemed to be constructed overnight: inflated like balloons.

The balloon frame spelled the beginning of the end for highly trained construction craftsmen. Costs of balloon frame construction were estimated in 1865 to be less than half that of traditional building, a result of the cheapness of materials and the reduced need for skilled workers. These lower costs greatly encouraged housing development in the Midwestern and Western states.

The Contractor System

Home construction in the later years of the 19th century involved specialized trades, often supervised by a carpenter. The demands of organizing and supervising a growing legion of specialists gave rise to the **contractor system**, under which a single supervisor oversees the building project. The specialists hired by the contractor are referred to as subcontractors.

Among the earliest subcontracting trades were painters, bricklayers, glaziers, stonemasons, and plasterers. By the 1880s, hot water and hot-air heating systems were available. By the end of the century, public health authorities were requiring sewer connections, so plumbers were added to the building trades.

Becoming a contractor in the 19th century was not difficult. A carpenter could buy an estimator's manual and submit a bid. Staying in business was another matter, however. Because it was so easy to break into the business, a highly competitive environment developed. Contractors were always looking for ways to cut costs and keep bids low. They experimented with new materials and labor-saving methods but often encountered resistance. The experimentation resulted in the refinement of existing materials, tools, and techniques and in the development of new technologies.

For instance, concrete rode a brief wave of popularity as the miracle material of the 1890s and early 1900s. Concrete was a favorite construction material of the visionary architect Frank Lloyd Wright. In some of his most famous buildings (such as Unity Temple in Illinois and the Falling Water residence in Pennsylvania), Wright developed a technique of building a wooden mold and casting an entire reinforced concrete structure in a single pour.

By World War I, a good contractor could build a house in one day, to the chagrin of the building-trades unions, whose members perceived threats to jobs and warned of diminished quality in housing as a possible consequence. The building trades grew increasingly organized to resist efficient new materials and technologies that threatened their livelihood. The general public, too, was wary of the more innovative construction techniques.

Nonetheless, housing construction materials, techniques, and technologies have continued to evolve. Greater efficiency has resulted in quicker construction, and many new materials are far sturdier and longer-lasting than traditional ones.

Architectural Styles

Through successive styles, U.S. history can be traced in its **housing stock**. Historic styles are important in today's market because they go in and out of fashion, affecting demand and prices for a given type of house. Figure 6.1 compares the characteristics of some popular housing styles.

FIGURE 6.1:   **Popular American Architectural Styles**

Name	Original Period	Key Characteristics
Greek Revival	1820–1860	columns, flat roof
Octagon	1850–1860	octagonal floor plan
Italianate	1860–1890	tall, narrow, arched windows
Stick	1880s	square bays, ornamental boards
Queen Anne	1880–1900	ornate, asymmetrical, "Victorian"
Craftsman	1890–1920	exposed structural timbers
Mission Style	1890–1920	stucco walls, tile roof, arcade
Colonial Revival	1895–1910	boxy style, classical detailing
Prairie School	1900–1920	low horizontal, geometric style
Bungalow	1900–1940	small, one-story, narrow lot
Art Deco	1920–1930s	curvilinear, streamlined form
California Ranch	1950–1960s	one-story, indoor-outdoor flow
Split Level	1940s–present	floors at different levels

Today, new housing is constructed using a wide variety of styles and combinations of styles to suit the taste of individual buyers and local markets.

Like real estate, the housing industry uses some specifically defined terms. It's important to understand this professional "jargon" in order to fully engage in a discussion about the residential housing market.

Housing Definitions

Housing Unit   A **housing unit** is a general term for any place where people live. Housing units have a number of general characteristics:

- An *enclosed physical space* or structure with a full range of living facilities, within which an individual, group, or family may live privately, separated from those in other units.

- A *single detached house,* an *apartment within or attached to a house,* a house *sharing a wall with another house,* an *apartment in a multiunit building,* or *manufactured housing.* It may be one room or many rooms.

- *Rented, owned outright,* or held in some form of common ownership such as a condominium, co-op, or group home.

The **Census Bureau** defines *housing unit* as "a house, an apartment, … a group of rooms, or a single room *occupied* … or *intended for occupancy as separate living quarters.*"[4] "Separate living quarters" are those in which the occupants do not live and eat with other persons in the structure and that have direct access from the outside of the building or through a common hall.

Under this definition, some types of living space are specifically excluded. Some exclusions include dormitories, bunkhouses, and barracks; quarters in transient hotels and motels (except for residential hotels); and quarters in institutions, general hospitals, and military installations (except those occupied by staff members or resident employees who have separate living arrangements).

Single Family   Any structure used as a dwelling unit for occupancy by one family—a private home. A single-family home may be detached (free-standing) or attached (such as a townhouse).

Multiunit Buildings, Two to Four Units   For purposes of housing statistics, multifamily residential buildings are distinguished on the basis of number of units. Small multiunit buildings include duplexes, triplexes, fourplexes, small apartment buildings, and rented rooms in single-family houses.

---

4.   United States Census Bureau, "Glossary," U.S. Census Bureau, www.census.gov/glossary/#term_Housingunit (accessed May 19, 2015).

Multiunit Buildings, Five or More Units   Larger multiunit buildings include apartment towers and complexes. Individual units in multiunit buildings may be rented (apartment buildings) or owned (as in condominiums and cooperatives).

U.S. Home Ownership

Since 1995, homeownership in the United States has ranged from 64–69% (see Figure 6.2).

FIGURE 6.2:   **Quarterly Homeownership Rates for the United States: 1995–2014**

Year	First Quarter	Second Quarter	Third Quarter	Fourth Quarter
1995	64.2	64.7	65.0	65.1
1996	65.1	65.4	65.6	65.4
1997	65.4	65.7	66.0	65.7
1998	65.9	66.0	66.8	66.4
1999	66.7	66.6	67.0	66.9
2000	67.1	67.2	67.7	67.5
2001	67.5	67.7	68.1	68.0
2002	67.8	67.6	68.0	68.3
2003	68.0	68.0	68.4	68.6
2004	68.6	69.2	69.0	69.2
2005	69.1	68.6	68.8	69.0
2006	68.5	68.7	69.0	68.9
2007	68.4	68.2	68.2	67.8
2008	67.8	68.1	67.9	67.5
2009	67.3	67.4	67.6	67.2
2010	67.1	66.9	66.9	66.5
2011	66.4	65.9	66.3	66.0
2012	65.4	65.5	65.5	65.4
2013	65.0	65.0	65.3	65.2
2014	64.8	64.7	64.4	64.0

Source: U.S. Census Bureau

According to the U.S. Census Bureau, single-family detached houses (the "American dream" home) made up more than 60% of the total U.S. housing inventory in 1960. Single-family detached houses continue to be the most popular type of housing and generally account for around 60% of the housing inventory.

Data from the Census Bureau shows different trends over time for various types of housing. For example, in 1940, townhouse-type homes made up more than 7% of the housing stock. By 1990, they accounted for only

5%. On the other hand, apartment buildings with five or more units have become more popular over time; they accounted for about 10% of the housing inventory in 1940 but for nearly 20% in the early 2000s.

A very dramatic change in Americans' housing preferences was the increase in popularity of manufactured housing. In 1940, manufactured housing was included in the Census Bureau's "Other" category along with boats, tents, and tourist cabins. In 1940 these made up less than 1% of the housing stock but by 1990, it was more than 7%.

Geographically, the north and east have seen a growth in single-family housing stock, while fast-growing southern and western regions are increasingly dominated by multifamily dwellings.

Housing data of many kinds are gathered by HUD and the Census Bureau in the American Housing Survey (AHS).

Unit Size

Statistics on unit size can be compiled for both the total housing stock and for trends in new construction. Two different measures are number of rooms and square footage.

FIGURE 6.3:   A Look Back at Percent of Americans Owning a Home by Decennial Census (2000)

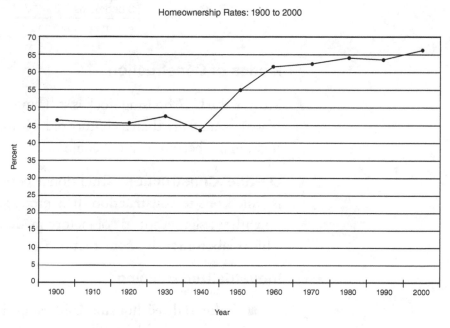

Homeownership Rates: 1900 to 2000

Source: U.S. Census Bureau

Rooms per Dwelling   In 1960, the median number of rooms in a U.S. dwelling was 4.9. In 1980, that had risen to 5.1, and by 1993 the average was 5.5 rooms.

The Census Bureau counts whole rooms (e.g., living rooms, dining rooms, bedrooms, and kitchens). A partially divided room, such as a living/dining room or dining "L," is counted as a separate room only if there is a partition from floor to ceiling.

The room count does not include bathrooms, halls, foyers or closets, alcoves, pantries, or laundry or furnace rooms. Unfinished attics or basements, open porches, storage space, manufactured housing or trailers used only as bedrooms, and offices used only by persons not living in the unit are not counted as "rooms."

Number of Bedrooms   The Census Bureau counts bedrooms as rooms used mainly for sleeping, even if they are used for other purposes. A living room with a sofabed is not counted as a bedroom. Likewise, a one-room apartment would be counted as having no bedroom. For information on the number of bedrooms in U.S. homes, see Figure 6.4.

FIGURE 6.4:   **Bedrooms in U.S. Homes (2013)**

Bedrooms	
2 or less bedroom	6%
3 bedrooms	43%
4 or more bedrooms	51%

Modes of Construction

Most of the U.S. housing stock is still built using traditional methods, many of which are more than a century old. However, various methods of prefabrication are becoming more common.

On-Site Construction   Traditional construction, built by contractors, is called **onsite construction**. It is produced on site from the foundation up without significant use of factory-made modular or panelized elements. This is labor-intensive construction.

Industrialized Housing

- **Industrialized housing** is housing that is factory-made or prefabricated to some degree.

■ **Modular Construction.** Sections of a house—whole rooms or groups of rooms—are built in a "factory," then brought to a site and quickly assembled on a permanent foundation. Finishing work may require a month. When completed, they are indistinguishable from onsite construction.

■ **Panelized Construction.** Two-dimensional parts of the house (interior and exterior walls and floor panels) are factory-produced and assembled on the site, as in modular construction.

■ **Manufactured Homes.** A special category of factory-built housing (commonly called "mobile homes," although the term was dropped from use by the federal government in 1980) are factory-built on a steel I-beam chassis, transported to a site, and placed on a foundation that includes hook-ups for plumbing and electricity. The I-beam chassis remains a part of the structure.

■ **Regulations.** Manufactured homes must meet federal construction and safety standards— **regulations** administered through **HUD**.

■ **Real property versus personal property.** Before 1980, manufactured homes were usually considered personal property. They were, after all, movable. In 1980, federal law mandated that any manufactured home affixed to a permanent foundation on privately owned land become real property and be taxed and financed as real estate.

■ **Zoning.** Community acceptance of manufactured homes has been growing, as measured by changes in state law, local **zoning** ordinances, and public attitude. Specifically, California law (Government Code Section 65852.3) now permits all manufactured homes built under HUD guidelines and on a foundation to be placed on lots zoned for conventional single-family residential dwellings. The manufactured homes must also conform to the same development standards applied to a conventional single-family residence.

A CLOSER LOOK   In 1981 the California legislature added section 65913 to the Government Code, preventing any city from categorically prohibiting the installation of manufactured housing on lots zoned for single-family dwellings:

In no case may a city...apply any development standards which will have the effect of totally precluding mobile homes from being installed as permanent residences.

WHO OWNS AMERICA'S HOUSING STOCK?

After a dramatic rise between 1940 and 1960, the proportion of housing units occupied by owners has been more or less on a plateau, ranging from 56–59% since 1968.

Figure 6.5 shows how the rate of home ownership has changed in the four major U.S. geographic regions.

FIGURE 6.5:   Home Ownership by Region (2008–2014)

Year/Quarter	United States	Northeast	Midwest	South	West
2014					
Fourth Quarter	64.0	61.9	68.3	65.5	58.6
Third Quarter	64.4	62.3	68.8	65.7	59.4
Second Quarter	64.7	62.1	69.6	65.9	59.6
First Quarter	64.8	62.4	69.3	66.5	59.4
2013					
Fourth Quarter	65.2	62.8	69.8	67.1	59.3
Third Quarter	65.3	63.6	69.6	66.9	59.5
Second Quarter	65.0	63.2	69.4	66.5	59.4
First Quarter	65.0	62.5	70.0	66.5	59.4
2012					
Fourth Quarter	65.4	63.9	69.7	67.0	59.5
Third Quarter	65.5	63.9	69.6	66.9	60.1
Second Quarter	65.5	63.7	69.6	67.4	59.7
First Quarter	65.4	62.5	69.5	67.5	59.9
2011					
Fourth Quarter	66.0	63.7	70.0	68.3	60.1
Third Quarter	66.3	63.7	70.3	68.4	60.7
Second Quarter	65.9	63.0	70.0	68.2	60.3
First Quarter	66.4	63.9	70.4	68.4	60.9
2010					
Fourth Quarter	66.5	64.1	70.5	68.5	61.0
Third Quarter	66.9	63.9	71.1	69.1	61.3
Second Quarter	66.9	64.2	70.8	69.1	61.4
First Quarter	67.1	64.4	70.9	69.2	61.9
2009					
Fourth Quarter	67.2	63.9	71.3	69.1	62.3
Third Quarter	67.6	64.0	71.6	69.7	62.7
Second Quarter	67.4	64.3	70.5	70.0	62.5
First Quarter	67.3	63.7	70.7	69.6	62.8
2008					
Fourth Quarter	67.5	64.0	71.4	69.8	62.7
Third Quarter	67.9	64.4	71.9	69.9	63.5
Second Quarter	68.1	65.3	71.7	70.2	63.0
First Quarter	67.8	64.7	72.0	69.7	62.8

Not surprisingly, in view of the financial means required, age is strongly correlated with home ownership. Older individuals, who were in their first homebuying phase before prices skyrocketed in the 1970s, are most likely to own their homes today (see Figure 6.6).

FIGURE 6.6:   **Home Ownership by Age (2004 to 2014)**

Year/Quarter	Home Ownership Rates					
	United States	Under 35 Years	35 to 44 Years	45 to 54 Years	55 to 64 Years	65 Years and Over
2014						
Fourth Quarter	64.0	35.3	58.8	70.5	75.8	79.5
Third Quarter	64.4	36.0	59.1	70.1	76.6	80.0
Second Quarter	64.7	35.9	60.2	70.7	76.4	80.1
First Quarter	64.8	36.2	60.7	71.4	76.4	79.9
2013						
Fourth Quarter	65.2	36.8	60.9	71.4	76.5	80.7
Third Quarter	65.3	36.8	61.1	71.3	76.2	81.2
Second Quarter	65.0	36.7	60.3	70.9	76.7	80.9
First Quarter	65.0	36.8	60.1	71.3	77.0	80.4
2012						
Fourth Quarter	65.4	37.1	60.4	72.1	77.6	80.7
Third Quarter	65.5	36.3	61.8	72.0	76.9	81.4
Second Quarter	65.5	36.5	62.2	71.4	77.1	81.6
First Quarter	65.4	36.8	61.4	71.3	77.8	80.9
2011						
Fourth Quarter	66.0	37.6	62.3	72.7	79.0	80.9
Third Quarter	66.3	38.0	63.4	72.7	78.6	81.1
Second Quarter	65.9	37.5	63.8	72.3	77.8	80.8
First Quarter	66.4	37.9	64.4	73.1	78.6	81.0
2010						
Fourth Quarter	66.5	39.2	63.9	72.7	79.0	80.5
Third Quarter	66.9	39.2	65.2	73.0	79.2	80.6
Second Quarter	66.9	39.0	65.6	73.6	78.7	80.4
First Quarter	67.1	38.9	65.3	74.8	79.1	80.6
2009						
Fourth Quarter	67.2	40.4	65.7	74.0	78.9	80.2
Third Quarter	67.6	39.8	66.5	74.5	79.4	80.9
Second Quarter	67.4	39.0	66.8	74.5	79.9	80.4
First Quarter	67.3	39.8	65.7	74.6	79.8	80.4
2008						
Fourth Quarter	67.5	40.3	66.6	74.5	79.7	80.4
Third Quarter	67.9	41.0	67.2	75.2	80.0	80.1

FIGURE 6.6:   **Home Ownership by Age (2004 to 2014) (cont.)**

Year/Quarter	Home Ownership Rates					
	United States	Under 35 Years	35 to 44 Years	45 to 54 Years	55 to 64 Years	65 Years and Over
Second Quarter	68.1	41.2	67.6	75.4	80.1	80.2
First Quarter	67.8	41.3	66.7	75.0	80.4	79.9
2007						
Fourth Quarter	67.8	41.0	67.2	75.1	80.4	80.3
Third Quarter	68.2	42.0	68.1	75.2	81.1	79.9
Second Quarter	68.2	41.9	67.6	75.5	80.6	80.5
First Quarter	68.4	41.7	68.3	75.8	80.4	80.9
2006						
Fourth Quarter	68.9	42.8	68.9	76.4	80.7	81.2
Third Quarter	69.0	43.0	68.8	76.4	80.7	81.5
Second Quarter	68.7	42.4	68.9	76.3	81.0	80.6
First Quarter	68.5	42.3	68.9	75.8	81.2	80.3
2005						
Fourth Quarter	69.0	43.1	69.7	76.7	80.6	80.6
Third Quarter	68.8	43.0	68.6	76.7	80.9	80.6
Second Quarter	68.6	42.8	68.7	76.3	81.3	80.3
First Quarter	69.1	43.3	70.1	76.5	81.8	80.8
2004						
Fourth Quarter	69.2	43.3	70.0	77.4	81.6	80.5
Third Quarter	69.0	43.1	68.6	77.4	81.2	81.8
Second Quarter	69.2	43.6	69.4	77.0	82.4	81.1
First Quarter	68.6	42.3	68.8	77.0	81.7	80.7

Source: U.S. Census Bureau

Households

A *housing unit* is a physical structure. A **household**, on the other hand, is a social unit. It consists of all the people who live together in a housing unit and helps define the character of the local market.

The relationship between household characteristics and housing units is influenced by marriage and divorce patterns, attitudes about independence for young adults and the elderly, costs of living separately, business conditions, available affordable housing and, of course, income levels. As lifestyles change in the United States, "traditional" patterns of two-parent, single-family, one-earner households have evolved accordingly. This process is not just of sociological interest, however. It has a real effect on the housing market in such areas as housing needs and design.

The composition of U.S. households has changed significantly since the early 1970s.

For instance, the share of households represented by families fell from about 81% in 1970 to 74% in 1980. In 1994, the number of family households reached 71%, or 68.5 million family households. Families traditionally have accounted for a majority of all U.S. households, but their share of the total is now significantly lower than in the past.

The U.S. Census Bureau defines a household, family household, and non-family household, respectively, as follows:

- A **household** is a person or group of people who occupy a housing unit. The householder is a person in whose name the housing unit is being bought or rented. A householder is the *designated head of household*.

- A **nonfamily household** consists of a person living alone or a householder who shares the home with non-relatives only (e.g., with roommates or an unmarried partner).

- A **family household** consists of a householder and one or more people living together in the same household who are related to the householder by birth, marriage, or adoption, and may also include people unrelated to the householder. If the householder is married and living with the spouse, then the household is designated a "married-couple household." The remaining types of family households not maintained by a married couple are designated by the sex of the householder.

What is meant by family households? The 2000 U.S. Census Bureau further defines the term as including

- married-couple families (approximately 52 million);

- families with a female householder, no husband present (approximately 12.9 million); and

- families with a male householder, no wife present (roughly 4.3 million).

A family consists of a householder and one or more other persons living in the same household who are related to the householder by birth, marriage, or adoption. Biological, adopted, and stepchildren of the householder who are under 18 are considered "own children" of the householder. Own children do not include other children present in the household, regardless of the presence or absence of the other children's parents. A family household may also contain people not related to the householder. A family in which the householder and a spouse of the opposite sex are enumerated as members of the same household is a husband-wife household.

According to the U.S. Census, people who were not related to the householder numbered 18.3 million in the 2010 census (6.1% of the household population), up from 14.6 million in 2000 (5.2% of the household population). In fact, 1 out of every 8 homes in 2010 contained one or more people not related to the householder. Roomers and boarders comprised 1.5 million individuals who represented a wide variety of people such as students, migrants to an area waiting for better accommodations, or people who could not afford to rent their own home.

CHARACTERISTICS OF THE MARKET

Certain general principles apply to the housing market and set it apart from markets for other commodities. They derive from the fact that buildings are fixed in place, durable, and varied.

Housing: A Unique Product

Housing is unlike other market commodities because *every unit is unique*. The uniqueness of housing results from a variety of factors, all of which boil down to location, location, location.

Value in Context   The value of a product such as real estate is determined only partly by its intrinsic qualities. The setting of the product is part of its value. This is a case where externalities (benefits and disabilities arising from the acts and omissions of neighbors) directly impact value. Whether these are positive or negative, the effect cannot be escaped because a house is fixed in place. One can remove a diamond from an ugly setting, but a house is stubbornly attached to its foundation, rooted to the ground. A fine, lovingly maintained house in a decaying neighborhood may lose value (a situation referred to as regression), while a more modest house in a desirable location appreciates in value (progression).

Further, remember that housing markets are intensely local. Although local communities are influenced by national and regional circumstances, each has its own geographic setting and environment, its own demographics, its own economic structure and markets, and its own policies on development—all with implications for local housing demand and supply. A community's power to draw and hold population is influenced by a number of factors.

- **Business Climate.** The fortunes of the local business community, as well as its sustained capacity to offer jobs and good incomes, is often dependent on the degree to which the economic base is diversified.

- **Infrastructure.** The general quality of roads, utilities, and transportation will attract or repel buyers.

- **Amenities.** Cultural, social, environmental, and recreational attractions will affect sales.

- **Public Sector.** The existence in or near the community of public-supported institutions or facilities that offer employment and purchase local goods and services, such as a state university, veterans' hospital, military base, or prison, will influence buyers' decisions.

- **Specialized Services.** Industries and businesses that attract outside dollars—one city may be renowned for its hospitals and medical specialists while another location may be synonymous with high-tech industries or aircraft manufacturing.

- **Neighborhoods.** The local nature of the housing market applies not only to the community as a whole but to its parts. Within the boundaries of a community are many submarkets, each with its own different populations and income levels. The reputation of particular neighborhoods or streets, scenic qualities, proximity to industry or airport noise, and a host of other factors will affect the value and desirability of housing.

- **Educational Facilities.** Quality educational facilities, including access to elementary, junior high, high school, community colleges, and universities will affect a community's attractiveness. A community may also draw people because of a school district's performance relative to minimum state achievement standards. Many communities throughout California have achieved a high level of performance relative to the quality of education provided and, in some cases, this becomes a drawing force for people desiring to live in a certain community.

Subjectivity

No two houses are alike in every way (design, features, location, and condition). Nor are any two buyers ever exactly the same. The match between house and buyer and, therefore, the value of the product will always include a large measure of **subjectivity**.

This does not mean that demand for housing with certain facilities and within a certain price range cannot be estimated. Developers and investors in income properties make such estimates all the time. However, a rich profusion of house and apartment types will usually be needed in the supply mix that satisfies demand.

Recent History of House Prices

By comparison, the median price of a single-family home in California in 2009 was about $292,960:

- The median price in the Los Angeles area was $339,982.

- The median price in the San Francisco Bay Area was $531,577.

- In Northern California, the median price was $255,597.

These figures demonstrate that the housing market is intensely regional and microcosmic. While it might be useful to know that the median price for a single-family home in the United States was $172,600 in 2009, the really significant number is the most local one.

By December 2014, the median price of a home in California was $452,570, compared to $402,760 in 2013 and $312,500 in 2012. As a historical comparison, in 1970, median home price in California was $24,640, while it was $23,000 in the United States. Figure 6.7 illustrates a historical look at home prices in various regions around the state relative to median price during the recession. Figure 6.8 compares the median price of a home throughout various regions in California from 2013 to 2014.

FIGURE 6.7:   **A Look Back at the Regional Sales and Price Activity During the Recession (2009)**

2009 Regional Sales and Price Activity Detached Single-Family Homes					
	Median Price Aug-09	Percent Change in Price from Prior Month Jul-09	Percent Change in Price from Prior Year Jul-09	Percent Change in Sales from Prior Month Jul-09	Percent Change in Sales from Prior Year Aug-09
Statewide					
California	$292,960	2.6%	−16.9%	−5.1%	9.0%
C.A.R. REGION					
Central Valley	$90,500	−16.8%	−29.4%	2.1%	−7.5%
High Desert	$111,771	1.0%	−33.9%	−13.2%	40.4%
Los Angeles	$339,982	0.2%	−13.9%	−10.6%	6/7%
Monterey Region	$298,935	5.4%	−19.3%	−8.7%	10.0%
Monterey County	$262,500	−14.3%	−30.7%	10.9%	48.8%
Santa Cruz County	N/A	N/A	N/A	N/A	N/A
Northern California	$255,597	−5.6%	−15.7%	−10.9%	−9.6%
Northern Wine Country	$347,916	−3.5%	−10.3%	−13.0%	−3.6%
Orange County	$499,437	−0.2%	−2.3%	−8.8%	5.9%
Palm Springs/Lower Desert	$169,076	3.7%	−23.8%	−19.8%	21.4%
Riverside/S. Bern.	$166,601	0.7%	−26.1%	−10.9%	−0.1%
Sacramento	$192,047	4.5%	−13.1%	−8.9%	−10.0%
San Diego	$375,706	0.8%	−3.3%	−13.4%	0.1%
San Francisco Bay	$531,577	−2.6%	−14.2%	−15.2%	7.6%
San Luis Obispo	$382,557	−3.0%	−7.8%	−9.0%	9.7%
Santa Barbara County	$376,086	0.0%	−10.0%	−15.0%	−5.7%
Santa Clara	$555,000	−5.5%	−14.6%	−20.7%	9.9%
Ventura	$466,197	2.1%	−2.6%	−6.9%	6.1%

Source: California Association of REALTORS® (September 2009)

FIGURE 6.8: **Sales and Price Activity—Existing Single-Family Homes (SFH)**

	Median Sales Price of Existing Single-Family Homes				
State/Region	Nov 14	Oct 14	Nov 13	Percent Change from Prior Month (MTM % Chg)	Percent Change from Prior Year (YTY % Chg)
CA SFH	$445,280	$450,270	$423,090	−1.1%	5.2%
CA Condo/ Townhomes	$369,040	$374,480	$374,050	−1.5%	6.3%
Los Angeles Metro	$417,270	$412,190	$396,790	1.2%	5.2%
Inland Empire	$276,950	$274,630	$261,490	0.8%	5.9%
SF Bay Area	$748,870	$760,610	$692,860	−1.5%	8.1%

SF Bay Area	Nov 14	Oct 14	Nov 13	MTM % Chg	YTY % Chg
Alameda	$710,370	$706,280	$652,070	0.6%	8.9%
Contra Costa	$654,410	$721,590	$698,110	−9.3%	−6.3%
Marin	$1,111,110	$969,700	$942,070	14.6%	17.9%
Napa	$652,000	$599,140	$528,410	4.3%	18.3%
San Francisco	$956,320	$986,260	$896,740	−3.0%	6.6%
San Mateo	$1,092,500	$1,071,000	$895,000	2.0%	22.1%
Santa Clara	$850,000	$870,000	$785,000	−2.3%	8.3%
Solano	$332,020	$327,400	$280,360	1.4%	18.4%
Sonoma	$487,110	$487,930	$463,820	−0.2%	5.0%

Southern California	Nov 14	Oct 14	Nov 13	MTM % Chg	YTY % Chg
Los Angeles	$433,850	$477,600	$405,470	−9.2%	7.1%
Orange County	$689,480	$692,390	$660,890	−0.4%	4.3%
Riverside County	$320,880	$321,750	$306,350	−0.3%	4.7%
San Bernardino	$213,780	$208,080	$192,470	2.7%	11.1%
San Diego	$491,690	$493,030	$473,360	−0.3%	3.9%
Ventura	$549,440	$583,810	$543,330	−5.9%	1.1%

Central Coast	Nov 14	Oct 14	Nov 13	MTM % Chg	YTY % Chg
Monterey	$460,000	$460,000	$420,000	0.0%	9.5%
San Luis Obispo	$453,950	$455,660	$486,510	−0.4%	−6.7%
Santa Barbara	$643,290	$570,000	$558,330	12.9%	15.2%
Santa Cruz	$689,500	$715,000	$666,000	−3.6%	3.5%

Central Valley	Nov 14	Oct 14	Nov 13	MTM % Chg	YTY % Chg
Fresno	$200,000	$200,600	$193,020	−0.3%	3.6%
Glenn County	$95,000	$167,500	$150,000	−43.3%	−36.7%
Kern (Bakersfield)	$211,450	$215,000	$190,000	−1.7%	11.3%
Kings County	$192,500	$168,670	$171,670	14.1%	12.1%
Madera	$235,710	$166,000	$160,000	42.0%	47.3%

Median Sales Price of Existing Single-Family Homes				
State/Region	Nov 14	Oct 14	Nov 13	Percent Change from Prior Month (MTM % Chg)	Percent Change from Prior Year (YTY % Chg)
Placer County	$369,490	$380,170	$361,166	–2.8%	2.3%
Sacramento	$266,260	$270,150	$246,900	–1.4%	7.8%
San Joaquin	$249,080	$263,270	$233,070	–5.4%	6.9%
Stanislaus	$230,950	$228,630	$198,400	1.0%	16.4%
Tulare	$187,000	$179,060	$161,300	4.4%	15.9%
Other Counties in CA	**Nov 14**	**Oct 14**	**Nov 13**	**MTM % Chg**	**YTY % Chg**
Butte County	$260,710	$247,580	$255,950	5.3%	1.9%
Del Norte	$127,500	$160,000	$135,000	–20.3%	–5.6%
Humboldt	$262,500	$260,340	$239,280	0.8%	9.7%
Lake County	$186,670	$190,000	$143,330	–1.8%	30.2%
Mendocino County	$332,140	$337,500	$300,000	–1.6%	10.7%
Shasta	$210,610	$220,920	$207,560	–4.7%	1.5%
Siskiyou County	$172,500	$161,670	$166,670	6.7%	3.5%

Source: California Association of REALTORS®, December 2014

Housing Starts

Housing starts are a measurement of the number of new residential construction projects begun in the United States during a given period, typically in the form of monthly, quarterly, or annual reports. Economists look to these housing starts to catch any trends developing in the housing industry. The housing starts figures published by the federal government include units built

- *for rent*;
- by *a contractor* on an owner's land;
- by *an owner* acting as the contractor; and
- for *condominium or co-op development*.

Housing starts are an extremely important leading indicator and are watched closely by government and private economists. Figures are usually derived from local building permits. Almost all permits lead to a construction start, usually within 30 to 60 days, with an average project completion time of six and one-half months.

Housing Start Cycle   The *business cycle* (discussed in Unit 3) is reflected in and influenced by the ups and downs of housing starts. The housing starts cycle leads the business cycle, on average, by about 13 months.

The housing starts cycle for each type of building (single-family, townhouse, condominium, or large apartment building) has its own average course, depending on differences in demand. The curves, however, usually show a similar direction and go up or down at roughly the same times.

Local Business Conditions

The real estate market is driven by the business climate in which it exists. As discussed in Unit 5, the key to economic health in an urban setting is the area's economic base. There are several components of this base.

Population Growth   People are attracted by an eclectic variety of factors, among them the availability of jobs, climate, local attractions for recreation and amusement, cultural needs, and educational opportunities.

Real Estate Development   Real estate development goes hand in hand with population growth. Without continuous population growth, housing development would be limited to simply replacing existing stock or even reducing overall housing stock. Another limiting factor is affordability, which has caused a reduction in development of detached housing and a surge in the development of condominiums, apartment buildings, and attached residences such as townhouses.

Employment Opportunities   Employment is spurred by a variety of factors and is an indicator of the stability of the economic base. If the local economy is strongly dependent upon one component, as in a "company town," this is an extremely fragile foundation and likely to lead to large swings in employment levels, retail sales, and demand for housing. Diversity in the economic base is desirable.

Diversity is the key to a strong local economy. If the economy is rooted in one industry, such as lumber in Oregon or automobiles in Detroit, it is extremely vulnerable to an overall economic downturn. If, on the other hand, there is a wide base of diversity within the industrial sector, prospects for weathering an adverse economic climate appear brighter.

Retail Sales   Retail sales are closely tied to population demographics (that is, the age, ethnicity, income, education, and other factors that define a social group) and employment patterns. If the local plant that employs

2,000 people lays off 500, retail activity is affected geometrically, not just arithmetically. In other words, for every basic industry job in town, there is a corresponding number, whether on a one-to-one basis or even more, of service and retail jobs that support and are supported by it. The basic industry may be a factory, banking, trucking, farming, or even an educational institution. Whatever it is, the loss of basic jobs has a ripple effect, reducing demand for gyms and suntan parlors, barber and beauty shops, TV and appliance repair, shoe stores, and computer stores—all the myriad goods and services that the base-industry employees consumed in their daily activities.

Interest Rates

Few people contemplating the purchase of a house can afford to buy outright. Such major purchases almost always require a loan. Buyer decisions to purchase and lender decisions to loan are both based primarily on the buyer's estimated ability to handle monthly payments, and interest rates have strong effects on monthly payments. During the early 1980s, house sales dropped off markedly when interest rates were high. The housing industry picked up again, however, when rates went down again.

THE NEXT STEP   This concludes our general statistical overview of the U.S. real estate economy. As we've said repeatedly, the real estate market is a local market. In the following units, we will focus specifically on the state of California—its economic structure and strength in general and its real estate market in particular.

SUMMARY

- **Housing** is a major factor in the U.S. economy, accounting for nearly 16% of the nation's overall economic activity. The U.S. home ownership rate is almost 65%, and roughly 42% of most homeowners' total wealth is made up of equity in their homes.

- Residential construction has evolved over the years, both technologically and stylistically. Greater efficiency has resulted in quicker construction, and many new materials are far sturdier than their traditional counterparts. More cost-efficient homebuilding methods have made home ownership a possibility for more people.

- A **housing unit** is *an enclosed space intended for occupancy as separate living quarters*, with a *full range of living facilities* in which an individual, group, or family may live privately, *separated from others*.

- There are a variety of **construction methods** available. The two basic forms are *on site* (traditional) and *industrialized*, which include modular, panelized, and manufactured homes.

- A **household** is a *social unit*. It consists of *all the people who live together in a housing unit*. A **householder** is the *designated head of household*, in whose name the home is owned or rented.

- The **housing market** is unlike other market commodities because every unit is *unique*.

- **Housing starts** are a measurement of *the number of new residential construction projects begun in the United States during a given period*. The housing starts cycle generally leads the business cycle by slightly more than a year.

- Among the factors that drive the real estate market are **local business conditions** and **mortgage interest rates**.

REVIEW QUESTIONS

1. How does California compare with the rest of the nation relative to housing starts?

2. What is the median household income for the rest of the country, and how does it compare with that of California and that of your area?

3. Discuss the role the U.S. Census plays in economics.

4. Discuss the evolution of housing units in your community relative to architecture, and indicate which style or theme is more popular in your neighborhood.

5. Do you believe that there will be a further population increase in California and, if so, why?

6. Discuss the three different types of households as defined by the U.S. Census Bureau, and see if you can determine the makeup of your community.

7. How has your local real estate market improved since the recession of 2009?

UNIT QUIZ

1. A household can be considered
    a. a physical unit.
    b. a social unit.
    c. an economic unit.
    d. a geographic unit.

2. When measuring or analyzing the differences between homes and properties, we view this as a measure of
    a. subjectivity.
    b. objectivity.
    c. value in context.
    d. none of these.

3. Which type of residential construction earned its name based on the speed with which houses were constructed?
    a. Modular
    b. Overnight
    c. Balloon
    d. Stick

4. Which architectural style is characterized by ornate, asymmetrical detailing?
    a. Octagon
    b. Bungalow
    c. Italianate
    d. Queen Anne

5. All of the following would be included in the U.S. Census Bureau's definition of *housing unit* EXCEPT
    a. a rented home.
    b. manufactured housing.
    c. an efficiency apartment.
    d. a motel room.

6. According to the U.S. Census Bureau, which type of housing has increased significantly in popularity since 1940?
   a. Large apartment buildings
   b. Single-family detached houses
   c. Townhouses
   d. Tourist cabins

7. Mr. and Mrs. Hopper's house has three bedrooms, a kitchen, two bathrooms, a den, a large foyer, and a combination living/dining room. There is a sofabed in the den. The house also includes a separate laundry room and a large pantry off the kitchen. According to the U.S. Census Bureau's methodology and based on these facts, how many rooms are in the Hoppers' house?
   a. 5
   b. 6
   c. 9
   d. 11

8. The construction method in which two-dimensional pieces of a house's interior and exterior walls and floors are factory-produced and then assembled at the building site is referred to as
   a. panelized construction.
   b. modular construction.
   c. balloon construction.
   d. traditional construction.

9. L, M, and N live together in an apartment. L and M are married. L signed the lease for the apartment, but only M is employed, so M pays the rent. N owns the apartment building. In this situation, who is the householder?
   a. L only
   b. M only
   c. N only
   d. L and M together

10. Housing is unlike other market commodities because
   a. housing must usually be purchased with borrowed money.
   b. every unit is unique.
   c. there is such a variety of styles and materials available to consumers.
   d. regulations control its quality.

CALIFORNIA'S ECONOMIC PROFILE

KEY TERMS

agriculture   foreign trade   trade balance

demographics   manufacturing   unemployment

diversity   per capita income   workforce

employment   personal income

LEARNING OBJECTIVES

- Understand how California's diverse climates, populations, and geography contribute to the state's economic condition

- Explain the importance of microeconomies to the overall economic health of the state

- Compare how California's various regions have different economic histories, conditions, and expectations

AT HOME IN CALIFORNIA

Each state has its own economy. Over the years, the people, organizations, and political leadership build on the state's natural and human resources and create a culture. They develop a distinctive transportation, communication, and educational infrastructure and create their own business, legal, and social climate. A state builds its own agricultural, labor, and trade policies and, to a significant degree, its own opportunities. The results can be impressive, as the following survey of the California economy demonstrates.

California's Diversity

When you think of California, think **diversity**. Geographically, California's land area—nearly 160,000 square miles—makes it the third largest state in the country. Its thousand miles of Pacific coastline runs from the sandy, Mediterranean-style beaches of the south to the rocky, fog-shrouded redwood forests of the northern part of the state. California has the highest peak in the continental United States, Mount Whitney in the Sierra Nevada mountains, and the lowest point in North America, Death Valley. There are glaciers and deserts and 6 million acres of fertile cropland in the Central Valley where farms and orchards grow more than 250 different types of crops.

California has the largest population in the United States. The state produces about 10.7% of the total U.S. GDP and is the port for 40% of all U.S. trade with Asia. Some $71 billion in imports and exports cross the California coastline annually, based on 2014 figures.

More than 1 million businesses call California home. Its industries are at the forefront of the electronics revolution, and California is a leading producer of computers, memory chips, semiconductors, communications, and automation. The defense industry, medical research, tourism (a $53 billion industry alone), and entertainment are vital components of the widely diversified California economy. California's largest exports come from aerospace, pharmaceuticals, other information technology sectors, and agriculture. However, imports outweigh exports by a 2 to 1 margin.

Demographics

There are 38.5 million people living in California. That **demographic** number represents not only the greatest number of people in any state but a 20% increase over the past 10 years.

California has one of the most diverse populations in the world. Currently ethnic minorities make up more than half of the state's population at 52%

of the total. Figure 7.1 through Figure 7.3 illustrate the international nature of California's population.

Between 1946 and 2002, California's population grew from 9.6 million to more than 34 million people. Population growth, including migration from other parts of the United States, slowed in the early 1990s as the state experienced a serious economic downturn. Nevertheless, the state's growth trend has continued upward.

FIGURE 7.1:   California's Diverse Population

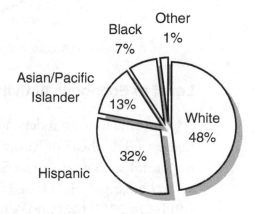

Source: U.S. Census Bureau

FIGURE 7.2:   California's Hispanic Population

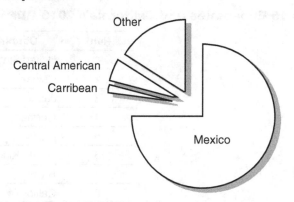

Source: U.S. Census Bureau

FIGURE 7.3:   **California's Asian/Pacific Population**

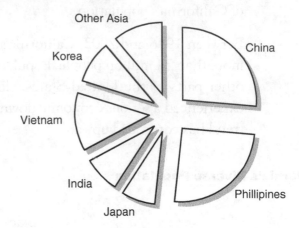

Source: U.S. Census Bureau

Level of Economic Activity

If California were an independent nation, it would have the world's eighth highest GDP, ahead of Russia and Italy (see Figure 7.4). In 2013, California's total state product was $2.05 trillion, up from $1.96 trillion in 2012. As a comparison, the United States' GDP was $16.2 trillion, up from $15.5 trillion in 2012. California's top three trading partners are Mexico, Japan, and Canada. By September 2014, the United States GDP stood at $17.56 trillion.

FIGURE 7.4:   **Top 15 Economies and California's 2013 GDP**

Rank	Countries	$ (Billions)
1	United States	$16,800
2	China	$9,181
3	Japan	$4,902
4	Germany	$3,636
5	France	$2,737
6	United Kingdom	$2,536
7	Brazil	$2,243
8	California	$2,203
9	Russia	$2,118
10	Italy	$2,072
11	India	$1,871
12	Canada	$1,825
13	Australia	$1,505
14	Spain	$1,359
15	Mexico	$1,259

Source: California Department of Finance/World Bank

Professional Workforce   Because of its physical and cultural amenities and its job opportunities, the state attracts well-educated professionals from other parts of the country and other parts of the world to its **workforce**. Thus, California is on the receiving end of a "brain drain" that makes these people's services and abilities available to business and to the general public.

Educational Institutions   Economic growth is often strongly related to the quality of a state's system of higher education. California has excellent public and private colleges and universities, staffed by renowned scholars. Their advanced research and teaching helps keep the state on the leading edge of ideas and technology.

High-tech companies often send their engineers back to school to keep abreast of the latest research. Such companies find it desirable to locate near universities and think tanks.

While recent tax and spending reforms may affect public universities' ability to continue to provide a broad, high-quality education, the perception of California's status as an educational powerhouse remains strong. As of 2012, California's higher education system was comprised of the following:

- *University of California*

  — 10 campuses, 5 medical centers, 3 national laboratories

  — 214,000 full-time equivalent (FTE) students

  — 138,000 FTE faculty and staff

  — $2.3 billion state general fund support

- *California State University*

  — 23 campuses

  — 340,000 FTE students

  — 37,000 FTE faculty and staff

  — $2 billion state general fund support

- *California Community Colleges*

  — 72 districts

  — 112 campuses

  — 1.2 million FTE students

— 62,000 FTE faculty and staff

— $5.8 billion Proposition 98 support

Hospitality to New Ideas   California has the reputation of being a trend-setting state. In fact, California has long had a culture that is hospitable to creativity, diversity, and unconventionality. Fashion trends, religious movements, social and tax reform ideas—all of these and more find their origins in California's "social laboratory." The natural result of such a climate is that innovative and risk-taking individuals find a natural home in the state. This has beneficial economic consequences, among them a business environment that encourages entrepreneurship.

This pro-entrepreneur environment is demonstrated by California's rapidly growing small business sector. A "small business" is defined by the Trade & Commerce Agency as any independently owned and operated company that is not dominant in its industry and has fewer than 100 employees.

Employment in California

In California as elsewhere, **employment** falls into four major categories of productive activity: service-providing, manufacturing, agriculture, and government (see Figure 7.5).

FIGURE 7.5:   **California Workers by Sector**

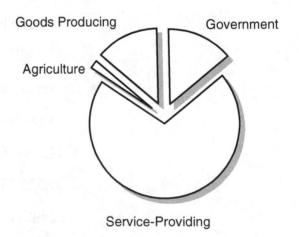

Source: California Employment Development Department

The federal government defines **employment** as those individuals who did any work for pay or profit, including part-time and temporary work. Individuals are counted as employed if they have a job but are not working due to vacations, sickness, childcare issues, taking care of family, maternity/paternity leave, industrial disputes, or were prevented from working by bad weather.[5] It defines **unemployed** individuals as those who do not have a job and have actively looked for work in the prior four weeks and are currently available for work.[6] While the unemployment rate has been over 10% in the past, the unemployment rate in 2010 peaked at an all-time historical high at 12.4% in California and 9.6% in the United States. According to the State Employment and Development Department (EDD), the February 2015 unemployment rate for California was at 6.8%, while the U.S. unemployment rate was 5.5%, a sign that the economy is recovering from the great recession. Figure 7.6 provides the unemployment rates for California and the United States from 1993–2013

FIGURE 7.6:   Unemployment Rates for California and the United States (1993–2013)

	California	U.S.
1993	9.5%	6.9%
1994	8.6%	6.1%
1995	7.9%	5.6%
1996	7.3%	5.4%
1997	6.4%	4.9%
1998	6.0%	4.5%
1999	5.3%	4.2%
2000	5.0%	4.0%
2001	5.4%	4.7%
2002	6.7%	5.8%
2003	6.8%	6.0%
2004	6.2%	5.5%
2005	5.4%	5.1%
2006	4.9%	4.6%
2007	5.4%	4.6%
2008	7.2%	5.8%
2009	11.3%	9.3%
2010	12.4%	9.6%
2011	11.8%	8.9%
2012	10.4%	8.1%
2013	8.9%	7.4%

Source: California Department of Finance

5.   United States Department of Labor, "Labor Force Statistics from the Current Population Survey," Bureau of Labor Statistics, www.bls.gov/cps/cps_htgm.htm (accessed June 3, 2015).
6.   Ibid.

By 2010, job losses continued to grow, and California's unemployment rate hit an all-time high of 12.4% (9.6% nationally). By 2013, California's unemployment rate had dropped to 8.9% (7.4% nationally). In November 2014, the national unemployment rate remained at 5.8%, and the labor force participation rate held at 62.8%. U.S. total non-farm jobs rose by 321,000 in November 2014, the biggest increase since January 2012, after an upward revision of the October 2014 number to 243,000 as reported by the California Department of Finance. California's non-farm payroll employment grew by 41,500 jobs in October 2014, higher than the 22,500 monthly average for the first nine months in 2014. Eight sectors gained jobs, while three lost jobs. The largest job gains were in professional and business services (12,500) and trade, transportation and utilities (12,400). Other sectors that gained jobs were leisure and hospitality (7,500), government (3,500), educational and health services (3,100), information (1,900), construction (800), and manufacturing (700). The three sectors that had small job losses were other services (400), financial activities (400), and mining and logging (100).

Both California and the United States continue to add jobs. The U.S. real GDP growth rate was revised up by 0.5% for the third quarter of 2014. The number of California housing permits issued in October 2014 was the highest since March 2007. Overall consumer price inflation has been low, averaging less than 2% in California during the first 10 months of 2014. Falling fuel prices have kept inflationary pressures mild across the nation.

Agriculture in California   California grows more than half of the nation's fruits, nuts, and vegetables. California **agriculture** is more than just food. California farmers also contribute to the creation of products related to manufacturing, health care, printing, education, recreation, transportation, construction, entertainment, and personal care. These products range from detergents, X-ray film, antibodies, paper, shampoo, toothpaste, footballs, shoes, flowers, tires, and antifreeze to baseball bats.

By 2012, California had 80,500 farms and ranches, which constitute about 3.7% of the nation's total. Some 350 crops are recognized in California, including seeds, flowers, and ornamentals. When compared to the rest of the nation, California ranks No. 1 among the top 5 agricultural producing states. Another reason why California ranks No. 1 is that roughly 67 major crops are grown on a large commercial scale in California. According to the 1997 Agricultural Census, ranking of market value products sold, 8 of the nation's top 10 producing counties are in California. California is also the nation's leader in agricultural exports, annually shipping more than $6.5 billion in both food and agricultural commodities around the world. It is estimated that nearly 18% of California's agricultural production is shipped to foreign markets.

Although California had experienced a recession, the sales value generated by California agriculture increased by 3.2 % between the 2011 and 2012 crop years. California's farms and ranches received a record $44.7 billion for their output, up from $43.3 billion in 2011. California's increase in revenue was led by the grape industry, followed by the cattle sector and almond production. In 2012, nearly 24% of California's farms generated commodity sales over $100,000, slightly greater than the national average of 18%. The amount of land devoted to farming and ranching in California remained constant at 25.4 million acres for the sixth consecutive year. The average farm size increased from 312 acres to 316, which is below the national average. California's top 20 crop and livestock commodities accounted for more than $36.4 billion in value in 2012. Eleven commodities exceeded $1 billion in value in 2012. The cash receipts of 13 of the top 20 commodities increased in value between 2011 and 2012. The growth in the cash receipts of grapes overshadowed that of almonds, as grapes became the second leading revenue-generating commodity in California.

Grape production generated $4.45 billion in cash receipts in 2012, up 15% from the previous record high received in 2011. Production was virtually the same, but process received by growers increased from $578 per ton of grapes in 2011 to $666 per ton in 2012. Revenue for the cattle sector improved to a record high for the third year in a row as cash receipts were nearly $3.3 billion for the crop year. Receipts increased nearly 17% from 2011 despite production increasing by only 5%. Almond cash receipts increased for the third year in a row despite decreased production. Cash receipts increased 8.5% due to a rise in prices from $1.99 per pound of almonds in 2011 to $2.20 per pound in 2012. [7]

Agricultural Exports California continues to set the pace for the rest of the nation as the country's largest agricultural producer and exporter. In dollar terms, California's agricultural exports reached a record-breaking $18.18 billion for 2012. Significantly, California is the nation's sole

---

7.   United States Department of Agriculture, "California Agriculture Statistics 2012, Crop Year," USDA National Agricultural Statistics Service, Pacific Region–California, www.nass.usda.gov/Statistics_by_State/California/Publications/California_Ag_Statistics/Reports/2012cas-all.pdf (accessed April 8, 2015).

exporter of many agricultural commodities, supplying 99% or more of the following: almonds, artichokes, dates, figs, grapes (raisins), kiwifruit, olives, peaches (clingstone), pistachios, plums (dried), pomegranates, rice (sweet), seed (Ladino Clover), and walnuts. [8]

FIGURE 7.7: California's Top 10 Agricultural Export Markets, 2012

Rank	Country	Export Value (Millions)	Leading Exports
1	Canada	$3,149	Wine, lettuce, strawberries
2	European Union	$2,511	Almonds, wine, pistachios
3	China/ Hong Kong	$2,341	Almonds, pistachios, walnuts
4	Japan	$1,532	Rice, almonds, hay
5	Mexico	$889	Dairy and products, table grapes, processed tomatoes
6	South Korea	$869	Oranges and products, almonds, walnuts
7	India	$374	Almonds, cotton, pistachios
8	United Arab Emirates	$332	Almonds, hay, walnuts
9	Turkey	$309	Almonds, walnuts, cotton
10	Taiwan	$309	Rice, almonds, walnuts

Source: California Department of Agriculture

California ranks first in the United States in its share of high-wage jobs such as management services, biomedical instruments, entertainment, computers, and engineering services. As in the rest of the country, California's service sector is growing while manufacturing, agriculture, and mining are becoming less important parts of the state economy.

Each of the four broad categories encompasses several major areas of employment. For example, goods-producing includes manufacturing, construction, and mining.

The Service Sector As illustrated in Figure 7.8, the service sector has been the largest source of employment in California. Figure 7.9 shows the relative sizes of the major components of the state's service sector.

8. California Department of Food and Agriculture, "California Agricultural Statists Review," CDFA, ftp://ftp.consrv.ca.gov/pub/oil/SB4DEIR/docs/AGF_CDFA_2014.pdf (accessed April 18, 2015).

FIGURE 7.8:   **A Historical Look Back at California Jobs by Industry (2002)**

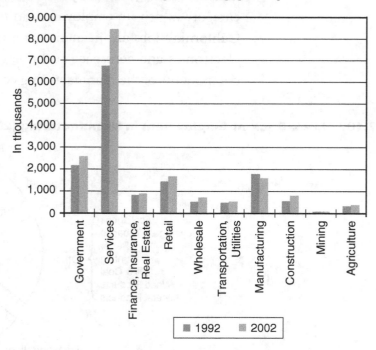

Source: California Employment Development Department

FIGURE 7.9:   **A Look Back at Service Sector Employment (2002)**

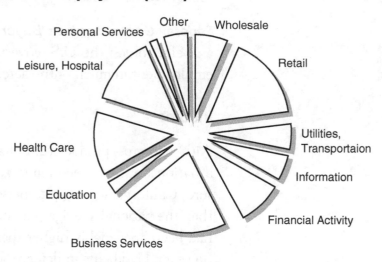

Source: California Employment Development Department

Manufacturing Employment Manufacturing is the second largest category of private employment in the state after services. About 15% of California's jobs are in manufacturing industries, mostly those related to electronics and aerospace technologies. Figure 7.10 illustrates the major components of the manufacturing economy.

FIGURE 7.10: Look Back at Employment in Manufacturing (2002)

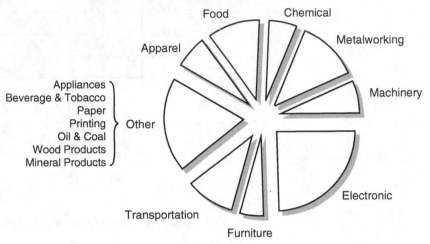

Source: California Employment Development Department

Federal Government as Buyer As a major buyer of aircraft, missiles, and electronics, the U.S. government supports (but does not guarantee) employment in much of the aerospace and electronics industries.

Income

Although gross product (in dollar terms) is the most common measure of a nation's or state's economic activity, **personal income** is another measure. California's per capita personal income had been 10 to 20% higher than the national average year after year. Historically, Californians' income had been appreciably higher than that of other Americans. In the 1990s, however, broad cuts in defense spending had a devastating effect on high-paying, defense-related jobs. At the same time, the state experienced a rapid growth in population among low wage earners. As a result, California's per capita income was no longer far ahead of the rest of the nation (see Figure 7.11).

FIGURE 7.11: Per Capita Personal Income (1980–2014)

Year	United States	California
1980	10,150	11,924
1981	11,260	13,126
1982	11,944	13,730
1983	12,649	14,536
1984	13,858	15,862
1985	14,717	16,766
1986	15,457	17,571
1987	16,263	18,489
1988	17,422	19,603
1989	18,647	20,569
1990	19,584	21,484
1991	19,976	21,816
1992	21,051	22,637
1993	21,690	22,957
1994	22,528	23,527
1995	23,551	24,578
1996	24,709	25,874
1997	25,929	27,125
1998	27,488	29,104
1999	28,611	30,639
2000	30,587	33,366
2001	31,524	34,066
2002	31,800	34,229
2003	32,677	35,303
2004	34,300	37,156
2005	35,888	38,964
2006	38,127	41,623
2007	39,804	43,152
2008	40,873	43,608
2009	39,379	41,587
2010	40,144	42,282
2011	42,332	44,479
2012	44,200	47,505
2013	44,765	48,434
2014	46,129	50,109

Per capita personal income is total personal income divided by total midyear population. All dollar estimates are in current dollars (not adjusted for inflation).

Source: U.S. Department of Commerce Bureau of Economic Analysis, www.bea.gov/itable/, accessed April 8, 2015.

Actual income, of course, varies widely across the state (as we'll discuss later, in the "Micro-economies" section of this unit). As a rule, incomes are higher in urban areas and lower in rural counties.

Sources of Personal Income   Employees earn wages and salaries. Stockholders receive dividends. Savers earn interest. Landlords receive rents. Retirees receive Social Security and pensions. Wages and salaries constitute, by far, the most significant source of personal income in California.

Agriculture

Although it accounts for only 2% of reported California employment, **agriculture** is still a major economic and physical presence in the state.

One of the strengths of California agriculture is that it is very diverse. This contrasts with the heavy dependence of some states on one or two crops. Because of California's extraordinarily diverse climate and geography, it offers ideal conditions for farming—dairy cows, beef cattle, sheep, orchards, vegetable farms, and fishing. More than 350 different agricultural products are farmed in California, with California being the nation's sole producer (99% or more) of a large number of specialty crops such as almonds, clingstone peaches, figs, persimmons, raisins, sweet rice, artichokes, dried plums, pomegranates, walnuts, and seed ladino clover. California is the leading producer of 75 different crops. On only 3% of the nation's farmland, Californians grow more than half the fruit, nuts, and vegetables consumed in the United States. California is also the nation's number one dairy state and produces 95% of domestic wines. Refer to Figure 7.12 for California's top 20 agricultural commodities.

FIGURE 7.12:   California's Top 20 Agricultural Export Commodities (2012)

Rank	Commodity	Millions
1	Almonds	$3,387
2	Dairy Products	$1,313
3	Wine	$1,273
4	Walnuts	$1,112
5	Pistachios	$1,073
6	Table grapes	$812
7	Rice	$688
8	Oranges and products	$664
9	Tomatoes, Processed	$574
10	Cotton	$483
11	Strawberries	$382
12	Raisins	$380
13	Beef and Products	$374
14	Lettuce	$345
15	Hay	$305
16	Seeds for Sowing	$303
17	Dried Plums	$177
18	Peaches and Nectarines	$166
19	Raspberries and Blackberries	$155
20	Lemons	$145

Source: California Department of Agriculture

Food Processing   Processing all those products is a major California industry. From food warehousing and transportation to wineries and baked goods, from producing beverages and sugar to fats and oils, California is the largest food processing employer in the United States, employing 200,000 people in more than 3,000 different businesses.

The Farm King   Fresno County, which became the U.S.'s top farming region during the Eisenhower administration, continued to lead in overall crop value in 2007. Fresno remained the number one county in the nation with $5.35 billion in agricultural value. It should be noted that Fresno County continued to hold the top title (with the exception in 2001 when Tulare County climbed to number one) as the nation's top county for agricultural production when it surpassed Los Angeles County in 1954.

In 2012, Fresno County still led all other California counties by continuing to rank number one with an agricultural production value of $6.59 billion. Kern County was second in value production with $6.21 billion, an increase of 11% from 2011. Tulare County fell to third in value with a production value of $6.21 billion, and Monterey County ranked fourth with a production value of $3.14 billion. [9]

California agriculture saw a 15% gain in the sales value of its products in 2007. The state's 80,000 farms and ranches received a record $36.6 billion for their output in 2007, up from $31.8 billion in receipts in 2006. The previous high was reached in 2005 when sales totaled $32.4 billion. California's largest-in-the-nation dairy industry saw a major recovery in 2007 from depressed milk prices that plagued the industry in 2006. Dairy producers received $7.33 billion for their milk production in 2007 compared to $4.49 billion in 2006. The dairy industry, California's leading commodity in cash receipts, generated $6.90 billion for milk production in 2012, down 10% from the record production of 2011. Milk production increased less than 1%, but a drop in process resulted in an overall reduction in cash receipts for the crop year. Milk prices received by producers fell from $18.54 per hundred pounds of milk sold in 2011 to $16.52 in 2012. As the leading dairy-producing state in the country, California produced nearly 21% of the nation's supply in 2012.

California remained the leading state in cash farm receipts in 2012 with more than 350 commodities representing 11% of the U.S. total. California's leading crops remained fruits, nuts and vegetables. Over a third of the country's vegetables and nearly two-thirds of the country's fruits and nuts were produced in California.[10]

Some counties include timber as part of their crop report. The total 2012 value of production reported by the counties, included timber, is $55.7 billion, up 7.3% from the prior year (2011). At $62.6 million, Humboldt County led the state with 23.4% of the state's total timber value in 2012.

California is home to the most productive agricultural counties in the nation. Twelve of the top 20 counties in the United States that produce agricultural products are in California.

---

9. United States Department of Agriculture, "California County Agricultural Commissioners' Reports 2012," USDA National Agricultural Statistics Service, Pacific Region–California, www.nass.usda.gov/Statistics_by_State/California/Publications/AgComm/201212cactb00.pdf (accessed April 8, 2015).

10. United States Department of Agriculture, "California Agricultural Statistics, Crop Year 2012," USDA National Agricultural Statistics Service, Pacific Region–California, www.nass.usda.gov/Statistics_by_State/California/Publications/California_Ag_Statistics/2012cas-ovw.pdf, (accessed April 8, 2015).

FIGURE 7.13: Agricultural California Counties (2012)

Rank	County & Commodity	Production Value
1	**Fresno** (grapes, almonds, milk, livestock)	$6,587,794,000
2	**Kern** (grapes, almonds, milk, vegetables)	$6,212,362,000
3	**Tulare** (milk, grapes, cattle, oranges)	$6,210,694,000
4	**Monterey** (lettuce, strawberries, broccoli, grapes)	$4,137,863,000
5	**Merced** (milk, chickens, almonds, cattle and calves)	$3,280,209,000
6	**Stanislaus** (milk, almonds, chickens, walnuts)	$3,277,843,000
7	**San Joaquin** (milk, grapes, almonds, walnuts)	$2,881,441,000
8	**Kings** (milk, cotton, cattle and calves, tomatoes)	$2,215,014,000
9	**Ventura** (strawberries, lemons, celery, raspberries)	$1,960,753,000
10	**Imperial** (cattle, hay, wheat, lettuce)	$1,945,759,000

Source: California Department of Agriculture

California ships agricultural product to more than 150 countries. The top 10 export destinations accounted for 85% of the 2006 export value of 48 commodities. The top three destinations included the European Union, Canada, and Japan, and accounted for 60% of the 48 commodity total. The primary market for California agricultural production is the rest of the United States. However, foreign markets have become relatively more important in recent years. In 1999, 16% of the state's production was shipped to overseas markets, whereas in 2006, this figure was 24%.

Foreign Trade

Exports are a major source of earnings for the California economy. Its geographic location makes it the nation's principal western port for both domestic export products and international imports. It is the primary seaport and airport for the Asian and Pacific markets, handling more than 20% of total U.S. trade. More than 75% of all goods shipped through West Coast ports move through California. The ports of Los Angeles and Long Beach are the nation's busiest.

California is more than just a doorway to the world, though. California is a major export power in its own right and a leader in **foreign trade**. Overall, one-third of the state's farm products are sent to foreign markets, principally Europe, Japan, Canada, and South Korea. Significant exports are also made to Mexico and Southeast Asia. The European Union (EU) accounts for more than 20% of California's exports. Japan alone accounts for more than 17%.

Technology   Most of California's "hard" exports fall into three categories:

- **Electronic Products:** telecommunications equipment and various electronic components

- **Industrial Machinery:** manufacturing technologies as well as computers and peripherals

- **Transportation Equipment:** automobiles, mass-transit vehicles, and aircraft

Agriculture   Beef is the state's biggest agricultural export product, but other agricultural exports include cotton, grapes, almonds, fish and, of course, oranges. Processed foods such as wine, dried fruit, milled rice, and soft drink syrups, constitute a considerable portion of California's agricultural export economy. One of the biggest consumers of California's milled rice crop is Southeast Asia.

Trade Balance   The **trade balance** is classified as positive (favorable) or negative (unfavorable). While this mercantilist interpretation is somewhat oversimplified for today's global economy, a nation's ratio of imports to exports has important effects on its production and purchasing power. As we've seen, the same is true of any other economic entity.

In 2014, California exported $174.1 billion to 229 foreign economies. California top export markets continue to be Mexico, Canada, China, Japan, and South Korea. Exports from California accounted for 10.7% of the total U.S. exports in 2014. Mexico continues to be California's number one export market. Mexico purchases 14.5% of all California exports. Figure 7.14 illustrates the nine major California global export markets expressed in U.S. (million) dollars between 2011 and 2014.

FIGURE 7.14: **Leading California Export Markets (in million USD)**

Partner	2011	2012	2013	2014
World Total	159,136	161,880	168,045	174,129
Mexico	25,807	26,370	23,904	25,419
Canada	17,261	17,424	18,887	18,249
Japan	13,096	13,033	12,733	12,263
South Korea	8,425	8,246	8,363	8,500
Hong Kong	7,664	7,826	7,793	8,502
Taiwan	6,245	6,318	7,519	7,467
Germany	5,307	4,979	5,591	5,427
Netherlands	4,417	4,344	4,755	5,370
India	3,793	3,209	5,264	5,276

Source: U.S. Department of Commerce

CALIFORNIA'S MICROECONOMIES

Demographics

Just as California is a part of the total U.S. economy, the California economy is made up of a number of microeconomic units: regions, counties, cities, and even neighborhoods.

No Mason-Dixon Line divides them, but Northern and Southern California have their own distinctive traits. Other parts of the state also have developed into clearly distinguishable microeconomies. Some of the key demographic differences include the following:

■ **Population.** Almost 60% of Californians live in the coastal urban areas—San Francisco and Los Angeles.

■ **Employment.** California experienced an enormous increase in migrants during the 1990s. Coupled with a disastrous recession in the early years of the decade, California's unemployment rate rose dramatically. For much of the mid-1990s, unemployment continued to be high in California, even as the rate fell in the United States as a whole. By 1996–1997, however, unemployment in California was declining.

California's Central Valley and northern regions typically have higher unemployment rates than the metropolitan regions to the south. This is largely a by-product of the region's seasonal job base in agriculture, lumber, and tourism. State unemployment is lowest in the Bay Area where high-tech industries provide fuel for rising employment.

The Los Angeles (L.A.) area's unemployment tends to be higher than that of other metropolitan areas as a result of its economic diversity and the strains resulting from the region's being unprepared for massive immigration.

■ **Per Capita Income.** While California has historically enjoyed a **per capita income** higher than that of the country as a whole, incomes vary substantially in various parts of the state. For instance, incomes tend to be higher in the major metropolitan areas (such as the Bay Area) than in rural or agricultural regions. Income also tends to track employment; where unemployment is high, incomes are lower than in areas where more people are working. Of course, the local economy has an important effect on income level.

Figure 7.15 contrasts the five California counties with the highest per capita incomes (Marin, San Francisco, San Mateo, Contra Costa, and Santa Clara) with the five counties having the lowest per capita incomes (Madera, Imperial, Merced, Tehama, and—with California's lowest per capita income—Del Norte). Interestingly, the top five are all clustered in the Bay Area, while two of the bottom five are in Northern California.

FIGURE 7.15:   Per Capita Income by County for 2013

Rank	County	Income
1	Marin	$97,124
2	San Francisco	$84,356
3	San Mateo	$79,893
4	Santa Clara	$70,151
5	Contra Costa	$63,403
54	Madera	$32,287
55	Imperial	$32,225
56	Merced	$31,935
57	Tehama	$31,810
58	Del Norte	$30,818

Source: U.S. Department of Commerce/California Department of Finance

THE NEXT STEP   In the next unit, we will focus on California's housing market. Like the state's economy in general, the housing market is highly diverse, with major differences among the various regional microeconomies.

SUMMARY

- **California** is the nation's *third largest state* geographically. With approximately 38.5 million people, it is the *most populous and ethnically diverse state in the United States*. It has one of the most *varied climates*, and its farms grow more than *250 different kinds of crops*.

- California is an **economic powerhouse**, producing almost *11% of the total U.S. GDP*. It is the port for *40% of all U.S. trade with Asia*. California is home to more than 1 million businesses, from fast-food restaurants and convenience stores to high technology, defense, and entertainment giants. If California were an independent nation, it would have *the world's eighth highest national GDP*.

- The **service sector** is the largest employer in California, followed by **manufacturing**.

- California's **agricultural economy** accounts for only 2% of the state's employment but plays a large role in the state's economic health. California is the world's leading producer of many different crops. On 3% of the nation's farmland, California grows *half of the U.S.'s produce*. California is the *number one dairy producer* in the United States.

- California's top 20 crop and livestock commodities accounted for more than $36.4 billion in value in 2012, and 11 commodities exceeded $1 billion in value in 2012 as well.

- **Exports** are a major source of earnings for the California economy. The state handles more than *20% of total U.S. trade*. The ports of Los Angeles and Long Beach are the *busiest in the nation*. California's **main exports** are electronics, industrial machinery, transportation equipment, processed food, agricultural crops, chemicals, and fabricated metals.

- California is composed of a number of **microeconomies**. The northern and southern parts of the state have distinct characteristics, and other regions have their own unique economic qualities and challenges.

REVIEW QUESTIONS

1. Who are the major employers in your community/area, and what is the total annual payroll that these employers generate for the community?

2. Is agriculture a major employer in your county? If so, what is the annual crop value of all commodities produced within the county?

3. What are the leading export commodities in your county as well as the leading import commodities? What is the destination of commodities that are exported from your county?

4. Looking at the most recent census information for your county, what is the total percentage of the population who have gone to college and obtained a degree (e.g., AA, BS, MA, PhD, etc.)?

5. What is the percentage of real estate licensees in your community compared to the rest of the employed population?

6. What is the unemployment rate in your community (i.e., city, county) and how does that compare to neighboring communities?

7. California produces a variety of specialty crops. What are some of these crops and are any of these crops found in your county?

UNIT QUIZ

1. In terms of geographical area, where does California rank among U.S. states?
   a. First
   b. Second
   c. Third
   d. Fifth

2. In 2012, what was the number one agricultural export commodity?
   a. Almonds
   b. Wine
   c. Oranges
   d. Lemons

3. The largest ethnic group in California is
   a. white.
   b. black.
   c. Hispanic.
   d. Asian.

4. Which California county is considered to be the farming king of the state?
   a. Tulare
   b. Los Angeles
   c. Riverside
   d. Fresno

5. Approximately what percentage of California's population resides in the coastal urban regions?
   a. 60%
   b. 25%
   c. 38%
   d. 80%

6. Which of the following job sectors is the largest in California?
   a. Government
   b. Goods-producing
   c. Service-providing
   d. Agriculture

7. All of the following are components of the service sector *EXCEPT*
   a. lodging.
   b. electronics.
   c. health care.
   d. education.

8. Which of the following is the largest recipient of California's state exports?
   a. Japan
   b. Canada
   c. The European Union
   d. Mexico

9. California's leading export commodity is
   a. processed food.
   b. electronics.
   c. chemicals.
   d. fabricated metals.

10. All of the following California counties are in the state's top five for highest per capita income *EXCEPT*
    a. San Mateo.
    b. Santa Clara.
    c. Contra Costa.
    d. Del Norte.

UNIT EIGHT

THE CALIFORNIA REAL ESTATE MARKET

KEY TERMS

absorption rate	geographic factors	occupancy
affordability	households	rental housing
availability	income	retail market
building types	income ratios	scarcity
climate	inventory	supply
Credit Crunch	market	trends
demographics	median home price	underground storage
economic cycle	mortgage	tanks
economic fluctuations	net absorption	vacancy rates
existing homes		

LEARNING OBJECTIVES

- Understand the volatile history of California's real estate economy

- Describe the demographics of the California real estate market

- Explain income and affordability issues, and the way they interact with California's unique economy

- Distinguish among the characteristics and special issues of the residential, commercial, and industrial real estate markets

BUILDING A MARKET

As we've said over and over, real estate is intensely local in nature. The value of any property is completely dependent on where the property is located. That is as true for an apartment in New York or an office building in Chicago as it is for an Iowa farm or a house in any suburb. It is also true of California. As in most things, however, California occupies a unique position in the real estate **market**. All states are different from one another, of course, but as we saw in the last unit, California's unique geography, demographics, income, and culture produce a vastly different picture from the national economy in general. The nature of California's housing market is a reflection of the state's uniqueness and diversity.

An Economic Roller Coaster

When the recession of the early 1980s ended, California underwent something of a second Gold Rush. Real estate and construction markets soared along with the rest of the state's economy. On the other hand, the Tax Reform Act of 1986 led to a steep decline in multifamily rental construction as investors lost significant tax benefits. In the early 1990s, the **economic cycle** started again; the recession returned, and the real estate market once again suffered. Home sales returned to their pre-recession levels, with the market being in an expansion period from 1999 to 2006. The previous real estate boom brought unprecedented increased prices in housing that resulted in the statewide median home price reaching $597,640 in April 2007 and remained near record levels for most of 2007. As the fall of 2007 rolled around, the housing market began to see a downturn as the negative effects of the **"Credit Crunch"** began to take a stronghold on the California economy and caused sales to fall further. As a result, record rates of decline in the statewide median price of housing fell.

Housing Patterns

According to the California Department of Finance, California now has approximately 13.7 million dwelling units. The lack of construction is a partial cause of the continual climb of **median home prices** (see Figure 8.1) throughout California. Those numbers put California housing growth behind much of the nation in housing growth.

FIGURE 8.1:   **Median Sales Price of Single-Family Homes (2005–2015)**

	Region		
Month/Year	Los Angeles Metro	San Francisco Bay Area	Inland Empire
February 2005	$460,694	$669,297	$332,436
February 2006	$526,395	$707,329	$378,514
February 2007	$541,005	$725,305	$382,167
February 2008	$417,616	$679,236	$286,437
February 2009	$239,459	$378,519	$167,587
February 2010	$265,239	$482,968	$172,226
February 2011	$266,830	$443,880	$174,041
February 2012	$264,430	$438,280	$172,600
February 2013	$326,460	$584,430	$212,300
February 2014	$383,080	$673,410	$260,360
February 2015	$409,810	$740,270	$282,400

Sales for California are seasonally adjusted and annualized. Existing single-family detached homes only.

L.A. Metro is a five-county region that includes Los Angeles County, Orange County, Riverside County, San Bernardino County, and Ventura County.

Inland Empire includes Riverside County and San Bernardino County.

San Francisco Bay Area has been redefined to include the following counties: Alameda, Contra Costa, Marin, Napa, San Francisco, San Mateo, Santa Clara, Solano, and Sonoma.

Source: California Association of REALTORS®.

Occupancy

California has a high level of renter **occupancy**, largely the result of high land costs in the state and the fact that many types of occupations demand a high degree of mobility. Figure 8.2 shows the number of occupied and vacant units in California from 2009 to 2013.

FIGURE 8.2:   **Housing Occupancy and Vacancy in California (2009–2013)**

Year	Total Housing Units	Occupied	Vacant
2009	13,268,682	12,187,191	1,081,491
2010	13,552,624	12,392,852	1,159,772
2011	13,631,129	12,433,172	1,197,957
2012	13,667,226	12,466,331	1,200,895
2013	13,726,869	12,542,460	1,184,409

Source: U.S. Census Bureau, 2009-2013 5-Year American Community Survey

Types of Housing Units

Renters are more likely to be in multiunit buildings, but the continuing trend toward condominiums (both new and conversions) has increased the percentage of owner-occupied multiunit dwellings. Across California, there are a variety of types of dwellings available.

Vacancy Rates

Housing vacancy rates in California are generally low for most of the states. For any commodity, **affordability** and merchandise appeal affect how much of the **inventory** is unsold at any time. However, the significance of vacancy rates varies from place to place with economic conditions, environmental appeal, and development patterns.

Geographic Factors **Geographic factors** such as **climate** and scenery are important in the California mystique. Californians prefer coastal areas, other things being equal, so demand for housing in those areas tends to be high and vacancy rates generally low. In recent years, transportation cost, time, and inconvenience have caused many consumers to reexamine their traditional fondness for the suburbs.

Economic Fluctuations A community in a normally low-vacancy region may suffer high vacancy rates because of some temporary **economic fluctuation** or a rash of overbuilding as occurred in the rapid growth areas of the Antelope Valley and Inland Empire (Riverside–San Bernardino County areas) in the 1980s. However, due to the recession, which contributed to high unemployment and a lack of new housing starts, with today's demand for rental housing as the economy has improved, rates for rental housing generally average between 2 to 3% in Riverside and San Bernardino counties.

Characteristics of Households

In 2013, there were close to 12.5 million **households** in California. A household, you'll recall from Unit 6, refers to all the people who occupy a housing unit. The **demographics** (factual characteristics) about these units help us better understand the California real estate marketplace.

Age Another way of looking at age composition is the age distribution of total heads of households. According to the California Department of Finance, there are approximately 3.6 million households in California where the head of the household is between the ages of 35 to 64 for owner-occupied residences. There are 1.9 million households where the head of household is between the ages of 35 to 64 for a renter-occupied residence. The total number of households where a child under 18 was living was 4.7 million based on the 2010 census. Another interesting fact for California is the number of children under the age of 18 living with a grandparent is 826,037, and the number of children under the age of 3 is 243,056.

Household Size   In general, the more people living together in a housing unit, the more space they will need. There are exceptions, of course, including cases of extreme poverty (in which large numbers of persons may live together in very small quarters) and extreme wealth (in which a small family may occupy a very large home). Nonetheless, there remains a direct relationship between household size and housing need. According to the U.S. Census Bureau (2010 Census), the average number of persons per household in California was 2.9, which is higher than any other state or region. The national average is 2.58

Income and Affordability

Income is obviously an important factor in shaping the California housing market; how much money buyers can afford to spend has much to do with establishing the fair market value of properties. As we saw in Unit 7, per capita income in California varies a great deal depending on which region is considered. On average, however, the state's per capita income in 2008 was around $42,696—higher than the national average of $39,751. According to the Department of Finance, California's per capita income in 2012 had risen to $47,505, and by 2013, it was $48,434.

On the other hand, it's almost necessary that California's per capita income exceed that of the United States as a whole; it represents one of the nation's most expensive housing markets. San Francisco, for instance, had the highest median home price in the United States, $719,660. That's nine times the median income for the Bay Area, or roughly four-and-a-half times the 2005 national median home price ($218,000). In the interior of the state, away from the coastal regions, housing affordability is slightly more than 60%, or roughly the national average. However, in 2015, Los Altos, California, represents the most expensive housing market, with the median price being $1,963,099.

Looking back at 2005, approximately 14% of California households were able to afford to purchase a median-priced home, compared with about 50% for the nation as a whole. While roughly 66% of all homebuyers earned $70,000 or more in 2001, compared with 57.3% in 2000, the median income of first-time buyers remained unchanged for the third year in a row at $60,000. California faced a loss of affordability of a large portion of its existing federally subsidized housing units, including a significant share of 92,000 Section 8 units, which have contracts that expired in 2005. While this was true in 2000, the affordability had been drastically reduced in California by 2005. At the end of 2005, the California Association of REALTORS® estimated that only 14% of households could afford a median-priced home, compared to 55% for the rest of the United States.

For historical purposes, the minimum household income needed to purchase a median-priced home at $538,770 in California in October of 2005 stood at $128,480, based on an average effective mortgage interest rate of 6.03% and assumed a 20% down payment. The minimum household income needed to purchase a medium-priced home was up from $106,490 in October 2004, when the median price of a home in California was $459,530 and the prevailing interest rate was 5.70%. The minimum household income needed to purchase a median-priced home at $218,000 in the United States in October 2005 was $51,990. This would later change by 2009, with affordability moving to an all-time high of about 69%. By the first quarter of 2014, the affordability index for California stood at approximately 30%, while nationally it stood at approximately 57%.

The Housing Affordability Index measures the percentage of households that can afford to purchase the median-priced home in the state and regions of California based on traditional assumptions. Specifically, the index looks at median price, assumes a down payment of 20%, and computes monthly principal, interest, taxes, and insurance (PITI). It is also assumed that the PITI does not exceed 30% of the household's income. These traditional factors are taken into consideration when computing the figures for the affordability index.

Looking back at the beginning of the recession in January 2009, the statewide median price stood at $281,100, which had dropped 41.5% from the prior median of $480,820. According to the California Association of REALTORS®, the significant decline in price was largely attributed to the dramatic change in the mix of sales since late 2007 and the increased share of distressed sales. For the year 2008, the annual median price had fallen approximately 39% from $560,270 in 2007 to $346,750. As the economy continued to deteriorate and financial markets struggled, distressed properties continued to impact the California real estate market.

Payment to Income Ratios   Lenders traditionally have used a "rule of thumb" formula to determine whether or not a prospective buyer can afford a certain purchase—the monthly cost of buying and maintaining a home (**mortgage** payments—both principal and interest—plus taxes and insurance impounds) should not exceed 28% of the borrower's gross (pretax) monthly income. The payments on all debts should not exceed 36% of monthly income. Expenses such as insurance premiums, utilities, and routine medical care are not included in the 36% **income ratio** figure but are considered to be covered by the remaining 64% of the buyer's monthly income. These formulas may vary, of course, depending on the type of loan program and the borrower's earnings, credit history, number of dependents, and other factors.

Based on this traditional rule of thumb, many Californians are effectively barred from any hope of ever buying their own home.

Nonetheless, housing affordability has generally increased throughout California. Only 14% of Californians could afford their own home in 1989; by 1997, that number rose to nearly 40%. However, by December 2001, that number was back down to 35.6%. This was due, in part, to a growth in higher-income jobs throughout the state and partly due to a decline in mortgage interest rates. In October 2005, the number further dropped to 15%, a significant decline from 2001. With the change in the economy, credit crunch, and number of distressed homes in California, the affordability in 2009 rose to 69%. By 2014, with an improving housing market in California, the affordability stood at roughly 30%. This was not as high as it stood in 2009, but it was much better than during 2005–2007. This is an indicator that, should things continue on the same track, the affordability of housing in California should continue to drop as we move into 2016.

RECENT TRENDS   The California Association of REALTORS® monthly affordability index measures the percentage of households that can afford to purchase a median-priced home in California. The index is the most fundamental measure of housing well-being in the state. For example, the Northern Wine Country is now much more affordable (59%) than in 2005, when affordability stood at 7%.

A CLOSER LOOK   A prospective California homebuyer wants to know how much house he can afford to buy. The buyer has a gross monthly income of $3,750. The buyer's allowable housing expense may be calculated as follows:

$3,750 gross monthly income × 28% = $1,050 **total housing expense** (referred to as front-end ratio)

$3,750 gross monthly income × 36% = $1,350 **total debt expenses** (referred to as back-end ratio)

(More lenient ratios are sometimes used for first-time homebuyers.)

Sales of Existing Homes

One obvious measure of a housing market is the number of existing homes that are sold. The term *existing homes* refers to previously occupied housing as opposed to new construction. Since 1970, the California market for existing homes has fluctuated wildly, peaking in the late 1970s, then falling in the early 1980s. By 1990, the market was back up again, only to slump in the middle of the decade. By the end of the 1990s, the market seemed to be adjusting itself upward once again. During the recession of 2009, sales of existing homes were also up, but this was mainly attributed to cash investors buying distressed properties (those in preforeclosure and in foreclosure). This was very similar to what had occurred during the Great Depression of the 1930s when cash investors also purchased distressed properties at a discount.

Housing Starts

As discussed in Unit 6, one measure of the vitality of a real estate market (whether local, state, or national) is the amount of residential construction activity, measured by projects started during a particular period. Despite periodic downturns, housing starts in California generally were higher by 1997 than they had been since 1989. California began to experience a decline in 2005, with significant declines occurring in 2008 and lasting through the end of the recession. Even after the recession, and though the economy has recovered, housing starts are still lagging in some parts of the country.

The concept of "housing starts" is simple and is key in the real estate market and just as important to investors. Housing starts are also referred to as "New Residential Construction Reports" for the month. These figures are typically released by the U.S. Commerce Department in the middle of the month and provide a comparison of the current month to the prior month as well as to the prior year. Surveys of home builders, as well as data compiled from city/county building departments around the country, are utilized to generate these monthly reports.

Why are housing starts important? Housing starts statistics are considered a critical indicator of the strength of the economy at a given point in time. Investors will watch the housing starts figures released each month, as they will have a significant effect on related industries such as mortgage and finance, manufacturing, raw materials, and real estate. Simply, in a strong economy, people are likely to purchase new homes; in a weak economy, people will hesitate to purchase new homes. Because housing is a key part of the U.S. economy, economists and investors alike are constantly watching for the release of new building permits each month, as it signals what is to come.

FIGURE 8.3:   **Housing Starts, 1993 to 2013**

	Housing Activity: California and United States						
	California			United States			
				Permits		Starts	
Year	Units (000)	% Change	CA % OF US	Units (000)	% Change	Units (000)	% Change
1993	85	–13.1%	7.1%	1,199	9.5%	1,288	7.3%
1994	97	14.6%	7.1%	1,372	14.4%	1,457	13.2%
1995	85	–12.1%	6.4%	1,333	–2.9%	1,354	–7.1%
1996	94	10.5%	6.6%	1,426	7.0%	1,477	9.1%
1997	112	18.5%	7.8%	1,441	1.1%	1,474	–0.2%
1998	126	12.5%	7.8%	1,612	11.9%	1,617	9.7%
1999	140	11.5%	8.4%	1,664	3.2%	1,641	1.5%
2000	149	6.0%	9.3%	1,592	–4.3%	1,569	–4.4%
2001	149	0.1%	9.1%	1,637	2.8%	1,603	2.2%
2002	168	12.8%	9.6%	1,748	6.8%	1,705	6.4%
2003	196	16.6%	10.4%	1,889	8.1%	1,848	8.4%
2004	213	8.8%	10.3%	2,070	9.6%	1,956	5.9%
2005	209	–1.9%	9.7%	2,155	4.1%	2,068	5.8%
2006	164	–21.4%	8.9%	1,839	–14.7%	1,801	–12.9%
2007	113	–31.2%	8.1%	1,398	–24.0%	1,355	–24.8%
2008	65	–42.5%	7.2%	905	–35.3%	906	–33.1%
2009	36	–43.9%	6.2%	583	–35.6%	554	–38.9%
2010	45	22.9%	7.4%	605	3.7%	587	5.9%
2011	47	5.2%	7.5%	624	3.2%	609	3.7%
2012	58	23.1%	7.0%	830	32.9%	781	28.2%
2013	83	42.6%	8.5%	976	17.7%	923	18.3%

Source: California Department of Finance & U.S. Department of Commerce, Bureau of the Census/February 2014 update

Rental Housing

There are many reasons why people rent their homes. Some consumers who would like to buy houses find it financially impractical to do so. Others prefer the relative freedom from maintenance and upkeep responsibilities offered by rental housing. Still, others work in jobs that require frequent travel or relocation. Because the decision to rent or buy is often based on personal preferences and fluctuating economic conditions, it is difficult to make broad demographic statements about "renters" as a group. Whatever the reason for renting, rental housing is a significant part of the California real estate economy.

Roughly one-quarter of California's population lives in rental housing. That's about half of all households, as defined by the Census Bureau.

By comparison, the national figure is less than 20%. The disparity reflects the constant affordability question as well as the diversity of California's economy. The number of renters as a percentage of households is highest in the Bay Area and in the southern coastal area, including Los Angeles. There are fewer renters in the central and northern parts of the state.

Renting versus Buying   By January 2013, the median price of a home in California had gone up to $337,040, approximately 24% higher than the previous year (2012) at the same time. With the recovering housing market, consumers began to contemplate whether it was more beneficial to buy property versus continuing to rent. The California Association of REALTORS® noted in 2013 that for the State of California, consumers could save 32% per month by buying a property. At the local level, buying in the Inland Empire or in Los Angeles County could save 40% per month, 15% in San Diego, and 12% in San Francisco. However, buying in other areas was not the best solution—it was still better to rent in Orange, Alameda, and Santa Clara counties, with monthly rent savings ranging from 7 to 11%.

Disadvantages of Renting   While there are many good reasons to rent housing, there are some significant disadvantages to the choice. Primary among these is the fact that once rental payments are made, they are gone; renters do not build up equity in their homes. There are also very real tax advantages to home ownership that are not enjoyed by renters, principally the ability to deduct mortgage interest payments from income taxes and to shelter gains on the sale of a primary residence. Contrary to the popular view, renters are not immune from increases in local property taxes or utility rates; the rent payment reflects prorated shares of property taxes and utilities paid by the landlord.

Housing is generally the greatest single expense for households. Current public standards measure housing cost in relation to gross household income. Those households spending in excess of about 30% of income are generally considered "cost burdened." Using this measure, housing cost burdens for owners and renters in 2013 were a significant source of strain for households throughout California. In 2013, more than 2.5 million rental households paid in excess of 35% of their incomes on housing, while more than 37.8% of homeowners (1.9 million households) paid in excess of 35% of their incomes.

OTHER HOUSING ISSUES FACED BY CALIFORNIA

Overcrowded Housing

Overcrowding continues to be a concern in California both in metropolitan and suburban areas and tends to impact renters more significantly than owners, regardless of household size. Overcrowding is generally more strongly related to family size (i.e., overcrowding tends to be a trend the larger a family is and/or the lower a family's income is, not the larger a household gets). Overcrowding can increase health and safety concerns and stresses the condition of the housing stock and infrastructure.

Overcrowding is also experienced by many of the state's agricultural works. California's strong agricultural sector functions with farm labor throughout the state. These employees and their families must have access to adequate housing while they are temporarily or permanently employed in an area. Far too often they are forced to occupy substandard "homes" because of the pure economics of housing. Very few California residents have seen the "homes" of many of these farmworkers or day laborers. Many of these farmworkers live out of sight to avoid harassment from permanent residents or passing motorists, often in undeveloped canyons, fields, and squatter camps, as well as motels, trailers, cars, and outbuildings.

Where Are They?   In 2012, California produced approximately 52% of all U.S. production of fruits, nuts and vegetables and employed over one-third of the U.S. hired farm labor workforce. According to the California

Employment and Development Department (EDD), the annual average employment in California agriculture was about 380,000 individuals in 2010 and had risen to 395,000 in 2011. Agricultural employment is still considered seasonal peaking to approximately 460,000 individuals in the month of June and a low of 300,000 in January. The peak-trough ratio decline of 1.5 is primarily attributed to growth in year-round production of fresh fruits and vegetables and increases in nut crop productions.

Recent surveys show that many farm workers in California have increased reliance on unsubsidized, private market, off-farm housing; however, their housing conditions have not improved. This has been a major shift in the responsibility of farmers by placing the cost of housing on to the workers themselves. On-farm housing and farm labor camps have reduced in numbers in recent years, yet there has been only a marginal increase in the number of subsidized farm labor housing units developed by either government agencies or non-profit groups. Today, most of the hired farm workers reside in California's cities.

The Census Bureau's American Community Survey (ACS) has recently released new findings indicating that most hired farm workers today likely reside in California's incorporated cities, especially those located in agricultural valleys outside of the coastal region's largest cities and those that have sizeable Hispanic populations. These include Bakersfield, Salinas, Oxnard, and Santa Maria, and each likely have more than 10,000 hired farm workers. There are significant concentrations of farm labor households in Bakersfield, Salinas, Oxnard, Santa Maria, Fresno, Madera, Delano, Stockton, Watsonville, Arvin, Avenal, and Lamont. While the concentration of farm labor housing in cities has been a notable recent trend, a sizeable share of the farm labor workforce still resides in the unincorporated areas as well as in smaller incorporated cities/communities. This trend is primarily attributed to the duration of seasonal farm employment becoming longer, which has encouraged many farm workers to permanently settle in communities.

The Homeless Population

Homeless individuals and families face ultimate housing deprivation. In the worst circumstances, these individuals and households may be living in places not meant for human habitation. "Homes" may include cars, parks, sidewalks, alleys, parking ramps, or door stoops; homeless individuals may also be squatters. Many of these individuals occupy abandoned buildings, roofs, stairwells, farm outbuildings, or garages (among other locations). In addition, homeless persons may be in "public" accommodations, including emergency shelters or transitional housing. These individuals share an attribute: a person is considered homeless when the person or family lacks a fixed and regular night-time residence, has a primary night-time residence that is a supervised publicly operated shelter designated for providing temporary living accommodations, or is residing in a public or private place not designated for, or ordinarily used as, a regular sleeping accommodation for human beings.

One other characteristic is common to the homeless: transience. It is very difficult to reliably estimate the numbers of homeless people. Because homeless people are generally on the move and sometimes illegally occupy space, it is difficult, if not impossible, to identify all locations where people find shelter.

Throughout the United States in 2013, approximately 610,042 people had experienced homelessness. Homelessness is described as a lagging indicator, or in other words, it takes time for economic and housing developments to impact trends in homelessness. Examining trends in populations that are plausibly at risk of homelessness is a valuable exercise in anticipating needs for housing and homeless assistance. People who become homeless often have strained financial resources and are challenged by the cost of housing, including rents, utilities, and other expenses.

In many cases, families, friends and other related and nonrelated individuals live together in one unit to reduce individual housing-related expenses. The phenomenon of living doubled up is often the last and final living situation of households that become homeless. There are four at-risk populations that would potentially lead to homelessness. These include poverty, unemployment, poor renter households with severe housing cost burdens, and people in poor households living doubled up. In 2012, there were approximately 6.3 million people living in poverty in California as compared to 6.1 in 2011, a 3.38% increase in one year.

In November of 2013, the U.S. Department of Housing and Urban Development (HUD) released its annual Homeless Assessment Report, which found that Southern California has the largest homeless population in the United States. The report found that the City of Long Beach, with a population of 460,000, has the fourth highest rate of people living without shelter. The report also found that California has 22% of the American homeless population and that 66.7% of the homeless in California lack shelter.

In order to address and place the responsibility of homelessness on local governments, the State of California adopted Senate Bill SB2, which became effective on January 1, 2008. Also called the Housing Accountability Act, SB2 is intended to strengthen housing element law and was adopted to ensure zoning encourages and facilitates emergency shelters and limits the denial of emergency shelters and transitional and supportive housing. SB2 requires that

- local agencies provide emergency shelters without a conditional use permit,

- there be sufficient capacity to accommodate the need for emergency shelters,

- emergency shelters be subject to the same standards as applied to residential uses, and

- zoning ordinances be flexible for such uses.

Local governments must provide for such provisions in their local regulations or risk having their housing elements not be approved by the State of California, which could have significant impact on the development of future residential uses.

SUMMARY OF CALIFORNIA HOUSING MARKET

The following key issues in the California housing market will have a significant impact on the future quality of life for California residents and summarize the state of California's housing crisis:

- Much higher levels of housing construction are needed to adequately house the state's population.

- High housing cost burdens are increasingly an issue for both owners and renters. The combination of upward price pressure in the housing market and relatively tight urban housing markets has led to increasing cost burdens, particularly for low-income renters.

- In addition to high housing cost burdens, overcrowding is a concern in some portions of the state.

- California has an extensive agricultural economy that depends on temporary workers to harvest and process crops. Significant numbers of these critical workers migrate throughout the state, facing housing challenges that impact their lives.

- The homeless individuals and households who have fallen through the cracks of society face significant difficulties in obtaining shelter and reintegrating themselves into the broader society.

- Falling home prices, worsening credit availability, shrinking equity values, and growing job losses delivered a crushing blow to both the national and California economies in 2008, thus impacting the housing market. However, by 2014, the housing market showed signs of a recovered market. Equity sales, not distress sales, were the majority of sales, and more than 126,000 building permits were issued in October 2014.

THE NEXT STEP   In focusing on the California real estate market, this unit has emphasized residential properties up to this point. Next, we'll consider two other very important components of the California real estate market: commercial and industrial real estate.

COMMERCIAL AND INDUSTRIAL TRENDS

California characteristically outstrips the rest of the country in industrial development, principally due to its attraction as a place to live and work. The California climate is famously appealing, the state's workforce is qualified and plentiful, and the regulatory environment, although demanding, does not drive away business. Even without artificial incentives for relocation of new industry as used in some states, such as tax incentives or state-provided infrastructure improvements, California fares extremely well. The ability to attract new industry is, in turn, a major force in creating the need for more office, retail, and temporary and permanent housing.

In California as a whole, the **availability** of real estate varies with the type desired. Commercial construction (including offices, retail centers, and hotels) exceeds industrial by a wide margin, paralleling the national pattern.

A key analysis that should be performed when determining whether to introduce or build new commercial or residential units into an existing market is to determine the **absorption rate**, which is the ability of the real estate market to absorb or sell all of the houses, office units, apartment units, and the like for sale or lease in a given amount of time. As an example, if there are 100 units sold each month and there are 1,200 units for sale, it will take 12 months to sell all of the units currently for sale. If there are 2,400 units for sale, the absorption rate will be 24 months or two years for all of the units for sale. However, this does not take into account the number of units that will eventually come on to the market in addition to those already for sale. **Net absorption** is the space tenants leased minus the space they gave up.

Major sectors of the commercial/industrial real estate market are

- single commercial properties (free-standing or street-front retail properties, restaurants, professional offices, or service providers, as well as hotels or motels);

- retail centers and malls;

- office buildings; and

- industrial buildings.

Each of these sectors has its own distinctive marketing issues, regional patterns, and economic strengths and weaknesses. Figure 8.4 shows how the different types of uses compare nationally.

FIGURE 8.4:   U.S. Commercial Building Use

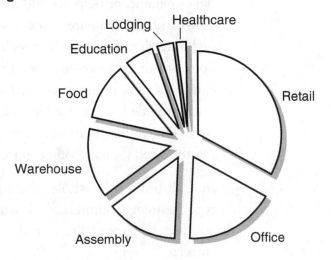

Commercial Structures

Commercial structures house retail stores, offices, motels/hotels, restaurants, commercial schools, warehouse facilities, medical offices, and many other businesses. About 90% of these structures are occupied by only one establishment.

Retail Market

The U.S. **retail market** has largely converted from the proverbial "general store," evolving from the retail strip and downtown commercial hub to a variety of planned retail centers that fall into seven general categories.

1. **Convenience Centers.** These are often found on corners formerly occupied by gas stations. During the 1970s, the oil industry concluded that major retail corner locations were no longer economically viable for gasoline and car repairs. Developers improved these locations (many well under an acre in size) as small retail centers with service-type tenants and fast food facilities. The principal tenant is often a liquor/deli store or a minimart. By the mid-1980s, the oil companies recognized a missed opportunity and started to expand their service station facilities with minimarts and began downplaying the auto service aspect.

2. **Neighborhood Centers.** Roughly four to ten acres in size, these centers serve a larger population than the convenience centers, which are supported by small, densely populated trading areas. In the neighborhood center, a major supermarket or drugstore is usually the principal tenant, with an array of service and specialty establishments. A recent trend finds some of the major supermarket chains providing for additional tenants within the market structure itself, such as drug stores, restaurants, banks, and clothing outlets, with direct access to potential customers whose principal destination has been the supermarket.

3. **Community Shopping Centers.** These usually occupy 10 to 30 acres and are anchored by a medium-sized department store or outlet of a major store. They require probably four to five times the service area needed to support a neighborhood center. However, as regional shopping centers proliferate, the community center is often becoming what is described as a "power center" where discounters gravitate.

4. **Regional Shopping Centers.** At the end of World War II, the flight to the suburbs spurred major department stores to relocate from their traditional downtown locations to the new, freeway-ori-

ented areas where potential shoppers lived. The plot size of these basically suburban centers (which are now often multistoried and enclosed instead of single story and exposed) runs from 30 to 100 acres with a major department store as the main or anchor tenant.

5. **Shopping Malls.** The rise of the shopping mall during the 1970s and 1980s caused a severe drainage of resources and revenues from downtown areas as retailers and service-providers moved out of urban areas and clustered themselves in and around the new suburban and outlying malls. Attracted by clean, pleasant, temperature-controlled environments and acres of free parking, the shoppers whose dollars had supported downtowns got in their cars and drove out to the malls, taking their dollars with them. As result of the recession, today many of these shopping malls have experienced a large number of vacancies, attributed to both the economy and the desire for many retailers to look at downtowns and mixed-use developments.

6. **Big Box Centers.** Big Box Centers typically contain single-level buildings and could, in most cases, consume 25 to 30 acres, with some of the larger centers accommodating over 1,500 vehicle parking spaces at a ratio of 3.75 per 1,000 square feet. Most big box centers resist multi-level stores because of the difficulty in moving shopping carts from one level to another. Many of these centers are also known as "single-use" centers, with only one big box store occupying the site. Many of these centers are anchored by such tenants as home improvement centers, home electronic centers, and warehouse outlets such as Home Depot, Lowes, Costco, Sam's Club, and Walmart.

7. **Outlet/Factory Outlet Malls.** Outlet malls or factory outlet malls are comprised of a large number of stores that sell clothing or other household goods and are typically located outside of a town or city. Some of the smaller factory outlet facilities may be located in a downtown corridor of a community with as a little as five stores. These facilities can be described as brick and mortar retail centers in which manufacturers sell their stock directly to the public. Typical factory outlet malls range in size from 100,000 to 600,000 square feet of retail space, with many averaging around approximately 215,000 square feet.

Downtown retailers attempted to reinvigorate themselves by supporting closed streets and pedestrian malls, but these too failed. By the mid-1990s, however, there were signs that the trend was reversing. Shopper preferences changed, and downtown areas began re-attracting retailers and shoppers even as the malls began to fail. Before and during the recession of 2009, many communities once again began to pursue land use, transportation, life style, urban design, and commerce back into their downtowns with an emphasis on mixed-use developments. Many of the communities that continued to re-energize their downtowns had four primary goals in mind: vitality, visibility, uniqueness, and safety. The trend continues throughout California and has been referred to as the "back to the downtown" movement.

According to the Urban Land Institute, today many of the larger retailers in America, such as Target, Walmart and Best Buy, that previously located in shopping malls or were stand-alone retailers, are now locating in the downtowns of many cities. With many cities embracing the concept of mix-use, this is becoming the trend in urban planning as well as in retail. Many of the large retailers are now moving back into the city centers. The new paradigm is mixed-use, accessible by both the automobile and pedestrians. An example of a very successful mixed-use development is Santana Row in San Jose, California, located in the heart of Silicon Valley. The facility is comprised of 680,000 square feet of retail space and restaurants. There are approximately 1,200 dwelling units (lofts and apartments), two hotels, and seven parks, all of which is configured along a 1,500-foot pedestrian-friendly main street. Some of the larger retailers include Best Buy, The Container Store, Crate & Barrel, and an array of smaller shops.

According to commercial real estate analysts, the 24-hour urban markets are slated to outperform other commercial real estate properties such as shopping malls. Today's trends show that tenants are willing to pay higher rents in return for more efficient design layouts and lower operating costs in LEED-rated , green projects.

The factory outlet mall phenomenon further contributes to the troubles facing traditional malls: shoppers are often willing to travel to remote locations to enjoy particularly steep discounts. One of the latest outlet malls to open in California opened its doors in November 2012 in Livermore, California, located along the Interstate 580 corridor. The facility includes 543,000 square feet and is comprised of 120 stores.

California is home to the nation's largest number of shopping centers according to the International Council of Shopping Centers. Three of the largest centers in the country are in California: Del Amo Fashion Center in

Torrance; South Coast/Crystal Court in Costa Mesa; and Lakewood Center in Lakewood.

Office Space

The availability of office space is a significant indicator of the overall vitality of the local commercial real estate market. For instance, when office vacancy is high, rents will be forced to low levels by the forces of supply and demand. There will be little motivation for investors and developers to add to an already glutted inventory of office properties. As a result, construction jobs will decline and employment and income will be affected across a broad range of industries. On the other hand, when office vacancy rates are low, developers will seize the opportunity to respond to increased demand by building more space. Rents will increase along with employment opportunities.

Figure 8.5 compares office vacancy rates for the United States generally with 10 California metropolitan areas, for both suburban and downtown office space in both Northern and Southern California Regions. Note how California's famous regional diversity is apparent here, too. In some cities, such as San Francisco, the downtown vacancy rate is lower than that of the outlying suburbs. In others, urban vacancies far surpass the suburban rate.

FIGURE 8.5: **A Look Back at Office Vacancy Rates, Suburban and Downtown (2013)**

	Office Vacancy Downtown		Office Vacancy _ Suburban		Office Vacancy _ Metropolitan	
	1Q13	1Q12	1Q13	1Q12	1Q13	1Q12
Northern and Central California:						
Oakland East-Bay	13.5	12.2	14.3	14.2	14.0	13.4
Sacramento	18.1	16.4	22.6	25.6	21.7	23.7
San Francisco	8.7	10.0	10.9	11.0	9.5	10.3
San Jose	22.7	23.5	10.2	11.4	12.0	13.2
Walnut Creek	NA	NA	13.7	16.9	13.7	16.9
Southern California:						
Inland Empire	NA	NA	21.2	22.7	21.2	22.7
Los Angeles Metro	18.8	18.3	16.4	16.9	16.8	17.2
Orange County	NA	NA	12.3	15.0	12.3	15.0
San Diego	17.8	18.6	14.3	16.2	14.9	16.6
Ventura County	NA	NA	24.7	24.0	24.7	24.0
National Average	12.4	12.8	17.0	17.8	15.3	16.1

Source: California Department of Finance

In January of 2014, downtown San Jose's office vacancy rates had dropped below 20%, as the office market began to experience a recovery and saw the most net absorption since 2013. In the third quarter of 2013, the office vacancy rate for San Jose stood at 19.5%, according to the Silicon Valley Business Journal. The downtown San Jose market experienced a net absorption of 114,488 square feet in the fourth quarter of 2013. In January 2014, average rents for office space in San Jose stood at $2.74 per square foot.

One building in particular has had a rather large impact on San Jose's office vacancy rates. Downtown San Jose's largest single vacancy was Riverpark II, which was completed in 2009 and is a 16-story high rise office building containing just under 300,000 square feet. This modern office tower was completed at the beginning of the recession and was vacant until 2014. It is estimated that if a full building user/tenant were to occupy this building today, the vacancy rate for downtown San Jose would drop to 15.9%. The last time the vacancy rate for office real estate was below 16% was in 2003.

A CLOSER LOOK   Silicon Valley—the phrase summons up images of high-tech industrial parks humming with white-suited workers building computer chips and disk drives in cool, sterile factories. Nevertheless, Silicon Valley (the popular nickname for the Santa Clara Valley/San Jose region) is not a simple success story. While home to such technology giants as Adobe Systems, Apple Corporation, Borland International, Hewlett Packard, Hitachi, IBM, Intel, Netscape, Novell, and Pacific Telesis, as well as aerospace giant Lockheed Missiles & Space Company, the Silicon Valley commercial and industrial real estate market has known its ups and downs.

The Silicon Valley commercial real estate market (measured in the figures in terms of research and development [R&D] space) underwent a recovery in the latter half of the 1990s from a slump earlier in the decade. The area thrived during a major recession in the early 1980s, when interest rates were in the high teens, resulting in an economic bonanza followed by a sharp decline due to oversupply.

The Industrial Market

California's industrial market includes all properties used for manufacturing and other industrial uses, such as research and development (R&D), on industrially zoned land. In the mid-1980s, 60% of industrial space was devoted to warehousing and distribution activities. Today, while California's vital national and international trade and commerce activities continue to drive demand for distribution centers, high-tech R&D properties are the "hot" niche.

Statewide, from the late 1970s to the mid-1980s and into the 1990s, measured in terms of building permit values, industrial construction activity was relatively flat, while commercial construction activity grew steadily, even during the two recessions that occurred during that period. The California Department of Finance looks at construction of nonresidential structures for commercial and industrial buildings as an economic indicator, specifically tracking authorized valuation through permits issued in millions of dollars. In June 2012, the valuation reported was $914 million, and in June 2013, it stood at approximately $101 billion—an overall annual increase of 30.5% according to the Department of Finance.

Vacancy Rates According to the National Association of REALTORS® (NAR), industrial **vacancy rates** fell from 9.0% to 8.9% nationwide in the first quarter of 2015. In California specifically, however, the regional nature of the real estate market is reflected in the demand for industrial properties.

If we look at specific markets, we can see the current trends in industrial properties in California. For 2014, in San Diego, vacancy rates for the industrial market closed at 6.8%. The San Diego industrial market experienced a robust positive net absorption of 587,379 square feet during the fourth quarter of 2014, or a total net absorption of approximately 2.6 million square feet for all of 2014. Average asking rents in the San Diego region stood at $0.82 per square foot at the end of 2014. Demand, along with a lack of new construction over the past several years due to the recession of 2009, resulted in a low vacancy rate and rents gaining an upward momentum.

In Los Angeles, the vacancy rate for industrial properties closed 2014 at a historic low of 1.6%. The Los Angeles industrial market experienced a positive net absorption of more than 4.7 million square feet for the entire year of 2014. The average asking rents closed at $0.62 per square foot in 2014, up 10.3% from the prior year. In comparison, in Northern California, the Silicon Valley industrial market also finished 2014 with exceptionally good growth, and vacancies decreasing from 10.28% to 9.6% from the prior year. Vacancy rates below 10% had not been seen in the Silicon Valley in over a decade. The fourth quarter of 2014 produced 402,114 square feet of positive net absorption with a total of 648,232 square feet for the entire year of 2014, signaling the industrial sector's strongest performance since

2011. The average asking for the region stood at $1.33 per square foot, up $0.16 per square foot from the prior year (2013).

The year 2012 signaled the beginning of a very tight market for industrial lands along the I-880 corridor. The Oakland/San Leandro, Hayward, and Union City submarkets showed extreme improvements with leasing and sales activity increasing overall from 2012 through 2014.

A CLOSER LOOK   Pursuant to SB 1171, which became effective January 1, 2015, the Agency Disclosure and Confirmation has been expanded to include commercial property. According to the California Association of REALTORS®, "under the new law, transactions involving any commercial, industrial, or vacant land property, and leases for longer than one year for any of those types of property, will now require the delivery of the Agency Disclosure form. Residential income property with five dwellings or more is still exempt."[11] The industry is moving toward more consumer protection for purchasers and commercial lessees.

THE NEXT STEP   Finally, we conclude our look at California real estate with an overview of the rural real estate market: agricultural properties, the lumber and mining industries, and open space protections.

CALIFORNIA'S RURAL REAL ESTATE MARKET

Through the years, rural land use has experienced a far-reaching metamorphosis, largely due to two distinct forces: advances in agricultural technology and the changing demographics of expanding suburban sprawl.

Technology has increased productivity, permitting less land and fewer workers to produce even more food products. As agriculture has receded from its primary role in the U.S. economy, rural lands are increasingly converted to other uses—orange groves are replaced by subdivisions, a ranch becomes an office park, or a strawberry field becomes a shopping center. The family farm of the past has, for the most part, succumbed to giant agribusiness operators, replacing small generational farmsteads with corporate savvy and factory-style efficiency.

This bleak image of picturesque rural Americana being gobbled up by parking lots is not the whole story, however. Agriculture is vitally important, and in California, it is still a very big business.

---

11.   Robert Bloom, Esq., "Agency disclosure and confirmation expanded to include commercial property," California Real Estate, January/February 2015, www.car.org/legal/miscellaneous-contacts/ca-re-magazine-legal-column/JanFeb2015/.

The Land

California ranks as one of the leading agricultural producers in the world. Some of the reasons for this leadership position follow:

- **Arable Soil.** The productive areas of the San Joaquin, Sacramento, Coachella, and Imperial valleys are widely known for the excellent quality of their soil. Soil determines the suitable type of crop and yield per acre. Thirty million acres of California land are under cultivation.

- **Extended Growing Season.** Due to California's mild climate, farmers can enjoy multiple harvests and increasing yields. Each crop has a particular growing cycle to reach fruition. It takes seven years for new citrus trees to produce. Considerable time, capital expenditure, effort, and luck are needed before there is any return in the form of crop yield. Other crops like strawberries may produce at once and have several yields per growing season, given proper conditions. California's climate makes the long-cycle products more economical and makes multiple yields possible.

- **Water Supply.** Natural water supply through adequate rainfall or irrigation by manmade systems, such as agricultural canals, is vital to agricultural productivity. While water has been problematic since the drought in 2013, the Sierra Nevada snow runoff plus water from the Colorado and Owens rivers have historically sustained crop development. In 1913, the Owens River was diverted by aqueduct to serve the Southern California citrus crops.

With growth and urban expansion came growing pains of new development. Additionally, years of drought that have plagued California put an even bigger strain on California's water supply. As a result, the state legislature and the governor assembled a package of legislation known as the Delta Reform Act that sought to improve water supply reliability throughout California, which was voted on in the November 2010 statewide general election. This landmark legislation resulted in the creation of the Delta Stewardship Council, which was charged with the adoption of the Delta Plan, which was adopted by the Delta Stewardship Council on May 16, 2013, and became effective on September 1, 2013. The Delta Plan is comprised of 14 regulatory policies and 61 recommendations. The key elements contained in the Delta Plan include ecosystem restoration; water delivery reliability; the protection and enhancement of cultural, recreational, natural and agricultural resources; and the reduction of flood risks in the delta.

The key features of the legislation include the following:

- **$19.4 billion in general obligation bonds** have been authorized by voters since 2013, and of which approximately $17.2 million have been allocated to drought relief, regional water supply projects, Delta sustainability projects, water storage, and water shed conservation.

- **Water Conservation.** Urban water suppliers would have until 2020 to cut average daily per capita urban water use by 20% statewide. Agricultural water suppliers have until 2012 to submit water management plans. Since 2014, approximately 60 agricultural suppliers have submitted to the Department of Water Resources their water management plans, with several more to follow.

- **Groundwater Monitoring.** The Department of Water Resources (DWR) will be required to do regular and systematic monitoring of groundwater levels in all groundwater basins throughout the state.

Additionally, the plan calls for a partnership of local, state, and federal agencies to participate in its implementation. This is necessary due to the complexities of the plan's goal and the funding required. The implementation will require participation by local cities and counties, special districts, flood control districts, the California Department of Water Resources, the State Water Resources Control Board, the California Department of Fish and Wildlife, the Bureau of Reclamation (federal), and the U.S. Army Corps of Engineers. Based on 2012–2013 expenditures by both California and the federal government, thus far it has been documented that expenditures have reached a combined total of $444.2 million. Since the enactment of the enabling legislation, implementation of the Delta Plan will require an array of funding sources, including the use of user fees and/or beneficiary fees that would be charged to land owners or those who would directly benefit from a project or service program. Such fees could have a significant economic impact on land owners depending how the fees are implemented in the future.

Grazing Land

Under leases from the U.S. Department of Agriculture (forest lands) and the Bureau of Land Management (usually desert areas) as well as in private ownership, twice as much agricultural land in California is devoted to grazing as to crops. The reasons are quite basic:

- Lands not adaptable to farming are still suitable for feeding livestock, particularly in the Coast and Sierra Nevada mountain ranges.

- Livestock require a large area per unit to provide adequate range feed.

- Livestock are a lower-maintenance form of agriculture than crops, which generally require more human resources and attention in their tending and reaping.

Inhibitors to Agricultural Development

Both politics and economics play a role in controlling, and sometimes inhibiting, California's agricultural economy. In certain instances, farmers are precluded from growing specific crops or are required to obtain permission. This is true of tobacco, cotton, and sugar beets. Farms located near urban areas, particularly Los Angeles, Inland Empire, San Diego, and Sacramento, have succumbed to the upward pressure on land value and the lure of developers' dollars. Environmental regulation of the use of pesticides and growth hormones, coupled with labor union activity among farmworkers, has also impacted the farm community.

LUMBERING AND MINING

Lumber rights alone (sold separately from the land) can be a valuable commodity in the marketplace. This resource has exerted considerable upward pressure on price levels and, thus, on the desirability of timber rights due to several factors:

- **Scarcity.** There is a long "gestation" period for the product. Reforestation after harvesting requires years for replenishment.

- **Government Control.** Through the national park system, the government exerts control on the California, Oregon, and Washington timber industries by limiting the stands of timber available for harvesting. Some three million acres may be set aside nationwide, reducing the amount of acreage available for lumbering.

- **Supply.** Timberlands are also undergoing conversion to urban, recreational, and commercial applications. Just as development reduces the amount of land available for agricultural purposes, it reduces the land available for lumbering.

- **Difficult Access.** Many timber areas have difficult topography and limited road access. In these cases, flumes and waterways may be used for transportation. Smaller timber stands do not warrant erection of a processing mill and, therefore, may not be economical for harvesting.

- **Transportation.** Because of the bulk of the product, mills are usually located close to the stands of timber, and the raw product is not transported over long distances for processing. For unfinished goods, trucks are the principal haulers. Trucks, vessels, and freight trains transport the finished products, and transportation adds to cost.

- **Demand.** Housing, paper, and other timber product requirements continue at brisk levels, with the current interest in recycling only slightly mitigating dependence on new timber harvests. Demand for the product is both national and international in scope, with net exports from most harvesting areas far exceeding the amount of harvest required for use in the immediate area.

- **Tax Treatment.** There are special tax benefits for logging operations in California and elsewhere. The Timberland Productivity Act of 1982 requires all counties and cities with productive private timberlands to establish Timberland Production Zones (TPZs) to discourage the premature conversion of timberland to other uses. Patterned after the Williamson Act, TPZs are rolling 10-year contracts that provide preferential tax assessments to qualified timberlands under the program. Assessments on timber are based on the value of the timber at the time of harvest rather than the annual assessment on the market value of standing timber.

Mining

California's mining sector is relatively modest, and most of the jobs are in oil and gas. The remainder of the industry is largely limited to stone extractions, such as quarries and sand and gravel operations, and some metals, such as gold.

Once an extractive resource is removed, it does not replenish itself like timber. Therefore, special tax treatment in the form of a depletion allowance (a mineral, oil, and gas version of depreciation) is permitted.

Certain factors are of particular importance for land devoted to mineral, oil, and gas activities. These include:

- **Quality of Resource.** If the resource is abundant and of good quality, it will command a higher price in lesser amounts than inferior quality resources.

- **Economic Conditions.** Precious minerals (such as gold, silver, and platinum) fluctuate in price based upon the degree of confidence that citizens place in their currency. As confidence wanes, prices of these metals increase; people feel that their wealth is "safer" in the form of a permanent metal. As confidence improves, prices for precious metals tend to decline. Precious metal prices are not, however, pure indicators of consumer confidence. Investors and traders can artificially manipulate the market for precious metals.

Environmental Concerns

Extractive processes disturb the land, lumbering leaves hillsides barren and eroded, and both industries' produce have toxic side effects. Since 1976, stringent state and federal environmental regulations have helped diminish such negative side effects while increasing operating costs.

In the case of California mining, the Surface Mining and Reclamation Act (SMARA) was enacted by the legislature in 1975. The act was the state's response to society's need for a continuing supply of mineral resources while preventing, as much as possible, damage from mining activities to public health, property, and the environment. SMARA is California's answer to two seemingly contradictory demands: (1) the need for a continuing supply of mineral resources and (2) the assurance that the significant adverse impacts of surface mining will be mitigated. SMARA requires cities and counties to address mineral recovery operations (including reclamation) through planning policies that harmonize the mineral resources needed from California with the maintenance of local environmental quality. SMARA requires that mine sites be reclaimed once the mining operation has been completed. Reclamation includes maintaining water and air quality and minimizing flooding, erosion, and damage to wildlife and aquatic habitats caused by mining. According to the State of California's Department of Conservation, the following are examples of successful reclamation projects:

- A mining company in Ventura County reclaimed its mining pit to a strawberry field.

- A gravel extraction site at Mississippi Bar in Sacramento County was returned to a riparian (water) wildlife habitat.

- An aggregate mine on agricultural lands in Yolo County operates in four phases. The intent is that not more than 95 acres is out of agricultural production at any time during the mine project's life.

Other mined lands have been reclaimed to grazing and production of crops such as alfalfa, corn, grapes, and tomatoes. In other parts of California, such as in Marin and Sonoma counties, former aggregate mine sites have been reclaimed to residential housing sites, thus providing for housing opportunities.

OPEN SPACE PROTECTION

Rural land applications are constantly under extreme pressure to convert to higher density uses. Urban sprawl is particularly evident in the so-called Sun Belt states where the climate serves as a lure to growing population. California is the most populous state in the country, and a growing population continues to exert pressure on the remaining open space.

Farmland Protections

State and federal legislators have deemed it a public good to provide incentives and protections to farmers. For example, special tax laws help to preserve the present land use by keeping assessments of farmlands low, reflecting their current use instead of the highest and best use to which the land could be put. Other tax laws protect remaining family farms.

The Williamson Act   The Williamson Act (included in the Land Conservation Act of 1965) is a voluntary land conservation program administered by counties and cities, with technical assistance from the California Department of Conservation. The purpose of the act is to

- preserve California farmland to ensure a secure food supply for the state, nation, and future generations;

■ maintain agriculture's contribution to local and state economies;

■ provide economic relief to tax-burdened farmers and ranchers; and

■ promote orderly city growth and discourage sprawl and the loss of farmland, while preserving open space for its scenic, social, aesthetic, and wildlife values.

The Williamson Act essentially creates a contract between the state and small farmers. Farmland is taxed a lower rate, using a scale based on the actual use of the land for agricultural purposes as opposed to its unrestricted market value. In exchange, the landowners agree to restrict the use of the land to agricultural and open space uses for 10 years. Counties and cities are compensated for the loss of property tax revenue through the Open Space Subvention Act of 1971. A budgetary nightmare for California counties occurred in 2009. The suspension of the Williamson Act Subvention payments to local governments was unfortunate and unexpected as a result of the state's fiscal constraints. While subvention payments to the counties have been customary for many years, they have never been guaranteed. Amendments to the Budget Act of 2009 reduced the Williamson Act Subvention payments budget to $1,000 to be divided among all of the participating counties, essentially suspending the payments to the counties. As a result, California counties saw little to no subvention funds come back to the individual counties to replace the lost revenue from the lack of subvention payments. What has allowed the Williamson Act to continue to be successful in maintaining open space and farmland is primarily due to the counties' desire to continue implementing the principals of the act despite the loss of tax and subvention revenues.

Natural and Recreational Land

Privately funded activist groups such as Sierra Club and The Nature Conservancy are diligent in their efforts to preserve open space and have ongoing campaigns to acquire open space for the use and enjoyment of future generations. Public park programs also allow these lands to be preserved in their natural state.

Open space preservation efforts are generally altruistic and, to some extent, represent an ideal situation. In recent years, many local governments have created regional habitat conservation programs and plans. The reverse side of this coin is that they further limit the amount of land available for future development. Because the laws of supply and demand still prevail, this puts inflationary pressure on the remaining lands and their products.

The California Coastal Act   The California Coastal Act of 1976 was enacted to protect, maintain, and, where feasible, enhance and restore the overall quality of the coastal zone environment and its natural and artificial resources. The act applies to the coastal zone, a strip along the California coastline generally extending seaward to the state's outer limit of jurisdiction, including all offshore islands, and extending inland generally 1,000 yards from mean high tide of the sea. The Coastal Commission regulates development within portions of the coastal zone and oversees coastal planning efforts along the entire coast. The Coastal Commission, in partnership within coastal cities and counties, plans and regulates the use of land and water in the coastal zone. Implementation of Coastal Act policies is accomplished primarily through the preparation of local coastal programs (LCPs) that are required by each of the 15 counties and 61 cities located in whole or in part in the coastal zone. The LCPs also include land use plans (LUPs), which are elements of the community's general plan.

THE OUTLOOK FOR CALIFORNIA

Looking back, the California housing market experienced significant strain throughout the 1990s. The recession of the early 1990s dampened construction during the early part of the recession through 1996. This resulted in weak construction activity throughout California during that period. While economic activities lagged in portions of the state (particularly in the Central Valley and many rural areas of California), strong economic growth occurred in the Bay Area, San Diego, and portions of the Sacramento and Los Angeles regions, which resulted in a residential construction upswing by 1998. Most of this growth was due to technology-based industry (dot-coms) expanding in these regions as well as a stock market fueled by the expansion of technology-based companies, which placed a significant demand on residential and office real estate in these regions. Most of the technology-based companies disappeared or filed for bankruptcy due to a volatile stock market during 2001 and 2002. However, demand for residential real estate continued to be high as low interest rates and short supply continued to keep the real estate market strong in many regions throughout the state.

Next came the "Credit Crunch of 2007" followed by the recession, which resulted in widespread unemployment in 2009. As a result, housing construction became sluggish, with single-family permits down 34.7% and multi-family permitting down 72% in 2009 as compared to 2008. The toll of the recession in California was most visible in labor markets. No region of the state, including the metropolitan areas, had been spared by the recession, and no region gained payroll jobs from March 2008 to March 2009.

In 2009, California's housing slump began to show signs of recovery. California home building fell for the fourth consecutive year in 2008. The number of units for which permits were granted was only 30% of the level in 2004, and few new homes were sold in 2008. However, existing single-family detached homes sales grew by 27%. Inventory of unsold new homes had been pared in 2009. According to the California Department of Finance, in 2009, some positive signs were seen in the national and California economies, including that monthly job losses fell in both the United States and California, consumers began to once again spend money, and conditions improved in the financial markets. The pace of contraction of both the U.S. and California economies slowed. The recovery was definitely impacted and slowed by troubled mortgages resetting in 2010 and 2011. In 2014, we once again began to see a near normal housing market, with sales moving at a moderate pace and home price appreciation growing at more sustainable levels.

A key note about residential markets is that California is not producing enough housing to keep pace with demand. Because of the shortage, it is anticipated that the median price for a home in California will continue to rise. It is assumed that by the year 2020, California will need to build homes for an additional 11.3 million people; however, the construction of new housing units will not be able to keep pace with the anticipated demand. According to the Department of Finance, more than 126,000 building permits were issued in October 2014, which was 44,000 higher than the January-to-September (2014) average of 82,000. Compared with September, single-family permits were unchanged at 34,000 and multifamily permits increased by 40,000 to 93,000. For residential valuation, the month-over and year-over growth rates were 18.9% and 6% respectively. Even with more housing starts recorded in 2014, it is still not enough units to meet the state's housing demand.

Among the reasons given why supply is not keeping pace with demand is California's environmental regulations, amongst the toughest in the nation. Laws passed in the 1970s, such as Proposition 13, limit local use of property tax revenue, which has led cities to promote retail development over housing to maximize their sales tax proceeds. Possible solutions to the housing crisis include promoting more housing to allow cities and counties providing new affordable housing to keep the entire property tax increase.

At this point, they must pass it to the state. Legislation could also provide more incentives to developers such as density bonuses, fee-reduction programs, joint ventures using federal grant monies, and tax credits.

SUMMARY

- California's housing market is a reflection of the state's unique and diverse economy.

- California has undergone steep rises and sharp falls in its housing market from the 1980s to the present. Housing vacancy rates vary across the state and are directly related to localized real estate markets.

- California continues to be one of the nation's most expensive housing markets.

- Lenders use a 28/36 "rule of thumb" in determining whether a prospective borrower can afford a particular home purchase.

- While there are many good reasons to rent housing, there are also significant disadvantages. These include the lack of equity buildup and the absence of tax advantages.

- Commercial construction exceeds industrial construction by a wide margin in California. The industrial vacancy rate in the state varies by region. Some parts of California have industrial vacancy rates at or above the national average; others are below it. Many previously vacant industrial and commercial buildings are being converted to other uses, including residential.

- Office vacancy and rental rates vary widely among the state's regions. Office vacancy is a sign of local economic health.

- The median price of a single-family detached home in California was $450,620 in October 2014, up from $396,220 in 2013.

- The greatest concentration of homeless people reside in the metropolitan areas of the state, particularly in the urban centers of Los Angeles and San Francisco.

- California has an extensive agricultural economy that depends on temporary workers to harvest and process crops. Many of these individuals live in substandard housing and are constantly facing difficulties finding housing.

- Agriculture, lumbering, and mining are major commercial uses of California's rural land. In the mining industry, or extraction sector, oil and gas are the primary products.

- The natural and recreational lands are preserved by state and federal laws and by the work of private activist groups. Examples of these include the Williamson Act and the California Coastal Act.

REVIEW QUESTIONS

1. What is the amount of revenue generated by the housing industry in your area?

2. What is the median price of existing homes in your area? Are new homes being constructed adhering to the median level?

3. Locally, are there any projections as to the number of affordable housing units needed to meet the anticipated demand for housing by 2017?

4. What lenders, if any, are involved in financing new small businesses in your community?

5. What is the condition of existing housing stock in your community? Is it being converted to other uses besides residences?

6. What, if anything, is being done in your community to provide housing for the homeless?

7. Discuss what land-use controls are presently in place in your community that have either encouraged or discouraged development of vacant lots.

8. In the neighborhood where you live, what is the ratio of owner-occupied to nonowner-occupied (renters) housing?

9. Does farming/agriculture play a major role in your area/county? If so, what are the major crops?

10. What do you believe the economic outlook will be for California, and, most important, your community after you have completed this course?

11. What non-farming industries are present in your community?

UNIT QUIZ

1. Lenders have traditionally utilized a payment to income ratio or a "rule of thumb" formula to determine whether a prospective buyer can afford the monthly cost of buying a home, which includes principal, interest, taxes, and insurance. What percentage of a borrower's gross monthly income should not be exceeded under this "rule of thumb"?
    a. 29%
    b. 28%
    c. 37%
    d. 15%

2. In an area where office vacancy rates are high
    a. construction jobs are likely to increase.
    b. rent for office space will be higher than usual.
    c. rent will decrease in order to fill the vacancies.
    d. developers will build more space to increase demand.

3. The average number of persons per household in California is
    a. higher than the national average.
    b. lower than the national average.
    c. higher than the national average but lower than the Midwest and Northeast.
    d. the same as the national average.

4. What is the absorption rate for office spaces in an area where there are 190 units leased each month and there are 810 units available?
    a. 4.3 months
    b. 3 months
    c. 5.5 months
    d. 8 months

5. Which of the following statements about the California residential housing market is *TRUE*?
    a. California is one of the nation's most affordable housing markets.
    b. Housing affordability has steadily declined in California since 1990.
    c. Since the mid-1980s, California's housing market has proven itself to be uniquely recession-proof.
    d. California's housing market is one of the least affordable in the United States.

6. Which of the following is generally an indication of a strong economy?
    a. A sustained high vacancy rate
    b. A sustained high absorption rate
    c. A sustained high number of housing starts
    d. A decrease in the sale of existing homes

7. Which of the following statements is *TRUE* regarding commercial and industrial properties in California?
    a. Since the mid-1990s, industrial construction has rapidly exceeded commercial construction.
    b. In the Los Angeles metropolitan area, industrial vacancy rates consistently exceed the national average.
    c. Commercial construction continued to increase during the recessionary years of the early 1990s.
    d. Commercial and industrial construction and vacancy rates are an exception to the usual regional differences among areas of California.

8. Which of the following is *TRUE* regarding absorption rates?
    a. A high absorption rate is desirable to sellers.
    b. A low absorption rate is desirable to sellers.
    c. A low absorption rate gives buyers a lot of flexibility in their property search.
    d. None of these statements are true.

9. In regional shopping centers, the main tenant, usually a department store, is referred to as
    a. the power center.
    b. the hub.
    c. the anchor.
    d. the "big box."

10. The purpose of the Williamson Act is to
    a. preserve California's farmland.
    b. protect the water supply to cities.
    c. acquire open land for public parks and preserves.
    d. develop technologies to prolong growing seasons.

UNIT NINE

LAND-USE PLANNING AND DEVELOPMENT

KEY TERMS

architect	easements	police power
availability	eminent domain	public use
budget	engineer	restrictions
building codes	exemptions	site
Daniel H. Burnham	feasibility study	specific plan
City Beautiful	Gantt chart	subdivider
Movement	general plan	subdivision
condemnation	land use	urban planning
conditional-use permit	liens	variance
contracts	The New Deal	zoning
developer	nonconforming use	zoning ordinances
due diligence	permanent financing	

LEARNING OBJECTIVES

■ Describe in detail the various steps involved in the planning and development process

■ Develop an understanding of the origins of land-use planning

■ Explain the types of zoning, their underlying objectives, and possible constitutional issues

■ Understand the ways in which local governments regulate land use and the strategies available to developers to work with government agencies and community organizations in planning successful projects

INTRODUCTION TO LAND-USE PLANNING

In order to understand why our cities have evolved in the ways they have, we must first gain a historical perspective of **urban planning**. The early period of city planning in the United States reflected a diversity of style and character. The first agrarian communities in North America were little more than forts or military outposts to protect the new settlers from Indian attacks. From these early settlements emerged the towns. These towns were simple, possessing modest homes grouped in a gridiron pattern around a park or a commons that was usually next to a meeting place.

The most notable exception to the gridiron approach in early U.S. urban planning was the Pierre L'Enfant Plan for Washington, D.C. A baroque-like plan of radial streets slashing through the gridiron, it was to be a monument to the new federal government, although it was reminiscent of Versailles or Napoleonic Paris.

Thus, the early pattern of urban planning in the United States, as would be expected, was not unlike European planning of the 17th and 18th centuries. The difference was that the early American settlers, who were not urban people, desired more space and openness in their cities. It was not until the middle of the 19th century that more than 20% of the U.S. population lived in cities.

The halcyon years of U.S. urbanization witnessed the great industrialization and foreign immigration of the late 19th and early 20th centuries. Adequate transportation, communications, cheap labor, abundant resources, and open space made the United States grow at an unprecedented rate. It can be described as chaotic growth. As a result, the industrial cities became drab, polluted, unsafe, and unhealthy. Greed and selfishness meant land was treated as a commodity to be traded for profit.

What Happened Next?

Daniel H. Burnham was the chief planner and architect for the 1893 Chicago World's Fair, called the Columbian Exposition. The Exposition was to commemorate the 400th anniversary of the discovery of America. Burnham was chosen to develop a *white city* as the antithesis of the dark U.S. industrial cities. The Exposition was held to honor the United States' new industrial might. Burnham used classical buildings and expansive esplanades, promenades, and open spaces on the Chicago waterfront. Burnham invoked an adage that became a manifesto for planners and their patrons:

> Make no little plans; they have no magic to stir men's blood... Make big plans...for a noble document once recorded will never die.

The white city of the Columbian Exposition was a commercial success, but more important, it showed the masses what could be achieved on a colossal scale. Thus, the **City Beautiful Movement** of U.S. urban planning was ushered in. Burnham also created plans for several other cities, including San Francisco and Cleveland, and revised the Washington, D.C. plan. Soon after, planning commissions were established throughout the country, and zoning was begun. Housing, subdivision, and public health codes were created.

A number of major reforms were quickly undertaken. In 1916, New York City adopted the first comprehensive zoning ordinance to control the use of land and the height and bulk of buildings. In 1922, the U.S. Department of Commerce, seeing land control as good for the economy, issued the first Standard State Zoning Enabling Act, by which states could grant such powers to cities. After the *Euclid v. Ambler Realty* case of 1926, in which the U.S. Supreme Court upheld the constitutionality of zoning, such ordinances became ubiquitous. By 1932, the growth of planning agencies in the United States appeared phenomenal. The reform movement had been so dynamic in its success that only a few areas in the south and the far west did not have planning or zoning agencies.

Ironically, urban planning appeared to be a solution to the vagaries of a *laissez-faire* economic system. Planning became an integral part of **The New Deal**. Franklin D. Roosevelt believed that national planning could channel the investments of the government in order to end the Depression and stabilize the economy. Much of this national-state planning effort was directed toward resolving urban problems.

Theories in Land-Use Planning

The evolution of cities has been described as the conversion of rural to urban uses using the following **land-use** planning theories illustrated in Figure 9.1.

FIGURE 9.1:   Ring, Sector, and Multiple-Nuclei Theories

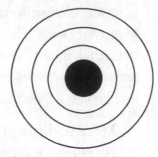

Concentric Ring Theory

Sector Theory

Multiple-Nuclei Theory

The Concentric Ring Theory   This theory is based on the pioneering work of Ernest Burgess, who identified five zones of land use. They are

1. a central business district (CBD) representing the center of activity, generally close to the site of the original settlement;

2. a zone of transition, mixing commercial and industrial uses;

3. a low-income housing zone in the metropolitan area, containing older housing units;

4. a middle-income housing zone, frequently including some older suburbs; and

5. the outlying zone of newer suburban developments.

With decline, the outer zone remains static while the transition zone enlarges into the central zone. Although this model is very simple, it does have a certain descriptive value.

The Sector Theory   This theory was first proposed by Homer Hoyt in 1939. It suggests that cities grow not in strict concentric zones but rather in sections of similar types of development. For example, residential areas might expand outward along existing transportation links, topographic features, natural amenities, or the like.

The Multiple Nuclei Theory   This theory, developed in 1945 by Chauncy Harris and Edward Ullman, states that the downtown area is not considered the only focal point for growth. Land-use patterns are likely to develop as a series of nuclei, each with a different function. For example, manufacturing and transportation uses may form one nucleus. Likewise, hotels, offices, and trans-shipment facilities may develop around an airport.

These theories were developed over a 25-year period from 1920 to 1945, with each adding to the knowledge of cities.

STEPS IN THE DEVELOPMENT PROCESS: AN OVERVIEW

The conversion of raw land to an improved state is the ultimate in risk taking. Success lies at the end of a long and convoluted path of regulations, due diligence reports, contractual negotiations and obligations, financial arrangements, scheduling challenges, public relations hurdles, and infinite details involved in the development process. This unit will examine how the elements of land, labor, and capital are combined to bring a project to fruition.

The process begins long before ground is broken on the site. In broad outline, there are five stages in a development project:

1. **Site Identification.** A **site** must first be identified that meets the specifications of the development. Housing developers do not normally seek sites in industrial areas, and vice versa. In order to properly identify a suitable site, locators investigate a number of factors affecting a property's development potential.

2. **Zoning.** The local planning department will indicate which areas are currently zoned or have the potential of being rezoned (such as agricultural to residential) in keeping with the needs of the project.

3. **Economic Conditions.** Discussions with the local Chamber of Commerce can reveal the general economic health of the area as well as economic stratification by neighborhood.

4. **Real Estate Values.** Local real estate brokers and appraisers can provide useful, current data concerning the tiers of value by neighborhood and their relative stability or trends upward or downward.

5. **Availability.** Upon identification of the target development area, local real estate firms should be contacted to determine **availability** of sites for consideration.

Site Acquisition

Once a site has been identified, the negotiation process begins.

Feasibility Study   A thorough economic analysis of the area (a **feasibility study**) is performed to evaluate the following, as relevant to the type of project:

- Local amenities

- Utility availability

- Transportation availability

- Economic trends of the area

- Housing price levels and/or rent comparables

- Retail sales activity

- Shopping, schools, and houses of worship

- Actual or potential project competition

- Financing terms available on competing projects

- Current vacancy rates

- Demographic/population trends

Sales Contract

Once a price has been negotiated with the land owner, the terms of the sales contract can be structured to reduce the developer's risk. Even when a comprehensive study indicates a project at the particular site is feasible, there are many hurdles yet to overcome. For this reason, the developer should consider three possible routes:

1. **Option Agreement.** The most cautious approach is merely providing option money on the site while the **due diligence** process takes place.

2. **Lease with Option to Purchase.** If the transaction initially appears to be fairly solid, the developer may want more control of the land than a mere option, and this instrument is such an intermediate device.

3. **Escrow Instructions with Contingencies.** This is, in effect, another form of option, as normally these escrow instructions will call for an extended escrow period (sometimes as much as a year or 18 months), subject to rezoning of the property, approval of a preliminary tract map, availability of utilities, and satisfactory soil and geological tests. In an area such as Malibu where there are no sewers, this would include the ability of the land to accept septic discharge.

4. **Other Conditions of Due Diligence.** Items such as building permits also may be necessary to the intended use of the site.

Interim Activities

During the option period, certain expenditures are required in order to ascertain the viability of the project. Some of these activities are

- hiring a professional *subdivision engineer* to prepare maps and coordinate map approvals with local authorities;

- engaging an **architect** to design building plans, taking into consideration the lot configuration designed by the subdivision **engineer** as well as local regulations and market realities;

- obtaining appropriate *legal documentation* that may be required for the development, such as articles of incorporation, by-laws, protective restrictions, and leases;

- soliciting bids from *subcontractors* for various construction elements, such as foundation, framing, plumbing, electrical, masonry, plastering, and roofing;

- preparing a project **budget**;

- making preliminary arrangements for *construction financing* on the project; and

- negotiating for **permanent financing**, either for qualified purchasers (in the case of residential developments) or for the developer directly if ownership is to be retained (in the case of commercial and industrial property).

Project Financing

Once the sale is complete and final subdivision maps and permits have been obtained, the construction process begins with funds impounded by the construction lender to be disbursed upon satisfactory progress.

Lender's Investigation Before the construction lender consummates a credit extension, many of the preliminary steps that were performed by the developer will be independently repeated by the construction lender to verify the financial feasibility of the project. In addition, the condition of title will be examined for the following:

- **Restrictions.** Existing recorded **restrictions** may preclude the intended development unless it wins approval of architectural committees or a holder of reversionary rights.

- **Easements. Easements** on the property may interfere with proposed improvements.

- **Contracts.** Agreements or **contracts** with local authorities may not be in concert with the proposed project. For instance, a prior owner may have signed an agreement with the city reserving the site for development of low- to moderate-income housing, while market-rate housing is planned.

- **Liens.** Prior financing arrangements (such as **liens**) that affect the equity requirements of the lender may have to be paid off or subordination arranged.

- **Other Conditions.** Other title items may affect the ability of the lender to be in a first lien position or otherwise violate the lender's underwriting requirements.

Construction Scheduling

Once the construction loan is consummated and construction commences, the developer converts to a scheduling phase, which may be based on the Gantt charts used by manufacturers in scheduling production. A **Gantt chart** is a bar-style chart in which project activities are illustrated on a horizontal time scale. Each bar corresponds to an item in the task list. By comparing the horizontal bars to the current date, a developer can see clearly whether or not the project is on schedule. Figure 9.2 illustrates a sample Gantt chart for reviewing this book so far.

FIGURE 9.2:   Gantt Chart

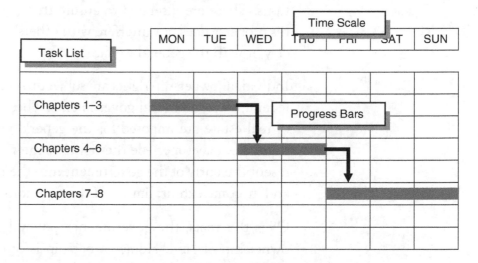

A successful scheduling process should bring the project to completion at or before the contemplated date. Credit checks and background investigations of the subcontractors are essential to avoid mechanics' liens and production delays, which can be disastrous.

Permanent Financing   Once construction is complete, the developer will want to convert the construction loan to permanent financing at the earliest possible date. Early conversion to a permanent loan is important to the developer because

- it *reduces overall project cost* due to the elimination of the risks involved during construction; and

- it *increases the developer's profit* in the event the project is sold.

There is still some risk involved in obtaining permanent financing for a development project. Commercial and industrial loan funds have become harder to obtain since the restructuring of the financial market due to the savings and loan crisis of the early 1980s. Lenders are also reluctant to become involved in projects in which environmental issues are involved. This concern will be discussed in Unit 10.

GOVERNMENT REGULATION OF LAND USE

In Unit 5, we saw that an extensive *bundle of rights* goes along with owning real estate. However, those rights are not absolute. That is, a landowner's power to control his property is subject to other interests. Even the most complete ownership the law allows is limited by public and private restrictions. These are intended to ensure that one owner's use or enjoyment of his property does not interfere with others' use or enjoyment of their property or with the general welfare.

Individual ownership rights are subject to certain powers, or rights, held by federal, state, and local governments. These limitations on the ownership of real estate are imposed for the general welfare of the community and, therefore, may supersede the rights or interest of the individual. They represent the entry of the government into the marketplace to act as regulator and, to some extent, limiter of the functioning of a free real estate market.

Over the years, the government's policy has been to encourage private ownership of land. Home ownership is often referred to as "the American Dream." It is necessary, however, for a certain amount of land to be owned by the government for such uses as municipal buildings, state legislative houses, schools, and military stations. Government ownership may also serve the public interest through urban renewal efforts, public housing, and streets and highways. Often the only way to ensure that enough land is set aside for recreational and conservation purposes is through direct government ownership in the form of national and state parks and forest preserves. Beyond this sort of direct ownership of land, however, most government controls on property occur at the local level.

In this chapter, we will look at government controls of land use that directly affect economic development of real estate. In the next chapter, we will consider more indirect regulation, such as fair housing laws and environmental regulation.

Police Power

Every state has the power to enact legislation to preserve order, protect the public health and safety, and promote the general welfare of its citizens. That authority is known as the state's **police power**. The states delegate to counties and local municipalities the authority to enact ordinances in keeping with general laws. The increasing demands placed on finite natural resources have made it necessary for cities, towns, and villages to increase their limitations on the private use of real estate. There are now controls over noise, air and water pollution, and population density.

In California, the state's police power may be exercised "for the protection of the welfare, health, and peace of the people of this state." The California Constitution (Article XI, § 7) delegates police powers to counties and cities to enforce ordinances and regulations that are "not in conflict with the general laws."

Eminent Domain

Eminent domain is not a police power; it is the constitutional right of the government to acquire privately owned real estate for public use. **Condemnation** is the process by which the government exercises this right by judicial or administrative proceedings. The Fifth Amendment of the U.S. Constitution allows for private property to only be taken for public use. The government may only take private property if

- the use is for the public;

- just compensation is paid to the owner; and

- the rights of the property owner are protected by due process of law.

Public use has been defined very broadly by the courts to include not only public facilities but also property that is no longer fit for use and must be closed or destroyed.

A CLOSER LOOK   One of the most significant court cases dealing with eminent domain that affects private property rights was decided on June 23, 2005, by the U.S. Supreme Court: *Kelo v. City of New London, Connecticut.*

After approving an integrated development plan designed to revitalize its ailing economy, the city of New London, Connecticut, through its development agent, purchased most of the property earmarked for the project from willing sellers but initiated condemnation proceedings when the owners of the rest of the property refused to sell. The unwilling sellers argued that the taking of their properties would violate the "public use" restriction in the Fifth Amendment's Takings Clause. The city of New London argued that the city carefully formulated a development plan that believed would provide appreciable benefits to the community, including, but not limited to, new jobs and increased tax revenue. The city's plan served to coordinate a variety of commercial, residential, and recreational land uses providing for cohesive integrated development. To effectuate the city's plan, the city invoked a state statute that specifically authorized the use of eminent domain to promote economic development. The unwilling sellers further argued that economic development did not qualify as a public use and that it was not supported by precedent or logic. The Supreme Court rejected the argument and stated that promoting economic development is a traditional and accepted governmental function, and there is no principled way of distinguishing it from other public purposes.

In response to the Supreme Court's decision in the *Kelo v. New London* case, the U.S. Senate passed an Eminent Domain amendment to the Transportation, Treasury, Housing and Urban Development, Judiciary and District of Columbia (TTHUD) appropriations bill. The amendment permits states and cities to use federal funds for projects that involve eminent domain for public use. However, the amendment bars federal funds to be utilized for any economic development project that primarily benefits private entities, proclaiming such projects not for public use.

Taking

The concept of *taking* comes from the takings clause of the Fifth Amendment to the U.S. Constitution. The clause reads, "nor shall private property be taken for public use, without just compensation." This means that when land is taken for public use through the government's power of eminent domain or condemnation, the owner must be compensated.

In general, no land is exempt from government seizure. The rule, however, is that the government cannot seize land without paying for it. This payment is referred to as *just compensation*—compensation that is just, or fair.

Of course, it is sometimes very difficult to determine what level of compensation is fair in any particular situation. The compensation may be negotiated between the owner and the government, or the owner may seek a court judgment setting the amount.

One method used to determine just compensation is the *before-and-after method*. This method is used primarily where a portion of an owner's property is seized for public use. The value of the owner's remaining property after the taking is subtracted from the value of the whole parcel before the taking. The result is the total amount of compensation due to the owner.

Dolan v. City of Tigard, Oregon: In 1994, the U.S. Supreme Court reinforced that there must be a "nexus," or direct relationship, when property is exacted from property owners. Ms. Florence Dolan sought from the city of Tigard permission to expand her appliance and hardware store, including an expansion of the existing parking lot. Her property was located partially in a flood plain. The city of Tigard required that Dolan dedicate a portion of her property (approximately 10%) to the city for a bike path and public greenery. In this case, the Supreme Court ruled against the city of Tigard saying that the city had not proven the relationship between additional traffic the new store would generate and the need for a bike path. In essence, the court determined that local governments must prove there is a direct relationship between actual projects and the exactions that have been imposed on developers. This case changed the way exactions upon developers in California are handled.

Zoning

Zoning ordinances are local laws that regulate and control the use of land and structures. Zoning ordinances are, in effect, tools used by local governments to implement the master (or general) plan and ensure orderly growth and development. In general, **zoning** affects such things as

- permitted uses of each parcel of land;

- lot sizes;

- types of structures;

- building heights;

- setbacks (the minimum distance away from streets or sidewalks that structures may be built);

- lot coverage (how much of a lot may be covered by structures);

- style and appearance of structures, including architectural compatibility;

- density (the ratio of land area to structure area);

- protection of natural resources; and

- protection of man-made resources (i.e., architectural heritage and archaeological resources/artifacts).

Zoning ordinances cannot be static; they must remain flexible to meet the changing needs of society. For example, in many large cities, factories and warehouses sit empty. Some cities have begun changing the zoning ordinances for such properties to permit new residential or commercial developments in areas once zoned strictly for heavy industrial use. Coupled with tax incentives, the changes lure developers back into the cities. The resulting housing is modern, conveniently located, and affordable. Simple zoning changes can help revitalize whole neighborhoods in big cities.

Zoning Objectives

Zoning ordinances have traditionally divided land use into residential, commercial, industrial, and agricultural classifications. These land-use areas are further divided into subclasses. For example, residential areas may be subdivided to provide for detached single-family dwellings, semi-detached structures containing not more than four dwelling units, walkup apartments, highrise apartments, and so forth.

To meet both the growing demand for a variety of housing types and the need for innovative residential and nonresidential development, municipalities are adopting ordinances for subdivisions and planned residential developments. Some municipalities also use buffer zones, such as landscaped parks and playgrounds, to screen residential areas from nonresidential zones. Certain types of zoning that focus on special land-use objectives are used in some areas. These include

- **bulk zoning** to control density and avoid overcrowding by imposing restrictions such as setbacks, building heights, and percentage of open area or by restricting new projects;

- **aesthetic zoning** to specify certain types of architecture for new buildings; and

- **incentive zoning** to ensure that certain uses are incorporated into developments, such as requiring the street floor of an office building to house retail establishments.

Inclusionary zoning results in a condition that a limited percentage of the purchasers buy at market prices, and the remainder buy at a reduced price reserved for low- to moderate-income buyers. The economic effect, in practice, is that the price level of the "market price" units is raised to compensate for the profit lost in offering the price reductions.

Exclusionary zoning results in a limitation of residential, commercial, and other use types over large areas. Exclusionary zoning has been utilized to limit the expansion of affordable housing and even adult businesses in many communities. The primary purpose of zoning is to segregate uses that are thought to be incompatible with one another through outright prohibition of certain uses or the establishment of excessive performance standards.

Figure 9.3 shows part of one city's zoning map.

FIGURE 9.3:   Sample Zoning Map

C: Commercial Zone
MU: Mixed–Use Zone
P-SF: Planned Single-Family Residential Development
R-1: Single-Family Residential Zone
R-2, R-3: Low-Density Multifamily Residential Zone

A Closer Look at Zoning   Why has zoning not been challenged? A landmark U.S. Supreme Court case heard in 1926 is why zoning continues to be applied today. In the case of *Village of Euclid Ohio v. Ambler Realty Company* 272 U.S. 365 (1926), the practice of zoning has served to reinforce zoning ordinances even today throughout the United States and Canada. Ambler Realty Co. owned 68 acres of land in the Village of Euclid, a suburb of Cleveland. In order to keep the industrial areas of Cleveland from encroaching upon Euclid, the Village enacted a zoning ordinance based on six classes of land use, three classes of height, and four classes of area. The property owned by Ambler Realty was divided into three use classes, thereby preventing Ambler Realty from developing the land as industrial. Ambler Realty sued the Village, arguing that the zoning ordinance had substantially reduced the value of the land by limiting its use, amounting to a deprivation of Ambler Realty's liberty and not allowing for due process (thus, arguing a taking). The Supreme Court argued that the zoning ordinance was not an unreasonable extension of the Village's police power and did not violate the 14th Amendment's due process clause. It should be noted that since 1926, the Supreme Court has never heard a case regarding zoning or even a case that would overturn Euclid.

Comprehensive (or General) Plan   Local governments establish development goals by creating a *comprehensive plan* or **general plan**. This is also referred to as a *master* (or *general*) *plan*. Municipalities and counties develop plans to control growth and development as well as the management of their resources. The plan includes the municipality's objectives for the future and the strategies and timing for those objectives to be implemented. For instance, a community may want to ensure that social and economic needs are balanced with environmental and aesthetic concerns.

The general plan forms the foundation of local land-use planning. When a local agency adopts a general plan, it creates a vision into objectives, goals, policies, and implementation programs for the community's development. Today, many communities embark on efforts to revise or update their general plans, including weaving health considerations throughout their plan's elements. In recent years, some communities have added an optional health element to their general plans to address linkages between health and the built environment. It has been determined by health officials and urban planners that land use can influence health outcomes positively by presenting opportunities for healthy behavior or negatively by restricting access to healthy options. Key land-use characteristics that affect health include

- patterns of land use within a community,

- the design and construction of spaces and buildings within a community, and

- the transportation systems that connect people to places.

A CLOSER LOOK AT CALIFORNIA   California state law requires each city and county to adopt a general plan "for the physical development of the county or city, and any land outside its boundaries which…bears relation to its planning" (Gov. Code Section 65300). The role of the community's general plan is to act as a "constitution," a basis for rational decisions regarding a city or county's long-term physical development. The general plan expresses the community's development goals and embodies public policy relative to the distribution of future land uses, both public and private.

The general plan must include the seven basic elements or subject categories of land use, circulation, housing, conservation, open space, noise, and safety. The seven mandated elements must address the following:

- **Land Use.** This element designates the type, intensity, and general distribution of uses of the land for housing, business, industry, open space, education, public buildings and grounds, waste disposal facilities, and other categories of public and private uses.

- **Circulation.** This element is correlated with the land-use element and identifies the general location and extent of existing and proposed major thoroughfares, transportation routes, terminals, and other public utilities and facilities.

- **Housing.** This element is a comprehensive assessment of current and projected housing needs for all segments of the jurisdiction and all economic groups. In addition, it embodies policies for providing adequate housing and includes action programs for that purpose. By statute, the housing element must be updated every five years.

- **Conservation.** This element addresses the conservation, development, and use of natural resources including water, forests, soils, rivers, and mineral deposits.

- **Open Space.** This element details plans and measures for preserving open space for natural resources, the managed production of resources, outdoor recreation, public health and safety, and the identification of agricultural land.

- **Noise.** This element identifies and appraises noise problems within the community and forms the basis for land-use distribution.

- **Safety.** This element establishes policies and programs to protect the community from risk associated with seismic, geologic, flood, and wildfire hazards.

A local general plan may also include other topics of local interest. For instance, a city or county may choose to incorporate into the land-use element a detailed program for financing infrastructure and timing of capital improvements. The safety element of a city or county that suffers from wildfire hazards may contain certain strategic fire protection planning policies to mitigate such hazards.

In addition to the statutory seven elements, a city or county may also adopt any other elements that relate to its physical development. Common themes for optional elements include recreation and parks, air quality, capital improvements, community design, and economic development.

Of Special Interest: Economics in Planning. Assessing economic trends is very important in preparing a realistic general plan. Municipalities may undertake one or more economic studies on such subjects as employment, market demand, and the benefit-cost ratio of development. The projections that result from these studies will form the basis for planning assumptions.

The Importance of the General Plan. A 1984 California appellate court decision held that a local government may not grant a conditional use permit if the general plan inadequately addresses pertinent state-mandated issues. Other decisions of the late 1970s and the 1980s have also prohibited various development projects due to the inadequacy of local general plans. Consequently, it is now in the best interest of real estate professionals, developers, local governments, and the public to make sure that general plans are legally adequate and that their implementing actions meet the consistency requirements.

The Specific Plan as a Land-Use Tool

In addition to the general plan, many communities have adopted **specific plans** to aid in the planning and development of specific areas in the community. As noted earlier, the general plan provides for an overall guidance for the physical development of a community. The general plan sets forth goals, objectives, policies, and programs for the entire jurisdiction/community. The same areas are included in specific plans to the extent that apply but for a localized or specific area and in more detailed policy guidance. The specific plan actually establishes development regulations and can include customized zoning standards for the affected area in the community.

A specific plan effectively establishes a direct link between the community's general plan and individual development proposals. A specific plan also creates a comprehensive vision, theme, and land-use plan for a given area, bringing all individual land-use projects/proposals under one plan. The specific plan can also amend zoning ordinances to establish more appropriate land-use designations used to address specific areas of concern (i.e., hillside development) and environmentally sensitive areas. It can serve as the basis for development agreements, which serve as contractual agreements for development rights/uses, financing responsibilities, and timing of required improvements between a local community and the developer.

Specific plans go beyond traditional land use planning tools (i.e., zoning, general plan, etc.) in that they identify more precise rules for how an area will develop, build flexibility beyond typical zoning ordinances, tailor regulations to address issues of a specific area without changing city or county ordinances, and can be used to formulate development agreements, just to name a few. Specific plans are often used when there are multiple property owners in a given area, and the goal is to achieve consistency between all of the future developments within the area. They are also used when it is appropriate and desirable to coordinate private funding or cooperative public/private financing of the plan's preparation.

Constitutional Issues and Zoning Ordinances   Zoning can be a highly controversial issue. Among other things, it often raises questions of constitutional law. The preamble of the U.S. Constitution provides for the promotion of the general welfare, but the 14th Amendment prevents the states from depriving "any person of life, liberty, or property, without due process of law."

Section 19, Article 1 of the California Constitution states that:

> Private property may be taken or damaged for public use only when just compensation, ascertained by a jury unless waived, has first been paid to, or into court for, the owner. The Legislature may provide for possession by the condemnor following commencement of eminent domain proceedings upon deposit in court and prompt release to the owner of money determined by the court to be the probable amount of just compensation.

Any land-use legislation that is destructive, unreasonable, arbitrary, or confiscatory usually is considered void.

Nonconforming Use   Frequently, a lot or an improvement does not conform to the zoning use because it existed before the enactment or amendment of the zoning ordinance. Such a **nonconforming use** may be allowed to continue legally as long as it complies with the regulations governing nonconformities in the local ordinance, until the improvement is destroyed or torn down, or the current use is abandoned. If the nonconforming use is allowed to continue indefinitely, it is considered to be grandfathered in to the new zoning.

Variances and Conditional-Use Permits   Each time a plan or zoning ordinance is enacted, some property owners are inconvenienced and want to change the use of their property. Generally, these owners may appeal for either a conditional-use permit or a variance to allow a use that does not meet current zoning requirements.

- A **conditional-use permit** (also known as a *special-use permit*) is usually granted to a property owner to allow a special use of property that is defined as an allowable conditional use within that zone, such as a house of worship or day care center in a residential district. For a conditional-use permit to be appropriate, the intended use must meet certain standards set by the municipality.

- A **variance** permits a landowner to use the property in a manner that is strictly prohibited by the existing zoning. Variances provide relief if zoning regulations deprive an owner of the reasonable use of the property. To qualify for a variance, the owner must demonstrate the unique circumstances that make the variance necessary. In addition, the owner must prove that she is harmed and burdened by the regulations. A variance might also be sought to provide relief if existing zoning regulations create a physical hardship for the development of a specific property. For example, if an owner's lot is level next to a road but slopes steeply 30 feet away from the road, the zoning board may allow a variance so the owner can build closer to the road than the setback allows.

Both variances and conditional-use permits are issued by zoning boards only after public hearings. The neighbors of a proposed use must be given an opportunity to voice their opinions. A property owner can also seek a change in the zoning classification of a parcel of real estate by obtaining an amendment to the district map or a zoning ordinance for that area. That is, the owner can attempt to have the zoning changed to accommodate the owner's intended use of the property. The proposed amendment must be brought before a public hearing on the matter and approved by the governing body of the community.

Building Codes

Most municipalities have enacted ordinances to specify construction standards that must be met when repairing or erecting buildings. These are called **building codes**, and they set the requirements for kinds of materials and standards of workmanship, sanitary equipment, electrical wiring, fire prevention, and the like.

A community's building and housing codes implement primarily the land use, housing, noise, and safety elements. Building and housing codes have their greatest effect on new construction and rehabilitation, but certain parts of the codes apply to the use, maintenance, change in occupancy, and public health and safety hazards of existing buildings. State housing law (Health and Safety Code Section 17910, et seq.) requires cities and counties to adopt regulations imposing substantially the same requirements as those contained in the various uniform industry codes: Uniform Housing Code, Uniform Building Code, the Uniform Plumbing Code, the National Electric Code, and the Uniform Mechanical Code. State housing law applies to buildings such as apartments, hotels, lodging houses, manufactured housing, and dwellings. In addition to meeting the requirements of state housing law, local codes must also comply with other state requirements applicable to fire safety, noise insulation, earthquake protection, energy insulation, and access for the disabled.

A property owner who wants to build a structure or alter or repair an existing building usually must obtain a building permit. Through the permit requirement, municipal officials are made aware of new construction or alterations and can verify compliance with building codes and zoning ordinances. Inspectors will closely examine the plans and conduct periodic inspections of the work. Once the completed structure has been inspected and found satisfactory, the municipal inspector issues a certificate of occupancy or occupancy permit. A building permit is evidence of compliance with municipal regulations.

Similarly, communities with historic districts or those that are interested in maintaining a particular "look" or character (such as the "painted lady" areas of San Francisco), may have aesthetic ordinances. These laws require all new construction or restorations to be approved by a special board. The board ensures that the new structures will blend in with existing building styles. Owners of existing properties may need to obtain approval to have their homes painted or remodeled. In recent years many more communities throughout California have adopted design or architectural review ordinances, which further allow for the regulation of height, bulk, mass, and aesthetics.

A CLOSER LOOK   Here is a section of the California Government Code regarding zoning:

§ 65850. The legislative body of any county or city may, pursuant to this chapter, adopt ordinances that do any of the following:

(a) Regulate the use of buildings, structures, and land as between industry, business, residences, open space, including agriculture, recreation, enjoyment of scenic beauty, use of natural resources, and other purposes.

(b) Regulate signs and billboards.

(c) Regulate all of the following:

   (1) The location, height, bulk, number of stories, and size of buildings and structures.

   (2) The size and use of lots, yards, courts, and other open spaces.

   (3) The percentage of a lot which may be occupied by a building or structure.

   (4) The intensity of land use.

(d) Establish requirements for off-street parking and loading.

(e) Establish and maintain building setback lines.

(f) Create civic districts around civic centers, public parks, public buildings, or public grounds and establish regulations for those civic districts.

(g) (1) Regulate, pursuant to a content-neutral zoning ordinance, the time, place, and manner of operation of sexually oriented businesses, when the ordinance is designed to serve a substantial governmental interest, does not unreasonably limit alternative avenues of communication, and is based on narrow, objective, and definite standards. The legislative body is entitled to rely on the experiences of other counties and cities and on the findings of court cases in establishing the reasonableness of the ordinance and its relevance to the specific problems it addresses, including the harmful secondary effects the business may have on the community and its proximity to churches, schools, residences, establishments dispensing alcohol, and other sexually oriented businesses.

REGULATION OF LAND DEVELOPMENT

Laws governing subdividing and land planning are controlled by the state and local governing bodies where the land is located. Rules and regulations developed by federal government agencies have provided certain minimum standards. Many local governments, however, have established standards that are higher than the minimum standards.

California Government Code Section 66424 defines a subdivision as the division, by any subdivider, of any unit or units of improved or unimproved land, or any portion thereof, shown on the latest equalized county assessment roll as a unit or as continuous units for the purpose of sale lease or financing whether immediate or future. Property shall be considered as continuous units, even if separated by roads, streets, utility easements, or railroad rights-of-way.

Development Plan

Most communities have adopted subdivision and land development ordinances as part of their comprehensive (or general) plans. An ordinance includes provisions for submitting and processing subdivision plats. A major advantage of subdivision ordinances is that they encourage flexibility, economy, and ingenuity in the use of land.

In California the Subdivision Map Act and Subdivided Lands Act establish certain procedures for public protection that must be followed by developers. These laws regulate subdivision map processing as well as informational reports that must be provided (public report or "white report") to potential consumers detailing area amenities as well as any potential hazards (such as earthquakes or flooding) that may exist in the area.

Of special note, California Government Code Section 66434.5 requires that when a soils report, geologic report, or soils and geologic report has been prepared specifically for a subdivision, each report shall be kept on file for public inspection by the city or county having jurisdiction.

A **subdivider** is a person who buys undeveloped acreage and divides it into smaller lots for sale to individuals or developers or for the subdivider's own use. A **developer** (who may also be a subdivider) improves the land, constructs homes or other buildings on the lots, and sells them. Developing is generally a much more extensive activity than subdividing.

Before the actual subdividing can begin, the subdivider must go through the process of land planning. The resulting land development plan must comply with the municipality's comprehensive (or general) plan. Although comprehensive (or general) plans and zoning ordinances are not necessarily inflexible, a plan that requires them to be changed must undergo long, expensive, and frequently complicated hearings.

Subdivision Consistency   Before a city or county may approve a subdivision map and its provisions for design and improvements, the city or county must find that the proposed **subdivision** map is consistent with the General Plan and any applicable Specific Plan. These findings can only be made when the local agency has officially adopted a General Plan and the proposed subdivision is compatible with the objectives, policies, general land uses, and programs specified in that plan.

FIGURE 9.4:   **Steps in Processing a Subdivision in California**

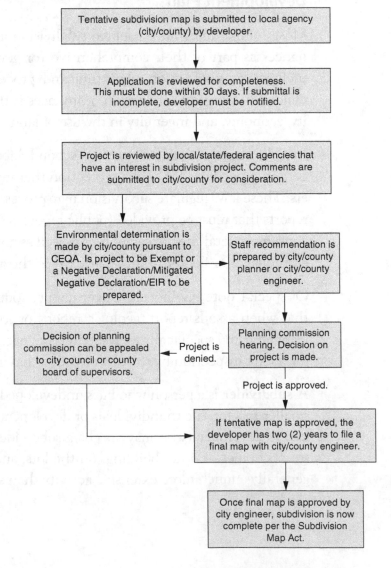

Pursuant to California Government Code Section 66474 and 66474.61, a city or county is required to deny approval of a subdivision tentative map if it makes either of the following findings:

- The proposed map is not consistent with the applicable General Plan and Specific Plan.

- The design or improvement of the proposed subdivision is not consistent with applicable general and specific plans.

Plats   From the land development and subdivision plans, the subdivider draws plats. A plat is a detailed map that illustrates the geographic boundaries of individual lots. It also shows the blocks, sections, streets, public easements, and monuments in the prospective subdivision. A plat may also include engineering data and restrictive covenants. The plats must be approved by the municipality before they can be recorded. A developer may be required to submit an environmental impact report with the application for subdivision approval if the proposed development will have a significant effect on traffic, noise, or pollution. This report explains what effect the proposed development will have on the surrounding area.

Subdivision Plans   In plotting out a subdivision according to local planning and zoning controls, a subdivider usually determines the size as well as the location of the individual lots. The maximum or minimum size of a lot is generally regulated by local ordinances and must be considered carefully.

The land itself must be studied, usually in cooperation with a surveyor, so that the subdivision takes advantage of natural drainage and land contours. A subdivider should provide for utility easements as well as easements for water and sewer mains. Most subdivisions are laid out by use of lots and blocks. An area of land is designated as a block, and the area making up this block is divided into lots.

One negative economic aspect of subdivision development is the potential for increased tax burdens on all residents, both inside and outside the subdivision. To protect local taxpayers against the costs of a heightened demand for public services, many local governments strictly regulate nearly all aspects of subdivision development.

Subdivision Density   Zoning ordinances control land use. Such control often includes minimum lot sizes and population density requirements for subdivisions and land developments. For example, a typical zoning restriction may set the minimum lot area on which a subdivider can build a single-family housing unit at 10,000 square feet. This means that the subdivider can build four houses per acre.

Many zoning authorities now establish special density zoning standards for certain subdivisions. Density zoning ordinances restrict the average maximum number of houses per acre that may be built within a particular subdivision. If the area is density zoned at an average maximum of four houses per acre, for instance, the subdivider may choose to cluster building lots to achieve an open effect. Regardless of lot size or number of units, the subdivider will be consistent with the ordinance as long as the average number of units in the development remains at or below the maximum density. This average is called *gross density*. For a subdivider and/or developer to realize the maximum economic benefit from a project, it is vital that the greatest legally allowable number of units be included.

Street Patterns   By varying street patterns and clustering housing units, a subdivider can dramatically increase the amount of open or recreational space in a development. Two of these patterns are the gridiron and curvilinear patterns (see Figure 9.5).

FIGURE 9.5:   Sample Zoning

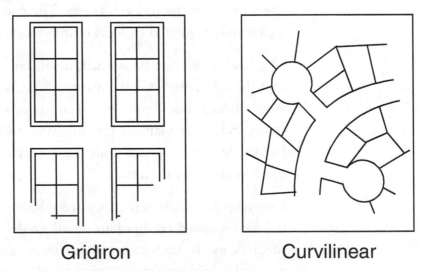

Gridiron   Curvilinear

The gridiron pattern features large lots, wide streets, and limited-use service alleys. Sidewalks are usually adjacent to the streets or separated by narrow grassy areas. While the gridiron pattern provides for little open space and many lots may front on busy streets, it is an easy system to navigate.

The curvilinear system integrates major arteries of travel with smaller secondary and cul-de-sac streets carrying minor traffic. Curvilinear developments avoid the uniformity of the gridiron but often lack service alleys. The absence of straight-line travel and the lack of easy access tend to make curvilinear developments quieter and more secure. However, getting from place to place may be more challenging.

Clustering for Open Space   By slightly reducing lot sizes and clustering them around varying street patterns, a subdivider can house as many people in the same area as could be done using traditional subdividing plans but with substantially increased open space.

Private Land-Use Controls

Not all restrictions on the use of land are imposed by government bodies. Certain restrictions to control and to maintain the desirable quality and character of a property or subdivision may be created by private entities, including the property owners themselves. These restrictions are separate from, and in addition to, the land-use controls exercised by the government. No private restriction can violate a local, state, or federal law.

Restrictive covenants set standards for all the parcels within a defined subdivision. They usually govern the type, height, and size of buildings that individual owners can erect, as well as land use, architectural style, construction methods, setbacks, and square footage. Restrictive covenants cannot be for illegal purposes, such as for the exclusion of members of certain races, nationalities, or religions. Private restrictions are also known as covenants, conditions and restrictions (CC&Rs). Such restrictions become part of the title, and the real estate professional should be aware that these will be typically referenced in a preliminary title report when escrow is opened. It would be wise for all parties, including the agent and purchaser of the property, to familiarize themselves with the CC&Rs.

Private restrictions can be enforced in court when one lot owner applies to the court for an injunction to prevent a neighboring lot owner from violating the recorded restrictions. The court injunction will direct the violator to stop or remove the violation. The court retains the power to punish the violator for failing to obey. If adjoining lot owners stand idly by while a violation is committed, they can lose the right to an injunction by their inaction. The court might claim their right was lost through *laches*—that is, the legal principle that a right may be lost through undue delay or failure to assert it.

REGULATION OF LAND SALES

Just as the sale and use of property within a state are controlled by state and local governments, the sale of property in one state to buyers in another is subject to strict federal and state regulations.

Interstate Land Sales Full Disclosure Act

The federal Interstate Land Sales Full Disclosure Act regulates the interstate sale of unimproved lots. The act is administered by the Secretary of Housing and Urban Development (HUD) through the office of Interstate Land Sales registration. It is designed to prevent fraudulent marketing schemes that may arise when land is sold without being seen by the purchasers. (You may be familiar with stories about gullible buyers whose land purchases were based on glossy brochures shown by smooth-talking salespersons. When the buyers finally went to visit the "little pieces of paradise" they'd bought, they frequently found worthless swampland or barren desert.)

The act requires developers to file statements of record with HUD before they can offer unimproved lots in interstate commerce by telephone or through the mail. The statements of record must contain numerous disclosures about the properties.

Developers are also required to provide each purchaser or lessee of property with a printed report before the purchaser or lessee signs a purchase contract or lease. The report must disclose specific information about the land, including

- the type of title being transferred to the buyer,

- the number of homes currently occupied on the site,

- the availability of recreation facilities,

- the distance to nearby communities,

- utility services and charges, and

- soil conditions and foundation or construction problems.

If the purchaser or lessee does not receive a copy of the report before signing the purchase contract or lease, the purchaser may have grounds to void the contract.

Exemptions

The act provides a number of **exemptions**. For instance, it does not apply to subdivisions consisting of fewer than 25 lots or to those in which the lots are of 20 acres or more. Lots offered for sale solely to developers also are exempt from the act's requirements, as are lots on which buildings exist or where a seller is obligated to construct a building within two years.

California Subdivided Land Sales

Section 11010 of the California Business and Professions Code requires that anyone who intends to offer subdivided land within this state for sale or lease must file a notice of intention and apply for a public report with the Bureau of Real Estate. The notice of intention must contain certain information about the subdivided land and the proposed offering, including:

- the name and address of the owner, the subdivider, and a legal description of the land;

- a statement of the condition of the title to the land, particularly including any encumbrances;

- a statement of the terms and conditions on which it is intended to dispose of the land, together with copies of any contracts intended to be used, and a statement of the use or uses for which the proposed subdivision will be offered and any limits on the use or occupancy of parcels;

- a statement of any provisions that have been made for public utilities in the proposed subdivision, including water, electricity, gas, telephone, and sewerage facilities; and

- a statement, if applicable, referencing any soils and/or geologic report that have been prepared specifically for the subdivision, as well as whether or not fill is proposed to be used in the subdivision.

ECONOMIC COOPERATION

Developers must deal with the realities of the marketplace. The ultimate input in the planning process comes from the community itself, and increasingly activist citizens have considerable influence on the development process. Even in unplanned communities, developers must deal with powerful and organized forces of public opinion.

- **Establishing Rapport.** Developing a rapport within the community as well as with the governing bodies is important. This means some form of liaison and dialogue in community and governmental forums. An understanding of the cultural, economic, and political demographics of a community is vital to knowing how to communicate effectively with citizens. Look for "common ground" issues and "mutual benefit" perspectives. Consider the kind of unspoken messages that development may send and how those messages may be interpreted by the public. For instance, what does a gated subdivision say to the surrounding community?

- **Willingness to Compromise.** In order to carry out a development project, many times tradeoffs must be arranged. Developers must be willing to compromise in order to see their projects to fruition.

- **Infrastructure.** Infrastructure issues have high priority in most communities; as more citizens arrive, more services are required. To alleviate some of these problems, developers often donate land for parks, schools, roads, flood control, and recreation. Developers are asked for these "donations" in the form of *dedications or exactions*. In general, the power to exact concessions from developers is part of a city/county's police power. Exactions, if properly used and secured, can implement a legitimate public goal or interest for a community. Because exactions are an exercise of police power, the process of exacting concessions from a developer can be derived from the General Plan and Zoning Ordinance. However, the oldest tool available to public agencies has been the Subdivision Map Act and the subdivision approval process. In the case of the subdivision approval process, "Caesar giveth and Caesar taketh." This simply means your subdivision might be approved, but you will have to make concessions.

- **Participation in the Planning Process.** Rather than opposing a comprehensive (or general) plan after the fact, the developer might seek to become involved and, thus, have some control of her own destiny. The developer can serve as a consultant to the community in reaching its development goals.

- **Understanding Community Goals.** Ideally, site selection criteria should include ascertaining that community goals are in harmony with the developer's own. One of the areas where tension arises between the development process and the community is the "slow growth" mode that many communities have embraced in recent years. Once the developer understands that the goal of master (or general) plans of this nature is to preserve the value of existing improvements, frustration can be eased somewhat. The self-image a community promotes through zoning regulations might be an urban financial center, an industrial giant, or a residential village.

Benefits to Community

The development process is indeed challenging. However, along with the challenges come both private and public rewards. Improvement of raw land provides needed housing and business structures and enhances the tax base, thus enabling local and state governments to provide the services their citizens need.

THE NEXT STEP   In the next unit, we will consider the ways in which government regulations in a more "social" arena influence the real estate market and the economics of land development.

SUMMARY

- The **development process** includes several distinct issues, each with its own analysis and considerations: *site identification, zoning, economic conditions, real estate values, and availability.*

- Individual ownership rights are subject to powers exercised by federal, state, and local governments. A state's power to *preserve order, protect public health,* and *promote the general welfare* is its **police power**.

- **Eminent domain** is the government's *right* to acquire privately owned real estate. The *process* by which that right is exercised is called **condemnation**.

- A government may **take** private real estate only for the *public good*. **Just compensation** must be paid to the owner, and the owner's rights must be protected by *due process of law*.

- **Zoning ordinances** are local laws that *regulate and control the use of land and structures*—to carry out the objectives of a **comprehensive (or general) plan** for the community.

- A **conditional-use permit** allows a *special use of property allowable within a zone*. A **variance** permits a landowner to use the property in a manner that is *strictly prohibited by existing zoning regulations*.

■ Through subdivision and land development laws, developers and subdividers must follow strict procedures to protect the public interest by *disclosing* specific information and following rules regarding hearings and compliance with the comprehensive (or general) plan.

■ Developers can comply with density requirements and maximize the profitable use of land through the use of various **street patterns** and **clustering** strategies.

■ The *sale* of **subdivided land** is regulated by both state and federal law.

■ The Subdivision Map Act sets forth conditions for approval of a subdivision map and requires enactment of subdivision ordinances by which local governments have control over the types of subdivisions to be undertaken. The Subdivided Lands Law is administered by the California Real Estate Commissioner and is intended to protect purchasers from fraud, misrepresentations, or deceit in the initial sale of subdivided land.

REVIEW QUESTIONS

1. Which of the three land-use theories best describes the community you live in?

2. How important is it for a community to have an up-to-date, legally defensible General Plan? What would be the consequences if a big box retailer operation, which would bring jobs and a solid tax base to the community, had an inadequate General Plan?

3. What are the seven basic elements of a General Plan? Does your community's General Plan contain these elements?

4. What steps would you undertake before submitting a development application to city hall?

5. What are the main differences between the *Subdivided Lands Act* and the *Subdivision Map Act*?

6. How have recent Supreme Court cases dealing with "takings" and eminent domain influenced land use as well as community politics in your community?

7. When are specific plans used? Provide an example of where such a planning tool can be used in your community to facilitate future development.

UNIT QUIZ

1. An economic analysis of a site, including utility availability, economic trends, and competition, is
   a. a plat.
   b. a feasibility study.
   c. a Gantt chart.
   d. a comprehensive (or general) plan.

2. All of the following steps would be taken by a developer during the option period *EXCEPT*
   a. engaging an architect.
   b. preparing a budget.
   c. soliciting subcontractor bids.
   d. filing an ILFDA report with HUD.

3. The process by which the government may acquire privately owned real estate for public use is
   a. eminent domain.
   b. condemnation.
   c. police power.
   d. zoning.

4. Local laws that regulate and control the use of land and structures within designated land-use districts are
   a. zoning ordinances.
   b. takings.
   c. conditional-use permits.
   d. subdivision plans.

5. Zoning with the primary intent of controlling density and avoiding overcrowding through setbacks, building height restrictions, and limits on new construction is which type of zoning?
   a. Bulk
   b. Aesthetic
   c. Incentive
   d. Inclusionary

6. All of the following are relevant to the government's power to take private property for public use *EXCEPT*
   a. the 14th Amendment to the U.S. Constitution.
   b. the Preamble to the U.S. Constitution.
   c. the 5th Amendment to the U.S. Constitution.
   d. the Declaration of Independence.

7. The city of Onion Lake has passed a new zoning ordinance that prohibits all commercial structures more than 30 feet high. A developer wants to construct an office building that will be 52 feet high. Under these facts, the developer must apply for
   a. a nonconforming use permit.
   b. a zoning permit.
   c. a conditional-use permit.
   d. a variance.

8. A homeowner would like to operate a day care business in her home. If she lives in an area zoned for residential, noncommercial use only, she must do which of the following?
   a. Request that the zoning board declare her home to be a nonconforming use
   b. Ask a court to grant an injunction against the zoning board
   c. Seek a conditional-use permit from the zoning board
   d. Apply to the zoning board for a variance

9. A detailed map that illustrates the geographic boundaries of individual lots in a subdivision is
   a. a plan.
   b. a plat.
   c. a gridiron.
   d. a disclosure.

10. The California Business and Professions Code requires that anyone who intends to offer subdivided land in California for sale or lease must file a notice of intention with
    a. the Secretary of Housing and Urban Development.
    b. the California Bureau of Real Estate.
    c. the Governor.
    d. the Office of Land Use Planning and Development.

10

FAIR HOUSING AND ENVIRONMENTAL REGULATIONS

KEY TERMS

accessibility

accommodations

Americans with
Disabilities Act
(ADA)

asbestos

California
Environmental
Quality Act (CEQA)

civil rights

color

Comprehensive
Environmental
Response,
Compensation,
and Liability Act
(CERCLA)

disability

dwelling units

electromagnetic fields
(EMFs)

Environmental Impact
Report (EIR)

Environmental Impact
Statement (EIS)

Fair Housing Act

family status

Federal Emergency
Management Agency
(FEMA)

Flood Insurance Rate
Maps (FIRMs)

friable

groundwater

handicap

hazards

landfill

lead

mold

National
Environmental
Policy Act of 1969
(NEPA)

National Flood
Insurance Program
(NFIP)

Negative Declaration

race

radon

Regional Water Quality
Control Board
(RWQCB)

sex

Supreme Court

underground storage
tanks (USTs)

LEARNING OBJECTIVES

- Understand the economic impact of fair housing laws on the real estate industry

- Identify the most common environmental considerations that influence buying and investing decisions

- Explain the liability issues arising under federal Superfund laws

FAIR HOUSING LAWS

The purpose of **civil rights** laws that affect the real estate industry is to create a marketplace in which all persons of similar financial means have a similar range of housing choices. The goal is to ensure that all people have the opportunity to live where they choose. Owners, real estate licensees, apartment management companies, real estate organizations, lending agencies, builders, and developers must all take a part in creating this single housing market. Federal, state, and local fair housing or equal opportunity laws affect every phase of a real estate transaction, from listing to closing. The intended effect of all these various regulations is to create a freer real estate market.

The U.S. Congress and the **Supreme Court** have developed a legal framework that preserves the constitutional rights of all citizens. However, while the passage of laws may establish a code for public conduct, centuries of discriminatory practices and attitudes are not so easily changed. Failure to comply with fair housing laws is both a civil and criminal violation and grounds for disciplinary action against a violator.

Evolution of Equal Housing

The federal government's effort to guarantee fair and equal housing opportunities to all U.S. citizens began with the passage of the Civil Rights Act of 1866. This law prohibits any type of discrimination based on race.

The U.S. Supreme Court's 1896 decision in *Plessy v. Ferguson* established the "separate but equal" doctrine of legalized racial segregation. A series of court decisions and federal laws in the 20 years between 1948 and 1968 attempted to address the inequities in housing that resulted from *Plessy*. Those efforts, however, tended to address only certain aspects of the housing market (such as federally funded housing programs). As a result, their impact was limited. Title VIII of the Civil Rights Act of 1968, however, prohibited specific discriminatory practices throughout the real estate industry.

The U.S. Supreme Court has since expanded the definition of the term *race* to include ancestral and ethnic characteristics, including certain physical, cultural, or linguistic characteristics that are commonly shared by a national origin group. These rulings are significant because discrimination on the basis of race, as it is now defined, affords due process of complaints under the provisions of the Civil Rights Act of 1866.

Jones v. Mayer In this 1968 U.S. Supreme Court case, the court held that Congress could regulate the sale of private property in order to prevent racial discrimination. Joseph Lee Jones, a black man, charged that a real estate company (Alfred H. Mayer Company) in Missouri's St. Louis County refused to sell him a home in a particular neighborhood on account of his race. The court sided with Jones and held that Section 1982 of the Congressional Act was intended to prohibit discrimination in the sale and rental of property, including governmental and private discrimination.

Fair Housing Act

Title VIII of the Civil Rights Act of 1968 prohibited discrimination in housing based on race, color, religion, or national origin. In 1974, the Housing and Community Development Act added sex to the list of protected classes. In 1988, the Fair Housing Amendments Act included disability and familial status (that is, the presence of children). Today, these laws are known as the federal **Fair Housing Act**. The Fair Housing Act prohibits discrimination on the basis of **race**, **color**, religion, **sex**, **handicap**, familial status, or national origin. The act also prohibits discrimination against individuals because of their association with persons in the protected classes. The law is administered by the Department of Housing and Urban Development (HUD).

A CLOSER LOOK The following are prohibited by the Federal Fair Housing Act, along with examples of each:

■ **Refusing to sell, rent, or negotiate the sale or rental of housing**

K owns an apartment building with several vacant units. When an Asian family asks to see one of the units, K tells them to go away.

■ **Changing terms, conditions, or services for different individuals as a means of discriminating**

S, a Roman Catholic, calls about a duplex, and the landlord tells her the rent is $400 per month. When she talks to the other tenants, she learns that all the Lutherans in the complex pay only $325 per month.

■ **Advertising any discriminatory preference or limitation in housing or making any inquiry or reference that is discriminatory in nature**

A real estate agent places this ad in a newspaper: "Just listed! Perfect home for white family, near excellent parochial school!" A developer places this ad in an urban newspaper: "Sunset River Hollow—Dream Homes Just for You!" The ad is accompanied by a photo of several African American families.

■ **Representing that a property is not available for sale or rent when in fact it is**

J, who uses a wheelchair, is told that the house J wants to rent is no longer available. The next day, however, the For Rent sign is still in the window.

■ **Profiting by inducing property owners to sell or rent on the basis of the prospective entry into the neighborhood of persons of a protected class**

N, a real estate agent, sends brochures to homeowners in the predominantly white Ridgewood neighborhood. The brochures, which feature N's past success selling homes, include photos of racial minorities, population statistics, and the caption "The Changing Face of Ridgewood."

■ **Altering the terms or conditions of a home loan, or denying a loan, as a means of discrimination**

A lender requires M, a divorced mother of two young children, to pay for a special in-depth credit report. In addition, her father must cosign her application. After talking to a single male friend, M learns that he was not required to do either of those things, despite his lower income and poor credit history.

■ **Denying membership or participation in a multiple listing service, a real estate organization, or another facility related to the sale or rental of housing as a means of discrimination**

The Topper County Real Estate Practitioners' Association meets every week to discuss available properties and buyers. None of Topper County's black or female agents is allowed to be a member.

Disability   A **disability** is a physical or mental impairment. The term includes having a history of, or being regarded as having, an impairment that substantially limits one or more of an individual's major life activities. Persons who have AIDS are protected by the fair housing laws under this classification.

The federal fair housing law's protection of disabled persons does not include those who are current users of illegal or controlled substances. Nor are individuals who have been convicted of the illegal manufacture or distribution of a controlled substance protected under this law. However, the law does prohibit discrimination against those who are participating in addiction recovery programs.

It is unlawful to discriminate against prospective buyers or tenants on the basis of disability. Landlords must make reasonable **accommodations** to existing policies, practices, or services to permit persons with disabilities to have equal enjoyment of the premises. For instance, it would be reasonable for a landlord to permit support animals (such as service animals) in a normally no-pets building or to provide a designated handicapped parking space in a generally unreserved lot.

People with disabilities must be permitted to make reasonable modifications to the premises at their own expense. Such modifications might include lowering door handles or installing bath rails to accommodate a person in a wheelchair. Failure to permit reasonable modification constitutes discrimination.

However, the law recognizes that some reasonable modifications might make a rental property undesirable to the general population. In such a case, the landlord is allowed to require that the property be restored to its previous condition when the lease period ends.

The law does not prohibit restricting occupancy exclusively to persons with handicaps in dwellings that are designed specifically for their accommodation. For new construction of certain multifamily properties, a number of accessibility and usability requirements must be met under federal law. Access is specified for public and common-use portions of the buildings, and adaptive and accessible design must be implemented for the interior of the **dwelling units**.

Exemptions   The federal Fair Housing Act provides for certain exemptions. It is important for developers, investors, and licensees to know in what situations the exemptions apply. However, no exemptions involve race and no exceptions apply when a real estate licensee is involved in a transaction.

- The sale or rental of a single-family home is exempt when the home is owned by an individual who does not own more than three such homes at one time, a real estate broker or salesperson is not involved in the transaction, and discriminatory advertising is not used.

- The rental of rooms or units is exempted in an owner-occupied, one- to four-family dwelling.

- Dwelling units owned by religious organizations may be restricted to people of the same religion if membership in the organization is not restricted on the basis of race, color, or national origin. A private club that is not open to the public may restrict the rental or occupancy of lodgings that it owns to its members as long as the lodgings are not operated commercially.

- The Fair Housing Act does not require that housing be made available to any individual whose tenancy would constitute a direct threat to the health or safety of other individuals or that would result in substantial physical damage to the property of others.

While the Fair Housing Act protects families with children, certain properties can be restricted to occupancy by elderly persons.

Equal Credit Opportunity Act

The federal Equal Credit Opportunity Act (ECOA) prohibits discrimination based on race, color, religion, national origin, sex, marital status, or age in the granting of credit. Note how the ECOA protects more classes of persons than the Fair Housing Act. The ECOA bars discrimination on the basis of marital status and age. It also prevents lenders from discriminating against recipients of public assistance programs such as food stamps and Social Security. As in the Fair Housing Act, the ECOA requires that credit applications be considered only on the basis of income, net worth, job stability, and credit rating.

Americans with Disabilities Act

The **Americans with Disabilities Act (ADA)** was signed into law in 1990; its accessibility guidelines were enacted in 1991. This piece of legislation, perhaps the most important U.S. civil rights law since 1964, was enacted to ensure that disabled citizens enjoy the same rights and opportunities as all Americans, including access to everyday activities such as commerce, recreation, travel, and housing accommodations.

The ADA requires employers to make reasonable accommodations that enable an individual with a disability to perform essential job functions. Reasonable accommodations include making the workplace accessible, restructuring a job, providing part-time or flexible work schedules, and modifying equipment that is used on the job. The provisions of the ADA apply to any employer with 15 or more employees.

The ADA also applies to accessibility to commercial buildings. The law addresses privately owned businesses and entities (including the government) that own or lease space and operate a facility that serves the public. The ADA further provides that public accommodations providing goods and services may not discriminate against individuals with disabilities. It should be noted that public entities, including state and local governments, are held to a higher standard under the ADA. Private businesses such as stores, restaurants, hotels, theaters, museums, schools, and recreational facilities are covered under the provisions of the ADA.

Real estate has been impacted by the ADA because new construction and alterations to existing facilities must comply with the ADA. Although existing facilities are subject to less stringent requirements than newly constructed buildings, the law does not totally exempt the existing structures, as do many zoning and building codes. The ADA requires the "readily achievable" removal of physical barriers if it can be done without much difficulty or expense. Moreover, in order to achieve the "barrier removal," the Internal Revenue Service (IRS) grants tax credits and deductions to businesses that remove the physical barriers to allow easier access.

Fair Housing Advertising Practices

No advertisement of property for sale or rent may include language indicating a preference or limitation. The media used cannot target one population to the exclusion of others. For instance, advertising property in a Korean-language newspaper only tends to discriminate against non-Koreans. Similarly, limiting advertising to a cable television channel available only to white suburbanites may be construed as a discriminatory act. However, if an advertisement appears in general-circulation media as well, it may be legal. Figure 10.1 outlines HUD's various restrictions.

Those who prepare appraisals or any statement of valuation, whether they are formal or informal, oral, or written (including a competitive market analysis), may consider any factors that affect value. However, race, color, religion, national origin, sex, handicap, and familial status are not factors that may be considered.

FIGURE 10.1: Fair Housing Law

Category	Rule	Permitted	Not Permitted
Race Color National Origin	No discriminatory limitation/preference may be expressed	"master bedroom" "good neighborhood"	"white neighborhood" "no French"
Religion	No religious preference/limitation	"chapel on premises" "kosher meals available" "Merry Christmas"	"no Muslims" "nice Christian family" "near great Catholic school"
Sex	No explicit preference based on sex	"mother-in-law suite" "master bedroom" "female roommate sought"	"great house for a man" "wife's dream kitchen"
Handicap	No exclusions or limitations based on handicap	"wheelchair ramp" "walk to shopping" "nonsmoking"	"no wheelchairs" "able-bodied tenants only"
Family Status	No preference or limitation based on family size or nature	"two-bedroom" "family room" "quiet neighborhood"	"married couple only" "no more than two children" "retiree's dream house"
Photographs or Illustrations of People	People should be clearly representative and nonexclusive	Illustrations showing a mix of races, family groups, singles, etc.	Illustrations showing only singles, black families, elderly white adults, etc.

California Fair Housing Laws

California's fair housing laws include essentially the same prohibitions against discrimination, panic selling, redlining, steering, and blockbusting contained in the federal law. Under the California Government Code, Section 12955, it is illegal for the owner of any housing accommodation to discriminate against any person because of race, color, religion, sex, marital status, national origin, ancestry, **family status,** or disability. Through subsequent amendments in 2007 and in 2012, Government Code Section § 12955 has been expanded to include sexual orientation, source of income, genetic information about individuals, gender identity, and gender expression. No advertisement for the sale or rental of housing may indicate a preference, limitation, or discrimination based on the protected classes.

It is illegal for any person, bank, mortgage company, or other institution that provides financial assistance for the purchase, organization, or construction of any housing accommodation to discriminate against any person or group of persons because of their race, color, religion, sex, marital status, national origin, ancestry, familial status, or disability in the terms, conditions, or privileges relating to the obtaining or use of that financial assistance.

Accessibility   Under California law, "discrimination" includes the failure to design and construct a multifamily dwelling of four or more units in a manner that provides access to and use by persons with disabilities. Multifamily dwellings must have at least one accessible building entrance, unless the terrain or other unusual characteristic of the site prohibits **accessibility** by persons with disabilities. All the doors designed to allow passage into and within all premises must be sufficiently wide to allow passage by persons in wheelchairs. Public and common areas must be accessible, and light switches, electrical outlets, thermostats, and other environmental controls must be in accessible locations.

California law requires newly constructed multifamily residential housing units to include reinforced bathroom walls to allow later installation of grab bars around the toilet, tub, shower stall, and shower seat; kitchens and bathrooms must be designed so that an individual in a wheelchair can maneuver about the space.

Barrows v. Jackson   This 1953 California decision (later affirmed by the U.S. Supreme Court) held that a property owner may not recover damages from another for breach of a racially restrictive covenant. The California Civil Code § 782 (enacted in 1961) subsequently provided that any provision in any deed that purports to restrict the right to sell, lease, rent, use, or occupy real property to persons of a particular racial, national, or ethnic group is void.

The Rumford Act   The California Fair Employment and Housing Act (Government Code §§ 12900–12996) prohibits discrimination in housing accommodations (sale, rental, lease or financing) on the basis of race, color, religion, sex, marital status, national origin, or ancestry. The act prohibits an owner or the owner's licensed agent from discriminating, asking prospective buyers or lessees about prohibited discriminatory factors, indicating preference in ads, or discriminating against someone who opposed the owner's prior discriminatory practices.

California Civil Rights Act   California Civil Code §§ 51–52, enacted in 1959, prohibits discrimination in California business establishments based on sex, race, color, religion, ancestry, and national origin. "Business establishments" includes all professional services of real estate licensees, as well as the "business" of renting or selling property, even if this is not how the owner earns a living.

California law prohibits other types of discrimination, such as discrimination against children in apartment complex rentals and discrimination based on sexual preference.

ENVIRONMENTAL ISSUES

Most states have recognized the need to balance the legitimate commercial use of land with the need to preserve vital resources and protect the quality of air, water, and soil. Preservation of a state's environment both enhances the quality of life and helps strengthen property values. The prevention and cleanup of pollutants and toxic wastes not only revitalizes the land but creates greater opportunities for responsible development.

Hazardous Substances

Pollution and hazardous substances in the environment are important considerations in the real estate economy because they affect the attractiveness, desirability, and market value of cities, industrial, commercial, and residential properties. An environment filled with **hazards** is not a place where anyone would want to live or work.

Hazardous substances include the following:

Asbestos. A mineral that was once used as insulation because it was resistant to fire and contained heat effectively, **asbestos** was banned in 1978. Prior to that year, it was a component of more than 3,000 types of building materials. It was used to cover pipes, ducts, and heating and hot water units. Its fire-resistant properties made it a popular material for use in floor tile, exterior siding, and roofing products. The Environmental Protection Agency (EPA) estimates that about 20% of commercial and public buildings in the United States contain asbestos.

Asbestos is highly **friable**: as it ages, its fibers break down easily into tiny filaments and particles. When these particles become airborne, they pose a risk to humans; exposure to microscopic asbestos fibers can result in a variety of respiratory diseases. Airborne asbestos contamination is most prevalent in public and commercial buildings, including schools, although asbestos contamination can also be found in residential properties. If the asbestos fibers in the indoor air of a building reach a dangerous level, the building becomes difficult to lease, finance, or insure. No safe level of asbestos exposure has been determined.

Asbestos is costly to remove because the process requires licensed technicians and specially sealed environments. In addition, removal itself may be dangerous; improper removal procedures may further contaminate the air within the structure. The waste generated must be disposed of at a licensed facility, which further adds to the cost of removal. Encapsulation, or the sealing off of disintegrating asbestos, is an alternate method of asbestos control that may be preferable to removal in certain circumstances.

■ **Lead.** For many years, **lead** was used as a pigment and drying agent in alkyd oil-based paint. Lead-based paint may be on any interior or exterior surface, but it is particularly common on doors, windows, and other woodwork. The federal government estimates that lead is present in about 75% of all private housing built before 1978; that's approximately 57 million homes, ranging from low-income apartments to million-dollar mansions.

An elevated level of lead in the body can cause serious damage to the brain, kidneys, nervous system, and red blood cells. The degree of harm is related to the amount of exposure and the age at which a person is exposed. Lead dust can be ingested, inhaled, or consumed in the water supply because of lead pipes or lead solder. Soil and groundwater may be contaminated by everything from lead plumbing in leaking landfills to discarded skeet and bullets from an old shooting range. High levels of lead have been found in the soil near waste-to-energy incinerators. The air may be contaminated by leaded gasoline fumes from gas stations or automobile exhausts.

The use of lead-based paint was banned in 1978. Licensees who are involved in the sale, management, financing, or appraisal of properties constructed before 1978 face potential liability for any personal injury that might be suffered by an occupant. Numerous legislative efforts affect licensees, sellers, and landlords. Known lead-based paint hazards must be disclosed to prospective buyers and tenants.

■ **Radon.** A radioactive gas, **radon** is produced by the natural decay of other radioactive substances. Although radon can occur anywhere, some areas are known to have abnormally high amounts. The eastern United States is especially rich in radon. When radon enters buildings and is trapped in high concentrations (usually in basements with inadequate ventilation), it can cause health problems. Opinions and scientific evidence differ as to both minimum safe levels and the actual danger posed by exposure. Radon may be the most underestimated cause of lung cancer, particularly for children, individuals who smoke, and those who spend considerable time indoors.

Interestingly, the modern practice of creating energy-efficient homes and commercial buildings with practically airtight walls and windows may increase the potential for radon gas accumulation.

■ **Urea-formaldehyde.** Urea-formaldehyde was first used in building materials, particularly insulation, in the 1970s. Gases leak out of the urea-formaldehyde foam insulation (UFFI) as it hardens and become trapped in the interior of a building. In 1982, the Consumer Product Safety Commission banned the use of UFFI. The ban was reduced to a warning after courts determined that there was insufficient evidence to support a ban. The National Toxicology Program within the Department of Health and Human Services added formaldehyde to its list of known human carcinogens in 2011. Formaldehyde does cause some individuals to suffer respiratory problems as well as eye and skin irritations.

■ **Carbon Monoxide.** Carbon monoxide (CO) is a colorless, odorless gas that occurs as a by-product of burning such fuels as wood, oil, and natural gas due to incomplete combustion. Furnaces, water heaters, space heaters, fireplaces, and wood stoves all produce CO as a natural result of their combustion of fuel. However, when these appliances function properly and are properly ventilated, their CO emissions are not a problem. When improper ventilation or equipment malfunctions permit large quantities of CO to be released into a residence or commercial structure, it poses a significant health hazard. More than 200 deaths from carbon monoxide poisoning occur each year.

■ **Electromagnetic Fields.** One of the most hotly debated environmental problems today is the issue of **electromagnetic fields (EMFs).** EMFs are generated by the movement of electrical currents. The use of any electrical appliance creates a small field of electromagnetic radiation; clock radios, blow-dryers, televisions, and computers all produce EMFs. The major concern regarding electromagnetic fields involves high-tension power lines. The EMFs produced by these high-voltage lines, as well as by secondary distribution lines and transformers, are suspected of causing cancer, hormonal changes, and behavioral abnormalities. There is considerable controversy (and much conflicting evidence) about whether EMFs pose a health hazard.

Groundwater Contamination

Groundwater is the water that exists under the earth's surface within the tiny spaces or crevices in geological formations. Groundwater forms the water table, the natural level at which the ground is saturated. This may be near the surface (in areas where the water table is very high) or several hundred feet underground. Surface water can also be absorbed into the groundwater.

Any contamination of the underground water can threaten the supply of pure, clean water for private wells or public water systems. If groundwater is not protected from contamination, the earth's natural filtering systems may be inadequate to ensure the availability of pure water.

Water can be contaminated from a number of sources. Run-off from waste disposal sites, leaking underground storage tanks, uncapped dry wells, and use of pesticides and herbicides are some of the main culprits. Because water flows from one place to another, contamination can spread far from its source. Numerous regulations are designed to protect against water contamination. Once contamination has been identified, its source can be eliminated. The water may eventually become clean. However, the process can be time-consuming and extremely expensive.

In response to the ever-growing threat to California's water, the Porter-Cologne Water Quality Control Act established a state Water Resources Control Board and nine regional water quality control boards. This board is referred to as the **Regional Water Quality Control Board (RWQCB).** The act establishes guidelines for controlling the discharge of effluents, which may affect the quality of water. Many communities throughout the state have curtailed their growth due to their inability to expand their waste water treatment facilities that have traditionally discharged into waters of the state (i.e., streams, creeks, and rivers, etc.). This, in turn, has limited the supply of available housing as well as commercial development in many areas. Not only are private property owners held liable in the contamination of California's water resources but so are local governments.

Underground Storage Tanks Approximately 3 to 5 million **underground storage tanks (USTs)** exist in the United States. Underground storage tanks are commonly found on sites where petroleum products are used or where gas stations and auto repair shops are located. They also may be found in a number of other commercial and industrial establishments—including printing and chemical plants, wood treatment plants, paper mills, paint manufacturers, dry cleaners, and food processing plants—for storing chemical or other process waste. Military bases and airports are also common sites for underground tanks. In residential areas, they are used to store heating oil and propane.

Some tanks are currently in use, but many are long forgotten. It is an unfortunate fact that it was once common to dispose of toxic wastes by simple burial—out of sight, out of mind. Over time, however, neglected tanks may leak hazardous substances into the environment. This permits contaminants to pollute not only the soil around the tank but also adjacent parcels and groundwater.

Some warning signs include the presence of fill pipes, vent lines, stained soil, and fumes or odors. Detection, removal, and cleanup of surrounding contaminated soil can be an expensive operation.

Recent state and federal laws impose very strict requirements on landowners where underground storage tanks are located to detect and correct leaks in an effort to protect the groundwater. The federal UST program is regulated by the EPA. The regulations apply to tanks that contain hazardous substances or liquid petroleum products and that store at least 10% of their volume underground. UST owners are required to register their tanks and adhere to strict technical and administrative requirements. Owners are also required to demonstrate that they have sufficient financial resources to cover any damage that might result from leaks.

Waste Disposal Sites

Americans produce vast quantities of garbage every day. Despite public and private recycling and composting efforts, huge piles of waste materials—from beer cans, junk mail, and diapers to food, paint, and toxic chemicals—must be disposed of. Old tires are most commonly disposed of in landfill operations, such as abandoned quarries. Landfill operations have become the main receptacles for garbage and refuse. Special hazardous waste disposal sites have been established to contain radioactive waste from nuclear power plants, toxic chemicals, and waste materials produced by medical, scientific, and industrial processes.

Perhaps the most prevalent method of common waste disposal is simply to bury it. A **landfill** is an enormous hole, either excavated for the purpose of waste disposal or left over from surface mining operations. The hole is lined with clay or a synthetic liner to prevent leakage of waste material into the water supply. A system of underground drainage pipes permits monitoring of leaks and leaching.

Waste is laid on the liner at the bottom of the excavation, and a layer of topsoil is then compacted onto the waste. The layering procedure is repeated again and again until the landfill is full, the layers mounded up sometimes as high as several hundred feet over the surrounding landscape. *Capping* is the process of laying two to four feet of soil over the top of the site and then planting grass or some other vegetation to enhance the landfill's aesthetic value and to prevent erosion. A ventilation pipe runs from the landfill's base through the cap to vent off accumulated natural gases created by the decomposing waste.

Federal, state, and local regulations govern the location, construction, content, and maintenance of landfill sites. Test wells around landfill operations are installed to constantly monitor the groundwater in the surrounding area, and soil analyses can be used to test for contamination. Completed landfills have been used for such purposes as parks and golf courses. Rapid suburban growth has resulted in many housing developments and office campuses being built on landfill sites.

A CLOSER LOOK A suburban office building constructed on an old landfill site was very profitable until its parking lot began to sink. While the structure itself was supported by pylons driven deep into the ground, the parking lot was unsupported. As the landfill beneath it compacted, the wide concrete lot sank lower and lower around the building. Each year, the building's management had to relandscape to cover the exposed foundations. The sinking parking lot eventually severed underground phone and power lines and water mains. Computers were offline for hours, and flooding was frequent on the ground floor. Finally, leaking gases from the landfill began causing unpleasant odors. The tenants moved out, and the building was left vacant.

Hazardous and radioactive waste disposal sites are subject to strict state and federal regulation to prevent the escape of toxic substances into the surrounding environment. Some materials, such as radioactive waste, are sealed in containers and placed in "tombs" buried deep underground. The tombs are designed to last thousands of years, built according to strict federal and state regulations. These disposal sites are usually limited to extremely remote locations, well away from populated areas or farmland. (Phase I and Phase II Environmental Assessments are also previously covered in Unit 8.)

Of particular concern in California is the geologic stability of hazardous waste sites. Careful studies must be conducted to ensure that such sites are not built on or near active fault lines.

Environmental issues have a significant impact on the real estate economy. In 1995, a jury awarded $6.7 million to homeowners whose property values had been lowered because of the defendant tire company's negligent operation and maintenance of a hazardous waste dump site. The 1,713 plaintiffs relied on testimony from economists and a real estate appraiser to demonstrate how news stories about the site had lowered the market values of their homes.

CERCLA and Environmental Protection

The majority of legislation dealing with environmental problems was instituted between the 1980s and 1990s. Subsequent amendments took place in 2002, known as the Small Business Liability Relief and Brownfields Revitalization Act, and in 2007 to the 1990 Oil Pollution Act. Although the

EPA was created at the federal level to oversee such problems, several other federal agencies' areas of concern generally overlap.

The **Comprehensive Environmental Response, Compensation, and Liability Act (CERCLA)** was created in 1980. It established a fund of $9 billion, called the Superfund, to clean up uncontrolled hazardous waste sites and to respond to spills. It created a process for identifying potential responsible parties (PRPs) and ordering them to take responsibility for the cleanup action. CERCLA is administered and enforced by the federal EPA.

A landowner is liable under CERCLA when a release or a threat of release of a hazardous substance has occurred on the landowner's property. Regardless of whether the contamination is the result of the landowner's actions or those of others, the owner can be held responsible for the cleanup. This liability includes the cleanup not only of the landowner's property but also of any neighboring property that has been contaminated. A landowner who is not responsible for the contamination can seek recovery reimbursement for the cleanup cost from previous landowners, any other responsible party, or the Superfund. However, if other parties are not available, even a landowner who did not cause the problem could be solely responsible for the costs.

After determining that hazardous material has been released into the environment, the EPA is authorized to begin remedial action. First, it attempts to identify the potentially responsible parties (PRPs). If the PRPs agree to cooperate in the cleanup, they must agree about how to divide the cost.

If the PRPs do not voluntarily undertake the cleanup, the EPA may hire its own contractors to do the necessary work. The EPA then bills the PRPs for the cost. If the PRPs refuse to pay, the EPA can seek damages in court for up to three times the actual cost of the cleanup.

Liability under the Superfund is considered to be *strict, joint and several,* and *retroactive. Strict liability* means that the owner is responsible to the injured party without excuse. *Joint and several liability* means that each of the individual owners is personally responsible for the total damages. If only one of the owners is financially able to handle the total damages, that owner must pay the total cost and collect the proportionate shares from the other owners whenever possible. *Retroactive liability* means that the liability is not limited to the current owner but includes people who have owned the site while it was contaminated.

In 1986, the U.S. Congress reauthorized the Superfund. The amended statute contains stronger cleanup standards for contaminated sites and five times the funding of the original Superfund, which expired in September 1985. The amended act also sought to clarify the obligations of lenders. As mentioned, liability under the Superfund extends to both the present and all previous owners of the contaminated site. Real estate lenders found themselves either as present owners or somewhere in the chain of ownership through foreclosure proceedings.

The amendments created a concept called innocent landowner immunity. It was recognized that in certain cases, a landowner in the chain of ownership was completely innocent of all wrongdoing and, therefore, should not be held liable. The innocent landowner immunity clause established the criteria by which to judge whether a person or business could be exempted from liability. The criteria included the following:

- The pollution was *caused by a third party*.

- The property was *acquired after the fact*.

- The landowner had *no actual or constructive knowledge* of the damage.

- *Due care* was exercised when the property was purchased (the landowner made a reasonable search, called an *environmental site assessment*) to determine that no damage to the property existed.

- *Reasonable precautions* were taken in the exercise of ownership rights.

Federal Environmental Regulation

The **National Environmental Policy Act of 1969**, or **NEPA**, as it is commonly called, declared environmental protection to be a national policy in which all agencies of the federal government shall, to the fullest extent possible, directly promote efforts to prevent or eliminate damage to the environment. The most significant aspect of NEPA is the requirement that all federal agencies (e.g., Army Corps of Engineers, U.S. Forest Service, U.S. Department of the Interior, etc.) prepare, file, and consider an **Environmental Impact Statement (EIS)** before approving any major federal action that could have a significant effect on the environment, such as the construction of several miles of roadway through a national forest or the construction of a dam across a major river.

This requirement includes any action (project) in which a federal agency has proprietary or financial interest, or in which government action will have a direct or indirect effect on the environment. An example of the types of actions or projects that would be subject to NEPA include the following:

- The construction of a new federal prison

- The expansion or widening of an interstate highway

- The construction of a new housing project funded by the Department of Housing and Urban Development (HUD)

- Any amendments to existing federal legislation affecting the environment, such as the Clean Water Act, Clean Air Act, etc.

- The paving of existing roads within a national forest

- The removal or harvesting of timber from a national forest

- The construction of a coal mine on land owned and operated by the

- Interior Department

- The construction/establishment of a casino on federal trust lands

California Environmental Regulation

Such projects would fall within the parameters of NEPA and thereby would require an Environmental Impact Statement to be prepared and circulated for public review prior to approval.

As in many other trends, California has always been in the forefront in environmental protections. While the environmental problems faced in California are the same as in other states, some issues are particularly important. These include

- *air quality* (a problem in urban regions with automobile-based cultures and little public transportation);

- *agricultural toxins* linked to crop-dusting operations and pesticide manufacturers;

- abandoned and operational *mines;*

- abandoned and operational *military installations;*

- *oil* exploration and extraction sites;

- *wood treatment* plants; and

- *scrap metal* operations.

In addition to state versions of the federal laws already discussed, *more than 750* different California Code sections regulate the use of land and resources for environmental protection purposes.

CEQA   The **California Environmental Quality Act (CEQA)** was enacted in 1970, approximately one year after NEPA was enacted at the federal level. It requires local governments and state agencies to conduct environmental reviews on all public and private developments to determine their environmental impact. CEQA's basic goal is to protect California's environment. CEQA accomplishes this by

- taking all action necessary to protect, rehabilitate, and enhance the environmental quality of the state;

- identifying the significant effects of projects on the environment; and

- providing feasible mitigations where possible.

CEQA applies to projects proposed to be undertaken or requiring approval by state and local government agencies. Major projects often require approvals from more than one public agency. In these instances, CEQA requires one of these public agencies to serve as the lead agency in disclosing potential environmental effects.

Under the law, "projects" include the enactment of zoning ordinances, the issuance of conditional use permits, and the approval of tentative subdivision maps. A "significant environmental effect" is one that will significantly impact a rare or endangered species of animal or plant or its habitat; the movement of any resident or migratory fish or wildlife species; and the habitat of any fish, wildlife, or plants. Most recently, the courts have also ruled that CEQA applies to the review of timber harvest plans under the jurisdiction of the California Department of Forestry and Fire Protection (CDF) for the cutting of timber.

How Does CEQA Work?   Because most projects or developments involve local municipalities exercising their authority, CEQA is the environmental law that will be used. Under CEQA, local governments follow a three-step process in applying CEQA to proposed development projects. A project, depending on its impact, size, and scale may become exempt or may require that an **Environmental Impact Report (EIR)** be prepared, with the developer paying for the cost of the environmental analysis. (See Figure 10.2 and 10.3.)

FIGURE 10.2:   California Environmental Quality Act (CEQA) Process Flowchart

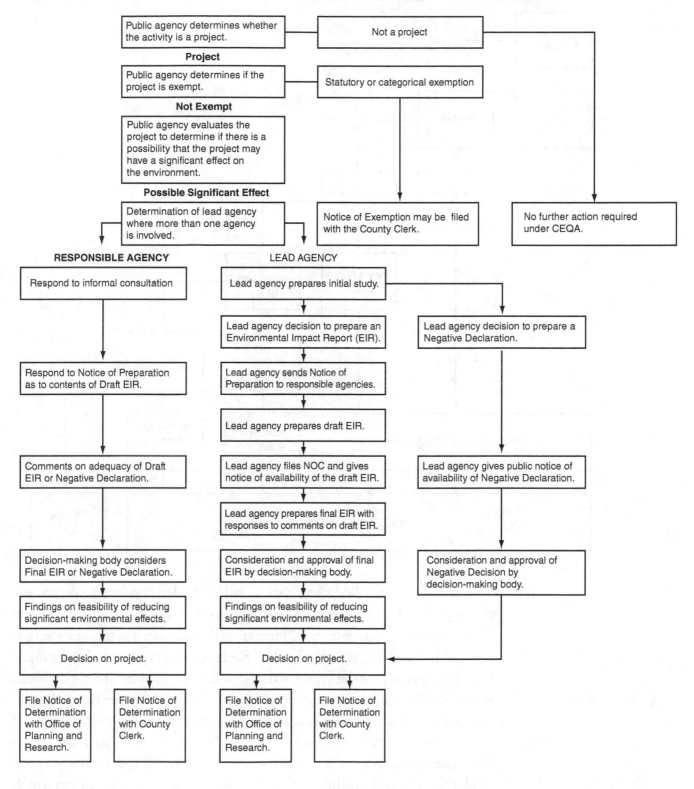

FIGURE 10.3: CEQA Decision-Making Process

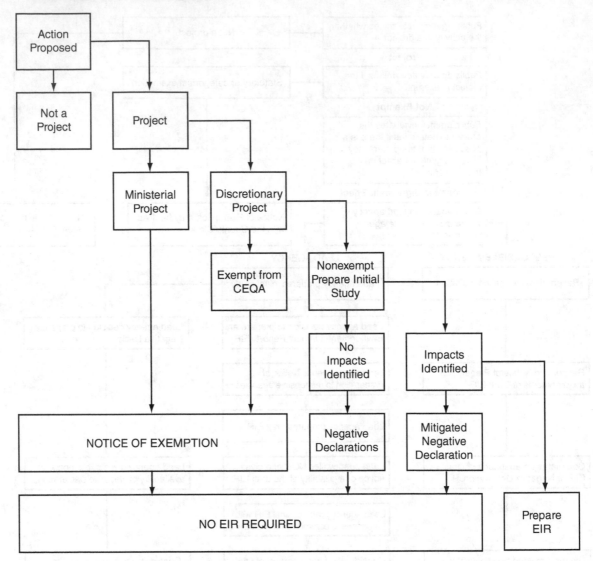

The first step in the "CEQA Process" is for the lead agency to determine if the proposal is a "project" as defined under CEQA. According to the California CEQA guidelines, a "project" is defined as a discretionary action involving the physical environment. Such actions could involve a conditional-use permit for the construction of a day care center or a subdivision, which would result in the creation of 100 lots. On the other hand, actions that are not discretionary (issuance of a building permit in an approved subdivision) are not considered projects. It should be noted that even a discretionary action is sometimes exempt from the CEQA review process. Under the CEQA guidelines, the state has identified 33 categories in which certain projects or actions would be exempt.

Once a project is determined to be a project under CEQA, and not exempt, the local government then must assess the proposal and determine if the project will have a significant effect on the environment. A lead agency may determine that a **Negative Declaration** or Mitigated Negative Declaration may be adopted, which is a written statement that briefly describes how a project will not have a significant effect on the environment, including where mitigations are incorporated to minimize the potential impacts. In the final step, if the analysis concludes that the project will have a significant environmental impact, the lead agency (city or county agency) must prepare an Environmental Impact Report. An EIR is merely an informational document, which is prepared to provide the decision makers (Planning Commission, City Council, or Board of Supervisors) with enough information to make a decision on a proposal. Even if an EIR is prepared, the approval of a proposal is not guaranteed. CEQA also applies to other agencies and districts involved in approving a "project." For example, a school district contemplating a new school site would also be subject to the provisions of CEQA. Therefore, both private and public projects are subject to the California Environmental Quality Act.

The following are contained in an EIR:

- Discussion of significant environmental effects

- Discussion of unavoidable environmental effects

- Discussion of significant irreversible environmental effects

- Discussion of alternatives to the proposed project

- Discussion of cumulative impacts the project might have in combination with other projects

- Discussion of any growth-inducing impacts associated with the project

- Discussion of mitigation measures that will minimize the environmental effects

If an EIR is prepared for a development, and it identifies significant environmental impacts, the governmental agency (e.g., city or county) has the following options:

- Deny the project

■ Approve an alternative to the proposed project

■ Approve the project, with mitigation measures

■ Approve the project in spite of the identified environmental impacts

In addition to local interested public agencies, the following is a list of state agencies that might be interested in reviewing potential development projects in California:

■ The Department of Boating and Waterways

■ The California Coastal Commission

■ State Coastal Conservancy

■ Department of Conservation

■ Department of Forestry and Fire Protection

■ Office of Historic Preservation

■ Department of Parks and Recreation

■ San Francisco Bay Conservation and Development Commission

■ Department of Water Resources

■ Department of Fish and Game

■ The California Highway Patrol

■ California Department of Transportation (Caltrans)

■ California Energy Commission

■ The Public Utilities Commission

■ State Lands Commission

■ Santa Monica Mountain Conservancy

■ Air Resources Board

■ California Integrated Waste Management Board

■ Regional Water Quality Control Board

■ Department of Health Services

■ Department of Toxic Substance Control

■ Department of Alcohol Beverage Control (ABC)

An EIR is a disclosure report. It only provides information and does not approve or deny a project based on its findings.

Other Environmental Considerations

Mold in California   Perhaps nowhere is the growing environmental concern more apparent than with **mold**. The fungal growth, found in damp or wet conditions, has been linked to health problems.

As a result of the ever-growing concerns associated with mold and its health risks, on September 3, 2001, the California Legislature passed Assembly Bill (AB) 284 and Senate Bill (SB) 732, known as the *Toxic Mold Protection Act of 2001*. Both laws mandated the California Department of Health Services (now the California Department of Public Health) to study and provide a report on the toxic mold risk and remediation to the State Legislature by July 1, 2003.

SB732 further directed the California Department of Health Services to

- adopt permissible exposure limits for mold in indoor environments, based on the latest scientific data and any existing standards by authoritative bodies;

- adopt mold identification standards for environmental assessment of mold in indoor environments; and

- adopt mold remediation, based on permissible levels of exposure.

The law was intended to establish programs and the development of guidelines for assessing mold and cleanup procedures, as well as establishing disclosures for residences. However, these provisions were dependent on the state's Public Health Department establishing permissible exposure limits (PELs). It wasn't until April 2005 that the California Department of Public Health released its report to the legislature, which found, based on its research, that sound scientific-based, permissible exposure levels for indoor molds could not be established. The report further noted that the state's Public Health Department concurred with building and other health professionals that indoor dampness, water intrusions, or fungal growth should be eliminated in a safe and efficient manner. Since then, the California Department of Public Health has been focusing on public education relative to identification, exposures, and cleanup of molds and fungi.

What does this mean for the California real estate industry? In addition to requiring that the California Department of Health Services study the effects of mold and develop standards for exposure, the Toxic Mold Protection Act will require landlords and sellers of residential and commercial properties to provide written disclosure to potential tenants and buyers. Landlords and sellers will also have to identify the current or prior existence of mold and disclose whether it exceeds the permissible exposure limits. The law also authorizes the Department of Industrial Relations to respond to mold complaints and enforce standards in the workplace.

In November of 2001, a California jury awarded $2.7 million in a personal injury lawsuit brought by a single family (*Darren Mazza v. Raymond Schwartz*) alleging damages against the landlord for exposure to mold in their apartment. The case, centered in Sacramento, found that the apartment owners and the property manager were liable for ignoring the family's complaints regarding water intrusion and failing to properly maintain and repair their apartment unit.

In May of 2001, a Delaware Supreme Court had also upheld a $1.04 million award to two women whose landlords had failed to address mold problems in their apartment, resulting in asthma attacks. In July of 2001, the Supreme Court in Nebraska also held a contractor liable for negligence and breach of warranty in a case involving mold contamination in a new home.

In 2012, former NBA player Rudy Tomjanovich and his wife were ordered by a Los Angeles Superior Court to pay $2.7 million in compensatory damages (*Bardack v. Tomjanovich*). The plaintiff, Bardack, purchased the Tomjanovich Pacific Palisades home in 2007 and alleged that the defendants had failed to disclose the existence of water leaks and mold in the home.

As a result of litigation taking place in California and elsewhere in the United States, insurance companies in California as early as 2002 began to exclude coverage and/or not renew homeowners' policies where mold had been involved or a claim has been filed within the previous five years related to mold damage. This has undoubtedly had a major impact on homeowners throughout California with insurance companies extending this practice nationwide.

Flood Zones   Special Flood Hazard Areas are designated by the **Federal Emergency Management Agency (FEMA)** and are delineated on **Flood Insurance Rate Maps (FIRMs)** published by FEMA.

Congress created the **National Flood Insurance Program (NFIP)** in 1968 to reduce future flood damage through flood plain management and to provide people with flood insurance through individual agents and insurance companies. FEMA defines a flood as a general and temporary condition of partial or complete inundation of two or more acres of normally dry land area or two or more properties from

- overflow of inland or tidal waters;

- unusual and rapid accumulation of runoff of surface waters from any source;

- mudflows; or

- collapse or subsidence of land along the shore of a lake or similar body of water as a result of erosion or undermining caused by waves or currents of water exceeding anticipated cyclical levels that result in a flood.

Most real estate lenders will require flood insurance coverage for the amount of the loan. Typically, this is a requirement prior to granting the loan when properties are in a flood zone. It should also be noted that even if the property is not currently in a flood zone but FEMA subsequently places it within a flood zone through a map change or a flood event occurs, a lender may subsequently come back to the borrower and impose the requirement for flood insurance. This requirement would then result in an unanticipated charge to the borrower. A standard flood insurance policy is considered a single-peril (flood) policy that pays for direct physical damage to the insured property up to replacement cost or actual cash value (ACV) of the actual damages or the policy limit of liability, whichever is less.

What is covered by flood insurance and what is not covered?   Generally, physical damage to buildings or personal property "directly" caused by a flood is covered by flood insurance. FEMA encourages people to have both building and personal property coverage.

What is insured under building property coverage?

- The insured building and its foundation

- The electrical and plumbing systems

- Central air-conditioning equipment, furnaces, and water heaters
- Refrigerators, cooking stoves, and built-in appliances
- Permanently installed carpeting over an unfinished floor
- Permanently installed paneling, wallboard, bookcases, and cabinets
- Window blinds
- Detached garages (up to 10% of building property coverage)
- Debris removal

What is not insured under building property coverage?

- Damage caused by moisture, mildew, or mold that could have been avoided by the property owner
- Currency, precious metals, and valuable papers such as stock certificates
- Property and belongings outside of a building, such as trees, planters, wells, septic systems, walks, decks, patios, fences, seawalls, hot tubs, and swimming pools
- Living expenses, such as temporary housing
- Financial losses caused by business interruption or loss of use of insured property
- Most self-propelled vehicles, such as automobiles

How is flood insurance obtained? Individuals may typically purchase a flood insurance policy from any licensed property insurance agent or broker who is in good standing in the state in which the agent is licensed. The insurance agent completes the required forms and submits them to the NFIP along with the necessary elevation certificate and full premiums. It should be noted that the elevation certificate must be completed by a licensed civil engineer, land surveyor, or architect.

Another question most often asked by the real estate industry and individuals is, how are flood insurance premiums calculated? According to FEMA, a number of factors are considered in determining the premium for flood insurance coverage. They include the following: the amount of coverage purchased, location, age of the building(s) in the SFHA, elevation of the building(s) in relation to the base flood elevation (BFE), building occupancy, and design of the building. Buildings may be eligible for special low-cost coverage at predetermined, reduced premium rates for residences, one- to four-family dwellings, and nonresidential buildings located in moderate-risk Zones B, C, and X, with specified loss limitations.

Changes for 2014 Flood Insurance Policy Holders   The Homeowner Flood Insurance Affordability Act of 2014 (HFIAA) was signed into law by President Obama on March 21, 2014. This law makes changes to the National Flood Insurance Program (NFIP) by repealing and modifying some provisions of the Biggert-Waters Flood Insurance Reform Act of 2012, including repealing certain rate increases that already went into effect. As a result, many policy holders became eligible for a refund of a portion of their flood insurance premium.

Specifically, the refunds due to policy holders under HFIAA restore the subsidized rate for flood policies covering pre-Flood Insurance Rate Map (FIRM) buildings whose owners were required to pay the full-risk rate because the building was newly insured or newly purchased effective on or after July 6, 2012, or for coverage effective on or after October 4, 2012, that reinstated a policy covering a pre-FIRM building. The changes also call for reduction of the premium for most flood policies that increased more than 18% effective on or after March 21, 2014.

Note that the National Flood Insurance Act of 1968 authorized the use of rates that were less than the full-risk premium rate determined by actuarial principles for buildings constructed before a community adopted the initial FIRM into local building ordinance. These discounted rates are considered subsidized. Under the recent changes, the 18% cap on flood insurance premium increases does not apply to certain subsidized flood policies covering buildings in the following categories:

- Non-primary residences

- Businesses

- Severe repetitive loss properties

Refunds under HFIAA do not apply to those policies where the full-risk rate is less than the subsidized rate.

THE NEXT STEP This unit has focused on the social and regulatory environment in which the real estate economy operates. In the next unit, we will consider a more "economic" but nonetheless equally "limiting" issue that governs how real estate is owned, transferred, and used—financing and taxation.

SUMMARY

- The purpose of **state and federal fair housing laws** is to create a *colorblind marketplace* in which all persons of *similar financial means* have a *similar range of housing choices*.

- State and federal fair housing laws prohibit **discrimination in housing** based on *race, color, religion, sex, disability, familial status,* or *national origin*. There are certain exemptions to compliance and strict rules governing the way in which real property is advertised.

- Under the *Fair Housing Act*, persons with disabilities must be permitted to make **reasonable modifications** to rented premises *at their own expense*. The landlord may require that the property be returned to its original condition at the end of the lease period. The **Americans with Disabilities Act (ADA)** applies to *commercial properties and employer-employee relationships*.

- Hazardous environmental substances include **asbestos, lead, radon, UFFI, CO,** and (perhaps) **EMFs.** Owners of existing or former industrial properties must be especially concerned about toxic materials buried in **underground storage tanks.** Californians must be particularly aware of the geologic stability of hazardous waste disposal sites.

- Under **CERCLA**, a landowner is liable for toxic pollution cleanup costs if a release or threat of release of a hazardous substance occurred on the property. Liability under Superfund is strict, joint and several, and retroactive. Innocent landowner immunity, however, offers a shield for landowners who are completely innocent of any involvement in the conditions giving rise to the hazard.

- The purpose of the National Flood Insurance Program (NFIP) is to reduce future flood damage through flood plain management and to provide people with the opportunity to purchase flood insurance through individual insurance agents.

REVIEW QUESTIONS

1. Discuss the impacts on a community when the largest employer files for bankruptcy, suddenly closes its doors, and states it can no longer compete in the marketplace. It is soon discovered that the same employer left a contaminated facility, which also affects those properties immediately adjacent to the contaminated facility.

2. Does your community have a "rent control" ordinance? If so, when was the last time a major apartment or multifamily housing development was built? Does your local government offer any incentives to developers to construct multifamily housing units?

3. Can you name all the communities in California that have "rent control" ordinances?

4. A manufacturing plant being proposed in your community will bring in over 500 new good-paying jobs. However, after an Environmental Impact Report (EIR) was prepared for the proposed project, it was determined that the new manufacturing plant will result in several significant adverse environmental impacts, specifically centered around inadequate infrastructure and the destruction of wildlife habitat. Should the city council approve the project, and, if so, how is the approval justified?

5. At what point in the development process will a local municipality require an EIR on a new shopping mall? What do you believe are the steps involved in the evaluation of the project?

6. What economic impacts to the real estate industry will insurance companies have as coverage for mold becomes more difficult to obtain?

7. What percentage of your community is located within a floodplain or flood zone as designated on the Flood Insurance Rate Map for your community?

UNIT QUIZ

1. What is the underlying purpose of the civil rights laws that affect the real estate industry?
   a. To give certain groups an advantage over others in the real estate marketplace
   b. To ensure that everyone who wants to own a home can do so, regardless of race or financial means
   c. To create a marketplace in which all persons of similar financial means have a similar range of housing choices
   d. To require that homeowners sell their property to anyone who offers to buy it

2. Which of the following is *TRUE* regarding California's fair housing laws?
   a. The protected classes are the same as the federal law.
   b. The protected classes include age and sexual orientation.
   c. It is less stringent than the federal law.
   d. The protected classes include sexual orientation, source of income, genetic information about individuals, gender identify, and gender expression.

3. The federal Fair Housing Act prohibits discrimination in housing on the basis of all of the following *EXCEPT*
   a. religion.
   b. disability.
   c. national origin.
   d. sexual preference.

4. A landlord permits a disabled tenant to lower door handles and install bath rails. This is an example of
   a. a reasonable accommodation.
   b. a reasonable modification.
   c. a coercive mandate.
   d. a taking.

5. Which of the following protects the most classes of persons against discrimination?
   a. ECOA
   b. ADA
   c. Civil Rights Act of 1896
   d. Title VIII

6. All of the following have been proven to be environmental hazards *EXCEPT*
    a. lead.
    b. asbestos.
    c. carbon monoxide.
    d. electromagnetic fields.

7. If the EPA identifies a hazardous site, but the potential responsible parties (PRPs) refuse to cooperate in the cleanup or reimburse EPA for the cost of doing so, what can the EPA do?
    a. Nothing; one of the primary criticisms of CERCLA is that it fails to provide an enforcement mechanism
    b. Seek reimbursement, but not punitive damages, in a lawsuit
    c. Seek damages in court for up to three times the actual cost of the cleanup
    d. Arrest the PRPs, who will be subject to up to 10 years' imprisonment

8. Liability under Superfund is
    a. strict only.
    b. strict and several, but not joint.
    c. strict, joint and several, but not retroactive.
    d. strict, joint and several, and retroactive.

9. In order to qualify for the innocent landowner immunity offered by CERCLA, landowners must prove all of the following *EXCEPT*
    a. the pollution was caused by a third party.
    b. the property was polluted when purchased.
    c. being unaware that their actions would result in the release of toxic materials.
    d. having no actual or constructive knowledge of the damage.

10. Superfund is administered and enforced by
    a. CERCLA.
    b. EPA.
    c. PRP.
    d. CEQA.

11

FINANCING AND TAXATION

KEY TERMS

adjustable-rate
  mortgage (ARM)
ad valorem
allocation
American Recovery
  and Reinvestment
  Act
amortize
balloon payment
Cal-Vet
cash
credit unions
creditor
Department of
  Veterans Affairs
  (VA)
discount rate
equity

Fannie Mae
Farm Service Agency
  (FSA)
Federal Housing
  Administration
  (FHA)
Federal Reserve
  System
Freddie Mac
finance charges
Ginnie Mae
investor
liquidity
money
mortgage brokers
pension funds
private mortgage
  insurance (PMI)

poverty guidelines
primary mortgage
  market
prime rate
Proposition 13
rate cap
Real Estate Settlement
  Procedures Act
  (RESPA)
Regulation Z
reserve funds
savings banks
thrifts
servicing
wraparound loan
yield

LEARNING OBJECTIVES

- Identify the participants in and characteristics of the primary and secondary mortgage markets

- Describe the different types of private and government financing plans available and the advantages and disadvantages of each

- Understand the requirements of the Truth in Lending Act, the Equal Credit Opportunity Act, the Community Reinvestment Act, and RESPA

- Discuss the types of federal and state taxation relevant to real property and the effects of taxation on the real estate economy

INTRODUCTION TO REAL ESTATE FINANCE

Most real estate transactions require some sort of financing. Few people have the **cash** in hand necessary to buy a house or another large property. Also, as economic conditions change, the forces of supply and demand reshape the real estate market. Both factors have combined to create a complex and rapidly evolving mortgage market. One of the greatest challenges today's real estate licensees face is how to maintain a working knowledge of all the financing techniques available.

Availability of Funds

Money   Just like any other resource, money is limited in its availability. Availability is affected by the level of savings accumulated by individuals and businesses, which can then be converted into a variety of competing investment alternatives, ranging from interest-bearing bank accounts and money market instruments to business acquisition and real estate investment. It should be noted that the concept of disintermediation plays an important role in economics and real estate finance. Disintermediation occurs when there is a removal of intermediaries in the supply of real estate funding. Intermediaries include distributors, wholesalers, brokers, and agents.

Allocation   The **allocation** of these limited resources generally reflects the level of interest rates available from the various investment alternatives. Decisions to allocate funds to real estate financing are dictated by the three measurements for any investment:

- **Yield**—*Yield* is *adequate return* based on the relative risk of the investment.

- **Safety**—*Safety* means proper protective measures in the form of *sound underwriting* of the credit supported by the real estate value.

- **Liquidity**—*Liquidity* is the principal *disadvantage* of real estate as an investment, due to its heterogeneous nature. Real estate is simply not a highly liquid investment; it takes time to convert a real property asset into a cash asset.

Investor Expectations Participants in real estate lending—the **investors**—will normally demand a higher yield than they would from a high-quality corporate bond of equal risk, which requires much less servicing.

In Unit 4, we discussed the Federal Reserve System and its role in the U.S. economy. Here, we will review the operation of the Fed, with particular emphasis on its role in real estate financing.

Federal Reserve System

The purpose of the **Federal Reserve System** (the *Fed*) is to maintain sound credit conditions, help counteract inflationary and deflationary trends, and create a favorable economic climate.

The Federal Reserve System divides the country into 12 Federal Reserve districts, each served by a federal reserve bank. All nationally chartered banks must join the Fed and purchase stock in its district reserve banks.

The Federal Reserve regulates the flow of money and interest rates in the marketplace indirectly through its member banks by controlling their reserve requirements and discount rates.

Reserve Requirements The Federal Reserve requires that each member bank keep a certain amount of assets on hand as **reserve funds**. These reserves are unavailable for loans or any other use. This requirement not only protects customer deposits but also provides a means of manipulating the flow of cash in the money market.

By increasing its reserve requirements, the Federal Reserve, in effect, limits the amount of money that member banks can use to make loans. When the amount of money available for lending decreases, interest rates (the amount lenders charge for the use of their money) rise. By causing interest rates to rise, the government can slow down an overactive economy by limiting the number of loans that would have been directed toward major purchases of goods and services.

The opposite is also true; by decreasing the reserve requirements, the Fed can encourage more lending. Increased lending causes the amount of money circulated in the marketplace to rise while simultaneously causing interest rates to drop.

EXAMPLE

1. Increasing reserve requirements by 10% to 80% would mean that for every dollar deposited, only $0.80 is available for loans and interest rate increases.

2. Decreasing reserve requirements by 10% means that for every dollar deposited, $0.90 is available for loans and interest rate increases.

Discount Rates   Federal Reserve member banks are permitted to borrow money from the district reserve banks to expand their lending operations. The interest rate that the district banks charge for the use of this money is called the **discount rate.** This rate is the basis on which the banks determine the percentage rate of interest they will charge their loan customers.

The **prime rate** (the short-term interest rate charged to a bank's largest, most creditworthy customers) is strongly influenced by the Fed's discount rate. In turn, the prime rate is often the basis for determining a bank's interest rate on other loans, including mortgages. In theory, when the Federal Reserve discount rate is high, bank interest rates are high. When bank interest rates are high, fewer loans are made and less money circulates in the marketplace. On the other hand, a lower discount rate results in lower interest rates, more bank loans, and more money in circulation.

Primary Mortgage Market

The **primary mortgage market** is made up of the lenders that originate mortgage loans. These lenders make money available directly to borrowers. From a borrower's point of view, a loan is a means of financing an expenditure; from a lender's point of view, a loan is an investment. All investors look for profitable returns on their investments. For a lender, a loan must generate enough income to be attractive as an investment.

Income on a loan is realized from two sources:

- **Finance charges** collected at closing, such as loan origination fees and discount points

- **Recurring income**—that is, the interest collected during the term of the loan

An increasing number of lenders look at the income generated from the fees charged in originating loans as their primary investment objective. Once the loans are made, they are sold to investors. By selling loans to investors in the secondary mortgage market, lenders generate funds with which to originate additional loans.

In addition to the income directly related to loans, some lenders derive income from servicing loans for other mortgage lenders or the investors who have purchased the loans.

Servicing involves such activities as the following:

- Collecting payments (including insurance and taxes)

- Accounting

- Bookkeeping

- Preparing insurance and tax records

- Processing payments of taxes and insurance

- Following up on loan payment and delinquency

The terms of the servicing agreement stipulate the responsibilities and fees for the service.

Participants   Some of the major lenders in the primary market include the following:

- **Thrifts**, savings associations, and **savings banks** are known as fiduciary lenders because of their fiduciary obligations to protect and preserve their depositors' funds. Mortgage loans are perceived as secure investments for generating income and enable these institutions to pay interest to their depositors. Fiduciary lenders are subject to standards and regulations established by government agencies, such as the Federal Deposit Insurance Corporation (FDIC).

  The Financial Institutions Reform, Recovery, and Enforcement Act of 1989 (FIRREA) created the *Office of Thrift Supervision (OTS)* specifically to govern the practices of fiduciary lenders. The various government regulations (which include reserve fund, reporting, and insurance requirements) are intended to protect depositors against the reckless lending that characterized the savings and loan industry in the 1980s. On July 21, 2011, the OTS ceased to exist when it became part of the **Office of the Comptroller of Currency (OCC)**.

As of 2011, the OCC is responsible for regulating both national banks and federal savings associations (thrifts). The merger was part of the restructuring of the nation's economic system under the Frank-Dodd Act.

- **Insurance companies.** Insurance companies accumulate large sums of money from the premiums paid by their policyholders. While part of this money is held in reserve to satisfy claims and cover operating expenses, much of it is free to be invested in profit-earning enterprises, such as long-term real estate loans. Although insurance companies are considered primary lenders, they tend to invest their money in large, long-term loans that finance commercial and industrial properties rather than in single-family home mortgages.

- **Credit unions. Credit unions** are cooperative organizations whose members place money in savings accounts. In the past, credit unions made only short-term consumer and home improvement loans. Recently, however, they have branched out to originate longer-term first and second mortgage and deed of trust loans.

- **Pension funds. Pension funds** usually have large amounts of money available for investment. Because of the comparatively high yields and low risks offered by mortgages, pension funds have begun to participate actively in financing real estate projects. Most real estate activity for pension funds is handled through mortgage bankers and mortgage brokers.

- **Endowment funds.** Many commercial banks and mortgage bankers handle investments for endowment funds. The endowments of hospitals, universities, colleges, charitable foundations, and other institutions provide a good source of financing for low-risk commercial and industrial properties.

- **Investment group financing.** Large real estate projects, such as high-rise apartment buildings, office complexes, and shopping centers, are often financed as joint ventures through group financing arrangements such as syndicates, limited partnerships, and real estate investment trusts. These forms of group investment strategies are discussed in greater detail in Unit 12.

- **Mortgage banking companies.** Mortgage banking companies originate mortgage loans with money belonging to insurance companies, pension funds, and individuals with funds of their own. They make real estate loans with the intention of selling them to investors and receiving a fee for servicing the loans. Mortgage banking companies are generally organized as stock companies. As a source of real estate financing, they are subject to fewer lending restrictions than are commercial banks or savings associations. Mortgage banking companies often are involved in all types of real estate loan activities and often serve as intermediaries between investors and borrowers.

- **Mortgage brokers. Mortgage brokers** are not lenders. They are intermediaries who bring borrowers and lenders together. Mortgage brokers locate potential borrowers, process preliminary loan applications, and submit the applications to lenders for final approval. Frequently, they work with or for mortgage banking companies. They do not service loans once they are made. Mortgage brokers may also be real estate brokers who offer these financing services in addition to their regular brokerage activities. Many state governments are establishing separate licensure requirements for mortgage brokers to regulate their activities. In California, for instance, mortgage brokers are regulated by the Bureau of Real Estate.

The Secondary Market

In addition to the primary mortgage market, where loans are originated, there is a secondary mortgage market. Here, loans are bought and sold only after they have been funded. Lenders routinely sell loans to avoid interest-rate risks and to realize profits on the sales. This secondary market activity helps lenders raise capital to continue making mortgage loans. Secondary market activity is especially desirable when money is in short supply; it stimulates both the housing construction market and the mortgage market by expanding the types of loans available.

When a loan is sold, the original lender may continue to collect the payments from the borrower. The lender then passes the payments along to the investor who purchased the loan. The investor is charged a fee for servicing the loan.

Warehousing agencies purchase a number of mortgage loans and assemble them into packages (called *pools*). Securities that represent shares in these pooled mortgages are then sold to investors. Loans are eligible for sale to the secondary market only when the collateral, borrower, and documentation meet certain requirements to provide a degree of safety for the investors. The major warehousing agencies are discussed in the following paragraphs.

A CLOSER LOOK...   As a result of the subprime mortgage crisis that began in 2007, Goldman Sachs profited from the collapse in the subprime mortgage bonds by short-selling (or selling and then repurchasing) subprime mortgage-backed securities. In essence, Goldman Sachs earned a $4 billion profit by hedging or gambling on the collapse of the subprime market and shorting mortgage-backed securities. As a result of the 2008 financial crisis, many large Wall Street firms were forced into bankruptcy and out of business. On September 15, 2008, Lehman Brothers filed for bankruptcy, with $639 billion in assets and $619 billion in debt, making it the largest bankruptcy in U.S. history. Others, such as American International Group, Inc. (AIG), survived due to taxpayer bailouts, while Goldman Sachs not only survived but was also the recipient of $10 billion through the Troubled Asset Relief Program (TARP). Today Goldman Sachs is an $87 billion dollar company, while Lehman's bankruptcy led to more than $46 billion of its market value being wiped out.

Fannie Mae   Formerly known as the Federal National Mortgage Association, **Fannie Mae** is a quasi-governmental agency. It is organized as a privately owned corporation that issues its own common stock and provides a secondary market for mortgage loans. Fannie Mae deals in conventional and FHA and VA loans. Fannie Mae buys a block or pool of mortgages from a lender in exchange for mortgage-backed securities, which the lender may keep or sell. Fannie Mae guarantees payment of all interest and principal to the holder of the securities.

Federal Home Loan Mortgage Corporation (FHLMC, Freddie Mac)   Created in 1970, **Freddie Mac** is a federally chartered corporation owned primarily by the savings association industry. Its function is very similar to Fannie Mae and is overseen by the Department of Housing and Urban Development (HUD). Freddie Mac is composed of an 18-member board of directors, of which five are appointed directly by the President of the United States. Freddie Mac differs from Fannie Mae in that it scrutinizes rather than purchases loans for its portfolio. However, Freddie Mac acquires its loans through purchases from its approved sellers/servicers. While these sellers are mostly savings associations, the right to do business with Freddie Mac is open to any loan originator. The originator, however, must meet Freddie's qualifications. Most of the purchases that Freddie Mac makes are conventional loans that must carry private mortgage insurance (PMI) unless there is a 20% down payment. Freddie Mac also acquires FHA and VA loans, but almost all of these are now handled by Ginnie Mae. Freddie Mac has the authority to purchase mortgages, pool them, and sell bonds in the open market with mortgages as security. However, FHLMC does not guarantee payment of Freddie Mac mortgages.

Many lenders use the standardized forms and follow the guidelines issued by Fannie Mae and Freddie Mac. In fact, the use of such forms is mandatory for lenders that wish to sell mortgages in the agencies' secondary mortgage market. The standardized documents include loan applications, credit reports, and appraisal forms.

Government National Mortgage Association Unlike Fannie Mae, the Government National Mortgage Association (GNMA or **Ginnie Mae**) is entirely a governmental agency. GNMA is a division of the Department of Housing and Urban Development (HUD), organized as a corporation without capital stock. GNMA administers special-assistance programs and works with Fannie Mae in secondary market activities.

In times of tight money and high interest rates, Fannie Mae and Ginnie Mae can join forces through their tandem plan. The tandem plan provides that Fannie Mae can purchase high-risk, low-yield (usually FHA) loans at full market rates, with GNMA guaranteeing payment and absorbing the difference between the low yield and current market prices.

Ginnie Mae also guarantees investment securities issued by private offerors (such as banks, mortgage companies, and savings and loan associations) and backed by pools of FHA and VA mortgage loans. The Ginnie Mae pass-through certificate is a security interest in a pool of mortgages that provides for a monthly pass-through of principal and interest payments directly to the certificate holder. Such certificates are guaranteed by Ginnie Mae.

Financing Techniques

Now that you understand *where* real estate financing comes from, we'll turn to the *what*—the types of financing available. As mentioned at the beginning of this unit, real estate financing comes in a wide variety of forms. While the payment plans described in the following sections are commonly referred to as *mortgages*, they are really loans secured by either a mortgage or a deed of trust.

Straight Loans ("Interest Only")

A straight loan (also known as a term loan) essentially divides the loan into two amounts to be paid off separately. The borrower makes periodic interest payments followed by the payment of the principal in full at the end of the term. Straight loans were once the only form of mortgage available. Today, they are generally used for home improvements and second mortgages rather than for residential first mortgage loans.

Amortized Loans The word **amortize** literally means "to kill off slowly, over time." Most mortgage and deed of trust loans are *amortized loans*. That is, they are paid off slowly, over time. Regular periodic payments are made over a term of years, such as 15 or 30 years, although 20-year and 40-year mortgages are also available. Unlike a straight loan payment, an amortized loan payment partially pays off both principal and interest. Each payment is applied first to interest owed; the balance is applied to the principal amount. At the end of the term, the full amount of the principal and all interest due is reduced to zero. Such loans are also called *direct reduction loans*. Most amortized mortgage and deed of trust loans are paid in monthly installments. However, some are payable *quarterly* (four times a year) or *semiannually* (twice a year).

Different payment plans tend alternately to gain and lose favor with lenders and borrowers as the cost and availability of mortgage money fluctuate. The most frequently used plan is the fully amortized loan, or *level-payment loan*. The mortgagor pays a constant amount, usually monthly. The lender credits each payment first to the interest due then to the principal amount of the loan.

As a result, while each payment remains the same, the portion applied to repayment of the principal grows and the interest due declines as the unpaid balance of the loan is reduced. If the borrower pays additional amounts that are applied directly to the principal, the loan will amortize more quickly. This benefits the borrower who will pay less interest if the loan is paid off before the end of its term. Of course, lenders are aware of this, too, and may guard against unprofitable loans by including penalties for early payment. The amount of the constant payment is determined from a prepared mortgage payment book or a mortgage factor chart.

Adjustable-Rate Mortgages (ARMs) An **adjustable-rate mortgage (ARM)** is generally originated at one rate of interest. That rate then fluctuates up or down during the loan term based on some objective economic indicator. Because the interest rate may change, the mortgagor's loan repayments may also change. Details of how and when the interest rate will change are included in the note.

- The interest rate is tied to the movement of an objective economic indicator called an *index*. Most indexes are tied to U.S. Treasury securities.

- Usually, the interest rate is the index rate plus a premium, called the *margin*. The margin represents the lender's cost of doing business. For example, the loan rate may be 2% higher than the U.S. Treasury bill rate.

A CLOSER LOOK   Lenders charge borrowers a certain percentage of the principal as interest for each year a debt is outstanding. The amount of interest due on any one payment date is calculated by computing the total yearly interest (based on unpaid balance) and dividing that figure by the number of payments made each year.

For example, assume the current outstanding balance of a loan is $70,000. The interest rate is 7.5% per year, and the monthly payment is $489.30. Based on these facts, the interest and principal due on the next payment would be computed as shown:

$70,000 loan balance × 0.075 annual interest rate = $5,250 annual interest

$5,250 annual interest ÷ 12 months = $437.50 monthly interest

$489.30 monthly payment – 437.50 monthly interest = $51.80 monthly principal

$70,000 loan balance – 51.80 monthly principal = $69,948.20

This process is followed with each payment over the term of the loan. The same calculations are made each month, starting with the declining new balance figure from the previous month.

- **Rate caps** limit the amount the interest rate may change. Most ARMs have two types of rate caps—periodic and aggregate. A periodic rate cap limits the amount the rate may increase at any one time. An aggregate rate cap limits the amount the rate may increase over the entire life of the loan.

- The mortgagor is protected from unaffordable individual payments by the payment cap. The payment cap sets a maximum amount for payments. With a cap, a rate increase could result in negative amortization—that is, an increase in the loan balance.

- The adjustment period establishes how often the rate may be changed. For instance, the adjustment period may be monthly, quarterly, or annually.

■ Lenders may offer a conversion option, which permits the mortgagor to convert from an adjustable-rate to a fixed-rate loan at certain intervals during the life of the mortgage. The option is subject to certain terms and conditions for the conversion.

Balloon Loan When the periodic payments are not enough to fully amortize the loan by the time the final payment is due, the final payment is larger than the others. This is called a **balloon payment**. It is a partially amortized loan because principal is still owed at the end of the term. It is frequently assumed that if payments are made promptly, the lender will extend the balloon payment for another limited term. The lender, however, is not legally obligated to grant this extension and can require payment in full when the note is due.

Growing-Equity Mortgage (GEM) A *growing-equity mortgage (GEM)* is also known as a *rapid-payoff mortgage*. The GEM uses a fixed interest rate, but payments of principal are increased according to an index or a schedule. Thus, the total payment increases, and the loan is paid off more quickly. A GEM is most frequently used when the borrower's income is expected to keep pace with the increasing loan payments.

Reverse-Annuity Mortgage (RAM) A *reverse-annuity mortgage (RAM)* is one in which regular monthly payments are made by the lender to the borrower. The payments are based on the equity the homeowner has invested in the property, given as security for the loan. This loan allows senior citizens on fixed incomes to realize the equity they have built up in their homes without having to sell. The borrower is charged a fixed interest rate, and the loan is eventually repaid from the sale of the property or from the estate upon the borrower's death.

LOAN PROGRAMS

Computerized Loan Origination (CLO) and Automated Underwriting

A computerized loan origination (CLO) system is an electronic network for handling loan applications through remote computer terminals linked to several lenders' computers. With a CLO system, a real estate broker or salesperson can call up a menu of mortgage lenders, interest rates, and loan terms and then help a buyer select a lender and apply for a loan right from the brokerage office.

The licensee may assist the applicant in answering the on-screen questions and in understanding the services offered. The broker in whose office the terminal is located may earn fees of up to one-half point of the loan amount. The borrower, not the mortgage broker or lender, must pay the fee. The fee amount may be financed, however. While multiple lenders may be represented on an office's CLO computer, consumers must be informed that other lenders are available. An applicant's ability to comparison shop for a loan may be enhanced by a CLO system; the range of options may not be limited.

On the lenders' side, new automated underwriting procedures can shorten loan approvals from weeks to minutes. Automated underwriting also tends to lower the cost of loan application and approval by reducing lenders' time spent on the approval process by as much as 60%. The Federal Home Loan Mortgage Corporation uses a system called Loan Prospector. Fannie Mae uses a system called Desktop Underwriter, which reduces approval time to minutes and is based on the borrower's credit report, a paycheck stub, and a drive-by appraisal of the property. Complex or difficult mortgages can be processed in less than 72 hours. Through automated underwriting, one of a borrower's biggest headaches in buying a home—waiting for loan approval—is eliminated. In addition, prospective buyers can strengthen their purchase offer by including proof of loan approval.

Loan-to-Value Ratios

Mortgage loans are generally classified based on their loan-to-value ratios, or LTVs. The LTV is the ratio of debt to value of the property. Value is the sale price or the appraisal value, whichever is less. The lower the ratio of debt to value, the higher the down payment by the borrower. For the lender, the higher down payment means a more secure loan, which minimizes the lender's risk.

Determining LTV   If a property has an appraised value of $100,000, secured by a $90,000 loan, the LTV is 90%:

$$\$90,000 \div \$100,000 = 90\%$$

Conventional Loans

Conventional loans are viewed as the most secure loans because their loan-to-value ratios are lowest. Usually, the ratio is 80% or less of the value of the property because the borrower makes a down payment of at least 20%.

The security for the loan is provided solely by the mortgage; the payment of the debt rests on the borrower's ability to pay. In making such a loan, the lender relies primarily on its appraisal of the security real estate. Information from credit reports that indicate the reliability of the prospective borrower is also important. No additional insurance or guarantee is necessary to protect the lender's interest.

Lenders can set criteria by which a borrower and the collateral are evaluated to qualify for a loan. However, in recent years, the secondary mortgage market has had a significant impact on the borrower qualifications, standards for the collateral, and documentation procedures followed by lenders.

Loans must meet strict criteria in order to be sold to the Federal National Mortgage Association and the Federal Home Loan Mortgage Corporation. Lenders can be flexible in their lending decisions, but they may not be able to sell unusual loans in the secondary market.

Private Mortgage Insurance

One way a borrower can obtain a mortgage loan with a lower down payment is under a **private mortgage insurance (PMI)** program. Because the loan-to-value (LTV) ratio is higher than for other conventional loans, the lender requires additional security to minimize its risk. The borrower purchases insurance from a private mortgage insurance company as additional security to insure the lender against borrower default. LTVs of up to 95% of the appraised value of the property are possible with mortgage insurance.

PMI protects a certain percentage of a loan, usually 25 to 30%, against borrower default. Normally, the borrower is charged a fee for the first year's premium at closing. The borrower also pays a monthly fee while the insurance is in force.

Other methods of payment are available, however. The premium may be financed, or the fee at closing may be waived in exchange for slightly higher monthly payments. When a borrower has limited funds for investment, these alternative methods of reducing closing costs are very important. Because only a portion of the loan is insured, once the loan is repaid to a certain level, the lender may agree to allow the borrower to terminate the coverage. Practices for termination vary from lender to lender.

FHA-Insured Loans

The **Federal Housing Administration (FHA)**, which operates under HUD, neither builds homes nor lends money. The common term FHA loan refers to a loan that is insured by the agency. These loans must be made by FHA-approved lending institutions. FHA insurance provides security to the lender in addition to the real estate. As with private mortgage insurance, the FHA insures lenders against loss from borrower default.

The most popular FHA program is Title II, Section 203(b), fixed interest-rate loans for 10 to 30 years on one- to four-family residences. Rates are competitive with other types of loans even though they are high-LTV loans. Certain technical requirements must be met before the FHA will insure the loans. These requirements include the following:

- The borrower is charged a percentage of the loan as a premium for the FHA insurance. The up-front premium is paid at closing by the borrower or some other party. It may also be financed along with the total loan amount. A monthly premium may also be charged. Insurance premiums vary for new loans, refinancing, and condominiums.

- FHA regulations set minimum standards for type and construction of buildings, quality of neighborhood, and credit requirements for borrowers.

If the purchase price exceeds the FHA-appraised value, the buyer may pay the difference in cash as part of the down payment. In addition, the FHA has set maximum loan amounts for various regions of the country.

The FHA has characterized California as a "high cost area." The current county-by-county mortgage limits are shown in Figure 11.1.

FIGURE 11.1: FHA High-Cost Area Mortgage Limits by County (January 2014)

County Name	1 Living Unit	2 Living Units	3 Living Units	4 Living Units
Alameda	$625,500	$800,775	$967,950	$1,202,925
Alpine	$463,450	$593,300	$717,150	$891,250
Amador	$332,350	$425,450	$514,300	$639,150
Butte	$293,250	$375,400	$453,750	$563,950
Calaveras	$373,750	$478,450	$578,350	$718,750
Colusa	$271,050	$347,000	$419,425	$521,250
Contra Costa	$625,500	$800,775	$967,950	$1,202,925
Del Norte	$271,050	$347,000	$419,425	$521,250
El Dorado	$474,950	$608,000	$734,950	$913,350
Fresno	$281,750	$360,700	$436,000	$541,800
Glenn	$271,050	$347,000	$419,425	$521,250
Humboldt	$327,750	$419,550	$507,150	$630,300
Imperial	$271,050	$347,000	$419,425	$521,250
Inyo	$369,150	$472,550	$571,250	$709,900

FIGURE 11.1:   FHA High-Cost Area Mortgage Limits by County (January 2014) (cont.)

County Name	1 Living Unit	2 Living Units	3 Living Units	4 Living Units
Kern	$271,050	$347,000	$419,425	$521,250
Kings	$271,050	$347,000	$419,425	$521,250
Lake	$271,050	$347,000	$419,425	$521,250
Lassen	$271,050	$347,000	$419,425	$521,250
Los Angeles	$625,500	$800,775	$967,950	$1,202,925
Madera	$271,050	$347,000	$419,425	$521,250
Marin	$625,500	$800,775	$967,950	$1,202,925
Mariposa	$322,000	$412,200	$498,250	$619,250
Mendocino	$373,750	$478,450	$578,350	$718,750
Merced	$271,050	$347,000	$419,425	$521,250
Modoc	$271,050	$347,000	$419,425	$521,250
Mono	$529,000	$677,200	$818,600	$1,017,300
Monterey	$483,000	$618,300	$747,400	$928,850
Napa	$592,250	$758,200	$916,450	$1,138,950
Nevada	$477,250	$610,950	$738,500	$917,800
Orange	$625,500	$800,775	$967,950	$1,202,925
Placer	$474,950	$608,000	$734,950	$913,350
Plumas	$336,950	$431,350	$521,400	$648,000
Riverside	$355,350	$454,900	$549,850	$683,350
Sacramento	$474,950	$608,000	$734,950	$913,350
San Benito	$625,500	$800,775	$967,950	$1,202,925
San Bernardino	$355,350	$454,900	$549,850	$683,350
San Diego	$546,250	$699,300	$845,300	$1,050,500
San Francisco	$625,500	$800,775	$967,950	$1,202,925
San Joaquin	$304,750	$390,100	$471,550	$586,050
San Luis Obispo	$561,200	$718,450	$868,400	$1,079,250
San Mateo	$625,500	$800,775	$967,950	$1,202,925
Santa Barbara	$625,500	$800,775	$967,950	$1,202,925
Santa Clara	$625,500	$800,775	$967,950	$1,202,925
Santa Cruz	$625,500	$800,775	$967,950	$1,202,925
Shasta	$273,700	$350,350	$423,500	$526,350
Sierra	$304,750	$390,100	$471,550	$586,050
Siskiyou	$271,050	$347,000	$419,425	$521,250
Solano	$400,200	$512,300	$619,300	$769,600
Sonoma	$520,950	$660,900	$806,150	$1,001,850
Stanislaus	$276,000	$353,300	$427,100	$530,750
Sutter	$271,050	$347,000	$419,425	$521,250
Tehama	$271,050	$347,000	$419,425	$521,250
Trinity	$271,050	$347,000	$419,425	$521,250
Tulare	$271,050	$347,000	$419,425	$521,250
Tuolumne	$331,200	$424,000	$521,500	$636,900
Ventura	$598,000	$765,550	$925,350	$1,150,000
Yolo	$474,950	$608,000	$734,950	$913,350
Yuba	$271,050	$347,000	$419,425	$521,250

Source: U.S. Department of Housing and Urban Development/Federal Housing Administration

Other types of FHA loans are available, including one-year adjustable-rate mortgages, home improvement and rehabilitation loans, and loans for the purchase of condominiums. The FHA sets specific standards for condominium complexes and the ratio of owner-occupants to renters. These standards must be met for a loan on a condominium unit to be financed through the FHA insurance program. In 2015, FHA requires a minimum down payment of 3.5% for borrowers with a credit score of 580 and a minimum down payment of 10% for borrowers with credits scores below 580.

A borrower may repay an FHA-insured loan on a one- to four-family residence without penalty. For loans made before August 2, 1985, the borrower must give the lender written notice of intention to exercise the prepayment privilege at least 30 days before prepayment. If the borrower fails to provide the required notice, the lender has the option of charging up to 30 days' interest. For loans initiated after August 2, 1985, no written notice of prepayment is required.

The assumption rules for FHA-insured loans vary, depending on the dates the loans were originated:

- FHA loans originated before December 1986 generally have no restrictions on their assumptions.

- For an FHA loan originated between December 1, 1986, and December 15, 1989, a creditworthiness review of the prospective assumer is required. If the original loan was for the purchase of a principal residence, this review is required during the first 12 months of the loan's existence. If the original loan was for the purchase of an investment property, the review is required during the first 24 months of the loan.

- For FHA loans originated on December 15, 1989, and later, no assumptions are permitted without complete buyer qualification.

Discount Points The lender of an FHA-insured loan may charge discount points in addition to a loan origination fee. The payment of points is a matter of negotiation between the seller and the buyer. However, if the seller pays more than 6% of the costs normally paid by the buyer (such as discount points, the loan origination fee, the mortgage insurance premium, buydown fees, prepaid items, and impound or escrow amounts), the lender will treat the payments as a reduction in sales price and recalculate the mortgage amount accordingly. Points are tax deductible to the buyer regardless of which party pays them.

VA-Guaranteed Loans

The **Department of Veterans Affairs (VA)** is authorized to guarantee loans to purchase or construct homes for eligible veterans and their spouses (including non-remarried spouses of veterans whose deaths were service related). The VA also guarantees loans to purchase manufactured housing (mobile homes) and plots on which to place them.

The VA assists veterans in financing the purchase of homes with little or no down payments at comparatively low interest rates. The VA issues rules and regulations that set forth the qualifications, limitations, and conditions under which a loan may be guaranteed.

Like the term *FHA loan*, *VA loan* is something of a misnomer. The VA does not normally lend money; it guarantees loans made by lending institutions approved by the agency. The term *VA loan* refers to a loan that is not made by the agency but is guaranteed by it. There is no VA limit on the amount of the loan a veteran can obtain; this is determined by the lender. The VA limits the amount of the loan it will guarantee.

Prepayment and Assumption   As with an FHA loan, the borrower under a VA loan can prepay the debt at any time without penalty.

VA loans made before March 1, 1988, are freely assumable, although an assumption processing fee of ½ percent of the loan balance will be charged. For loans made on or after March 1, 1988, the VA must approve the buyer and assumption agreement. The original borrower remains personally liable for the repayment of the loan unless the VA approves a release of liability. The release of liability will be issued only if the buyer assumes all of the veteran's liabilities on the loan and the VA or the lender approves both the buyer and the assumption agreement.

Cal-Vet

The popular **Cal-Vet** program, administered by the California Department of Veterans Affairs, provides low-cost, low-interest loans to qualified veterans for up to $521,250 for single-family homes ($175,000 for housing in mobile home parks and $625,000 for farm properties). Cal-Vet is funded by California general obligation bonds and veterans' revenue bonds; it is not a tax-financed program. Interest rates for these loans will fluctuate based on bond sales that are authorized by the state of California and typically through the voters of the state. Currently, Cal-Vet also provides for home and loan protection plans. Cal-Vet provides comprehensive protection for its borrowers. Cal-Vet loan holders have full guaranteed replacement cost coverage for their homes. Loan holders are protected against floods and earthquake damage with a Cal-Vet loan. Cal-Vet currently requires a $500 deductible on flood claims and $500 or 5% of coverable loss (whichever is greater) on earthquake and mudslide claims. Most loans also include fire and hazard insurance coverage.

Farm Service Agency

The **Farm Service Agency (FSA)**, formerly the *Federal Agricultural Mortgage Corporation (FAMC, or Farmer Mac)*, is a federal agency of the Department of Agriculture. The FSA offers programs to help families purchase or operate family farms. Through the *Rural Housing and Community Development Service*, it also provides loans to help families purchase or improve single-family homes in rural areas (generally areas with populations of fewer than 10,000).

FSA loan programs fall into two categories: (1) guaranteed loans made and serviced by private lenders and guaranteed for a specific percentage by the FSA and (2) loans made directly by the FSA.

CREATIVE FINANCING TECHNIQUES

Because borrowers often have different needs, a variety of specialized financing techniques have been created. Other techniques apply to various types of collateral. The following are some of the loans that do not fit into the categories previously discussed.

Purchase-Money Mortgages

A *purchase-money mortgage* is a note and mortgage created at the time of purchase. Its purpose is to make the sale possible. The term is used in two ways. First, it may refer to any security instrument that originates at the time of sale. More often, it refers to the instrument given by the purchaser to a seller who takes back a note for part or all of the purchase price. The mortgage may be a first or a junior lien, depending on whether prior mortgage liens exist.

Package Loans

A *package loan* includes not only the real estate but also all personal property and appliances installed on the premises. In recent years, this kind of loan has been used extensively to finance furnished condominium units. Package loans usually include furniture, drapes, and carpets, and the kitchen range, refrigerator, dishwasher, garbage disposal, washer, dryer, food freezer, and other appliances as part of the sales price of the home.

Blanket Loans

A *blanket loan* covers more than one parcel or lot. It is usually used to finance subdivision developments. However, it can finance the purchase of improved properties, or it can consolidate loans. A blanket loan usually includes a provision known as a *partial release clause*. This clause permits the borrower to obtain the release of any one lot or parcel from the lien by repaying a certain amount of the loan. The lender issues a partial release for each parcel released from the mortgage lien. The release form includes a provision that the lien will continue to cover all other unreleased lots.

Wraparound Loans

A **wraparound loan** enables a borrower with an existing mortgage or deed of trust loan to obtain additional financing from a second lender without paying off the first loan. The second lender gives the borrower a new, increased loan at a higher interest rate and assumes payment of the existing loan. The total amount of the new loan includes the existing loan as well as the additional funds needed by the borrower. The borrower makes payments to the new lender on the larger loan. The new lender makes payments on the original loan out of the borrower's payments.

A wraparound mortgage can be used to refinance real property or to finance the purchase of real property when an existing mortgage cannot be prepaid. The buyer executes a wraparound mortgage to the seller, who collects payments on the new loan and continues to make payments on the old loan. The wraparound mortgage also can finance the sale of real estate when the buyer wishes to invest a minimum amount of initial cash. A wraparound loan is possible only if the original loan permits it. For instance, an acceleration and alienation or a due-on-sale clause in the original loan documents may prevent a sale under a wraparound loan.

How Does a Wraparound Loan Work? Let's look at the following examples:

EXAMPLE The sale of a $100,000 property with a $20,000 cash down payment by the buyer and an assumable senior loan balance of $60,000, creating a $20,000 shortage, can be financed by the seller who would carry back a new wraparound loan for $80,000. This type of wraparound loan is called a "purchase-money wraparound loan." This would require the borrower to make the payment on the $80,000, while the seller would retain the responsibility for making the required payment on the undisturbed existing $60,000 loan.

This form of financing can raise the effective yield to its holder because interest may be charged on the wrap that is more than the interest being paid on the underlying loan.

EXAMPLE If the $60,000 carries an interest rate of 10% and the wrap can be drawn for 12%, the wrap owner will be earning a full 12% on the $20,000 equity plus a 2% override on the $60,000, for an impressive 18% effective yield:

$$\$60,000 \times 0.02 = \$1,200; \$20,000 \times 0.12 = \$2,400;$$

$$\$1,200 + \$2,400 = \$3,600 \div \$20,000 = 0.18$$

Thus, a wraparound lender could benefit from a profit on an underlying lender's investment.

The use of the wraparound has diminished dramatically because most existing real estate loans cannot be easily assumed. Nevertheless, some individuals still use this type of financing to sell their properties. When it benefits the lender, they will use the wraparound to enhance their yields. In recent years, some lenders have offered their borrowers an opportunity to secure additional funds on the equities in their properties at less-than-market interest rates by arranging to "wrap" the existing loans at a one-point or two-point override. These loans are commonly known in many areas as "blends."

Open-End Loans

An open-end loan secures a note executed by the borrower to the lender. It also secures any future advances of funds made by the lender to the borrower. The interest rate on the initial amount borrowed is fixed, but interest on future advances may be charged at the market rate in effect. An open-end loan is often a less costly alternative to a home improvement loan. It allows the borrower to "open" the mortgage or deed of trust to increase the debt to its original amount, or the amount stated in the note, after the debt has been reduced by payments over a period of time. The mortgage usually states the maximum amount that can be secured, the terms and conditions under which the loan can be opened, and provisions for repayment.

Construction Loans

A *construction loan* is made to finance the construction of improvements on real estate such as homes, apartments, and office buildings. The lender commits to the full amount of the loan but disburses the funds in payments during construction. These payments are also known as *draws*. Draws are made to the general contractor or the owner for that part of the construction work that has been completed since the previous payment. Before each payment, the lender inspects the work. The general contractor must provide the lender with adequate waivers that release all mechanics' lien rights for the work covered by the payment.

This kind of loan generally bears a higher-than-market interest rate because of the risks involved for the lender. These include the inadequate release of mechanics' liens, delays in construction, or the financial failure of the contractor or subcontractors.

Construction loans are generally short-term or interim financing. The borrower pays interest only on the monies that have actually been disbursed. The borrower is expected to arrange for a permanent loan, also known as an *end loan* or *take-out loan*, that will repay or "take out" the construction financing lender when the work is completed. Some lenders now offer construction-to-permanent loans that become fixed mortgages upon completion. Participation financing is when a lender demands an equity position in the project as a requirement for the loan. Mortgage brokers can preapprove borrowers for a take-out loan and work in conjunction with a bank to secure a construction loan.

Sale-and-Leaseback

Sale-and-leaseback arrangements are generally used to finance large commercial or industrial properties. The land and building, usually used by the seller for business purposes, are sold to an investor. The real estate is then leased back by the investor to the seller, who continues to conduct business on the property as a tenant. The buyer becomes the lessor, and the original owner becomes the lessee. This enables a business to free money tied up in real estate to be used as working capital.

Sale-and-leasebacks involve complicated legal procedures, and their success is usually related to the effects the transaction has on the firm's tax situation. Legal and tax experts should always be involved in this type of transaction.

Buydowns

A buydown is a way to temporarily lower the initial interest rate on a mortgage or deed of trust loan. Perhaps a homebuilder wishes to stimulate sales by offering a lower-than-mortgage rate. A lump sum is paid in cash to the lender at the closing. The payment offsets (and so reduces) the interest rate and monthly payments during the mortgage's first few years. Typical buydown arrangements reduce the interest rate by 1–3% over the first one to three years of the loan term. After that, the rate rises. The assumption is that the borrower's income will also increase and that the borrower will be more able to absorb the increased monthly payments.

Home Equity Loans

Using the **equity** buildup in a home to finance purchases is an alternative to refinancing. Home equity loans are a source of funds for homeowners to use for a variety of financial needs, many of which have wide-ranging economic impact beyond the residence involved:

- To finance the purchase of expensive items

- To consolidate existing installment loans on credit card debt

- To pay medical, education, home improvement, or other expenses

The original mortgage loan remains in place; the home equity loan is junior to the original lien. If the homeowner refinances, the original mortgage loan is paid off and replaced by a new loan. (This is an alternative way to borrow the equity; it's not really a home equity loan.)

A home equity loan can be taken out as a fixed loan amount or as an equity line of credit. With the home equity line of credit, the lender extends a line of credit that the borrower can use at will. The borrower receives the money by a check, deposits made in a checking or savings account, or a book of drafts the borrower can use up to the credit limit.

The homeowner must consider a number of factors before deciding on a home equity loan. The costs involved in obtaining a new mortgage loan or a home equity loan, current interest rates, total monthly payments, and income tax consequences are all important issues to be examined.

FINANCING LEGISLATION

The federal government regulates the lending practices of mortgage lenders through the Truth in Lending Act, the Equal Credit Opportunity Act, the Community Reinvestment Act of 1977, and the Real Estate Settlement Procedures Act. This type of regulation of the marketplace represents the government's efforts to ensure free and fair behavior by participants.

Truth in Lending Act and Regulation Z

Regulation Z, promulgated pursuant to the Truth in Lending Act, requires credit institutions to inform borrowers of the true cost of obtaining credit. Its purpose is to permit borrowers to compare the costs of various lenders and avoid the uninformed use of credit.

Regulation Z applies when credit is extended to individuals for personal, family, or household uses. Regardless of the amount, recent amendments to Regulation Z not only apply to transactions secured by residences but to credit cards as well. The regulations do not apply to business or commercial loans or to agricultural loans, credit extended to other than natural persons (including credit to governmental agencies or instrumentalities), public utility credit, home fuel budget plans not subject to finance charges, and certain student loan programs.

Under Regulation Z, a consumer must be fully informed of all finance charges and the true interest rate before a transaction is completed. The finance charge disclosure must include any loan fees, finder's fees, service charges, and points, as well as interest. In the case of a mortgage loan made to finance the purchase of a dwelling, the lender must compute and disclose the annual percentage rate (APR). However, the lender does not have to indicate the total interest payable during the term of the loan. Also, the lender does not have to include actual costs such as title fees, legal fees, appraisal fees, credit reports, survey fees, and closing expenses as part of the finance charge.

Creditor A **creditor**, for purposes of Regulation Z, is any person who extends consumer credit more than 25 times each year or more than 5 times each year if the transactions involve dwellings as security. The credit must be subject to a finance charge or payable in more than four installments by written agreement.

Three-Day Right of Rescission In the case of most consumer credit transactions covered by Regulation Z, the borrower has three days in which to rescind the transaction by merely notifying the lender. The three-day "right of rescission" is applicable to all owner-occupied dwellings that are refinanced. It should be further noted that the three-day right of rescission rule does not apply to purchase money loans.

Advertising Regulation Z provides strict regulation of real estate advertisements that include mortgage financing terms. General phrases like "liberal terms available" may be used, but details that are given must comply with the act. The annual percentage rate (APR)—which is calculated based on all charges rather than the interest rate alone—must be stated.

Advertisements for buydowns or mortgages with reduced interest rates must show both the limited term to which the interest rate applies and the annual percentage rate. An advertisement for a variable-rate mortgage must include

- the number and timing of payments,

- the amount of the largest and smallest payments, and

- a statement of the fact that the actual payments will vary between these two extremes.

Specific credit terms, such as down payment, monthly payment, dollar amount of the finance charge, or term of the loan, may not be advertised unless the advertisement includes the following information:

- Cash price

- Required down payment

- Number, amounts, and due dates of all payments

- Annual percentage rate

- Total of all payments to be made over the term of the mortgage (unless the advertised credit refers to a first mortgage or deed of trust to finance the acquisition of a dwelling)

Amendments to Regulation Z—Advertising Effective October 1, 2009, the Truth in Lending Act was amended to prohibit the following seven deceptive or misleading practices in advertisements for closed-end mortgage loans:

- Advertisements that state "fixed" rates or payments for loans whose rates or payments can vary without adequately disclosing that the interest rate or payment amounts are "fixed" only for a limited period of time rather than for the full term of the loan

- Advertisements that compare an actual or hypothetical rate or payment obligation to the rates or payments that would apply if the consumer obtains the advertised product unless the advertisement states the rates or payments that will apply over the full term of the loan

- Advertisements that characterize the products offered as "government loan programs," "government-supported loans," or otherwise endorsed or sponsored by a federal or state government entity even though the advertised products are not government supported or sponsored loans

- Advertisements, such as solicitation letters that display the name of the consumer's current mortgage lender, unless the advertisement also prominently discloses that the advertisement is from a mortgage lender affiliated with the consumer's current lender

- Advertisements that make claims of debt elimination if the product advertised would merely replace one debt obligation with another

- Advertisements that create a false impression that the mortgage broker or lender is a "counselor" for the consumer

- Foreign-language advertisements in which certain information, such as a low introductory "teaser" rate, is provided in a foreign language, while required disclosures are provided only in English

Penalties Regulation Z provides penalties for noncompliance. The penalty for violation of an administrative order enforcing Regulation Z is $10,000 for each day the violation continues. A fine of up to $10,000 may be imposed for engaging in an unfair or a deceptive practice. In addition, a creditor may be liable to a consumer for twice the amount of the finance charge, for a minimum of $100 and a maximum of $1,000, plus court costs, attorney's fees, and any actual damages. Willful violation is a misdemeanor punishable by a fine of up to $5,000, one year's imprisonment, or both.

Equal Credit Opportunity Act

The federal Equal Credit Opportunity Act (ECOA), mentioned in Unit 10, prohibits lenders and others who grant or arrange credit to consumers from discriminating against credit applicants on the basis of any of the following factors:

- Race

- Color

- Religion

- National origin

- Sex

- Marital status

- Age (provided the applicant is of legal age)

- Dependence on public assistance

In addition, lenders and other creditors must inform all rejected credit applicants of the principal reasons for the denial or termination of credit. The notice must be provided in writing, within 30 days. The federal Equal Credit Opportunity Act also provides that a borrower is entitled to a copy of the appraisal report if the borrower paid for the appraisal.

Community Reinvestment Act

"Community reinvestment" refers to the responsibility of financial institutions to help meet their communities' needs for low-income and moderate-income housing. In 1977, Congress passed the Community Reinvestment Act of 1977 (CRA). Under the CRA, financial institutions are expected to meet the deposit and credit needs of their communities, participate and invest in local community development and rehabilitation projects, and participate in loan programs for housing, small businesses, and small farms.

The law requires any federally supervised financial institution to prepare a statement containing

- a *definition* of the geographical boundaries of its community;

- an *identification* of the types of community reinvestment credit offered (such as residential housing, housing rehabilitation, small business, and commercial and consumer loans); and

- *comments* from the public about the institution's performance in meeting its community's needs.

Financial institutions are periodically reviewed by one of four federal financial supervisory agencies: the Comptroller of the Currency, the Federal Reserve's Board of Governors, the Federal Deposit Insurance Corporation, and the Office of Thrift Supervision. The institutions must post a public notice that their community reinvestment activities are subject to federal review, and they must make the reviews public.

Real Estate Settlement Procedures Act

The federal **Real Estate Settlement Procedures Act (RESPA)** applies to any residential real estate transaction involving a new first mortgage loan. RESPA is designed to ensure that buyer and seller are both fully informed of all settlement costs.

New License Requirements in California for 2010

On January 1, 2010, the California Bureau of Real Estate (CalBRE) announced new requirements for those licensees who conduct mortgage loan activities.

Licensees who conduct activities as residential mortgage loan originators must now have an endorsement on their license. They must also register with the Nationwide Mortgage Licensing System and Registry (NMLS&R), which contains a single license record for each mortgage loan lender, broker, branch, and mortgage loan originator (MLO). The individual licensee must also satisfy the federal requirements for MLO licensure, which include new qualification assessments, federal and state examinations, and background checks, with no exceptions to or exemptions from these requirements for existing licensees. The law required that by January 1, 2011, a licensee engaged in mortgage loan activities must be issued an MLO endorsement, which will also carry a nationwide identification number, known as a "unique identifier," which will be assigned by the NMLS&R.

Why the Requirement in 2010?   Senate Bill 36 (SB 36), which was signed into law in October 2009, was enacted to identify real estate licensees conducting mortgage activities and to bring California into compliance with the Federal Secure and Fair Enforcement Mortgage License Act (SAFE Act) of the Housing and Economic Recovery Act of 2008. The SAFE Act requires all states to adhere to minimum residential mortgage loan originator license requirements. The Conference of State Bank Supervisors (CSBS) and the American Association of Residential Mortgage Regulators (AARMR) created, and will maintain, the National Mortgage Licensing System and Registry (NMLS&R) as the basis for state licensing.

SB 36 requires all CalBRE real estate licensees who conduct residential MLO activities to qualify for the MLO endorsement and to take and pass both the national and the California-specific component of the SAFE Act written examination and to complete 20 hours of prelicensing education. Licensees engaged in MLO activities will also be required to submit new sets of fingerprints and to authorize the NMLS&R to obtain a credit report from a consumer reporting agency, either as part of an online application process or within the first term of the license endorsement.

TAXATION

In order to provide services to citizens, governments take on many roles: welfare, police and fire protection, community planning and environmental concerns, employer to an increasingly large percentage of the population, utility provider in some cases, ombudsman, and others. To support this vast array of duties, government generates revenue from various sources.

Types of Taxes

Income, excise, property taxes, and bonds and assessments are all forms of taxation. Taxes are classified by economists into three distinct categories:

1. **Progressive tax.** In a *progressive tax system*, the tax rate increases in direct relation to income. Federal income tax, for example, is paid on the basis of taxable income. As income rises from one tax bracket to another, the percentage of taxation increases accordingly.

2. **Proportional tax.** In a *proportional tax system*, the tax rate remains the same regardless of the value of the item or amount of income. From time to time, proposals are made by politicians to change the U.S. income tax system from a progressive to a proportional

system, or "flat tax." Sales tax is an example of how a proportional tax system works. Whether one purchases a $50 radio or a $5,000 big-screen television, the percentage sales tax levied on the item remains the same. In an income tax context, the result is identical: a person who earns $50,000 in one year would pay the same tax rate as a person who earned $50 million in one year. Of course, the dollar amounts paid by each person would be significantly different.

3. **Regressive tax.** A *regressive tax system* is one in which the tax rate declines as the value of the taxable item or income increases. To some extent, real property under California's famous Proposition 13 (discussed in the following section) falls in this category because value for assessment purposes does not necessarily increase at the same rate as the market, which reduces the real tax obligation. Income tax might be considered regressive in practice because those with more income often have the ability to shelter more of it. Social Security and self-employment taxes are prime examples of regressive taxes because they do not apply to income above a certain level.

User Fees and Other Charges

Governments derive some income by charging fees for services. In the area of real estate, these include documentary tax stamps, recording charges, map filing and processing fees, building permit fees, annual levies based upon revenues generated by properties, license fees, and property registration for rent control.

Since the passage of Proposition 13 in 1978, more and more local jurisdictions (cities and counties and special districts) have resorted to parcel taxes. This now amounts to a significant proportion of the property tax bill (although parcel taxes are normally user taxes and are not *ad valorem* property taxes).

Parking fines, legal judgments, overdue book fines, and late charges of any nature are also revenue sources. The federal government derives substantial revenue from seigniorage, the difference between minting cost and the face value of the coin. Federal, state, and local agencies also generate revenue from various pamphlets, publications, and internet services that are sold to the public.

Ad Valorem Property Taxation

Ad valorem taxation means that tax levies are imposed by government in proportion to the value of the asset taxed (proportional tax). In the case of real property, tax assessors determine property value to establish the property tax base, which is then used to determine the tax rate to be imposed upon property owners in the county where the property is located.

Proposition 13

In California, **Proposition 13** (sometimes referred to as the "taxpayers' revolt initiative") passed in 1978. Since then, Proposition 13 has limited the ability of governing bodies to increase the tax base by increased valuation except when the property is sold. Despite cuts in services and facilities (such as education, health care, and public assistance) that resulted from its passage, Proposition 13 retained popularity primarily by delivering on its promise of limiting the tax rate.

Inequalities in Real Property Taxation Ad valorem tax assessments are based upon the tax collector's secured rolls (real property) and the unsecured roll (personal property). The owner of real property acquired prior to Proposition 13 has a definite advantage over persons who have recently purchased property in California. As long as property remains in the same hands, taxation is limited to a 2% annual increase in valuation without regard to the percentage increase in market value of the property. This produces considerable inequality of assessment between new and long-time owners.

Reassessment Procedure Any purchaser of property is assessed for the actual market price. Upon closing of the sale, the details of the transfer are made available to the assessor's office from the transfer statement provided by the purchaser. The property is then reassessed, and a supplemental tax bill is issued covering the period from the closing date until the next taxing period in order to avoid escaped revenues on the lower base. This reassessment also occurs when improvements are added between taxation periods and as a result of building permits.

Effect on Tax Structure To some extent, Proposition 13 means that California property tax is not strictly an ad valorem tax. To further complicate this issue, homeowners' and senior citizens' exemptions are available to certain taxpayers and not to the population as a whole. An appeals process is available to challenge assessors' valuations, but few citizens avail themselves of the opportunity because they don't understand the process or do not expect to benefit from it.

Reallocation of Resources

Some parties at both ends of the taxation spectrum provide minimal sources of tax revenue. These are individuals at the poverty level and the very rich who have the ability to shelter large amounts of income. This places a larger proportion of the tax burden on the large middle class to provide the revenues required to operate government at all levels, effectively subsidizing the benefits enjoyed by non-taxpayers at both ends. The net result is a reallocation of resources in directions determined by government policy.

Poverty Level   Income is redistributed to individuals who fall below the federally mandated poverty level group by the government through various welfare and public assistance programs, which are funded by taxes. Current "welfare reform" legislation at both the state and federal levels is designed to remove people from welfare dependence through job training programs and assistance.

The 2014 federal **poverty guidelines** are listed in Figure 11.2.

FIGURE 11.2:   2014 Federal Poverty Guidelines Table

Size of Family Unit	48 Contiguous States and D.C.	Alaska	Hawaii
1	$11,670	$14,580	$13,420
2	$15,730	$19,660	$18,090
3	$19,790	$24,740	$22,760
4	$23,850	$29,820	$27,430
5	$27,910	$34,900	$32,100
6	$31,970	$39,980	$36,770
7	$36,030	$45,060	$41,440
8	$40,090	$50,140	$46,110
For each additional person, add	$4,060	$5,080	$4,670

Source: U.S. Department of Health and Human Services

Working Poor   Between those dependent on government assistance for their day-to-day living and the financially self-sufficient middle class are those employed individuals who, while earning incomes above the federally mandated poverty levels, are nonetheless compelled to seek some assistance in order to survive.

Middle Class Proportionally higher taxes mean that this group has less disposable income available to generate savings and provide investment dollars for increasing capital. The term *middle class* is used broadly and popularly includes both social and economic characteristics. (Hard work and sound values, for instance, are the positive characteristics ascribed to the middle class. There are negative ones as well.) It may, however, be generally defined as the lower 60% of the population living above poverty level.

The productive segment of the economy, particularly the middle class, shifts a sizable segment of its income to government functions and to those who need assistance. While this is generally considered a socially beneficial purpose, it contributes to the problem of housing affordability for the middle class, where many households are unable to save enough for a down payment.

Upper Class Despite taxes, this group—generally considered those in the upper 20% of the U.S. income range—retains the highest degree of disposable personal income, which in turn generates faster percentage increases in personal net worth and future earning capacity.

Federal Tax Laws

In the past, and still today, investments in real estate have offered favorable taxation treatments that encourage ownership in real estate. In this day and age, income taxes play an important role in real estate. An owner's decisions, from buying or selling personal residences to decisions involving a variety of real estate investment properties, will determine the actions to be taken by many individuals as well as the tax implications imposed from the sale or purchase of real estate.

Historic Perspective The *Economic Tax Recovery Act of 1981* provided for the accelerated cost recovery system. This allowed a 15-year depreciation for real estate in order to stimulate real estate development. In 1984, the depreciation period was increased to 18 years, and a year later, in 1985, the depreciation period was further increased to 19 years. Under the *Tax Reform Act of 1986*, the depreciation period was established at 27½ years for residential property and 31½ years for nonresidential property. As a result of these changes, the extension of the depreciation periods resulted in real estate investors taking longer to recover their investments. To further add insult to injury, the *Revenue Reconciliation Act of 1993* further increased nonresidential property depreciation to 39 years. Because of the *Revenue*

Reconciliation Act of 1993, capital gains were taxed at 28% maximum tax rate if the capital assets were held more than one year, which affected many sellers of real estate prior to 1997.

The 1997 Tax Act reduced the top tax rate on capital gains of individuals and introduced new holding periods for real estate. After July 28, 1997, two different types of capital gains for noncorporate taxpayers were created:

- Short-term gains (on assets held for a year or less), which were treated as ordinary income rates

- Long-term capital gains (from the sale of assets held more than 12 months), which were treated at a maximum rate of 20% (10% for taxpayers in the 15% tax bracket)

The 1997 Tax Act did more than just modify the holding periods for both short-term and long-term capital gains. The act also increased the exclusion for gains on the sale of a personal principal residence. Prior to 1997, an individual could only exclude up to $125,000 of capital gains on the sale of a principal residence once per lifetime and only if age 55 or older.

What Is Considered a Personal Residence? A personal or principal residence is generally understood to be the taxpayer's primary personal residence, the dwelling that the taxpayer occupies most of the time. A taxpayer may have only one principal residence at a time, and it may be a

- single-family residence,

- mobile home,

- houseboat,

- motor home,

- condominium, or

- single unit within a multiple-unit dwelling.

The most significant change to occur in the tax code relative to the sale of real estate occurred with the 1997 Tax Act allowing a seller of any age (18 years or older) who has owned and used the home as a principal residence for at least two of the five years before the sale to exclude from income up to $250,000 of gain ($500,000 for joint filers). In general, the exclusion can be used only once every two years. More specifically, the exclusion does not apply to a home sale if, within the two-year period ending on the sale date, another home was sold by the same taxpayer to which the exclusion was applied.

Married couples filing jointly in the year of the sale may exclude up to $500,000 of the home-sale gain if either spouse owned the home for at least two of the five years before the sale. Both spouses must have used the home as their principal residence for at least five years before the sale. It should be noted that one spouse's inability to use the exclusion because of the once-every-two-year rule will not disqualify the other spouse from claiming the exclusion. However, the other spouse's exclusion cannot exceed $250,000. Further, the two-year occupancy need not be continuous. For example, a person could have occupied the property as a principal residence for six months and then rented it for a year but later moved back for an 18-month occupancy period. If the total occupancy is 24 months during the five-year period, the occupancy requirement is deemed to have been met.

California has adopted the federal U.S. universal exclusion of $250,000/ $500,000. If a sale gain meets the federal criteria for exclusion, it is also excluded from California income taxation.

The American Recovery and Reinvestment Act of 2009

To combat the Great Recession, the **American Recovery and Reinvestment Act of 2009**, commonly referred as the Economic Stimulus Program, was enacted by Congress in February 2009 at the urging of President Barack Obama. The American Recovery Reinvestment Act is intended to provide an economic stimulus boost to the U.S. economy. The stimulus, roughly worth $787 billion includes federal tax cuts; expansion of unemployment benefits; educational, health care, and infrastructure spending; and money for the energy sector.

Specifically, the bill provided a $780 billion package, with roughly 35% of the package devoted to tax cuts (mostly during 2009), and the remainder of the spending occurred in 2009 and 2010. Relative to real estate investments, the bill included provisions for a homebuyer tax credit; FHA, Fannie Mae, and Freddie Mac loan limits; neighborhood stabilization; commercial real estate; rural housing service; low-income housing grants; tax-exempt housing bonds; energy efficient housing and tax credits and grants; transportation investments; and broadband development.

Post Recession Era

Many changes occurred in 2014, including the expiration of some laws and the addition of new ones in an attempt to spur further economic growth. The most widely controversial legislation is the Patient Protection and Affordable Care Act (PPACA), often called ObamaCare. The main aspect of the law that will affect taxpayers is the mandate requiring individuals to purchase health insurance or receive a penalty. Under the Affordable Care Act, individuals must carry the qualified minimum coverage or incur a penalty that can amount to either $95 per adult plus $47.50 per dependent per household or 1% of the total household income, whichever is greater. The penalty's cap is the annual cost of a bronze-rated insurance plan for each family. Penalties are collected when individuals file taxes.

A deduction that affects many homeowners was eliminated in 2015. Since 2010, homeowners who pay private mortgage insurance (PMI) premiums have been able to deduct their premiums along with the mortgage interest homeowners pay on their homes. As of January 1, 2015, homeowners who put down less than 20% during the home purchase process and are required to carry mortgage insurance are not able to deduct their premiums. However, mortgage interest and property taxes will still remain as deductible expenses for homeowners.

Finally, another exemption that is also affecting homeowners is the primary residence cancellation of debt exclusion. In recent years, homeowners who had mortgage debt forgiven by a lender by way of a short sale have been exempted from paying tax on the forgiven debt. The Home Foreclosure Act, passed by Congress in 2007, was intended to improve liquidity and stabilization in the housing market but was not extended through 2014. Distressed homeowners now must include forgiven debt as income in the year the debt was forgiven. This will have an economic impact on the number of distressed properties that change hands nationwide and will dramatically increase the tax liability of homeowners who have all or a portion of their debt forgiven.

THE NEXT STEP   In Unit 12, we will expand on our basic discussion of finance and taxation and look at the economics of real estate investment.

SUMMARY

- The purpose of the **Federal Reserve System** is to maintain *sound credit conditions*, help *counteract inflationary and deflationary trends*, and create a *favorable economic climate*. It accomplishes this goal by regulating the flow of money and interest rates in the economy indirectly through member banks by controlling their *reserve requirements* and the *discount rate*.

- The **primary mortgage market** consists of lenders that *originate mortgage loans* as a means of generating profit. Some lenders in the primary mortgage market include thrifts, savings associations, and commercial banks; insurance companies; credit unions; pension funds; endowment funds; investment groups; and mortgage banking companies.

- The **secondary mortgage market** is where loans are *bought and sold by investors* after they have been funded. Participants in the secondary market include warehousing agencies, Fannie Mae, Ginnie Mae, and Freddie Mac.

- A variety of **mortgage loan structures** are available to borrowers. These include straight loans, amortized loans, adjustable-rate loans, balloon loans, growing-equity mortgages, and reverse-annuity mortgages.

- Mortgage loans are usually classified based on their **loan-to-value ratio (LTV)**, the *ratio of debt to the property's value*.

- **Conventional loans** are considered the most secure because they have the lowest LTV ratios. Other types of loans are **FHA-insured** and **VA-guaranteed**, both of which have specific qualification requirements.

- Because borrowers often have different needs, various **specialized finance techniques** are available (e.g., purchase-money mortgages, package loans, blanket loans, and wraparound loans). Open-end loans, construction loans, sale-and-leaseback loans, buydowns, and home equity loans are other popular alternatives.

- The federal government **regulates** the practices of mortgage lenders through the *Truth in Lending Act (Regulation Z)*, the *Equal Credit*

Opportunity Act, the *Community Reinvestment Act of 1977,* and the *Real Estate Settlement Procedures Act.*

■ In order to provide services to citizens, governments take on many roles: welfare, police and fire protection, community planning, and environmental protection, among others. To support this array of duties, government generates income through **taxation**, fees, and penalties.

■ Individuals at both ends of the income spectrum tend to provide minimal tax revenues; a larger proportion of the tax burden is placed on the **middle class**. Reallocation of income and resources is a result of government policy-making decisions.

■ The American Recovery and Reinvestment Act was passed in 2009 to create jobs and provide support to low-income and vulnerable households.

REVIEW QUESTIONS

1. What is the difference between the discount rate and the prime rate?

2. What are the maximum FHA loan limits in your area, and how do they differ from the surrounding counties?

3. Taxes are placed into three main distinctive categories. What are they? How do they differ from one another?

4. Which of the changes to the tax code in recent history have been the greatest stimulant on real estate development, and why?

5. Discuss the overall economic benefits of the American Recovery and Reinvestment Act and how you believe you/your community has benefitted.

UNIT QUIZ

1. All of the following would likely result from the Fed's decreasing its reserve requirements *EXCEPT*
   a. increased lending activity.
   b. increased circulation of money in the economy.
   c. decreased saving.
   d. decreased interest rates.

2. The prime rate is
   a. the rate lenders charge for a mortgage loan.
   b. a long-term interest rate charged to banks by the Fed.
   c. the short-term interest rate charged to a bank's most creditworthy customers.
   d. the rate paid by banks on the average passbook savings account.

3. All of the following are included in a lender's servicing of a loan *EXCEPT*
   a. bookkeeping.
   b. credit approval.
   c. processing payments.
   d. pursuing delinquent payments.

4. All of the following are lenders in the primary mortgage market *EXCEPT*
   a. pension funds.
   b. insurance companies.
   c. mortgage banking companies.
   d. mortgage brokers.

5. A mortgage loan in which the borrower makes periodic interest payments, followed by the payment of principal in full at the end of the loan term, is what kind of mortgage?
   a. Straight
   b. Amortized
   c. Balloon
   d. Growing-equity

6. In an adjustable-rate mortgage, a limit on the amount the interest rate may increase at any one time is called
   a. a payment cap.
   b. a periodic rate cap.
   c. an adjustment period.
   d. an aggregate periodic cap.

7. A property has a sales price of $280,000 and is appraised at $250,000. The buyer has obtained a loan for $210,000. What is the LTV?
   a. 72%
   b. 77%
   c. 84%
   d. 86%

8. Funds for Federal Housing Administration loans are usually provided by
   a. the Federal Housing Administration.
   b. the Federal Reserve.
   c. mortgage lenders.
   d. the seller.

9. A loan secures a note executed by a borrower to the lender. The loan also secures any future advances of funds made by the lender to the borrower. The interest rate on the original loan amount is fixed, but the future advances will be made at the market rate then in effect. This is what type of loan?
   a. Buydown
   b. Wraparound
   c. Package
   d. Open-end

10. Which statement correctly describes a proportional tax system?
    a. The tax rate increases in proportion to income.
    b. The tax rate declines proportionate to the increase in value of the taxable item or income.
    c. The tax rate remains the same regardless of the value of the item or the amount of income.
    d. It is the opposite of a so-called flat tax.

THE ECONOMICS OF REAL ESTATE INVESTMENT

KEY TERMS

appreciation
boot
cash flow
cost recovery
deduction
depreciation
exchanges
general partnership
inflation
intrinsic value

investment
Internal Revenue
   Service (IRS)
leverage
limited partnership
liquidity
pyramiding
real estate investment
   syndicate

real estate investment
   trust (REIT)
real estate mortgage
   investment conduit
   (REMIC)
tax credits
tax-deferred
taxpayer

LEARNING OBJECTIVES

■ Explain the reasons why real estate may—or may not—be a good investment for a particular investor

■ Understand the concepts of appreciation, income, leverage, equity, pyramiding, and depreciation

■ Identify the various forms of investment ventures: syndicates, REITs, and REMICs

WHAT IS REAL ESTATE INVESTMENT?

We perceive a real estate investment as a physical product or entity. Since the beginning of time as we know it, we have been programmed with the need to own and control physical objects. Many of us believe that land and man-made improvements (i.e., dwelling units, accessory buildings, etc.) are the essence of *real estate*. To own or control a diversified portfolio, which includes residential, commercial, and industrial properties, is the single biggest goal of many real estate investors.

INVESTING IN REAL ESTATE

Even though changes in the economy have increased risk or lowered returns, the investment market continues to devise innovative and attractive investment strategies, particularly for a popular investment such as real estate.

How Do Investors See Real Estate?

Generally, investors are concerned with the amount of money needed to acquire the asset (real estate) and with the cash flows they expect over some future time period. In recent years, investors have devised sophisticated models that utilize internal rates of return and present value techniques to convert space/time concepts into money/time projections. Thus, the essential of real estate analysis is learning the techniques by which we can develop reliable methods of converting space/time into money/time (*the concepts of investments are further discussed in Units 14 and 15*).

What Motivates the Investor?

A question frequently asked by many in the real estate field is why people generally invest. Some economists argue that individuals tend to save a portion of their current income(s) to provide future consumption and, thus, face investment decisions constantly (the nest egg). Rarely is the consumption argument stated by real estate investors. Rather, most cite the financial (including tax savings) and nonfinancial advantages and disadvantages of real estate investments. Investment incentives, motives, and returns are as diverse as the investors who acquire real estate. Motivations of individuals also differ significantly from those of large corporations. Perceived advantages of certain real estate investments may vary over time and may have to be reevaluated periodically as attitudes and strategies change.

Let's look at some of the more traditional motives behind real estate investing:

- **Pride of ownership.** Many people need to own and control real estate for ego gratification. Many individuals believe that real estate is a status symbol and a measure of importance or success. For others, owning property is an emotional experience and, thus, creates an important attribute to be recognized and dealt with.

- **Personal control.** Real estate, unlike the stock market, allows the investor to participate actively and exercise personal control.

- **Occupancy.** Most individuals acquire real estate for personal use. The purchase of a single-family residence is a form of investment that provides both a physical shelter and a tax shelter. In addition, the owner benefits from the appreciation of property value and freedom from rent payments.

- **Estate building.** An investor can begin to build an estate by acquiring leveraged real estate, reinvesting the cash proceeds, and, over time, allowing the buildup of equity through loan amortization and appreciation of property values.

- **Leverage.** One of the principal attractions of real estate is the investor's ability to control a large asset with a small amount of equity capital. Investors can use other people's money to parlay their equity yield to significantly higher levels. Leveraged financing is the key factor in most real estate investments.

- **Tax shelters.** The real estate investor generally seeks shelter from income tax burdens. An investor also seeks to generate tax losses that can be used to shelter earned income. After time, the investor might sell the property and seek favorable capital gain tax treatment on appreciated property value. In addition, taxable gains can be deferred through tax-deferred exchanges. Investors use tax-planning techniques to maximize after-tax cash flows over time.

- **Hedge against inflation.** In addition to the other benefits, the investor desires to receive a favorable return from increases in property values. Historically, real estate has been a good inflation hedge, outperforming stocks and other securities.

Advantages of Real Estate Investment

In recent years, real estate values have fluctuated widely in various regions of the country. As a result, some investments have failed to produce returns greater than the rate of inflation (i.e., serving as inflation hedges). Yet many real estate investments have shown above-average rates of return, generally greater than the prevailing interest rates charged by mortgage lenders. In theory, this means an investor can use the leverage of borrowed money to finance a real estate purchase and feel relatively sure that, if held long enough, the asset will yield more money than it cost to finance the purchase.

Real estate offers investors greater control over their investments than do other options, such as stocks, bonds, or other securities. Looking back at the fluctuations in the stock market during the 20th century and into the new millennium, a great deal of uncertainty had been created and many individuals turned to real estate as a safe means of investing.

The stock market hit an all-time high on September 4, 1929, and just a little over a month later, on October 29, 1929, the stock market lost $14 billion of wealth. The crash of 1929 was primarily due to stocks being over-valued and margin buying.

We saw yet another example of the markets peaking on August 25, 1987, followed by a market crash on October 19, 1987, where the market lost roughly 37% of its peaked value or a loss of $0.5 trillion. The October 1987 crash was primarily attributed to the lack of liquidity and overvalued stocks.

Between 1992 and 2000, the stock market and the economy experienced an expansion period. The expansion resulted from new Initial Private Offering (IPO) market, which had new companies trading at over $1 billion in revenue. In March of 2000, the Nasdaq hit a record high of 5,132.52 points, but by January 2, 2001, the Nasdaq had fallen almost 46% to 2,291.86 points. Subsequently, in October 2002, the Nasdaq had dropped even further to 1,108.49 points, a 78% drop from its high of 5,132.52 points in March of 2000. This resulted in losses of approximately $8 trillion due to the decline in the markets. The losses in 2002 were attributed, in part, to corporate corruption by companies inflating their profits by means of fraud and accounting loopholes and shielding company debt. As in prior historical examples, stocks were also overvalued, and the markets also experienced an influx of new, inexperienced day-traders and momentum investors. Conflicts of interest by research firms were also an issue. This was a result of analysts and investment bankers working closely together resulting in cases where, in companies that were trying to raise capital, the investment bankers would make sure that their research firms provided favorable ratings on their stocks. Oftentimes companies that were in financial trouble had favorable ratings on their stocks even prior to bankruptcy filings.

Although the real estate market did experience a downfall in value associated with large numbers of distressed sales nationwide, including California, the real estate markets showed a tremendous return in value and demand in 2014. Real estate is considered a cyclical investment and is often viewed as a preferred investment for many individuals, especially in times when the stock markets are in turmoil.

Real estate investors also receive certain tax benefits, including deferring taxes through exchanges and being able to depreciate investment properties. *Both leveraging and taxes are discussed in full later in this unit.*

Disadvantages of Real Estate Investment

Unlike stocks and bonds, real estate is not highly liquid over a short period. **Liquidity** refers to how quickly an asset may be converted into cash. For instance, an investor in listed stocks only has to call a stockbroker when funds are needed. The stockbroker sells the stock, and the investor receives the cash. In contrast, a real estate investor may have to sell the property at a substantially lower price than desired to ensure a quick sale. Of course, a real estate investor may be able to raise a limited amount of cash by refinancing the property.

Real estate investment is expensive. Large amounts of capital are usually required.

Investing in real estate is difficult without expert advice. Investment decisions must be based on careful studies of all the facts, reinforced by a thorough knowledge of real estate and the manner in which it is affected by the marketplace.

Real estate requires active management. A real estate investor can rarely sit idly by and watch investments grow. Management decisions must be made. How much rent should be charged? How should repairs and tenant grievances be handled? The investor may want to manage the property personally. On the other hand, it may be preferable to hire a professional property manager. Sweat equity (physical improvements accomplished by the investor personally) may be required to make the asset profitable. Many good investments fail because of poor management.

Finally, despite its popularity, real estate investment is far from a sure thing. In fact, it involves a high degree of risk, especially if leveraged. The possibility always exists that an investor's property will decrease in value during the period it failed or that it will not generate enough income to make it profitable or to service the debt.

The Investment

Real estate investors hope to achieve various investment objectives. Reaching their goals more effectively depends on the type of property and manner of ownership they choose. The most prevalent form of real estate investment is direct ownership. Both individuals and corporations may own real estate directly and manage it for appreciation or cash flow (income). Property held for **appreciation** is generally expected to increase in value during ownership and to show a profit when sold. Income property is just that: property held for current income as well as a potential profit upon its sale.

Appreciation Real estate is an avenue of investment open to those interested in holding property primarily for appreciation. Two main factors affect appreciation: inflation and intrinsic value.

- **Inflation** is a relative increase in the amount of money in circulation. When more money is available, its value declines. When the value of money declines, wholesale and retail prices rise. This is essentially an operation of supply and demand, as discussed in Unit 2.

- The **intrinsic value** of real estate is the result of the aggregate of all persons' individual choices and preferences for a given geographical area. As a rule, the greater the intrinsic value, the more money a property commands upon its sale.

Unimproved Land Quite often, investors speculate in purchases of either agricultural land or undeveloped land located in what is expected to be a major path of growth. In these cases, however, the property's intrinsic value and potential for appreciation are not easy to determine. This type of investment carries with it many inherent risks. How fast will the area develop? Will it grow sufficiently for the investor to make a good profit? Will the expected growth occur? More important, will the profits eventually realized from the property be great enough to offset the costs of holding it, such as property taxes? Because these questions often cannot be answered with any degree of certainty, lending institutions may be reluctant to lend money for the purchase of raw land.

Income tax laws do not allow the depreciation (cost recovery) of land. Also, such land may not be liquid (salable) at certain times under certain circumstances because few people will purchase raw or agricultural land on short notice. Despite all the risks, however, land has historically been a good inflation hedge if held long term. It can also be a source of income to offset some of the holding costs. For example, agricultural land can be leased for crops, timber production, or grazing.

A CLOSER LOOK A few years ago, a real estate investor learned from her friends in the state capital that the governor was about to announce that a major new international airport would be built at a rural site currently occupied by an abandoned industrial site. The investor immediately bought several large tracts near the proposed airport location. Once the airport was in place, she planned to sell the land to developers for the hotels, restaurants, and office buildings that would be in demand. The governor announced the airport, and the value of the investment soared. In an election before construction began, however, the governor was defeated. The newly elected governor decided that the proposed airport would be a waste of taxpayer money, and the project died for lack of political support, leaving the investor holding largely worthless land around a potentially toxic site.

Income Property The wisest initial investment for a person who wishes to buy and personally manage real estate may be rental income property.

Cash Flow The object of directing funds into income property is to generate spendable income, usually called cash flow. **Cash flow** is the total amount of money remaining after all expenses have been paid. These expenses include taxes, operating costs, and mortgage payments. The cash flow produced by any given parcel of real estate is determined by at least three factors: amount of rent received, operating expenses, and method of debt repayment.

Generally, the amount of rent (income) that a property may command depends on a number of factors, including the property's location, physical appearance, and amenities. If the cash flow from rents is not enough to cover all expenses, negative cash flow will result.

To keep cash flow high, an investor should attempt to keep operating expenses reasonably low. Such operating expenses include general maintenance of the building, repairs, utilities, taxes, and tenant services (switchboard facilities, security systems, etc.).

An investor often stands to make more money by investing with borrowed money, usually obtained through a mortgage loan or deed of trust loan. Low mortgage payments spread over a long period result in a higher cash flow because they allow the investor to retain more income each month; conversely, high mortgage payments contribute to a lower cash flow.

Investment Opportunities Traditional income-producing property includes apartment and office buildings, hotels, motels, shopping centers, and industrial properties. In the past, investors have found well-located, one- to four-family dwellings to be among the most favorable investments. However, in recent years, many communities have experienced severe overbuilding of office space and shopping centers. The result has been high vacancy rates.

Leverage   Leverage is the use of borrowed money to finance an investment. As a rule, an investor can receive a maximum return from the initial investment (the down payment and closing and other costs) by making a small down payment, paying a low interest rate, and spreading mortgage payments over as long a period as possible.

The effect of leveraging is to provide a return that reflects the result of market forces on the entire original purchase price, but that is measured against only the actual cash invested. For example, if an investor spends $100,000 for rental property and makes a $20,000 down payment, then sells the property five years later for $125,000, the return over five years is $25,000. Disregarding ownership expenses, the return is not 25% ($25,000 compared with $100,000), but 125% of the original amount invested ($25,000 compared to $20,000).

Risks are directly proportionate to leverage. A high degree of leverage translates into greater risk for the investor and lender because of the high ratio of borrowed money to the value of the real estate. Lower leverage results in less risk. When values drop in an area or vacancy rates rise, the highly leveraged investor may be unable to pay even the financing costs of the property.

Equity Buildup *Equity buildup* is that portion of the loan payment directed toward the principal rather than the interest, plus any gain in property value due to appreciation. In a sense, equity buildup is like money in the investor's bank account. This accumulated equity is not realized as cash unless the property is sold or refinanced. However, the equity interest may be sold, exchanged, or mortgaged (refinanced) to be used as leverage for other investments.

Pyramiding   An effective method for a real estate investor to increase holdings without investing additional capital is through **pyramiding.** Pyramiding is simply the process of using one property to drive the acquisition of additional properties. Two methods of pyramiding can be used: pyramiding through sale and pyramiding through refinance.

In *pyramiding through sale,* an investor first acquires a property and then improves the property for resale at a substantially higher price. The profit from the sale of the first property is used to purchase additional properties. Thus, the proceeds from a single investment (the point of the pyramid) provide the means for acquiring other properties. These properties are also improved and sold, and the proceeds are reinvested until the investor is satisfied with the return. Of course, the disadvantage is that the proceeds from each sale are subject to capital gains taxation, as discussed later.

The goal of *pyramiding through refinancing,* on the other hand, is to use the value of the original property to drive the acquisition of additional properties while retaining all the properties acquired. The investor refinances the original property and uses the proceeds of the refinance to purchase additional properties. These properties are refinanced in turn to enable the investor to acquire further properties, and so on. By holding on to the properties, the investor increases income-producing property holdings while simultaneously delaying the capital gains taxes that would result from a sale.

TAX BENEFITS

One of the main reasons real estate investments were popular and profitable in the past is that tax laws allowed investors to use losses generated by such investments to shelter income from other sources. Although laws have changed and some tax advantages of owning real estate investments are altered periodically, with professional tax advice, an investor can still make a wise real estate purchase.

Exchanges

Real estate investors can defer taxation of capital gains by making property **exchanges**. Even property that has appreciated greatly since its initial purchase may be exchanged for other property. A property owner will incur tax liability on a sale only if additional capital or property is also received. Note, however, that the tax is deferred, not eliminated. Whenever the investor sells the property, the capital gain will be taxed.

To qualify as a **tax-deferred** exchange under § 1031 of the Internal Revenue Code, the properties involved must be of *like kind*—that is, real estate for real estate of equal value. The fact that the real estate is improved or unimproved is immaterial. Any additional capital or personal property included with the transaction to even out the value of the exchange is called **boot**.

The **Internal Revenue Service (IRS)** requires tax on the boot to be paid at the time of the exchange by the party who receives it. The value of the boot is added to the basis of the property for which it is given. Tax-deferred exchanges are governed by strict federal requirements, and competent guidance from a tax professional is essential.

Depreciation

Depreciation, or **cost recovery**, allows an investor to recover the cost of an income-producing asset through tax deductions over the asset's useful life. While investors rarely purchase property without expecting it to appreciate over time, the tax laws maintain that all physical structures deteriorate (and lose value) over time. Cost recovery deductions may be taken only on personal property and improvements to land. Furthermore, they can be taken only if the property is used in a trade or business or for the production of income. Thus, a cost recovery deduction cannot be claimed on an individual's personal residence, and land cannot be depreciated. Technically, land never wears out or becomes obsolete.

Depreciation is calculated by dividing the improvement value by the useful life of the income property. For example, the formula for computing straight-line depreciation is as follows:

$$\frac{\text{improvement value}}{\text{useful life}} = \frac{\$250,000}{27.5 \text{ years}} = \$9,090.01 \text{ annual depreciation}$$

Depreciation taken periodically in equal amounts over an asset's useful life is called *straight-line depreciation*.

Deductions

In addition to tax **deductions** for depreciation, investors may be able to deduct losses from their real estate investments. The tax laws are complex. The amount of loss that may be deducted depends on whether an investor actively participates in the regular, day-to-day management of the rental property or makes management decisions. Other factors are the amount of the loss and the source of the income against which the loss is to be deducted. Investors who do not actively participate in the management or operation of the real estate are considered passive investors. Passive investors may not use losses to offset active income derived from active participation in real estate management, wages, or income from stocks, bonds, and the like. The tax code cites specific rules for active and passive income and losses and may be subject to changes.

Certain tax credits are allowed for renovation of older buildings, low-income housing projects, and historic property. A **tax credit** is a direct reduction in the tax due rather than a deduction from income before tax is computed. Tax credits encourage the revitalization of older properties and the creation of low-income housing. The tax laws governing these issues are also complex.

Real estate must be analyzed in conjunction with an investor's other investments and overall financial goals and objectives. Income tax consequences also have a significant bearing on an investor's decisions. Competent tax advice should be sought to help an investor carefully evaluate the ramifications of an investment decision.

Installment Sales

A **taxpayer** who sells real property and receives payment on an installment basis pays tax only on the profit portion of each payment received. Interest received is taxable as ordinary income. Many complex laws apply to installment sales, and a competent tax adviser should be consulted.

INVESTING WITH OTHERS

The expense and complexity of real estate investments often makes it desirable for investors to enter into coventuring agreements with others. This pooling of resources permits investment in larger, more lucrative projects, as well as a degree of risk sharing. These arrangements may take many forms, but some of the most popular are real estate investment syndicates, real estate investment trusts, and real estate mortgage investment conduits.

Real Estate Investment Syndicates

A **real estate investment syndicate** is a business venture in which people pool their resources to own or develop a particular piece of property. This structure permits people with only modest capital to invest in large-scale operations. Typical syndicate projects include highrise apartment buildings and shopping centers. Syndicate members realize some profit from rents collected on the investment. The main return usually comes when the syndicate sells the property.

Syndicate participation can take many legal forms. For instance, syndicate members may hold property as tenants in common or joint tenants. Various kinds of partnership, corporate, and trust ownership options are possible. Private syndication generally involves a small group of closely associated or experienced investors. Public syndication, on the other hand, involves a much larger group of investors who may or may not be knowledgeable about real estate as an investment. Any pooling of individuals' funds raises questions of securities registration under federal and state securities laws. These are commonly referred to as *blue-sky laws*.

To protect members of the public who are not sophisticated investors but who may still be solicited to participate in syndicates, securities laws govern the offer and sale of securities. Real estate securities that fall under the definition of a public offering must be registered with state officials and the federal Securities and Exchange Commission (SEC). Pertinent factors include the number of prospects solicited, the total number of investors, the financial background and sophistication of the investors, and the value or price per unit of investment.

Forms of Syndicates   A **general partnership** is typically organized so that some members of the group may be directly involved in the managerial decisions, profits, and losses involved with the investment. Certain members (or a member) of the syndicate may be designated to act as trustee for the group. The trustee holds title to the property and maintains it in the syndicate's name.

Under a **limited partnership** agreement, one party (or parties), usually a developer or real estate broker, organizes, operates, and holds responsibility for the entire syndicate. This person is called the *general partner*. The other members of the partnership are merely investors; they have no voice in the organization and direction of the operation. These passive investors are called *limited partners*.

The limited partners share in the profits, and the general partner is compensated out of the profits. The limited partners stand to lose only as much as they invest—nothing more. Like their level of participation, their risk of loss is limited. The general partner is totally responsible for any excess losses incurred by the investment.

The sale of a limited partnership interest involves the sale of an investment security as defined by the SEC. As a result, the sale is subject to state and federal laws concerning the sale of securities. Unless exempt, the securities must be registered with the SEC and the appropriate state authorities.

Real Estate Investment Trusts

By directing their funds into **real estate investment trusts (REITs),** real estate investors take advantage of the same tax benefits as do mutual fund investors. A real estate investment trust does not have to pay corporate income tax so long as 90% of its income is distributed to its shareholders. Certain other conditions must also be met. To qualify as a REIT, at least 75% of the trust's income must come from real estate. Investors purchase certificates in the trust which, in turn, invests in real estate or mortgages (or both). Profits are distributed to investors.

REITs are subject to complex restrictions and regulations. A competent attorney should be involved at all stages of a REIT's development.

Real Estate Mortgage Investment Conduits

A **real estate mortgage investment conduit (REMIC)** has complex qualification, transfer, and liquidation rules. For instance, the REMIC must satisfy the asset test. The asset test requires that after a start-up period, almost all assets must be qualified mortgages and permitted investments. Furthermore, investors' interests may consist only of one or more classes of regular interests and a single class of residual interests. Holders of regular interests receive interest or similar payments based on either a fixed rate or a variable rate. Holders of residual interests receive distributions (if any) on a pro rata basis.

THE NEXT STEP Lending, financing, investing, and taxation are all based on the value of a property. As we've seen, the operation of the marketplace is the ultimate determiner of value. The price a willing buyer pays for a property may be influenced, however, by subjective factors unrelated to the marketplace; the sales price may be inflated or understated in relation to market value. How do lenders, financiers, investors, and taxing bodies make an accurate determination of value? The appraisal process is the method, and its economic impact is significant. In the next unit, we'll look at how appraisal affects the real estate economy.

SUMMARY

■ There are many different reasons for owning real estate. The primary one is that *it provides us shelter against the elements*. However, *investors are motivated by personal control, estate building, the benefits of leverage, tax shelters*, and *protection against inflation*.

■ Investing in real estate has several distinct **advantages**: *above-average rates of return* (compared with other types of investment opportunities), *greater investor control*, and *tax benefits* (compared with the types of investment opportunities of comparable risk).

■ Investing in real estate has some **disadvantages**, too: *low liquidity, high capital requirements, complexity, intense management*, and relatively high *risk*.

■ Real estate is an avenue of investment especially attractive to those who are interested in holding property for **appreciation**. *Income tax laws do not allow the depreciation of land*, however.

■ **Cash flow** is the *total amount of money remaining after all expenses have been paid*. Traditional income-producing properties include apartment and office buildings, hotels, shopping centers, and industrial properties.

■ *The use of borrowed money to finance an investment* is called **leverage**. Leverage permits an investor to receive a maximum return from the initial investment by making a small down payment, paying a low interest rate on the loan, and spreading mortgage payments over a long period.

■ **Pyramiding** is *the process of using one property to drive the acquisition of additional properties*.

■ Real estate investors can defer taxation of **capital gains** by making **property exchanges**. Investors can **depreciate** *improvements on land* but not the land itself or a personal residence. Business or investment losses incurred in real estate investments may be **deducted** from the owner's *income taxes*.

■ Investors may choose to enter into coventuring agreements with others, including real estate investment syndicates, REITs, and REMICs.

REVIEW QUESTIONS

1. What are the advantages and disadvantages of investing in real estate?

2. In your area, how much has real estate appreciated in the last decade?

3. Who or which are the major real estate investors in your area/ community?

4. How have you prepared in recent years to become a real estate investor?

5. How would you minimize risk in purchasing real estate for investment?

6. What is the difference between speculation and investment?

UNIT QUIZ

1. All of the following are advantages to real estate investment *EXCEPT*
   a. liquidity.
   b. rate of return.
   c. investor control.
   d. tax benefits.

2. The increase in the amount of money available in circulation is referred to as
   a. liquidity.
   b. inflation.
   c. cash flow.
   d. leverage.

3. The use of borrowed money to finance an investment is called
   a. equity buildup.
   b. pyramiding.
   c. boot.
   d. leverage.

4. H is a real estate investor. H refinances one of her office buildings and uses the proceeds of the refinance to purchase a small shopping center. H then refinances the shopping center and uses the additional money to buy two office buildings and a vacant lot. What is H doing?
   a. Pyramiding through selling
   b. Leveraging
   c. Pyramiding through refinancing
   d. Investing through equity buildup

5. Two investors exchange unimproved properties. Because one property is worth more than the other, one of the investors also receives $50,000 in cash. What is the cash called?
   a. Cost recovery
   b. Like kind property
   c. Boot
   d. Leverage

6.   Depreciation taken periodically in equal amounts over the useful life of an asset is referred to as
   a.   equity buildup depreciation.
   b.   pyramiding through depreciation.
   c.   straight-line depreciation.
   d.   appreciation.

7.   X, Y, and Z enter into a business relationship in which all three will share equally in decision making, profits, and losses. What type of arrangement is this?
   a.   Limited partnership
   b.   Shared cooperation agreement
   c.   Limited venture
   d.   General partnership

8.   X and Y enter into a real estate investment partnership in which X will make all day-to-day decisions and Y will merely contribute capital and take a wholly passive role. What type of syndicate is this?
   a.   General partnership
   b.   Limited partnership
   c.   Passive partnership
   d.   Not any form of partnership

9.   A real estate investment trust does not have to pay corporate income tax as long as what percentage of its income is distributed to its shareholders?
   a.   75%
   b.   87%
   c.   90%
   d.   100%

10.   How is a REMIC different from a REIT?
   a.   At least 50% of a REIT's income must be derived from real estate; REMICs are not subject to any controls over the type of investments held.
   b.   Almost all of a REMIC's assets must be qualified mortgages.
   c.   A REIT invests in real estate loans; a REMIC invests in income properties.
   d.   REITs are subject to an asset test; REMICs are not.

13

THE ECONOMICS OF APPRAISAL

KEY TERMS

anticipation
appraisal
Appraisal Foundation
appraiser
Bureau of Real Estate
  Appraisers (BREA)
capitalization rate
change
competition
competitive market
  analysis (CMA)
conformity
contribution
cost approach
curable
data
demand
depreciation
Fannie Mae

Financial Institutions
  Reform, Recovery,
  and Enforcement
  Act of 1989
  (FIRREA)
Freddie Mac
gross rent multiplier
  (GRM)
Home Valuation
  Code of Conduct
  (HVCC)
income approach
incurable
lending
market price
market value
plottage
progression
reconciliation

regression
replacement
replacement value
sales comparison
  approach
scarcity
substitution
supply
taxation
transferability
*Uniform Standards of
  Professional Appraisal
  Practice (USPAP)*
utility
valuation
value
wealth

LEARNING OBJECTIVES

- Understand how the need for appraisal services evolved and how the modern appraisal industry is regulated

- Compare and contrast the three approaches to appraisal: what their distinguishing features are and when each one is used

- Describe the appraisal process from beginning to end

THE EVOLUTION OF PROPERTY VALUATION

At one time, people were nomadic and land was not owned or considered in terms of **wealth**. Western European colonists, for instance, laughed at the "simplistic" Native Americans who accepted beads and trinkets in exchange for land ownership. The Native Americans, on the other hand, were astonished that the Western Europeans were willing to pay valuable trade items for something the Native Americans did not consider "ownable" by anyone. This illustrates a clear clash in land **valuation** concepts.

When domestication of animals and crops began to emerge, land served as the basis for agricultural technologies. Still, its value as a commodity in its own right was not readily apparent because of its seeming abundance.

A widely recognized economic theory holds that all wealth is ultimately derived from land. Under this theory, ownership of land evolved as the main form of measuring wealth, even in strictly agricultural economies. The sale of land became the sale of the basic means for the production of wealth.

With the industrial revolution in the 19th century, land took on new meaning in the economic and social system. Factories needed fixed locations, and workers moved to where the jobs were. Mobility has important effects on real estate value. Value rises when properties sell more frequently. In other words, the shorter the turnover time, the more rapid the escalation of value. This partially explains why in the northeast and southern states, where homes frequently pass from generation to generation, the relative rise in real estate value is not as dramatic as in the more mobile Sun Belt states. One might say that mobility is a key factor in the enhancement of value.

How are Appraisals Different from CMAs and BPOs?

Competitive Market Analysis (CMA)   It is very important to realize the difference between formal appraisals and a **competitive market analysis (CMA)**. Each has a different purpose and use in real estate. A CMA is used for marketing or research. An **appraisal** is typically used for obtaining financing and is an estimate of property value that encompasses three appraisal approaches: the market approach, the cost approach, and the income approach. Each approach may yield different values. The **appraiser** reconciles the values using accepted appraisal methods and principles. In contrast, a CMA is an analysis of properties in the marketplace against which a subject property is competing. Although not a formal appraisal, many of the same principles apply. A CMA will consider other properties still on the market, as well as those properties recently sold or having expired listings. An appraisal is only concerned with sales that have actually closed and transferred, not listed properties. A CMA is similar to the market approach of an appraisal and is prepared in a like fashion.

Broker Price Opinion (BPO)   The broker price opinion (BPO) is a tool used by lenders and mortgage companies to value properties in situations where they believe the expense and delay of an appraisal is not necessary. Real estate brokers are typically given an order to do a BPO by a lender, mortgage company, or loss mitigation company. The broker either does a drive-by BPO or performs an internal BPO, in most cases. Reasons for performing a BPO instead of an appraisal might include (1) avoiding appraisal costs, (2) delinquent payments and pending foreclosure, and (3) refinance situations.

A lender who is considering a foreclosure, or even working with the borrower to come up with a solution, will typically order a BPO. This allows them to obtain a reliable estimate of the current value of the property, compare it to the mortgage balance, and recommend solutions.

The Need for Appraisal

As the United States became more mobile and property turned over more rapidly, the property valuation process gained in importance. Appraisal has evolved from mere personal observations and oral opinions of value to an orderly, formalized process of investigation and reporting.

Estimates of value have come to be required for

- *lending* on real estate to provide a margin of safety for lenders;

■ establishing *replacement value* of improvements for insurance purposes;

■ apportioning *taxation* of an individual property in relation to the total valuation of properties eligible for taxation on the assessment rolls;

■ *taking* of property for a public purpose (condemnation or eminent domain proceedings);

■ *partition* of property in the settlement of disputes over division of assets;

■ *inheritance tax*;

■ *benchmark of value* in the resolution of what a seller is willing to sell for and what a buyer is willing to pay; and

■ *confirmation of asset value* for a variety of other purposes, both personal and business.

THE APPRAISAL INDUSTRY

An **appraisal** is an opinion of value based on supportable evidence and approved methods. An **appraiser** is an independent person trained to provide an unbiased estimate of value. Appraising is a professional service performed for a fee.

The role of an appraiser is to estimate market value. An appraiser develops a supportable and objective report about the value of the subject property, relying on experience and expertise in valuation theories to evaluate market **data**. The appraiser does not establish the property's worth but instead verifies what the market indicates.

Regulation of Appraisal Activities

Title XI of the **Financial Institutions Reform, Recovery, and Enforcement Act of 1989 (FIRREA)** requires that any appraisal used in connection with a federally related transaction must be performed by a competent individual whose professional conduct is subject to supervision and regulation. Appraisers must be licensed or certified according to state law.

Each state adopts its own appraiser regulations, which must conform to federal requirements that follow criteria established by the Appraisal

Foundation. The Appraisal Foundation is a national body composed of representatives of major appraisal organizations. Appraisers are required to follow the **Uniform Standards of Professional Appraisal Practice (USPAP).**

A *federally related transaction* is any real estate-related financial transaction in which a federal financial institution or regulatory agency is engaged. This includes transactions involving the sale, lease, purchase, investment, or exchange of real property. It also includes the financing, refinancing, or use of real property as security for a loan or an investment, including mortgage-backed securities.

In California, appraisers are licensed and regulated through the **Bureau of Real Estate Appraisers (BREA).** *Appraisal* is defined by the California Business and Professions Code (§11302) as:

> a written statement independently and impartially prepared by a qualified appraiser setting forth an opinion in a federally related transaction as to the market value of an adequately described property as of a specific date, supported by the presentation and analysis of relevant market information.

California appraisers may be licensed in one of three classifications. Licensed Appraisers may appraise only noncomplex residential properties up to $1 million in value; Certified Residential Appraisers may appraise any residential property regardless of value; and General Certification Appraisers may appraise residential or commercial properties.

Initially on February 20, 2004, the Appraiser Qualifications Board of the **Appraisal Foundation** adopted changes to the *Real Property Appraiser Qualification Criteria* that became effective on January 1, 2008. These changes represented the minimum national requirements that each state must implement for individuals applying for a real estate appraiser license certification as of January 1, 2008. On December 9, 2011, the Appraisers Qualifications Board of the Appraisal Foundation adopted changes to the Real Property Appraisers Qualifications Criteria that became effective on January 1, 2015. These changes represent minimum national requirements that each state must have implemented no later than January 1, 2015. Figure 13.1 outlines the requirements. Note the following:

- Hours required include completion of the 15-hour *USPAP* course (or its equivalent)

■ Hours required include specific core curriculum courses and hours

■ College-level courses and degrees must be obtained from an accredited college or university

FIGURE 13.1:   National Requirements for Real Estate Appraisal License Certifications

AQB Minimum Real Property Appraiser Qualifying Criteria (Effective January 1, 2015)			
OREA License Levels	Basic Education Requirements	College Level Requirements	Experience
Trainee (AT)	150 Hours	N/A	N/A
Residential (AL)	150 Hours	30 semester credit hours from an accredited college or an associate's degree or higher (in any field)	2,000 hours (accumulated over at least a 12-month period)
Certified Residential (AR)	200 Hours	Bachelor's degree or higher (in any field) from an accredited college or university	2,500 hours (accumulated over at least a 30-month period)
Certified General (AG)	300 Hours	Bachelor's degree or higher (in any field) from an accredited college or university	3,000 hours that include at least 1,500 nonresidential hours (accumulated over at least a 30-month period)

Source: Appraisal Qualification Board of the Appraisal Foundation

Individuals gaining experience at the AT level must be supervised by a certified licensed level appraiser under the new criteria. No supervisor can supervise more than three trainees.

*In lieu of the associate's degree, an applicant can complete 21 college semester credits in courses covering specific subject matters: English composition; principles of economics (micro or macro); finance, algebra, geometry, or higher mathematics; statistics; introduction to computers; and business or real estate law.

**In lieu of the bachelor's degree, an applicant can complete 30 college semester credits in courses covering specific subject matters: English composition; microeconomics; macroeconomics; finance, algebra, geometry, or higher mathematics; statistics; introduction to computers; and business or real estate law; and two elective courses in accounting, geography, ag-economics, business management, or real estate.

Strengthening Appraiser Independence and Improving the Valuation Process

From 2005 to 2007, mortgage lending was too aggressive and placed pressure on the appraisal process. In many cases, this resulted in unrealistically high appraisals, which drastically impacted homebuyers as well as investors. As a result of an agreement between the attorney general of New York, the Office of Federal Housing Enterprise Oversight (OFHEO), Fannie Mae, and Freddie Mac, the Home Valuation Code of Conduct (HVCC) was created and became effective on May 1, 2009. The HVCC expanded existing enterprise appraisal standards, seeking to redress problems that contributed to the mortgage crisis and to improve the quality of the mortgage loans purchased by Fannie Mae and Freddie Mac. The HVCC's main purpose is to protect appraisers and the quality of appraisals from undue influence and conflicts of interest. The HVCC is designed to promote professional appraisals free from inappropriate pressure from lenders, borrowers, or brokers. It should be noted that HVCC does not apply to FHA and VA loans.

The HVCC states in part:

> No employee, director, officer, or agent of the lender, or any other third party acting as joint venture partner, independent contractor, appraisal management company, or partner on behalf of the lender, shall influence or attempt to influence the development, reporting, result, or review of an appraisal through coercion, extortion, collusion, compensation, instruction, inducement, intimidation, bribery, or in any other manner including but not limited to:

- withholding or threatening to withhold timely payment for an appraisal report;

- withholding or threatening to withhold future business for an appraiser, or demoting or terminating or threatening to demote or terminate an appraiser;

- expressly or impliedly promising future business, promotions, or increased compensation for an appraiser;

- conditioning the ordering of an appraisal report or the payment of an appraisal fee or salary or bonus on the opinion, conclusion, or valuation to be reached, or on a preliminary estimate requested from an appraiser;

- requesting that an appraiser provide an estimated, predetermined, or desired valuation in an appraisal report, or provide estimated values or comparable sales at any time prior to the appraiser's completion of an appraisal report;

- providing to an appraiser an anticipated, encouraged, or desired value for a subject property or a proposed target amount to be loaned to the borrower, except that a copy of the sales contract for purchase transaction may be provided;

- providing to an appraiser, appraisal management company, stock or other financial or non-financial benefits;

- allowing the removal of an appraiser from a list of qualified appraisers used by any entity, without prior written notice to such appraiser, which notice shall include written evidence of the appraiser's illegal conduct, a violation of the *Uniform Standards of Professional Appraisal Practice (USPAP)* or state licensing standards, substandard performance, or otherwise improper or unprofessional behavior;

- ordering, obtaining, using, or paying for a second or subsequent appraisal or automated valuation model in connection with a mortgage financing transaction unless there is a reasonable basis to believe that the initial appraisal was flawed or tainted and such basis is clearly and appropriately noted in the loan file, or unless such appraisal or automated valuation model is done pursuant to a bona fide pre-or-post-funding appraisal review or quality control process; or

- any other act or practice that impairs or attempts to impair an appraiser's independence, objectivity, or impartiality.[12]

The HVCC also contains additional provisions relative to communications with appraisers, low appraisals, appraisal management companies, unqualified or out-of-area appraisers, increased costs at closing, turnaround times for appraisals, and the transferring of appraisals. The HVCC also supports the critical role of appraisers and their central role in the underwriting process. Accurate appraisals produced in line with industry standards and legal requirements provide key protections for homeowners and investors who support the markets. It should also be noted that poor practices of the past are being corrected, and lessons learned are being addressed.

ESSENTIAL ELEMENTS OF VALUE

Like professionals in any industry, appraisers use certain terms that have specific meanings. *Value* is one of these. To understand appraisal, we must understand what is meant by *value*.

---

12 New York State Office of the Attorney General, "Home Valuation Code of Conduct," www .ag.ny.gov/sites/default/files/press-releases/archived/Code%20Final%203-2.pdf (accessed May 27, 2015).

Value

Value is defined as the present worth of all present and future benefits. For a property to have value in the real estate market—that is, to have monetary worth based on desirability—the following factors must come into play:

- **Demand**—the need or desire for possession or ownership of the property, backed by the financial means to satisfy that need.

- **Utility**—the property's usefulness for its intended purposes.

- **Scarcity**—a finite supply of the property.

- **Transferability**—the relative ease with which ownership rights can be transferred from one person to another.

Market Value

Generally, the goal of an appraiser is to estimate **market value**. The market value of real estate is the most probable price that a property should bring in a fair sale. This definition makes three assumptions:

- A competitive and open market exists.

- The buyer and seller are acting prudently and knowledgeably.

- The price is not affected by unusual economic circumstances.

The following are essential to determining market value:

- The *most probable price* is *not* the average or highest price.

- The buyer and seller must be *unrelated* and *acting without undue pressure*.

- Both buyer and seller must be *well informed* about the property's use and potential, including *defects* and *advantages*.

- A *reasonable time* must be allowed for exposure in the open market.

- Payment must be made *in cash* or *its equivalent*.

- The price must represent a *normal consideration* for the property sold, unaffected by special financing amounts or terms, services, fees, costs, or credits incurred in the market transaction.

Market Value and Market Price

Market value is an opinion of value based on an analysis of data. The data may include not only an analysis of comparable sales but also an analysis of potential income, expenses, and replacement costs (less any depreciation). **Market price**, on the other hand, is what a property actually sells for: its sales price. In theory, market price should be the same as market value. Market price can be taken as accurate evidence of current market value, however, only if the conditions essential to market value exist. Sometimes, property is sold below market value (e.g., when the seller is forced to sell quickly or when a sale is arranged between relatives).

Market Value and Cost

An important distinction can be made between market value and cost. One of the most common misconceptions about valuing property is that cost represents market value. Cost and market value may be the same. In fact, when the improvements on a property are new, cost and value are likely to be equal. More often, cost does not equal market value. "Cost" refers to *labor and materials*. For example, a homeowner may install a swimming pool for $25,000; however, the cost of the improvement may not add $25,000 to the value of the property.

Basic Principles of Value

A number of economic principles can affect the value of real estate. The most important are defined in the following text:

- **Anticipation.** According to the principle of **anticipation**, value is created by the expectation that certain events will occur. Value can increase or decrease in anticipation of some future benefit or detriment. For instance, the value of a house may be affected if rumors circulate that an adjacent property might be converted to commercial use in the near future. If the property has been a vacant eyesore, the neighboring home's value might increase. On the other hand, if the vacant property is perceived as a park or totlot that has added to the neighborhood's quiet atmosphere, the news might cause the house's value to decline.

- **Change.** No physical or economic condition remains constant. This is the principle of **change**. Real estate is subject to natural phenomena such as tornadoes, fires, and routine wear and tear. The real estate business is subject to market demands like any other business. An appraiser must be knowledgeable about the past and, perhaps, about the predictable effects of natural phenomena and the behavior of the marketplace.

■ **Competition.** The interaction of supply and demand creates **competition**. Excess profits tend to attract competition. For example, the success of a retail store may cause investors to open similar stores in the area. This tends to mean less profit for all stores concerned unless the purchasing power in the area increases substantially.

■ **Conformity.** The principle of **conformity** says that value is created when a property is in harmony with its surroundings. Maximum value is realized if the use of land conforms to existing neighborhood standards. In single-family residential neighborhoods, for instance, buildings should be similar in design, construction, size, and age.

■ **Contribution.** Under the principle of **contribution**, the value of any part of a property is measured by its effect on the value of the whole. Installing a swimming pool, greenhouse, or private bowling alley may not add value to the property that is equal to the cost. On the other hand, remodeling an outdated kitchen or bathroom probably would.

■ **Highest and best use.** The most profitable use to which a property may be put, or the use that is most likely to be in demand in the near future, is the property's **highest and best use**. The use must be

— physically *possible*,

— legally *permitted*,

— financially *feasible*, and

— maximally *productive*.

The highest and best use of a site can change with social, political, and economic forces. For instance, a parking lot in a busy downtown area may not maximize the land's profitability to the same extent an office building might. Highest and best use of the land is noted in every appraisal.

■ **Increasing and diminishing returns.** The addition of more improvements to land and structures increases value only to the asset's maximum value. Beyond that point, additional improvements no longer affect a property's value. As long as money spent on improvements produces an increase in income or value, the law of increasing returns applies. At the point where additional improvements do not increase income or value, the law of diminishing returns applies. No matter how much money is spent on the property, the property's value does not keep pace with the expenditures.

- **Plottage.** The principle of **plottage** or assemblage holds that merging or consolidating adjacent lots into a single larger one produces a greater total land value than the sum of the two sites valued separately. For example, two adjacent lots valued at $35,000 each might have a combined value of $90,000 if consolidated. The process of merging two separately owned lots under one owner is known as assemblage.

- **Regression and progression.** In general, the worth of a better-quality property is adversely affected by the presence of a lesser-quality property. This is known as the principle of **regression**. Thus, in a neighborhood of modest homes, a structure that is larger, better maintained, or more luxurious would tend to be valued in the same range as the less lavish homes. Conversely, under the principle of **progression**, the value of a modest home would be higher if it were located among larger, fancier properties. The larger property might be termed *overimproved*; the small one *underimproved*. Both would be detrimental conditions.

- **Substitution.** The principle of **substitution** says that the maximum value of a property tends to be set by how much it would cost to purchase an equally desirable and valuable substitute property.

- **Supply and demand.** As we learned in Unit 2, the principle of **supply** and **demand** says that the value of a property depends on the number of properties available in the marketplace—the supply of the product. Other factors include the prices of other properties, the number of prospective purchasers, and the price buyers will pay.

THE THREE APPROACHES TO VALUE

To arrive at an accurate estimate of value, appraisers traditionally use three basic valuation techniques: the sales comparison approach, the cost approach, and the income approach. The three methods serve as checks against each other. Using them narrows the range within which the final estimate of value falls. Each method is generally considered most reliable for specific types of property.

The Sales Comparison Approach

In the **sales comparison approach,** an estimate of value is obtained by comparing the property being appraised (the subject property) with recently sold comparable properties (properties similar to the subject). Because no two parcels of real estate are exactly alike, each comparable property must be analyzed for differences and similarities between it and the subject property. This approach is a good example of the principle of substitution, discussed previously. The sales prices of the comparables must be adjusted to the subject property to account for any dissimilarities. The principal factors for which adjustments must be made include the following:

- **Property rights.** An adjustment must be made when less than fee simple, the full legal bundle of rights, is involved. This includes land leases, ground rents, life estates, easements, deed restrictions, and encroachments.

- **Financing concessions.** The financing terms must be considered, including adjustments for differences, such as mortgage loan terms and owner financing.

- **Conditions of sale.** Adjustments must be made for motivational factors that would affect the sale, such as foreclosure, a sale between family members, or some nonmonetary incentive.

- **Date of sale.** An adjustment must be made if economic changes occur between the date of sale of the comparable property and the date of the appraisal.

- **Location.** Similar properties might differ in price from neighborhood to neighborhood or even between locations within the same neighborhood.

- **Physical features and amenities.** Physical features, such as age, size, and condition, may require adjustments.

The sales comparison approach is essential in almost every appraisal of real estate. It is considered the most reliable of the three approaches in appraising single-family homes, where the intangible benefits may be difficult to measure otherwise. Most appraisals include a minimum of three comparable sales reflective of the subject property.

Where Is the Comparison Data Found?   Comparables for an appraisal are drawn from the real estate office files of closed sales, the closed sales data of the multiple listing service (MLS), the county recorder's office, and other data bank sources that appraisers keep and maintain. The more recent the sale of a comparable, the more relevant it is to the appraisal. The degree of similarity of physical characteristics and the location are crucial to the appraisal. In selecting comparables, the appraiser must examine the *physical and nonphysical characteristics* of each comparable. The physical characteristics include *size, shape of property, type of construction, age, design,* and *any special features* (i.e., swimming pool). The nonphysical characteristics include the *date of sale, price, financing, time property was on the market,* and *what motivated the seller to sell the property.* The more characteristics that properties share, the better the comparable analysis will be.

The Cost Approach

The **cost approach** to value is also based on the principle of substitution. The cost approach consists of five steps:

1. Estimate the *value of the land as if it were vacant* and available to be put to its highest and best use.

2. Estimate the *current cost of constructing buildings and improvements.*

3. Estimate the *amount of accrued depreciation* resulting from the property's physical deterioration, functional obsolescence, and external depreciation.

4. Deduct the *accrued depreciation* (Step 3) from the *construction cost* (Step 2).

5. Add the *estimated land value* (Step 1) to the *depreciated cost* of the building and site improvements (Step 4) to arrive at the total property value.

There are two ways to look at the construction cost of a building for appraisal purposes: reproduction cost and replacement cost new.

Reproduction cost is the construction cost at current prices of an exact duplicate of the subject improvement, including both the benefits and the drawbacks of the property. *Replacement cost new* is the cost to construct an improvement similar to the subject property, using current construction methods and materials, but not necessarily an exact duplicate. Replacement cost new is more frequently used in appraising older structures because it eliminates obsolete features and takes advantage of current construction materials and techniques.

Determining Reproduction or Replacement Cost New   An appraiser using the cost approach computes the reproduction or **replacement** cost of a building using one of the following methods:

- **Square-foot method.** The cost per square foot of a recently built comparable structure is multiplied by the number of square feet (using exterior dimensions) in the subject building. This is the most common and easiest method of cost estimation.

- **Unit-in-place method.** In the unit-in-place method, the replacement cost of a structure is estimated based on the construction cost per unit of measure of individual building components, including material, labor, overhead, and builder's profit. Most components are measured in square feet, although items such as plumbing fixtures are estimated by cost. The sum of the components is the cost of the new structure.

- **Quantity-survey method.** The quantity and quality of all materials (such as lumber, brick, and plaster) and the labor are estimated on a unit cost basis. These factors are added to indirect costs (e.g., building permit, survey, payroll, taxes, and builder's profit) to arrive at the total cost of the structure. Because it is so detailed and time-consuming, this method is usually used only in appraising historical properties. It is, however, the most accurate method of appraising new construction.

- **Index method.** A factor representing the percentage increase of construction costs up to the present time is applied to the original cost of the subject property. Because it fails to take into account individual property variables, this method is useful only as a check of the estimate reached by one of the other methods.

Depreciation   In a real estate appraisal, **depreciation** is a loss in value due to any cause. It refers to a condition that adversely affects the value of an improvement to real property. Land does not depreciate—it retains its value indefinitely except in such rare cases as downzoned urban parcels, improperly developed land, or misused farmland.

Depreciation must also take age into consideration. Every structure has two different ages, chronological age and effective age. The chronological age of a structure is measured by the number of years the structure has existed. This is similar to the age of a person. The effective age refers to the age that the structure appears to be. A property that is well maintained may seem younger than it really is chronologically. Conversely, the effective age may be greater than the chronological age if the property has not been modernized or adequately maintained.

Depreciation is considered to be **curable** or **incurable**, depending on the contribution of the expenditure to the value of the property. For appraisal purposes, depreciation is divided into three classes, according to its cause:

1. **Physical deterioration**

   — *Curable:* An item in need of repair, such as painting (deferred maintenance), that is economically feasible and would result in an increase in value equal to or exceeding the cost.

   — *Incurable:* A defect caused by physical wear and tear. If its correction would not be economically feasible or contribute a comparable value to the building, the cost of a major repair may not warrant the financial investment.

2. **Functional obsolescence**

   — *Curable:* Outmoded or unacceptable physical or design features no longer considered desirable by purchasers; such features, however, could be replaced or redesigned at a cost that would be offset by the anticipated increase in ultimate value. Outmoded plumbing, for instance, is usually easily replaced. Room function may be redefined at no cost if the basic room layout allows for it. A bedroom adjacent to a kitchen, for example, may be converted to a family room.

   — *Incurable:* This type of depreciation, caused by negative factors not on the subject property (such as environmental, social, or economic forces) is more often uncurable than not.

3. **External obsolescence**

   — *Incurable:* A type of depreciation caused by negative factors not on the subject property (such as environmental, social, or economic forces) that is always incurable. The loss in value cannot be reversed by spending money on the property. For example, proximity to a nuisance, such as a polluting factory or a deteriorating neighborhood, is one factor that could not be cured by the owner of the subject property.

Straight-Line Depreciation   The easiest but least precise way to determine depreciation is the *straight-line method*, also called the economic age-life method. Depreciation is assumed to occur at an even rate over a structure's economic life, the period during which it is expected to remain useful for its original intended purpose. The property's cost is divided by the number of years of its expected economic life to derive the amount of annual depreciation.

The cost approach is most helpful in the appraisal of newer or special-purpose buildings such as schools, churches, and public buildings. Such properties are difficult to appraise using other methods because there are seldom enough local sales to use as comparables and because the properties do not ordinarily generate income.

The Income Approach

The **income approach** to value is based on the *present value of the rights to future income*. It assumes that the income generated by a property will determine the property's value. The income approach is used for valuation of income-producing properties such as apartment buildings, office buildings, and shopping centers. In estimating value using the income approach, an appraiser must take six steps:

1. *Estimate* annual potential gross income. An estimate of economic rental income must be made based on market studies. Current rental income may not reflect the current market rental rates, especially in the case of short-term leases or leases about to terminate. Potential income includes other income from the property from such sources as vending machines, parking fees, and laundry machines.

2. *Deduct* an allowance for vacancy and rent loss, based on published vacancy and rent loss rates (obtainable from management companies), to determine effective gross income.

3. *Deduct* the annual operating expenses from the effective gross income to arrive at the annual net operating income (NOI). Management costs are always included, even if the current owner manages the property. Mortgage payments (principal and interest) are debt service and not considered operating expenses.

4. *Estimate* the price a typical investor would pay for the income produced by this particular type and class of property. This is done by estimating the rate of return (or yield) that an investor will demand for the investment of capital in this type of building. This rate of return is called the **capitalization** (or "cap") **rate** and is determined by comparing the relationship of net operating income to the sales prices of similar properties that have sold in the current market. For example, a comparable property that is producing an annual net income of $30,000 is sold for $487,500. The capitalization rate is $30,000 divided by $487,500, or 6%. If other comparable properties sold at prices that yielded substantially the same rate, it may be concluded that 6% is the rate that the appraiser should apply to the subject property.

5. *Apply* the capitalization rate to the property's annual net operating income to arrive at the estimate of the property's value.

6. The capitalization rate is also determined by the level of risk, alternative investments, and interest rates.

With the appropriate capitalization rate and the projected annual net operating income, the appraiser can obtain an indication of value by the income approach.

Gross Rent or Gross Income Multipliers Certain properties, such as single-family homes and two-unit buildings, are not purchased primarily for income. As a substitute for a more elaborate income capitalization analysis, the **gross rent multiplier (GRM)** and gross income multiplier (GIM) are often used in the appraisal process. Each relates the sales price of a property to its rental income.

Because single-family residences usually produce only rental incomes, the gross rent multiplier is used. This relates a sales price to monthly rental income. However, commercial and industrial properties generate income from many other sources (rent, concessions, escalator clause income, and so forth), and they are valued using their annual income from all sources.

The formulas are:

- For five or more residential units, commercial, or industrial property:

$$\text{sales price} \div \text{gross income} = \text{GIM}$$

- For one- to four-residential units:

$$\text{sales price} \div \text{gross rent} = \text{GRM}$$

For example, if a home recently sold for \$382,000 and its monthly rental income was \$1,200, the GRM for the property would be computed as

$$\$382,000 \div \$1,200 = 318.3 \text{ GRM}$$

To establish an accurate GRM, an appraiser must have recent sales and rental data from at least four properties that are similar to the subject property. The resulting GRM can then be applied to the estimated fair market rental of the subject property to arrive at its market value. The formula would be

$$\text{rental income} \times \text{GRM} = \text{estimated market value}$$

Reconciliation

When the three approaches to value are applied to the same property, they normally produce three separate indications of value. **Reconciliation** is the art of analyzing and effectively weighing the findings from the three approaches.

The process of reconciliation is more complicated than simply taking the average of the three estimates of value. An average implies that the data and logic applied in each approach are equally valid and reliable and should, therefore, be given equal weight. In fact, however, certain approaches are more valid and reliable with some kinds of properties than with others.

For example, in appraising a home, the income approach is rarely valid, and the cost approach is of limited value unless the home is relatively new. Therefore, the sales comparison approach is usually given greatest weight in valuing single-family residences. In the appraisal of income or investment property, the income approach normally is given the greatest weight. In the appraisal of churches, libraries, museums, schools, and other special-use properties where little or no income or sales revenue is generated, the cost approach usually is assigned the greatest weight. From this analysis, or reconciliation, a single estimate of market value is produced.

THE APPRAISAL PROCESS

Although appraising is not an exact or a precise science, the key to an accurate appraisal lies in the methodical collection and analysis of **data**. The appraisal process is an orderly set of procedures used to collect and analyze data to arrive at an ultimate value conclusion. The data are divided into two basic classes:

- **General data:** Covers the nation, region, city, and neighborhood. Of particular importance is the neighborhood, where an appraiser finds the physical, economic, social, and political influences that directly affect the value and potential of the subject property.

- **Specific data:** Covers details of the subject property as well as comparative data relating to costs, sales, and income and expenses of properties similar to and competitive with the subject property.

The Appraisal Report

Once the approaches have been reconciled and an opinion of value has been reached, the appraiser prepares a report for the client. The report should

- identify the real estate and real property interest;

- state the purpose and intended use of the appraisal;

- define the value to be estimated;

- state the effective date of the value and the date of the report;

- state the extent of the process of collecting, confirming, and reporting the data;

- list all assumptions and limiting conditions that affect the analysis, opinion, and conclusions of value;

- describe the information considered, the appraisal procedures followed, and the reasoning that supports the report's conclusions—if an approach was excluded, the report should explain why;

- describe (if necessary or appropriate) the appraiser's opinion of the highest and best use of the real estate;

- describe any additional information that may be appropriate to show compliance with the specific guidelines established in the *Uniform Standards of Professional Appraisal Practice (USPAP)* or to clearly identify and explain any departures from these guidelines; and

- include a signed certification, as required by the *Uniform Standards.*

Formats of Appraisal Reports   There are three traditional formats for written reports. The choice depends on the amount of detail required by the client, the intended use of the report, and the appraisal standards to be met. The format also depends on the reporting option (self-contained, summary, or restricted). The three basic report formats are summarized as follows:

- **The Letter Format.** This is the least formal report form and is usually only one to five pages in length. The letter report contains the conditions of the assignment, a summary of the nature and scope of the appraiser's investigation, and an opinion of value. While this is a brief appraisal, the letter report must still contain a description of the extent of the appraisal process performed and clearly state its detail. This format is used when the client is familiar with the property and appraisal details are not required.

- **The Form Report.** The form report is an appraisal made on a pre-printed form. A checklist is frequently used to describe and rate property characteristics. These checklists or forms are typically standardized for each type of property being appraised, such as commercial, industrial, and residential. As these forms are standardized, they become the choice of lenders and, thus, are the most common type of report used for real estate transactions today.

- **The Narrative Report.** The narrative appraisal is the longest and most formal of the appraisal formats used. This is a step-by-step presentation of the facts used by the appraiser to arrive at a value. This report format also contains a detailed discussion of the various methods employed to interpret the data and facts presented in the report. The narrative report is used when the client needs to review each logical step taken by the appraiser. These types of reports are favored by many investors because they provide the greatest level of detail.

FIGURE 13.2: Uniform Residential Appraisal Report

UNIFORM RESIDENTIAL APPRAISAL REPORT File No.

Property Description

Property Address	City	State	Zip Code
Legal Description		County	
Assessor's Parcel No.	Tax Year	R.E. Taxes $	Special Assessments $
Borrower	Current Owner	Occupant: ☐ Owner ☐ Tenant ☐ Vacant	
Property rights appraised ☐ Fee Simple ☐ Leasehold	Project Type ☐ PUD	☐ Condominium (HUD/VA only)	HOA $ /Mo.
Neighborhood or Project Name	Map Reference	Census Tract	
Sale Price $	Date of Sale	Description and $ amount of loan charges/concessions to be paid by seller	
Lender/Client	Address		
Appraiser	Address		

				Predominant occupancy	Single family housing	Present land use %	Land use change
Location	☐ Urban	☐ Suburban	☐ Rural		PRICE $(000) / AGE (yrs)	One family ____	☐ Not likely ☐ Likely
Built up	☐ Over 75%	☐ 25-75%	☐ Under 25%			2-4 family ____	☐ In process
Growth rate	☐ Rapid	☐ Stable	☐ Slow	☐ Owner	Low	Multi-family ____	To: ____
Property values	☐ Increasing	☐ Stable	☐ Declining	☐ Tenant	High	Commercial ____	
Demand/supply	☐ Shortage	☐ In balance	☐ Over supply	☐ Vacant (0-5%)	Predominant		
Marketing time	☐ Under 3 mos.	☐ 3-6 mos.	☐ Over 6 mos.	☐ Vac. (over 5%)			

Note: Race and the racial composition of the neighborhood are not appraisal factors.

Neighborhood boundaries and characteristics: ____

Factors that affect the marketability of the properties in the neighborhood (proximity to employment and amenities, employment stability, appeal to market, etc.):

Market conditions in the subject neighborhood (including support for the above conclusions related to the trend of property values, demand/supply, and marketing time – such as data on competitive properties for sale in the neighborhood, description of the prevalence of sales and financing concessions, etc.):

Unacceptable Appraisal Practices

The following are examples of appraisal practices that Fannie Mae considers unacceptable:

- Inclusion of inaccurate factual data about the subject neighborhood, site, improvements, or comparable sales
- Failure to comment on negative factors with respect to the subject neighborhood, subject property, or proximity of the subject property to adverse influences
- Use of comparables the appraiser has not personally inspected by at least driving by them
- Selection and use of inappropriate comparable sales or the failure to use comparables that are locationally and physically the most similar to the subject property
- Use of data—particularly comparable sales data—provided by parties who have a financial interest in the transaction without verifying the information from a disinterested source. For example, it would be inappropriate to use comparable sales provided by the broker who is

handling the sale unless the appraiser verifies the data with another source and makes an independent investigation to determine that the comparables are the best ones available.

■ Use of adjustments to the comparable sales that do not reflect the market's reaction to the differences between the subject property and the comparables or failure to make adjustments when they are clearly indicated

■ Valuation that is based—either partially or completely—on the race, color, or national origin of either the prospective owners or occupants of the property or of the present owners or occupants in the vicinity of the subject property

■ Development of a valuation conclusion that is not supported by available market data

■ An appraisal fee based on a percentage of the appraised value of the property

THE NEXT STEP   The next unit continues our focus on the economic analysis of real estate. In "Analyzing Residential Income Property," we'll consider the tools used in performing a structured economic analysis of a particular segment of the market.

SUMMARY

■ An **appraisal** is *an opinion of value based on supportable evidence and approved methods.* An **appraiser** is *an independent person trained to provide an unbiased estimate of value for a fee.* FIRREA requires states to establish appraiser licensing procedures and industry regulations for appraisers who participate in **federally related transactions**.

■ For a property to have **value** in the real estate market, the following factors must come into play: *demand, utility, scarcity,* and *transferability.*

■ The appraiser's goal is to estimate **market value**. Market value is *an opinion of value based on an analysis of collected data.* **Market price** is what a property actually sells for.

■ A number of **economic principles** can affect the value of real estate. These include *anticipation, change, competition, conformity, contribu-*

tion, *highest and best use*, *increasing and diminishing returns*, *plottage*, *regression and progression*, *substitution*, and *supply and demand*.

■ The three approaches to value are the **sales comparison approach**, the **cost approach**, and the **income approach**. The art of analyzing and effectively weighing the findings from the three approaches is called **reconciliation**.

■ The **appraisal process** is an orderly set of procedures used to collect and analyze data to arrive at an ultimate value conclusion. The data are divided into two classes: *general* and *specific*. Once the approaches have been reconciled and an opinion of value has been reached, the appraiser prepares a detailed **appraisal report** for the client.

REVIEW QUESTIONS

1. How does the availability of money on a national scale affect the value of local real estate?

2. What is the difference between an appraisal and a competitive market analysis?

3. Discuss the diversification (or lack of it) of industry in your community. What would be the effect on local property values if the major industries in your community were to close down?

4. What do you think is the most important economic influence on the creation of local property values?

5. Discuss the different types of appraisal reports. Which would be used for a single-family residence?

6. As a person wishing to invest in commercial real estate in your area, what type of data would you need? How detailed must it be before you are willing to move forward with the investment?

7. What are the differences in value, in your community, of hillside lots over lots in the flatter areas?

8. Explain the use of gross rent multipliers (GRM) in valuing real estate. What are the strengths and the weaknesses of this method?

9. How do you believe that the Home Valuation Code of Conduct (HVCC) will affect how appraisals are performed?

UNIT QUIZ

1. An appraisal is
   a. a determination of a property's worth.
   b. an opinion of value.
   c. an opinion of market price.
   d. a "ballpark guesstimate" of worth.

2. Which of the following most completely defines a federally related transaction?
   a. Any real estate transaction in the United States
   b. Any real estate-related financial transaction in which federal property is bought or sold
   c. Any real estate-related financial transaction in which a federal financial institution or regulatory agency engages
   d. Any real estate-related transaction in which the federal government is the purchaser

3. J bought his house for $450,000. When J put the house up for sale, he asked $475,000. The house eventually sold for $462,500. An appraiser valued the house at $465,000. Based on these facts, what is the market value of J's house?
   a. $450,000
   b. $462,500
   c. $465,000
   d. $475,000

4. J bought his house for $450,000. When J put the house up for sale, he asked $475,000. The house eventually sold for $462,500. An appraiser valued the house at $465,000. Based on these facts, what is the market price of J's house?
   a. Cannot tell from these facts
   b. $462,500
   c. $465,000
   d. $475,000

5. "Value is created by the expectation that certain events will occur." This statement defines which economic principle?
   a. Conformity
   b. Highest and best use
   c. Anticipation
   d. Supply and demand

6. Q builds an eight-bedroom brick house with a tennis court, greenhouse, and indoor pool in a neighborhood of modest two-bedroom, aluminum-sided houses on narrow lots. The value of Q's house is likely to be affected by what economic principle?
   a. Conformity
   b. Assemblage
   c. Regression
   d. Change

7. Q builds an eight-bedroom brick house with a tennis court, greenhouse, and indoor pool in a neighborhood of modest two-bedroom, aluminum-sided houses on narrow lots. The owners of the more modest homes in Q's neighborhood may find that the value of their homes is affected by what economic principle?
   a. Contribution
   b. Increasing returns
   c. Substitution
   d. Progression

8. Location, physical features, and conditions of sale would be primary considerations in which of the approaches to value?
   a. Cost approach only
   b. Sales comparison approach only
   c. Income and cost approach only
   d. Income approach only

9. To air-condition an old 20-story office building would require removing all the stone from the building's facade, cutting large holes through its three-foot-thick interior walls, and rewiring the entire structure. When the job was completed, the building would not only lack historical charm but also be structurally unsafe for tenants. This is an example of which type of depreciation?
   a. Curable physical deterioration
   b. Curable functional deterioration
   c. External obsolescence
   d. Incurable functional obsolescence

10. A three-apartment building recently sold for $785,000. Its monthly income was $3,600. What is the GRM for this property?
    a. 0.0063
    b. 9.12
    c. 13.19
    d. 218.056

UNIT FOURTEEN

ANALYZING RESIDENTIAL INCOME PROPERTY

KEY TERMS

amenities	economic trends	net present value
calculation	equity	(NPV)
cash flow	improvements	ownership
community amenities	infrastructure	payback period
competition	internal rate of return	present value
cost analysis	(IRR)	price
dealer	interpretation	proceeds
design	investor	rehabilitation
developer	location	size
direct capitalization	market survey	strategies

LEARNING OBJECTIVES

- Describe and explain the four-step process of analyzing residential income property

- Demonstrate how investment performance may be analyzed using simple formulas

- Define net present value and internal rate of return as measures of investment performance and profitability

ANALYZING RESIDENTIAL INCOME PROPERTY: A PROCESS APPROACH

The decision to buy a personal residence is usually highly subjective. The economic benefits of **equity** buildup and appreciation are secondary to its utility and amenity value. Investment in residential income property, on the other hand, is an economic decision—as we discussed in Unit 12. In order to reach any conclusion on the purchase of a residential site in a given situation, it is important to establish the basic objective of the project.

Once the objective has been defined, a scientific approach to problem solving can be applied. The scientific method formulates a question, gathers data, analyzes it, forms a hypothesis, and tests it. In a real estate project, a modified version of this scientific process can be used to analyze the economic benefits of a particular project.

STEP ONE: CLARIFYING THE ISSUE

Before we can begin gathering data and developing an answer, we need to know what the question is. Formulating the question is based on five evaluations: location, financial goals, taxes, ownership structure, and development issues.

Location

Has careful consideration gone into the choice of neighborhood before any further investigation takes place? Is this **location** compatible with management objectives? It is important to remember when developing residential property that this will be someone's home. The importance of providing an appropriate residential environment appealing to the consumer is absolutely paramount.

Financial Goals

Is this property to be acquired for development and sale or held as an investment? What is an acceptable return on investment? If the property is to be held as an investment, will it be a long-term or short-term holding? What form of project financing is to be used? The financial goals may vary depending on whether the project is new construction or an existing residential property.

Tax Considerations

Is this property designed to attain **"dealer"** status for tax purposes by selling as a subdivision, or will it be subject to less harsh tax treatment as an **"investor"** with landlord status to be resold later?

Structuring of Ownership

Will the **ownership** be a corporation, a limited partnership, a trust, a general partnership, or in the names of individuals? If some form of joint entity is chosen, are the combined objectives of the owners compatible?

Development Issues

In the case of a project to be developed or the **rehabilitation** of an existing property, is the construction done by the developers or are the services of a general contractor to be used? This decision has a marked impact on the total project budget and scheduling.

STEP TWO: COLLECTING THE DATA

The scope of the study is dependent upon the size of the project and the developer's financial commitment to the undertaking. With this in mind, here are some of the sources of data that might be utilized in formulating an investment decision involving residential real estate.

Finding Current Economic Data

The most current economic data indicating potential growth patterns or clouds on the national or local economic horizon can be obtained free from the following sources (including their internet addresses on the web):

- U.S. Census Bureau: www.census.gov

- White House Economic Statistics: www.whitehouse.gov

- Bureau of Economic Analysis: www.bea.gov

- USDA Economics, Statistics, and Market Information: http://usda.mannlib.cornell.edu

- California Association of REALTORS®: www.car.org

- United States Department of Commerce: www.commerce.gov

■ California Department of Industrial Relations: www.dir.ca.gov

■ California Department of Finance: www.dof.ca.gov

Other excellent sources of timely residential housing data include the National Association of REALTORS® (www.realtor.com) and the National Association of Home Builders (www.nahb.com).

Traditional Sources

Direct and indirect information about the area can be gleaned from newspapers of all types—from the *Wall Street Journal* to neighborhood publications—promotional pieces for local developments, sales studies conducted by local economic groups, economically oriented publications of local firms such as banks or public utilities, and other publicity brochures.

Local television also serves to provide a feel for the character of the area and general price levels. Local chambers of commerce have a wealth of information about local economies, amenities, attractions, and resources. Local tastes and price levels of residential real estate can be learned from licensees and appraisers who are active in the area.

Along with print and visual media, local radio stations, businessowners, newspaper archives, libraries, and museums can all add to the investigator's knowledge of the area.

Local Government   Local government bodies such as housing authorities, economic development departments, and planning and building departments can provide good, strong, credible information about a community's commitment to housing development and rehabilitation as well as clarify land use, zoning, and infrastructure issues.

Other useful local authorities include road departments, commonly referred to as public works departments, or city/county engineering departments (for information about present access and future planned transportation developments). Local school districts and administrators also do projections and do their own school site planning. This information would provide a developer knowledge of where housing is most needed in the community. Another source is local utility companies; in many cases these are also part of city departments (the electric or water/sewer departments). These departments maintain data on customer base usage, infrastructure needs, and future projections of community needs as well as the cost of development and infrastructure improvements, which developers are required to install as part of the development.

Other Local Sources   The developer cannot afford to overlook any local source that might have a bearing on the project. For example, if one company is the major employer in the area, its future plans for expansion or contraction would bear heavily on the decision to go ahead or abandon plans. Influential political or environmental groups should also be sounded out at this stage. This is also the point at which to consult with neighborhood and community associations, both to create a cooperative atmosphere and to identify potential areas of contention.

Your Local Library   Because so many development projects in California are discretionary, requiring public notification and public hearings, a variety of environmental documents are prepared for such developments/ projects and are sent to the library to allow everyone access to the documents. Many of these documents will include basic environmental, social, and economic information that will prove useful. Additionally, copies of local ordinances and long-range planning documents (i.e., The General Plan) are also kept in the reference sections of the library. Many of these documents can allow a person to compile the necessary data and information to decide whether to develop a site.

Chamber of Commerce   These are local organizations that tend to lobby for business owners on a variety of issues. As many of these "chambers" also promote the areas or communities in order to attract businesses, information usually found in a summary form is typically made available to the general public.

Market Surveys   The **developer** may decide to conduct a custom-tailored **market survey** to determine local housing preference, especially if a specialized market is being targeted. For example, in certain recreational areas, manufactured and modular housing may be more popular than conventional "stick built" housing. Are the probable customers looking for garden kitchens, spacious yards, spas, swimming pools, air-conditioning, solar applications, golf courses, tennis courts, and other recreational facilities?

Research design studies will vary depending on whether the project is multiunit, such as apartments, cooperatives or condominiums; traditional detached single-family homes; or something in between. The nature of the project has a definite bearing on the type of data that will influence the decision of purchase or pass.

STEP THREE: INTERPRETING THE DATA

A developer can collect mountains of facts, figures, and opinions, but unless all those elements can be assimilated and arranged in a meaningful pattern, they are worthless. One of the principal concerns is the site under study itself. If the objective of the study is to determine the most suitable site, the factors outlined here will prove useful in making the selection. If there is just one site under study, reducing the data down to this level will help determine whether to proceed, abandon, or modify the project.

FIGURE 14.1:   Subdivision Plat Map

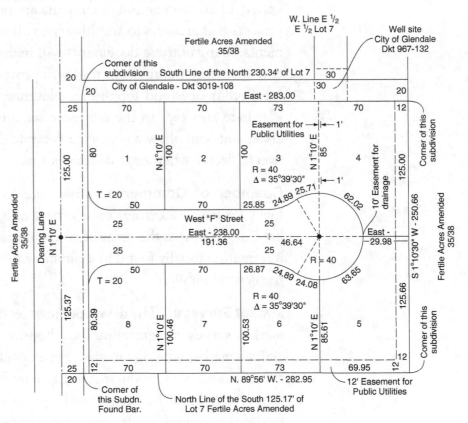

Analysis would normally consist of a feasibility study including the following:

- Project description
- Area description
- Competition
- Cost analysis

Project Description

- **Improvements:** A physical description of the existing or proposed **improvements** is a basic requirement of the analysis. This can vary from a simple purchase of an existing home to the development of hundreds of new homes or apartments.

- **Prices:** The local market as well as development costs will determine **price** ranges or rent levels. The study may cease at this point if it is determined that the costs of production are not adequately rewarded due to unattractive prevailing price levels.

- **Amenities:** This analysis will be based on a study of average **amenities** for the area. If every housing project has built-in appliances, a fireplace, and two or three bedrooms, then product differentiation will probably be in the area of additional amenities or **design** features within these parameters.

- **Lot, Unit, and Room Size:** If the surrounding area features half-acre house lots and the developer seeks to create postage-stamp lots, demand will be questionable. If local zoning requires a certain lot **size**, of course, that creates the minimum legal boundaries. Developers should be aware that room-size expectations are different in urban and suburban markets.

Area Description

- **Economic Trends: Economic trends** is an extremely broad topic that includes employment, median income, tax rates, ethnic mix, lifestyle, absorption rates of new projects, retail sales, future trends, and essentially any other issues the developer can think of.

- **Infrastructure, Transportation, and Services:** Capacity as well as availability of utilities and services (**infrastructure**) should be emphasized in the analysis. All aspects of transportation and access need to be assimilated and discussed in logical order. Not only are public utilities and appropriately lighted and signed street arterials essential, police and fire protection and other public services must be adequate to present and future needs.

- **Shopping:** Commercial centers from regional malls right down to the local grocery or mini-mall should be noted. If the project involves a sizable investment, this should be analyzed for a to 7–10-mile radius from the project. Remember that in U.S. culture, grocery stores and shopping centers are the "hunting grounds" for the local population. Just as a herd of predatory animals will establish a territory where there are plentiful prey and accessible water, modern urbanites and suburbanites require access to their sources of food and clothing.

- **Schools and Houses of Worship:** The entire spectrum of educational facilities should be listed in detail, including day care centers and preschools; public and private elementary and high schools; and local community colleges, business schools, and universities. The proximity of churches, temples, mosques, and other religious institutions is often a competitive advantage. Whether or not the consumers are spiritually oriented, the presence of religious institutions is often interpreted as a positive sign of stability and tradition.

- **Other Community Amenities:** These include recreational and athletic facilities (such as parks, health clubs, and public playgrounds); health care (hospitals and clinics); and special features such as cultural institutions and events (museums, orchestras, theaters, and fairs). There must be a good match between **community amenities** and the project's intended customers. For instance, if the target group is composed of older or retired persons, the proximity of playgrounds may be of less relevance than the quality of local health care facilities. On the other hand, the absence of places to take the grandchildren may be off-putting to potential buyers.

Competition   Just as when one is seeking a personal residence and wants to compare prices, the best approach is to look at price levels of similar housing in the same area, or **competition**. Of particular concern in a development project is the financing available on competitive merchandise and its availability for the project in question. If, for example, government funds are available for a competing project and not for the project in question, it might affect the price that must be charged to the consumer.

Cost Analysis   Budgetary concerns are not necessarily the last item addressed, as failure to pass the test of affordability may kill the project at once. Affordability applies to both the consumer and the developer. It is important through **cost analysis** to realistically examine the amount of capital available compared to the total capital outlay required for acquisition, development, marketing, and all other costs attributable to the objective of the investment.

STEP FOUR: MAKING THE DECISION

Before the ultimate decision of whether or not to buy, the accumulated data must be put to the test. Once arranged in orderly fashion, do the facts support the decision to purchase? The answer to this question is how we test our "hypothesis" that a particular investment decision is a sound one. If the facts support the purchase, then interim methods of landholding may be pursued for a proposed project while the balance of the due diligence process takes place. In the case of a home or condominium purchase, it may be time for an acceptable offer and entry into escrow.

If the answer to our hypothetical question supports going the final step, decision making involves two elements—factual conclusions and recommended strategies for action. Over the coming days, months, and years, the project can be monitored by repeating these steps in a continuing cycle of assessment and follow-up.

Conclusions

It is important to have a clear and logical summary of the results of the study leading to the decision to buy or pass. As with other types of income properties, an appropriate return on investment and appreciation of invested capital must be ensured. In order to maximize these items, proven approaches to investment analysis must be undertaken.

Strategies

Following from the conclusions are a series of **strategies** for carrying out the decision in the most profitable manner. Specific choices at this point include the number of units to be produced and, if in phases, how many units to each phase. There may be recommendations as to unit and room sizes, amenities, and community facilities that affect the marketability of the product. There will also be recommendations about the type of financing and terms to be made available to buyers, such as buydowns, graduated payments, and adjustable rates.

The decision-making process for individual unit purchase for investment or personal consumption is along the same lines, with additional attention to possible remodeling or additional amenities.

Assessment and Follow-Up

Nothing in life remains static. To assume that conditions will remain as they are is dangerously naive on the part of any developer. Once the property has been brought under the developer's preliminary control (through a lease-option, option to purchase, or escrow with contingencies), there may still be discoveries in the due diligence process (such as unavailability of water, downzoning, or local "slow growth" initiatives) that might affect the project. In the case of an existing property, inspection might uncover serious structural flaws or environmental hazards that affect value. The prudent developer will remain flexible and not stubbornly stick to a project that proves unfeasible at this stage.

MEASURES OF INVESTMENT PERFORMANCE

There are several commonly used calculations that an investor may employ to evaluate a property or project. For the purchase of an existing property, real figures should be available based on past performance. For proposed construction or a purchase where significant changes will be made, the same approaches are used with projected figures in a pro forma analysis.

Direct Capitalization

As a measure of economic productivity, **direct capitalization** is expressed in this formula:

$$R = \frac{i}{V}$$

where

R = overall rate of return
i = projected annual net operating income
V = value

For example, a property purchased for $300,000 ($V$) that produces an annual net operating income of $36,000 ($i$) may be said to produce an overall rate of return of 12% (R):

$$\$36,000 \div \$300,000 = 0.12, \text{ or } 12\%$$

This overall rate is a device used in valuation of a property in the income approach, assuming that normal financing is available, and such rates are established in the market through the interaction of buyers and sellers. This rate would tend to evaluate the investment only with 100% equity investment, a rare occurrence, and reversion (future sale) is not considered.

Cash-on-Cash Return

The same technique that is used in **direct capitalization** can be applied to the evaluation of equity investments by using cash-on-cash returns. The cash-on-cash return method gives a prospective investor a much better evaluation of the investment than an estimate of value based on direct capitalization alone.

This analysis uses the same formula as direct capitalization:

$$R = \frac{i}{V}$$

where

   R = rate of return on cash invested
   i = cash flow after debt service
   V = equity investment

For example, a property purchased for $300,000 with $75,000 cash down payment, and producing a net annual operating income of $36,000, would require a debt service of $23,700 on a $225,000 mortgage at 10%, leaving a cash flow of $12,300.

$$\$12,300 \div \$75,000 = 0.164, \text{ or } 16.4\%$$

While this technique presents a better analysis of the investment, it still fails to take into consideration the fact that debt service includes some equity build-up through amortization, and that there is a possibility of reversion in the property. The reversion will come from the sale of the property at some predicted time in the future.

Band of Investment Analysis

If the purchase of the property is financed, each component of financing represents a band of investment. By analyzing the proportion of an overall capitalization rate that is allocated to each band of investment, an equity yield rate can be established.

For example, assume that an investment property can be purchased at an overall capitalization rate of 12%. If a first trust deed loan of 80% of the purchase price can be obtained for 30 years at an annual interest rate of 10%, this represents the first band of investment. The equity band is the remaining 20% of the purchase price.

Assume the first loan has a mortgage constant of 0.105309 (the annual debt service divided by the original principal amount of the loan). By multiplying the percentage of the total purchase price that this band of investment represents (80%) by the mortgage constant for this available financing (0.105309), a capitalization rate is derived for this band of investment.

This capitalization rate is then subtracted from the overall capitalization rate to determine what portion of the overall rate is available to apply to the next band of investment, the equity band.

$$80\% \times 0.105309 = 0.0842$$

(or 8.42% of the capitalization rate to apply to the first band of investment)

$$
\begin{array}{ll}
12.00\% & \text{(overall capitalization rate)} \\
-\ 8.42\% & \text{(applied to the first band)} \\
=\ 3.58\% & \text{(to apply to the equity band)}
\end{array}
$$

$$0.0358 \div 0.20 = 0.179, \text{ or } 17.9\% \text{ (equity yield)}$$

This greatly increased equity yield, significantly higher than the overall capitalization rate, reflects the advantage of leverage and shows clearly that a capitalization rate alone does not analyze a leveraged investment. It also becomes clear that an overall capitalization rate alone is not an adequate tool for a direct comparison between a real estate investment and other types of investments that will compete for the investor's funds.

Payback Period

The **payback period** is the length of time required for the stream of cash flows produced by the investment to equal the original cash outlay. By measuring this period, the investor determines how long the investment funds are at risk. The cash outlay is divided by the annual cash flow:

$$\$75,000 \div \$12,300 = 6.10 \text{ years}$$

Payback periods are used to compare investment opportunities. A different investment might have higher returns in early years and nothing thereafter. In general, the shorter the payback period, the more attractive the investment. However, the total return may be more significant to some investors.

Proceeds per Dollar Invested

An investment may be evaluated according to the total anticipated **proceeds** from income and reversion upon sale of the property. The problem with this technique is that each dollar received is treated the same, regardless of when received, even though it is generally recognized that a dollar to be received one year from now is worth less than a dollar received today.

Discounted Cash Flows

Based on the theory that a dollar to be received in the future is worth less than a dollar in hand today (compound interest theory), a discounted cash flow analysis can be used to evaluate a series of negative and positive **cash flows** over the anticipated ownership of a property. The cash flows used can be either before-tax or after-tax calculations, but the more complete investment analysis for the client would require the use of after-tax cash flows. The mathematics of this procedure is relatively simple but lengthy. It is accomplished by the following formula:

$$PV = \frac{CF_1}{(1+i)} + \frac{CF_2}{(1+i)^2} + ... + \frac{CF_n}{(1+i)^n}$$

where

PV = present value of the discounted cash flows
CF = *cash flow*
i = discount rate used to reflect the time value of money
n = number of years of the life of the investment

The calculation of PV, while laborious, is accomplished quickly and easily with a few keystrokes on a basic financial calculator.

Net Present Value

An evaluation of the investment is frequently accomplished by determining the **net present value (NPV)** of a series of negative and positive discounted cash flows, where the first cash flow is the initial cash outlay, subsequent cash flows are the after-tax cash flows projected for the property, and the final cash flow is the anticipated value of the reversion from the sale of the property in 5, 10, or 15 years.

Interpretation Interpretation of the NPV is straightforward. A positive NPV indicates that the financial value of the investor's assets would be increased by this investment. An NPV of exactly zero means that the future cash flows have been discounted exactly to **present value**. NPV for one investment can be compared with NPV for another investment, and these comparisons can provide useful data in investment decision making. The greater the NPV, the greater the increase in the value of the investor's assets.

Internal Rate of Return

Internal rate of return (IRR) is the annual rate of return on capital generated by an investment over the entire period of its ownership.

Calculation   A series of discount rates is applied to a projected series of negative and positive cash flows to determine the net present value (NPV) of the cash flows at each discount rate. First, a high discount rate is used, then a low discount rate. Next, a slightly lower high rate is used, then a slightly higher low rate, and so on. These calculations continue in a reiterative process until a certain discount rate produces a NPV of approximately zero. This discount rate is the internal rate of return (IRR). *The calculation of IRR, being a reiterative process, is accomplished quickly and easily with a financial calculator.*

Application   The procedure enables a prospective investor in real estate to make direct comparisons of the real estate investment with other investments, such as bonds, notes, and other securities.

THE NEXT STEP   In the next and final unit, we'll focus on analyzing commercial investment property and compare the various types of analysis appropriate for different kinds of properties.

SUMMARY

- The **first step** in analyzing a potential residential income property is to make five preliminary evaluations: location, financial goals, tax considerations, ownership structure, and development considerations.

- The **second step** in analyzing a potential residential income property is to collect the data necessary for making a sound financial decision.

- The **third step** in analyzing a potential residential income property is to interpret the data based on the nature of the project, the area under consideration, the actual and potential competition, and a cost analysis.

■ The **final step** in analyzing a potential residential income property is to determine whether the accumulated and interpreted data support a decision to purchase.

■ There are several common **calculations** that an investor may use to evaluate a property or project. These include direct capitalization, cash-on-cash return, band of investment analysis, payback period, proceeds per dollar invested, and discounted cash flows. An evaluation of the investment is frequently accomplished by determining its net present value and internal rate of return.

REVIEW QUESTIONS

1. The housing sector tends to lead the rest of the economy. What are the "housing starts" in your community/and or county? (For this exercise, you may wish to visit your local building department and find out the total number of new residential unit building permits issued.)

2. Changes in housing starts are also triggered by mortgage rates. Currently, what is the status of mortgage rates in your area? Have they had a significant impact in the construction on new housing units in your area?

3. How many building permits for new residential units were issued this year compared with last year or the last two years? What catalyzed the difference, if any?

4. What questions would you ask and to whom before deciding to invest in a residential housing project in your county?

5. What types of development impact fees does your city charge/levy on new residential developments? Are these fees waived for affordable housing units? If fees are charged, what is the cost per unit?

6. How much commercial/office space has been developed in your community in the last two years?

UNIT QUIZ

1. In the first step of analyzing a residential income property, all of the following are considerations *EXCEPT*
   a. location.
   b. financial goals.
   c. ownership structure.
   d. cost analysis.

2. Which of the following sources of information would be likely to have the least current economic data about a particular location?
   a. www.census.gov
   b. Local chamber of commerce
   c. State housing authority
   d. Encyclopedia yearbook

3. In a feasibility study performed during Step three of a residential income property analysis, which of the following items would normally be first?
   a. Competition
   b. Cost analysis
   c. Project description
   d. Area description

4. Which of the following correctly expresses the formula for measuring direct capitalization?
   a. $R = i \times V$
   b. $V \div R = i$
   c. $C = R \times i$
   d. $R = i \div V$

5. If a property purchased for $250,000 produces an annual net operating income of $28,000, what is the property's overall rate of return?
   a. 8.9%
   b. 11%
   c. 70%
   d. $222,000

6. Which of the following correctly expresses the formula used to evaluate equity investments using the cash-on-cash return method?
    a. $R = i \times V$
    b. $V \div R = i$
    c. $C = R \times i$
    d. $R = i \div V$

7. What is the payback period?
    a. The time during which a borrower is permitted to repay a mortgage loan
    b. A term that refers to the practice of leveraging one project to finance another at a more acceptable rate of interest
    c. The length of time required for the stream of cash flows produced by an investment to equal the original cash outlay
    d. The contractual length of time demanded by a buyer during which he or she is permitted to a full refund of any down payment

8. A dollar to be received in the future is worth
    a. less than a dollar in hand today.
    b. more than a dollar in hand today.
    c. the same as a dollar in hand today.
    d. the value of today's dollar minus the difference between its value and the value of the future dollar $[(PV) - (F - P) = FV]$.

9. What does a positive NPV mean?
    a. The future cash flows have been discounted to exactly present value.
    b. The investor's assets will be unlikely to increase in value.
    c. The financial value of the investor's assets will be increased by the investment.
    d. The greater the NPV, the less the investor's assets will grow.

10. The annual rate of return on capital generated by an investment over the entire period of its ownership is referred to as its
    a. total rate of return (TRR).
    b. internal rate of return (IRR).
    c. net present value (NPV).
    d. annualized net return (ANR).

UNIT FIFTEEN

15

ANALYZING COMMERCIAL INVESTMENT PROPERTY

KEY TERMS

big box	industrial	parasite structures
capitalization rate	industrial park	retail
cash flow	infrastructure	return on investment
economy	mini-mall	shopping center
employment	net rentable space	special purpose
general purpose	NIMBY	start-up
income potential	office	

LEARNING OBJECTIVES

- Describe the characteristics of various classes of commercial property: office, retail, industrial, and special purpose

- Apply a process approach to commercial property analysis

- Explain the different issues arising in new construction versus existing structures

FUNDAMENTAL PRINCIPLES

Investment or income-producing property is designed to do just that—produce income. The degree to which income-producing property achieves this goal is measured by whether it provides a satisfactory return relative to risk for the investor. Rapid changes in the real estate investment arena today, ranging from tax law changes to overseas investment, make adherence to basic proven investment principles more important than ever.

Many of the analytical principles outlined for residential property in the previous unit also apply to commercial and industrial investment properties as well. Figure 15.1 reviews the systematic investigative approach described in Unit 14.

FIGURE 15.1: Systematic Investigative Approach

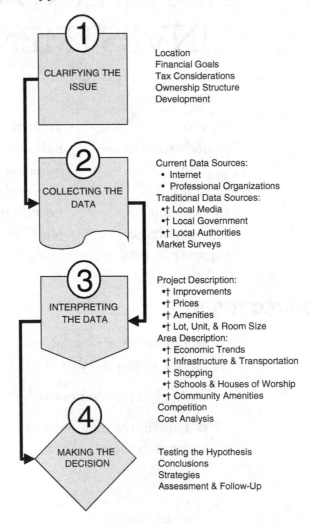

① CLARIFYING THE ISSUE
Location
Financial Goals
Tax Considerations
Ownership Structure
Development

② COLLECTING THE DATA
Current Data Sources:
• Internet
• Professional Organizations
Traditional Data Sources:
•† Local Media
•† Local Government
•† Local Authorities
Market Surveys

③ INTERPRETING THE DATA
Project Description:
•† Improvements
•† Prices
•† Amenities
•† Lot, Unit, & Room Size
Area Description:
•† Economic Trends
•† Infrastructure & Transportation
•† Shopping
•† Schools & Houses of Worship
•† Community Amenities
Competition
Cost Analysis

④ MAKING THE DECISION
Testing the Hypothesis
Conclusions
Strategies
Assessment & Follow-Up

TYPES OF PROPERTY

The scientific approach outlined in Figure 15.1 should be applied at the outset in selecting the type of investment. There is a wide range of choices for investment property, each with its own highly specialized characteristics. Investors in this area have formed many specific professional groups, which can be valuable sources of information. The array of investment property types can be grouped under four major headings: **office**, **retail**, **industrial**, and **special purpose**.

Office Property

This type of property is composed of several distinct classifications.

General Purpose The **general purpose** (generic) office building is for general offering to business, professional, and financial occupants. Typically, a large tenant, such as a bank or retailer, will occupy most of the ground floor space. The upper floors are typically leased as office space to professional and medical service providers.

Special Purpose Some office buildings are designed to accommodate the specific space, electrical, or other needs of a particular type of tenant (e.g., physicians or communications companies). They may have special construction, utility, and permit requirements that add to project costs in new developments.

Community-of-Interest Facilities In some buildings, common tenant goals are involved. Garment or jewelry wholesalers, interior decorators, art galleries, or furniture wholesalers may cluster in a single structure.

"Parasite" Structures **Parasite structures** enable firms that do business with a common large company, or whose noncompetitive businesses appeal to the large company's customers, to locate on the same parcel or in the same building as the "host" company.

Retail Property

From the traditional central business districts and commercial strips that dotted the landscape after World War II, retailing has gone through a variety of changes that have introduced the **mini-mall**, **"big box"** retailer, **shopping center**, and the superregional center with a variety of intermediate categories. These were described in detail in Unit 8. Of course, many retail properties are free-standing buildings, too.

Mini-mall This usually represents the conversion of a corner service station site into a row of stores. The size of the site may be from less than an acre to two or three acres. The building(s) may be configured in a variety of ways: parking in front and stores in back, L shapes, U shapes, subterranean parking and rooftop parking, single story, and multistory—all with the objective of maximizing the available space. Because of limited available space, many of these facilities lack adequate parking. As a result, they have difficulty maintaining a stable tenancy and experience comparatively high turnover rates.

Neighborhood Shopping Center These are usually four to ten acres in size with a single large store (typically a supermarket or drugstore) as the principal (anchor) tenant, supporting a variety of smaller stores and services.

Community Shopping Center Stepping up from groceries to consumer goods, this is a 10-acre to 30-acre site with a moderate-sized department store or factory outlet as the principal tenant.

Regional and Superregional Centers Often enclosed, these are large malls containing two or more major department stores. These anchors serve as drawing power for the smaller mall shops, referred to as "satellites."

"Big Box" Power Centers This type of mall focuses on a new class of discount stores, such as Walmart, Sam's Club, Costco, Home Depot, and so forth that deal in volume sales at bargain prices. It is usually on a site about the size of a community center. A variation of this concept is the upscale manufacturer's outlet, for those with elegant tastes and limited means.

Industrial Property

The classification *industrial property* includes such properties as manufacturers, assemblers, distributors, warehouses, and research-and-development facilities. The construction of an industrial facility is usually very closely linked to its intended use. Most of them, however, include the following features:

- Floors and foundations that are capable of bearing higher-than-normal weight loads (such as those involving heavy machinery)

- High ceilings (to accommodate large equipment, catwalks, and overhead conveyors)

- Independent power generators, or higher-than-normal utility service, as well as specialized plumbing, electrical, or other power systems

- Loading docks and shipping and receiving bays

- Multimode accessibility—that is, the site is accessible by various forms of transportation; a site may include its own rail spur, for instance, in addition to roadways and proximity to airports or seaports

Incubator Buildings   Often, small or **start-up** manufacturing businesses do not have the financial strength of larger companies, although they still have specific needs for industrial space. Incubator facilities are typically existing large industrial properties that are subdivided into multiple smaller units. The tenants cluster in the "incubator" and are able to establish themselves commercially and financially before they leave the nest. The shorter-term leases (offered at higher rates) give the investor in incubator projects an increased rate of return—along with the greater risk of vacancy and tenant default.

Industrial Parks   **Industrial parks** are collections of industrial buildings, often covering very large campuses. The parks are sometimes based on a common theme, such as technology industries or warehousing and distribution. Some associated office space is included.

Office Parks   These are mixed-use facilities that are conglomerate in nature. There may be light manufacturing, office space, related service businesses (such as stationery and fast printing), warehousing, and restaurants, all within the same facility.

Special Purpose Property

Management is the key element in the success of any income-producing property. In the case of special purpose properties, however, it is doubly critical. Most of the categories listed are businesses as well as buildings, and the decisions that management makes with respect to the conduct of the business represent the difference between success and failure. Some of the properties in this category include:

- Hotels and motels

- Parking structures

- Service stations

- Multiscreen motion picture theaters
- Bowling alleys
- Sports and other recreational facilities
- Private airplane hangars

Other Specialized Uses   These vary from food freezer operations in the fields to amusement parks like Great America, Marine World, SeaWorld, and, of course, Disneyland. Some uses—like the trampoline parks, skate parks, water parks, outdoor recreation/zipline parks, and drive-in theaters of the past and ministorage facilities of today—might be classified as transitory, a way of deriving revenue from temporarily underdeveloped land while some more permanent form of income production is considered.

COMMERCIAL PROPERTY INVESTMENT: AN ANALYTICAL APPROACH

Before any specific project can be properly analyzed economically, the factors of value that affect the investment decision must be identified and weighed. The basic economic strengths and weaknesses of the area under study are of particular importance in the decision to commit investment dollars. To make sure the purchase meets the investment objectives of the acquiring entity, a number of pertinent factors of value must be considered.

Economic Base of the Area

Land, labor, and capital are the key tools that any entrepreneur needs to derive a profit from an investment of assets and ingenuity. Adequate acreage in a configuration suitable to the planned development (or to service existing improvements) is essential. So is a sufficient labor pool with suitable skills. In some developments, labor may have to be imported if the area does not have built-in appeal; compensatory measures must be taken. Finally, adequate capital (that is, the financial resources to see the entire investment reach fruition) is a prime consideration.

Infrastructure Availability

The availability of adequate **infrastructure** is essential. Transportation is especially critical in the case of industrial properties, which require considerable capacity for electrical generation, water supply, road access, natural gas, and waste disposal. Communications, fire and police protection, transportation facilities, and a variety of other factors all play a part in selection of a suitable property.

Attitude of Government

Companies are dissuaded from locating in many areas because of government attitudes. In other areas, local governments actively welcome newcomers. Some states, particularly in New England, have undertaken aggressive programs to attract business. California has been able to function as a magnet due to the appeal of the state's economy, culture, resources, and environment. Attitudes toward development throughout California continue to vary. While some communities are sympathetic toward affordable housing needs in their communities and provide developer incentives to create housing, other communities provide expedited permit processing for those developments that continue to generate sales tax, such shopping centers, car dealerships, and big box retail stores. This is especially true in communities that have passed sales tax initiatives to maintain roads, police, and fire infrastructure.

"NIMBY"

Like their local governments, citizens sometimes welcome new companies into their neighborhoods and, other times, actively oppose the move-in. This is a particular issue for companies that are politically controversial, socially unpopular, or associated with the generation of unpleasant or toxic side-effects. The tendency of citizens to oppose disagreeable neighbors—which can include a wide array of entities, from small businesses such as funeral parlors, fast-food restaurants, bars, and dry cleaners to nuclear power plants, waste incinerators, and airports—is known among planners as the "**NIMBY** phenomenon." (NIMBY is an acronym that stands for "Not In My Back Yard.")

Environmental Matters

The environmental and worker safety concerns that have been raised since the mid-1970s have altered the attitude of commercial and industrial investors. This change in perspective is due to the considerable liability that ownership of such property might entail. Hidden problems may arise from contaminated ground, water, or air from prior activity on the property. These issues were discussed at length in Unit 10.

Competitive Factors

In many locations, office and retail space is in a state of oversupply. In others, new construction goes on almost daily. This local condition plays a key role in any investment decision. In general, a glut of office or commercial space affects value negatively through the simple operation of supply and demand. If there are many vacant spaces from which to choose, the competition rate is high, and the result is lower rents and lower rates of return for investors.

SAMPLE ECONOMIC ANALYSIS: NEW CONSTRUCTION

The Back Story

A developer proposes to build a 15-story steel and concrete office building containing 300,000 total square feet, roughly 85% of which will be rentable. The project will include three levels of underground parking containing 60,000 square feet. An office building development site has been selected containing 50,000 square feet.

Project Cost

The cost of the development is as follows:

Land Improvements	50,000 sq. ft. @ $125 / sq. ft.	=	$ 6,250,000
Shell (15 stories)	300,000 sq. ft. @ $150.00 / sq. ft.	=	$45,000,000
Underground garage	60,000 sq. ft. @ $70.00 / sq. ft.	=	$ 4,200,000
Net rentable space	255,000 sq. ft. @ $25.00 / sq. ft.	=	$ 6,375,000
Total Cost of Improvements		=	$55,575,000
TOTAL PROJECT COST	(land plus improvements)	=	**$61,825,000**

Income Potential

The costs previously outlined are then compared with the potential economic productivity of the building **income potential**, based upon comparable rentals and vacancy rates in the area, to derive the following data:

255,000 rentable sq. ft. × $2.50 / sq. ft.		
× 12 months		$7,650,000
– Vacancy Allowance		($ 700,000)
Effective Income	=	$6,950,000
+ Net Parking Revenue		$ 900,000
Net Before Expenses	=	$7,850,000
– Expenses	=	($1,850,000)
Net Income Before Debt Service	=	**$6,000,000**

Cap Rate Analysis for Value

Assuming that a **capitalization rate** of 9.5% is acceptable, use the following formula to derive an economic value for the property:

$$\text{value} = \frac{\text{income}}{\text{rate}}$$

So, in this example, the value of the property is

$$\$6,000,000 \div 0.095 = \$63,157,894$$

Financing Terms

The property qualifies for a \$43,370,000 permanent loan. Based upon the cost figures previously given, this would require an equity investment by the developer of \$18,455,000. A permanent loan is available, with a fixed rate based on a 30-year amortization, with annual principal and interest installments of approximately \$4,260,000.

Return on Investment

The costs, income, and terms previously outlined leave a net spendable income after debt service of \$557,400, a rather pale 3% **return on investment**. Each developer or investor must decide, on a case-by-case basis, whether the projected return is acceptable given his or her goals.

SAMPLE ECONOMIC ANALYSIS: EXISTING PROPERTY

The Back Story

This investment opportunity is a 15-story steel and concrete office structure containing 300,000 square feet of gross space, total **net rentable space** consisting of 255,000 square feet leased at an average of \$1.85 per square foot per month. In addition, the structure contains an underground parking garage that can accommodate 615 vehicles. Approximately 60% of the parking is used by tenants for an additional monthly fee of \$60 per space. Half the remaining parking adds revenue of \$150 per space per month, and the remaining spaces are used by the general public at an average of \$250 per space per month. Expenses for the building, after allowing 71/2% for depreciation and maintenance, amount to 35% of the effective income of the structure. A cap rate of 9.5 is acceptable.

Cash Flow Analysis

The first step is to convert the raw data to a **cash flow** analysis. This is done by taking income from all sources and measuring it against incurred expenses to derive net operating income.

Net Rentable Space	255,000 sq. ft. × $1.85	= $471,750 × 12	=	$5,661,000
Parking Revenue	369 spaces @ $60	= $ 22,140		
	123 spaces @ $150	= $ 18,450		
	123 spaces @ $250	= $ 30,750		
		$ 71,340 × 12	=	$856,080
	Total Monthly Revenue			$6,517,080
	Vacancy and Maintenance (7.5%)		–	**($488,781)**
	Effective Income			**$6,028,299**
Expense Allowance	Parking: 60%		=	$513,648
	Building: 35%		=	$1,981,350
	Total Expense	$2,494,998		($2,494,998)
	Net Operating Income (NOI)		=	**$3,533,301**

Valuation

The net operating income (NOI) figure obtained from the historical data would tend to support an economic valuation of:

$$\$3,533,301 \div 0.95 = \$37,192,604$$

This figure would represent the investor's "bottom line" offer. It would probably be difficult for a seller to justify an asking price significantly higher than $3,800,000 or so for this property.

Financing

A loan is available for financing this project in the amount of $27,900,000 with a 30-year term and fixed interest at the current rate of 8%. Annual mortgage payments on this debt would be $2,790,719, the majority of which would be interest.

Return on Investment

Assuming that the $9,300,000 difference between the loan and the indicated value would be provided in cash, the return on the cash flow after debt service would be approximately 8% (representing the difference between the NOI and the mortgage payments divided by the $9,300,000 investment).

Tax Considerations

The investment should be considered from the standpoint of the investor's tax exposure. If the replacement value of the improvements is estimated to be $19,000,000, the annual straight-line depreciation (based on the building's remaining useful life of 27½ years) would be reported as $51,463. This represents the difference between net income after debt service and the depreciation amount. The figure of the investor's reportable income is still positive and passive; thus, other projects that may be reporting negative cash flow figures after depreciation could be offset against this positive after-tax figure. Because this is an office building, in this example, we have used a recovery life of 30 years and not 27½ years as would normally be used for residential real estate.

THE NEXT STEP   This concludes our discussion of commercial real estate and our general introduction to real estate economics. Now let's turn our attention from the real estate economy as it is today and do a little forward-thinking toward the coming years.

THE STATE OF THE STATE

The recession years brought falling home prices, the difficulty of obtaining credit, shrinking equity values, and the ever-growing job losses in all sectors. All of these significantly impacted the national and California economies in 2008. Consumer and business spending, which is the very core of both the national and state economies, experienced a downturn in 2008. According to the Department of Finance, the committee of economists that officially dates the troughs and peaks of the national economy, declared that in late 2008, the United States was in a recession and had been since December 2007. While there is no official dating of business cycles for states, it was unlikely that the California economy fared better than the national economy in this trying economic environment.

By the summer of 2013, California had experienced a break in the two-year series of drops in the unemployment rate with a slight uptick in July. The number of jobs continued to rise, and the real estate market continued to improve. In July 2013, California's unemployment rate increased to 8.7%, a rise of 0.2% from June 2013. However, the year-over-year drop of 1.9 is still one of the largest decreases on record. The number of unemployed Californians rose by 29,000 over the month but had fallen 328,000 since July 2012. The number of employed Californians also dropped by 65,000 from June 2013 but had risen by 468,000 year over year. The number of non-farm payroll jobs increased by 38,100 in July 2013, the 25th consecutive month of adding jobs. The year-over-year growth was 236,400 jobs. The total private job growth was higher than total non-farm, with 42,000 jobs added in July 2013 and 245,600 since July 2012. This was attributed to the continuing loss of government jobs on a monthly (3,900) and year-over-year (9,200) basis, which offset private job growth somewhat. Most sectors had continued to add jobs; apart from government, only mining and logging (down 200) and construction (7,300) lost jobs. The loss of construction jobs was puzzling given the strong recovery in the housing sector, but there are anecdotal reports that projects slowed as skilled construction workers were in short supply. However, construction was still up 17,800 jobs on a year-over-year basis.

The Department of Finance also reported that financial activities were flat in July 2013. On a month-to-month basis, professional and business services added 15,000 jobs, while trade, transportation, and utilities added 12,100 jobs. Educational and health services added 6,600 jobs, information added 6,100 jobs, and leisure and hospitality added 5,200 jobs. Manufacturing added 2,600 jobs, and other services added 1,900 jobs. The residential real estate markets continued to recover in July 2013. The median price of existing single-family homes sold in July 2013 was $433,760, an increase of $96,700 from January 2013, and almost 30% higher than July 2012. However, this remained 27% below the prerecession peak.[13]

When developers and real estate analysts take on the task of determining if a project is feasible, they must ask Where? Who? and When? Looking at demographics and trends is key to developers as they analyze the feasibility of a development.

In December 2014, the California Department of Finance reported that both California and the United States continued to add jobs. The U.S. real gross domestic product growth rate was revised upward by 0.5% to 3.9% for the third quarter of 2014. The number of California housing permits issued in October 2014 was the highest since March 2007. The U.S. unemployment rate remained at 5.8% of the labor force in November 2014. California's unemployment rate was unchanged in October 2014 at 7.3%. California's non-farm payroll employment grew by 41,500 jobs in October 2014, higher than the 22,500 monthly average for the first nine months of 2014. Eight sectors gained jobs, and three lost jobs. The largest job gains were in professional and business services (12,500) and trade, transpor-

13. California Department of Finance, "Finance Bulletin, September 2013," California Department of Finance, www.dof.ca.gov/finance_bulletins/2013/september/ (accessed April 2015).

tation, and utilities (12,400). Other sectors that gained jobs were leisure and hospitality (7,500), government (3,500), educational and health services (3,100), information (1,900), construction (800), and manufacturing (700). The three sectors that had small job losses were other services (400), financial activities (400), and mining and logging (100).

Relative to the real estate market, the median sales price of an existing single-family home fell in October 2014 by 2.3% to $450,620. Compared to the prior year (2013), the median price was up by 5.4%. With job growth and solid economic expansion, household formation experienced a boost, and demand for rental and owner-occupied housing increased. As the economy continues to improve, there are promising signs for the housing industry because housing demand results in the creation of jobs and, in turn, fosters additional demand for construction. While prices have continued to rise on average, they have done so at a slower rate over the course of 2014, and that trend is expected to continue in 2015. [14]

Trends for the 21st Century

Let's take a look at the economic challenges that lie ahead for real estate professionals. We won't worry about the challenge of selling time-share properties on Mars or how many people will fit in a hover-car. We will, however, consider how the real estate market is likely to change over the next 30 years and ask what those changes may mean for the industry and for you. Those with foresight and imagination can respond creatively to the constant changes in the economic environment.

Population   Here are some projections from the U.S. Census Bureau about the changing population of the nation, the region, and California itself between now and the year 2025:

- Over the next 30 years, the West is projected to grow at nearly twice the national average, while the Northeast and Midwest are projected to grow at one-half the U.S. total rate.

- International migration is expected to play a dominant role in the population growth of the West, while both international and domestic migration will be important contributors to growth of the South.

---

14. California Department of Finance, "Finance Bulletin, December 2014," California Department of Finance, www.dof.ca.gov/finance_bulletins/2014/december/ (accessed April 2015).

- California, currently the most populous state, was home to 12% of the U.S. population in 1995. By 2025, more than 15% of Americans will live in California, which will add 17.7 million people—almost as if the entire population of the state of New York packed up and switched coasts. California's population in 2025 will be somewhere between 41 and 46 million people.

- California is projected to add the largest number of international migrants (8 million)—more than one-third of the total population of immigrants to the United States—between the mid-1990s and 2025.

- After 2015, Florida is projected to replace New York as the third most populous state, with Texas ranked second.

- Racially, the white population is projected to be the slowest-growing ethnic group between now and 2025. The African-American population is projected to be the second slowest-growing in all regions except the South, where it will rank third. The Asian population is the fastest-growing group in all regions. The Asian population is projected to have the greatest gains in the West with an increase of 7 million persons. Of the total added to the U.S. Asian population by 2025, 56% will be in the Western states. California will be home to 41% of the Asian population, the largest concentration in the country.

- The U.S. population of Hispanic origin will increase rapidly by 2025, accounting for 44% of the total U.S. population growth. The population of Hispanic origin is the second fastest-growing population. In 1995, California had the largest share of the nation's Hispanic population (9 million) followed by Texas, New York, Florida, and Illinois. California's Hispanic population will more than double over the projected period, to 21 million.

- In 2025, Alaska will be the state with the highest proportion of its population younger than 20 (34%), followed closely by California (33%).

Note: An official Census Bureau report detailing these and other projected population changes (as well as details explaining how the information was gathered, compiled, and adjusted) is included in Appendix II. While the real estate industry's product is land, its market is people, and that market is changing rapidly.

California's Recent Population Growth   California added 371,107 residents in 2014 to a total population of 38,802,500 as of July 1, 2014, according to the new city and county population data released by the U.S. Census Bureau.

With more than 38 million people as of 2014, California's population continues to grow. Despite a slowdown in the 1990s, the state of California has continued to grow in excess of 1% each year since 1997. Natural increase (more births than deaths) will account for three times as much growth (76% versus 24%) as net migration (people moving into the state, less those moving out).

How did California's communities do as of January 1, 2013? The San Francisco Bay Area is the fastest growing region in the state, with San Jose's population already surpassing 1 million residents and home construction placing the city of Dublin among the fastest growing cities in California. Santa Clara County and Alameda County were the two fastest growing counties in California.

San Francisco, the state's fourth-largest city, grew by 10,000 people in 2013. Over the past four years, demographic data shows that San Francisco's population grew by more than 31,000 people. During that time, only 5,000 new housing units were added, which explains why the new units added were not able to keep up pace with the new population moving into the city and why prices for homes and apartments in San Francisco have been driven upward. Overall, as a state, California only added 59,000 housing units in 2013, compared with 45,000 in 2012.

Four of the six fastest-growing cities in California made the list because of an increase in the number of prison inmates housed in those cities. Those cities are McFarland in Kern County, whose population increased 8.9%, Chowchilla in Madera County, up 8.7%, Calipatria in Imperial County, up 5.5%, and Adelanto in San Bernardino County, up 4.3%. Dublin ranked as the third-fastest growing city in 2013, following a 7.1% increase attributed to 1,100 new housing units.

FIGURE 15.2:   Population Estimates for California Cities

10 Largest Cities		
City	**Population January 1, 2010**	**Percent Change 2009–2010**
1. Los Angeles	4,094,764	1.1
2. San Diego	1,376,173	1.3
3. San Jose	1,023,083	1.6
4. San Francisco	856,095	1.1
5. Fresno	502,303	1.4
6. Long Beach	494,709	0.8
7. Sacramento	486,189	1.0
8. Oakland	430,666	1.2
9. Santa Ana	357,754	0.7
10. Anaheim	353,643	1.6
10 Fastest Growing Cities Based on Percent Change		
City	**Population January 1, 2013**	**Percent Change 2012–2013**
1. McFarland	13,745	8.9
2. Chowchilla	18,971	8.7
3. Dublin	53,462	7.1
4. Calipatria	7,517	5.5
5. Irvine	242,651	4.9
6. Adelanto	32,511	4.3
7. Campbell	41,993	4.0
8. Rio Vista	7,934	3.9
9. Imperial	16,708	3.8
10. San Marcos	90,179	3.5

Source: The California Department of Finance

Land Supply   Land is becoming a scarce commodity, reduced in supply by a variety of influences at the same time, that it must be allocated among an ever increasing number of people. Land scarcity, combined with increased population pressure, will cause increased emphasis on density and siting.

The growing acceptance of home offices and the technological feasibility of telecommuting for many in the workforce will have a definitive effect on housing design, dictating consideration for work as well as living space.

Land acquisition and development in the Sun Belt states will continue, but the nation's older northern and eastern urban areas may enjoy a renaissance as flexibility of residential location is afforded through the magic of electronics. Consumers will be attracted to these places by the generally lower housing prices, resulting from population shifts, and the unusual varieties of housing available.

Transportation Mobility has become a serious problem, particularly in urban areas, during the last decade of the 20th century. National, state, and local governments maintain streets and arterial systems; governments control land, sea, and air transport and space exploration. Billions of dollars have been spent on studies of different ways to link where people live and where they work. Today, with some people living literally thousands of miles from their work stations, transportation needs take on an entirely new dimension. Transportation is also closely linked to the issue of environmental quality, which, as we've seen, is an economic issue directly related to property values. Similarly, transportation issues may make or break residential, commercial, retail, and industrial developments. Rising fuel costs may eventually force people who currently live in suburbs far from their work to move closer to city centers—or alternatively, city-based jobs could move out to where the "stranded" employees live, further crippling the nation's urban centers.

Employment By the end of the first quarter of the 21st century, the **employment** picture may be far different from today's. Electronics and high-tech service industries will continue to experience the phenomenal growth we see currently, while heavy industries such as steel and automobile manufacturing will continue to be dominated by overseas expansion. With an explosion of the service economy, more and more U.S. workers will require retraining, and the typical office-based 9-to-5 job of today is likely to be a thing of the past. Mobile offices, home offices, satellite offices, and shared facilities are likely to replace more individual and localized workplaces. The number of part-time and temporary employees will grow rapidly as companies bring in outside expertise to perform individual tasks on projects rather than retraining existing workers. What will this mean for the real estate economy and for people's ability to afford housing? Will the scattering of once-centralized work sites lead to a more mobile population, one less linked to a specific geographic location? If so, what will that mean for the housing industry?

The Future

The future can be projected with statistics and models, but we will only know what the U.S. economy will look like in 30 years when we get there. No matter what direction the economy takes, however, the fundamental principles you've learned here, combined with old-fashioned entrepreneurial savvy, foresight, and a willingness to take risks and act ahead of the curve will help ensure your success in the real estate marketplace of the 21st century.

NOW LET'S TRY IT

The Feasibility Study for the Development of Land

As a developer or a real estate professional working with developers, you must perform a variety of studies and analysis before actually developing a parcel of land. Most developments begin with the acquisition and the subdivision of the land. Subsequently the land may be improved to satisfy market trends/needs (residential, multifamily, shopping centers, industrial parks, etc.).

As most people will look at residential properties for potential investments and developments, this exercise will help you analyze your investment. However, this exercise can also be utilized for analyzing commercial developments.

For your final class project you are to choose a property and prepare a feasibility study for the development of the property.

1.   Prepare a brief description of your project/development. (Under this section please define your project.)

2.   Next, analyze your project using Figure 15.1 (Systematic Investigation Approach). Using this flowchart as a guide, prepare a brief discussion for each of the headings.

3.   Some basic questions need to be explored and analyzed:
    a.   Is the use/development allowed/permitted? Does it comply with the General Plan/zoning? Is an EIR required? What is the political sentiment toward the type of project/proposal and will it be supported in a public forum?
    b.   As a result of the proposed project, are there any perceived environmental issues that will have to be mitigated and what are the mitigations? For example, a proposal will cause increased traffic on Street X, necessitating a traffic signal at an intersection. The traffic signal would be a mitigation to either additional traffic or traffic that wasn't there before. When a new development stresses a system beyond its capacity, the level of service is impacted. A developer today would be expected to mitigate or pay their fair share of the impact they have caused upon the system. In this case, the developer might be required to pay for the traffic signal.
    c.   Will you need to subdivide the property?

d. Are utilities available to the site, such as water, sewer, electric power, telephone, cable TV, and so forth? Or will the infrastructure improvements need to be brought in at a significant cost to the developer?

e. Can you obtain financing for the development?

f. What other alternatives are there for development?

g. Is there a market for your project/development? Who will be your consumers/clients? What will your consumers pay? Can your proposal be absorbed into the current market for such properties?

h. Is your project to be phased? When will certain phases of your project be completed? Prepare a timeline of the various events (development plan).

i. What will it cost you?

j. What is the best financing available for your purchasers?

k. Will your project result in a profit/loss or will you just break even?

l. Your final decision: was your proposal feasible? What would you have done different? Are there any other alternatives to the proposed development/project that may be more feasible given politics, financing, or other issues in the community?

4. Your project analysis should be prepared as follows:

a. Cover Page

b. Table of Contents

c. Introduction and Description

d. Analysis

e. Conclusion

f. Appendix, which contains supporting materials and information such as graphs, tables, photos, subdivision maps, zoning maps, architectural renderings, and so forth.

g. Your project should be typed and well suited for presentation. The presentation can be placed into a PowerPoint for greater impact on your audience.

5. The instructor may use this exercise as a final project or exam and, therefore, may require you to submit a written report or present an oral report to the class. In doing an oral presentation, you may wish to use any medium such as PowerPoint, video, or overhead transparencies. It is suggested that written reports be kept to a maximum of 15 pages excluding supporting materials; this allows the developer or investor to quickly go through the materials and make an informed decision. Additionally, the instructor may wish to assign this project as a class project, with each person responsible for certain tasks. Good luck!

SUMMARY

- **Office buildings** include a variety of classifications: *general purpose, special purpose, community of interest facilities*, and *parasite structures*.

- **Retail property** includes *free-standing facilities* as well as such developments as *mini-malls, neighborhood shopping centers, community shopping centers, regional centers*, and *"big box" power centers*.

- **Industrial property** includes traditional *factory and R&D facilities* as well as *incubator buildings, industrial parks*, and *office parks*. Industrial real estate is characterized by *load-bearing floors and foundations, high ceilings, independent power generators, loading docks, shipping bays*, and *multimodal accessibility*.

- **Special purpose properties** are businesses as well as buildings (e.g., *hotels and motels, parking structures, service stations*, and *bowling alleys*).

- Before any specific property can be analyzed, the **factors of value** that affect the investment decision must be identified and weighed: the area's *economic base*, available *infrastructure, government and neighborhood attitudes, environmental issues*, and *competitive factors*.

- Different **analytical expectations** apply to *existing properties* and *new construction*.

- The big trend for the **21st century** is *growth*: growing populations, growing ethnic diversity, a growing service economy, and growing transportation headaches. Land is becoming a scarce commodity, and the growth of telecommuting may change consumers' expectations for their homes.

REVIEW QUESTIONS

1. What are different types of shopping center classifications? Which one would be best suited for the community you reside in? Do you believe it will be successful in the long run?

2. What is the difference between an *appraisal* and a *feasibility study*?

3. What is being done in your community to entice or attract new industry or major employers to the area? Who are the key players? Government? The Chamber of Commerce?

4. What types of questions should a real estate investor ask before purchasing commercial real estate?

5. Discuss the implications of environmental laws on commercial real estate, such as warehouses, industrial parks, shopping centers, and, most important, service stations and supermarkets.

6. Where in your community could you obtain information on economic development data relative to commercial and industrial projects?

7. What is the difference between a *dealer* and an *investor*?

8. Explain the difference between *risk* and *return*.

9. How has the increase in the state prison population changed the demographics in your region/county?

UNIT QUIZ

1. General purpose, special purpose, and "parasite" structures are all classifications of which type of property?
    a. Retail
    b. Industrial
    c. Office
    d. Special purpose

2. Several importers agree to rent separate space in the same building in order to reduce their costs. What kind of building is this?
    a. General purpose
    b. Special purpose
    c. Community of interest
    d. Parasite

3. Garland Towne Centre is on a 25-acre site. It has 12 stores and a mid-sized factory outlet as an anchor tenant. What type of retail property is this?
    a. Neighborhood shopping center
    b. Community shopping center
    c. Regional center
    d. Power center

4. An industrial development in which new manufacturers are able to establish their businesses is known as
    a. an industrial park.
    b. a special purpose building.
    c. a start-up center.
    d. an incubator.

5. Someone interested in purchasing or investing in an industrial property would be looking for all of the characteristics below *EXCEPT*
    a. weight-bearing floors and foundations.
    b. high ceilings.
    c. an independent power generator.
    d. site isolation from transportation systems.

6. The tendency of neighboring property owners to oppose any development or industry that is perceived to threaten their property values or quality of life is a phenomenon known by what acronym?
   a. BYOB
   b. NIMBY
   c. NIDDI
   d. NOMYB

7. In the town of San Salmon, there were 100 potential tenants looking for office space and 380 available vacant units. In Bryrwood Clyffs, there were 20 potential tenants in search of office space and 12 available vacant units. Based on these facts, which of the following statements is *TRUE*?
   a. Rents will be higher in San Salmon than in Bryrwood Clyffs.
   b. Rents will be higher in Bryrwood Clyffs than in San Salmon.
   c. Because San Salmon has more potential tenants than Bryrwood Clyffs, it has a stronger office property market.
   d. If a developer adds 60 more office units to the Bryrwood Clyffs market, rental rates will probably increase.

8. Total project cost =
   a. revenue + income.
   b. land + improvements.
   c. improvements + net income before debt service.
   d. land + expense allowance.

9. An existing small office building has a total monthly revenue of $380,000. Vacancy and maintenance expenses are $97,500. Other expenses total $104,000. Assuming a capitalization rate of 0.93 is acceptable to the investor, what is the net operating income of this property?
   a. $166,005
   b. $178,500
   c. $276,000
   d. $353,400

10. A developer analyzing whether to build a new "big box" retail facility in the community should first determine
    a. if there is a demand for the type of development.
    b. if the city council is supportive of the development.
    c. if there is a population base to support the new development.
    d. all of these.

16

REAL ESTATE TRENDS IN CALIFORNIA

KEY TERMS

adjustable-rate
   mortgages (ARMs)
affordable housing
blight
business incubators
formaldehyde
general plan
green building
greenhouse gas
   emissions (GHGs)

greyfields
housing element
Leadership in Energy
   and Environmental
   Design (LEED)
location-efficient
   mortgages (LEMs)
multifamily
mixed-use
property tax increment

redevelopment
smart growth
subprime loans
tax increment
   financing
volatile organic
   compounds (VOCs)

LEARNING OBJECTIVES

- List and describe the various affordable housing programs in California and the role the state plays in the housing market

- Develop an understanding of how the state of California works with local communities (cities/counties) in working with at-risk groups (such as those with low income and the handicapped) for housing assistance

- Understand the importance of second units in our state's housing market

- Learn how redevelopment was originally established in California and how it has helped finance and rehabilitate many local communities

- Explain the three fundamental objectives of green building

- Recognize smart growth principles and how smart growth will change the face of real estate in California

- Understand the consequences of subprime loans to the economy and how real estate sales were affected

- Identify environmental issues that exist in California and explain how they affect the real estate market

AFFORDABLE HOUSING IN CALIFORNIA

In the past 30 years, California's housing prices have steadily outpaced residents' incomes. Housing production hasn't kept up with job growth within California, and the location and type of housing does not meet the needs of many new California households. As a result, fewer households can afford a typical house in California, which has led to overcrowding, and many California households pay more than they can afford for their housing.

At the end of 2014, housing markets in California appeared to have rebounded, with the coastal regions almost fully recovered, leaving inland regions well behind in recovery. There are now two common denominators in California's economy: (1) rents are on the rise, and (2) rental vacancy rates are down, creating a tight rental housing markets throughout the state.

Renters' wages have not kept up with spiking rents. Cumulatively between 2005 and 2013, the two-bedroom fair market rents increased by 17%, while renters' median incomes increased slightly by only 5%. According to the National Low Income Housing Coalition, the rent affordable to a median renter income earner was $935 in 2013, which could not even cover the fair market rent of $1,046 for a one-bedroom apartment in California. Typically lower-income households cannot afford increasing rents to secure affordable, adequate, and stable housing for their families, and they are being squeezed out of the rental market by middle and upper income households seeking better affordability. This is a significant trend for the California rental market, as lower-income households comprise almost 2/3 of all renter households, and the extremely low-income households represent one quarter of the total renters. These lower-income households bear heavy housing costs, often paying more than half of their incomes towards rents.

According to the State of California, 57% of all renters are paying more than 30% of their income for housing; among lower-income households, as many as 78% of renters are paying more than 30% of their income for housing. What is contributing to the tightening of the rental market is an increase of middle-income households choosing or finding it necessary to rent. This primary attributed to lending standards that tightened as a result of the recession and the continued decline in housing inventories due to the lack of new development statewide.

What we have also seen over the last several years and, most noticeably since the recent recession, is the shift of more single-family housing units being converted to investment rental housing stock to meet the rising rental demand, along with rising rents. New housing construction continues to be slow to fully rebound with residential permitting activity currently at less than half of the 2004 peak level. The existing housing stock is not adequate in meeting the emerging needs of housing stock continuing to age.

California's residential building permits peaked in 2004 at approximately 212,960, and then began to spiral downward by 84% in 2009 to just over 38,010, the lowest in 55 years. Multifamily permits also experienced a decrease by 80%, from 62,000 in 2004 to just over 11,000 in 2009. Although by 2013 we had seen a rebound in residential construction, it still lagged behind the 2004 peak, at 83,725 permits, or only 40% of the 2004 peak. The trend of the highest proportion of multifamily permits in total permits continued into 2013, as the multifamily sector comprised more than half of all the residential permits issued in 2013. Single-family development continued to lag.

In 2014 there were approximately 37,000 foreclosures in California, which is much lower than in 2013 but still significant for California. Many households experiencing foreclosure or economic downturn resorted to "doubling-up" with family and friends often resulting in overcrowded arrangements. The 2012 American Community Survey reported that over 1 million households were living in overcrowded conditions of which three-quarters were renter households, and the remaining quarter were homeowners. As a result of the economic downturn, including the increase in the number of foreclosures in California following the housing boom, there was a significant shift from homeownership to renting, which further created a strong opportunity for investment in California's housing market. Investment properties make up an important part of the single-family existing stock, representing almost 78% of the investment properties that become part of the rental housing stock in California, with the majority being located in the suburbs. In 2012, suburbs accounted for 73% of the home mortgages that ended in foreclosure nationwide. Many investors bought foreclosed suburban homes not to flip but to turn them into rentals.

California is projected to continue to experience steady population growth with steady gains of approximately 330,000 persons annually to 2020. The 2010 census revealed that most of the significant growth in the prior decade occurred in the Hispanic and Asian populations, at 28% and 31%, respectively, a trend that is likely to continue in the coming decades. The California Department of Finance projects that while the non-Hispanic White group will grow less than 1% by 2020, the Hispanic group is projected to grow by 21% and the Asian group by 11%. Geographically, the inland areas of California will experience particularly high population growth rates.

In the current decade, foreign-born ownership demand is projected to remain a majority of the growth in demand in California, at 71% of the total growth. Foreign-born rental demand is expected to slow down from 53.5% in the last decade to just over 38% during the current decade, due to upward mobility of immigrant households. The two dominant forces on the housing market will continue to be the aging baby-boomers and the younger Generation Y group. Their mix of preferences and needs of the state's diverse population will be drivers for more diverse housing demand in decades to come.

With or without private or state intervention, the housing sector cannot be successful alone. An integrated approach to housing policy and investment by engaging cross-sector partners, such as transportation, health, education, and economic development, will be necessary to move toward greater housing opportunities coupled with access to economic opportunity, health, and education, particularly for vulnerable populations.

Meanwhile, the federal government has significantly reduced the number of programs that were once used to assist local agencies and governments in accommodating growth. Voter-imposed property taxes and spending freezes have further constrained local governments from responding effectively to new residential growth. **Affordable housing** development, while still funded in part by the federal government, requires a larger local commitment than ever before. As such, it is no surprise that many communities no longer welcome population growth with open arms. In recent times, it has been noted throughout the state that when anyone proposes the development of affordable or **multifamily** housing, ambivalence about growth often shifts to hostility. Hostility feeds and strengthens certain myths and perceptions toward affordable housing.

Although some of these myths and perceptions may be positive, the negatives are usually highlighted in order to discourage growth. When people argue against affordable housing, often the decision makers are convinced that new development and new residents do not belong there. For example, they claim that traffic will become too heavy and unbearable, schools will become overcrowded, new buildings will clash with existing neighborhoods, people will not fit in, and maybe a criminal element will be attracted. The criminal element is a perception many people have about some of the federal government's unsuccessful endeavors (i.e., "the projects," as they have been known throughout the eastern and midwestern areas of the United States).

For affordable housing to make economic sense, more units per acre must lower the cost per unit. This can be accomplished if local governments allow developers meaningful density bonuses, which translates into smaller units costing less than larger ones. In order to encourage housing affordability, cities in California need to promote higher densities. One of the biggest misconceptions has been that high-density developments will result in greater traffic impacts on an area. However, people who live in affordable housing generally own fewer automobiles and drive less than their suburban counterparts.

In California, in the six largest metropolitan areas, two-thirds of the renters and over three-quarters of the households living below the poverty line own no vehicles or only one car, compared to 54% of all households and 44% of homeowner households. With lower car-ownership rates come fewer trips and fewer single-occupant auto commuters.

What Does This Mean Economically?

High-density housing can encourage nearby retail development, along with commercial development and ease of walking and transit use. Mixing housing with commercial developments is even more crucial with today's high cost of gasoline. It is worth noting that over three-quarters of the trips in Southern California are non-work-related. If high-density development is encouraged, stores serving neighborhood residents are more likely to move into the area, thus allowing residents to walk rather than drive to purchase groceries or other services typically offered by a neighborhood center.

Transit connections also become more common when neighborhood density increases, as transit is only cost effective at densities above eight to ten units per acre.

A CLOSER LOOK In an attempt to address the housing crisis on a local level, in 2006, the city of Los Angeles attempted to regulate condominium conversions through a moratorium on conversions. According to the Los Angeles Central City Association, there are currently approximately 800,000 rental units in the city, and the number of condominium conversions has ranged from approximately 3,000 to 4,500.

The city of Los Angeles has been considering a moratorium on conversions, demolition caps, and tripling the relocation fees that developers must pay to individuals who are displaced by such conversions. In February 2007, the city's planning commission recommended to the city council several ordinances that would set up stepladder fees that would be income-based and take the length of tenancy into account as follows:

1. Pay relocation fees of $14,500 to tenants who are over age 62, have children, or are disabled, and a $6,810 fee to all other tenants who lived in the residence for less than five years

2. Pay relocation fees of $17,080 for tenants who are over age 62, have children, or are disabled, and a $9,040 fee to all other tenants who have lived in their residences for five years or longer

3. Pay relocation fees of $17,080 to tenants who are over age 62, have children, or are disabled, and a $9,040 fee to all tenants whose income is 80% or below the area median income as defined by the U.S. Department of Housing and Urban Development

The city of Los Angeles's planning department also recommended placing a cap on condominium conversions at 734 units based on the median number of condominium conversions over a five-year period. In addition to the cap, owners requesting to convert their rental units to condominiums would have to participate in a lottery held quarterly. Projects that set aside 20% of the units for sale to low- and very low-income households would be considered first in any drawing for such units.

Between 2001 and 2003, the city of Los Angeles's planning department had not received any applications for conversions. However, in 2004, the city approved 1,083 applications, with the number of approvals dropping to 1,025 in 2005, and as of April 2006, decreasing further to 899 conversions. By 2007, the number of condominium conversion permits had dropped to only 208, a sign that the condominium market had finally begun to cool in Los Angeles. As the recession was coming to an end in 2012, the city had only issued 38 permits compared to 1,038 in 2004. Looking back at the prerecession days when the Los Angeles City Council was being asked to institute a moratorium on condominium conversions, it was determined it would discourage development at the beginning of the recession and was not instituted. Apartment owners in Los Angeles and throughout California are once again looking at conversions but nowhere near the numbers in 2004 through 2006. As with every revived economic and housing boom and a tightening rental market, we can expect housing advocates and politicians to come back in the future with yet another ordinance to cap the number of condominium conversions.

What Happens in One Community Does Not Always Occur in Another

While moratoriums on condominium conversions were being considered by the city of Los Angeles, just 25 miles south in Anaheim, California (the home of Disneyland), a different scenario for affordable housing existed. In August 2006, the Anaheim city council adopted an overlay zone that would allow the development of residential units in conjunction with hotels of 300 or more rooms in targeted areas of the resort city. According to news articles, a developer approached the city of Anaheim to amend the overlay zone. The developer sought the amendments for a major residential development it wanted to construct on a former manufactured home park site located southeast of Katella Avenue. The proposal would have allowed development of residential projects that dedicated a maximum of 15% of the units to rental housing affordable to low- and very low-income families.

However, in January 2007, Anaheim's planning commission unanimously voted to deny the requested amendments and expressed concerns about maintaining the integrity of the resort as a desirable place for tourism and conventions. This is an example of how affordable housing is viewed differently from region to region and from county to county.

As the housing industry slowed down, few investors were seeking to do condominium conversions in 2007. To add to this, very few lenders were willing to make loans on conversion projects, so many developers once again turned to apartments.

During the height of the condominium conversion craze in Southern California, the multifamily housing market in Orange County remained one of the strongest in the United States. This was primarily due to the low housing affordability keeping many people in the renter population. Since then, rents have continued to increase, vacancies have remained low, and investors still seek the opportunity to purchase real estate in Orange County.

New development activity throughout Orange County has been primarily focused on Class A properties, which offer an array of amenities including technology and building upgrades. This has also added to higher rents as developers expect a greater return on their investments.

What Is the State Doing About Housing?

California is at risk of losing 57,000 federally subsidized affordable apartments through conversion to market rate in the next five years, of which 35,000 are at risk of expiring in 2015. An additional 74,000 units are at risk of expiring in the following 15 years. The top five counties with the largest share of at-risk units within the upcoming five years are Los Angeles with 24,739 units (or 43% of total), followed by San Diego with 5,392, Orange with 4,112, San Francisco with 3,597, and Santa Clara with 2,380 units. A third of all of the units at risk of conversion are rented by senior citizens and disabled persons, who are often on fixed incomes. Almost 3,500 at-risk units are located in rural counties that are hardest hit by drought and at risk of remaining without adequate supply of water in the near future. There are another 8,000 units with subsidized mortgages in the state reaching their affordability term by 2017 and with the owners at risk of losing their homes and being displaced. The potential loss of these units directly impacts the affordable housing stock and compounds problems for many communities in California, in some instances, increasing the incidence of homelessness.

Preserving California's existing affordable housing is critical to its economy. We must ask the question, why preserve the existing rental housing? The answer is that it generally costs half as much and takes half the time than building new units. On average, it serves much lower-income households than new construction, and new construction alone cannot produce enough affordable housing stock to meet demand in most markets in California. In 2012, the California Department of Housing and Community Development utilized federal HOME Investment Partnerships Program (HOME) funds to assist 29 affordable properties (home to over 2,000 of the state's lowest-income tenants) in 20 counties in California. The units, which were previously funded by the state's Rental Housing Construction Program, Rural Rental Assistance (RHCP/RRA), were losing rental assis-

The mission statement of the California Department of Housing and Community Development is "Provide leadership, policies and programs to preserve and expand safe and affordable housing opportunities and promote strong communities for all Californians."

tance. While a temporary solution limited to two years, the state's assistance has gone a long way in allowing vulnerable very low-income tenants to remain in their homes while longer-term solutions are crafted.

Persons at Risk

As noted in Unit 9, state law requires every city and county to adopt a **general plan**. State law also requires that all cities and counties are required to prepare and adopt a **housing element** as part of their general plan. The housing element must include, among other things:

- Identification and analysis of existing and projected housing needs

- An identification of resources and constraints to address these needs

- Goals, policies, and scheduled programs for the maintenance, improvement, and development of housing for all economic segments of the community

California state law was amended pursuant to Government Code Section 65008, which requires the following in the preparation and the adoption of a housing element:

1. As part of a governmental constraints analysis, a housing element must analyze potential and actual constraints upon the development, maintenance, and improvement of housing for persons with disabilities and demonstrate local efforts to remove governmental constraints that hinder the local government (city/county) from meeting the need for housing for persons with disabilities.

2. As part of the required constraints program, the element must include programs that remove constraints or provide reasonable accommodations for housing designed for persons with disabilities.

According to the State Department of Housing and Community Development, the following list of questions should be asked to analyze the housing element as it relates to constraints on the development, maintenance, and improvement of housing for persons with disabilities:

1. Does the city/county have any processes for individuals with disabilities to make requests for reasonable accommodation with respect to zoning, permit processing, or building laws?

2. What is the process for requesting a reasonable accommodation?

3. Has the municipality made any efforts to remove constraints on housing for persons with disabilities, such as accommodating procedures for the approval of group homes, ADA retrofit efforts, an evaluation of the zoning code for ADA compliance, or other measures that provide flexibility?

4. Does the municipality make information available about requesting a reasonable accommodation with respect to zoning, permit processing, or building laws?

5. Has the city/county reviewed all of its zoning laws and policies for compliance with fair housing law?

6. Are residential parking standards for persons with disabilities different from other parking standards? Does the municipality have a policy or program for the relocation of parking requirements for special needs housing if a project proponent can demonstrate a reduced need for parking?

7. Does the municipality restrict the siting of group homes? How will this affect the cost and development of housing?

8. What zoning districts provide for group homes other than residential zones covered by state law? Are group homes with over six people allowed?

9. Does the municipality have occupancy standards in the zoning code that apply specifically to unrelated adults and not to families? Do the occupancy standards comply with Fair Housing Laws?

10. Does the land-use element of the General Plan regulate the siting of special needs housing in relationship to one another? Specifically, is there a minimum distance required between two or more special-need housing establishments?

11. How does the municipality process a request to retrofit homes for accessibility (e.g., ramp request)?

12. Has the municipality adopted the Uniform Building Code? What year? Has the municipality made amendments that might diminish the ability to accommodate persons with disabilities?

13. Has the municipality adopted any universal design elements in the building code?

14. Does the municipality provide reasonable accommodation for persons with disabilities in the enforcement of building codes and the issuance of building permits?

In analyzing how local governments address special needs in their housing elements, the State of California reviews and assists local cities and counties in preparing goals and policies as well as programs for the implementation of Housing Element Law. There are a few questions that are typically asked by the state when evaluating local housing elements. The purpose of the questions that the state asks local agencies is to make sure that local plans are truly considering goals and objectives that will lead to successful implementation.

Other Solutions to Housing in California

Another way the State of California and local cities and counties have been proactive in addressing the housing crisis in California has been through encouraging the establishment of second units (otherwise known as granny units, in-law apartments, or accessory apartments), which provides an important source of affordable housing in California. By promoting the development of second units, a community can ease the rental housing deficit, maximize limited land resources and existing infrastructure, and provide low- and moderate-income homeowners with supplemental income.

The State Legislature's intent of the Second-Unit Law:

> The Legislature finds and declares that second units are a valuable form of housing in California. Second units provide housing for family members, students, the elderly, in-home health care providers, the disabled, and others, at below-market prices within existing neighborhoods. Homeowners who create second units benefit from added income and an increased sense of security. It is the intent of the Legislature that any second-unit ordinance adopted by local agencies have the effect of providing for the creation of second units and that provisions in these ordinances relating to matters including second unit size, parking, fees and other requirements, are not so arbitrary, excessive, or burdensome so as to unreasonably restrict the ability of homeowners to create second units in zones in which they are authorized by local ordinance.
>
> Source: California Government Code Section 65852.150

In the past it has been argued that second units can increase the property tax base of a community and, most importantly, contribute to the local affordable housing stock. The state's Second-Unit Law (Government Code Section 65852.2), enacted in 1982, allowed local governments to create second units in residential zones, set development standards (e.g., height, setbacks, lot coverage), require minimum unit sizes, and establish parking requirements. One of the most significant changes in the Second-Unit Law, in January 2003, was to require that second units be considered ministerially. Specifically, this change in the law outlined that if a second unit conformed to the community's development standards, it removed the discretionary approval/disapproval process and would allow such units to only have to apply for a building permit (i.e., no public hearings on such units).

Ministerial Review

For an application to be considered ministerially, the process must apply predictable, objective, fixed, quantifiable, and clear standards. These standards must be administratively applied to the application and not subject to discretionary decision making by a legislative body. Specifically, the application request should not be subject to excessively burdensome conditions of approval, a public hearing or public comment, or any discretionary decision making process. In addition, second units are typically exempt from the provisions of the California Environmental Quality Act (CEQA). (See the discussion in Unit 10 on CEQA and where it is applied.)

What Are the Implications of Restrictions?

Requirements restricting the occupancy of a second unit may be susceptible to legal challenge. In a 1984 decision, *Hubbart v. County of Fresno* voided a Fresno County zoning ordinance that required that occupancy of a second unit be limited to persons related to the main unit's owner. The court stated that the ordinance violated the plaintiff's right to privacy guaranteed by Article I, Section I of the California Constitution.

In a 2001 decision, *Coalition Advocacy Legal Housing Options v. City of Santa Monica,* a second-unit ordinance preventing nondependent adult children or relatives as well as unrelated persons from living in a second unit, while permitting dependents and caregivers, was declared unconstitutional under the right to privacy and equal protection clause of the California Constitution.

The Economics of Second Units

As previously noted, second units do provide affordable housing and also allow for potential supplemental income for homeowners. Many individuals can simply convert existing space, while others may add rooms above garages or, if space permits, construct a new unit on the property. In many rural areas of California, manufactured homes have served as an alternative to a traditionally built second unit, thus greatly reducing the cost of the second unit.

REDEVELOPMENT

Redevelopment law in California was adopted in 1945 as the Community Redevelopment Act. Initially, the law was patterned after the federal housing acts adopted during the Depression era of the 1930s to deal with slums and inadequate housing throughout the United States. Funds for the original program were largely federal and later proved to be inadequate due to the number of cities nationwide competing for the funding. In 1952, a significant turning point occurred in California with the passage of a Constitutional Amendment. The voters of California approved a new financing technique that has become known as **tax increment financing**. Based on the increasing values of property created by activities of the redevelopment agency and resulting private investments, tax increment revenues weaned California governments away from the dependence on federal and state grants and loans.

The initial growth in redevelopment was slow, with only 46 redevelopment agencies statewide established by 1965. As the understanding of the redevelopment process grew, additional cities began to activate agencies and adopt project areas. By 1975, 158 agencies had been established with a total of 202 project areas. After the passage of Proposition 13 in 1978, the formation of redevelopment agencies accelerated throughout the 1980s. By 2011, there were over 400 active agencies.

Redevelopment is the process and program of activities undertaken by local governments to deal with the impact of blight and slums. The State Constitution and the Community Redevelopment Law established a complex process that provides a city or county with specific authority to establish a redevelopment agency as well as project areas. The primary criterion under the law that allows a city or county to initiate a redevelopment agency and project is known as blight. **Blight** is a legal term that encompasses a list of conditions. It is not only a prerequisite required for the adoption of a redevelopment agency, but it is what a redevelopment agency must spend its money to resolve.

Redevelopment Projects

Redevelopment agencies undertake a wide variety of projects and activities designed to improve a project area and eliminate blight. The redevelopment agency will determine the type of projects based upon the character of the neighborhood or district; the nature of the blight within the identified area; the needs and desires of property owners, businessowners, and tenants in an area; and the market support for the various types of projects. Redevelopment projects vary based on need or support, but they might include any or all of the following:

- Downtown revitalization

- Retail development

- Industrial development

- Residential development

- Development of public facilities

A CLOSER LOOK   The centerpiece of downtown Sacramento is the Downtown Plaza, which was developed by the Hahn Company of San Diego, California. This was a joint venture with the Downtown Plaza Association, a local investment group. The project itself was not entirely a new venture but an expansion and renovation of a redevelopment project that began in the 1960s when redevelopment was in the infancy stage in California. The redevelopment agency's original actions included slum clearance of blighted downtown office buildings, service stations, and other buildings. The agency initiated the building of an open-air mall consisting of 52 stores and 3,540 parking spaces. This mall was anchored by Macy's on one end and a J.C. Penney store on the other end. Since the time the mall opened, it has also gone through a transformation and modernization as well as the addition of new tenants. The mall originally opened in September 1971, employing approximately 1,200 area residents and generating over $245,000 in annual sales tax revenues for the city of Sacramento. The mall was later remodeled in 1993, which involved correcting some of the problems related to the 1971 original mall in that it opens up attractive corridors to Old Sacramento, the remainder of K Street, Capitol Mall, and the city's former Main Street (J Street). The reconfigured project combines elements of a traditional

Italian city with a series of piazzas (courtyards) or rooms with traditional American Main Street ambiance.

Due to changing economic conditions and the recession, the current mall has been reduced to 400,000 square feet of leasable space including 60 retailers, 3 restaurants, and a multiplex theater remain today. The J.C. Penney, the Hard Rock Café, and many other retailers are long gone. The eastern portion of the mall is being transformed into a new NBA Basketball Arena at a cost of $447 million in an effort to keep the Sacramento Kings team in Sacramento and not have the team move to Seattle, Washington. This new addition and renovation is not being done under redevelopment; it is economic development for the city's downtown with the use of private capital monies. The new sports complex is slated to open in October 2016. Redevelopment initially served as a catalyst for reviving downtown Sacramento, but this mall fell victim to the recession of 2009 and would need a different type of boost now that redevelopment is no longer an available tool.

Other major improvements in the area included new office buildings and hotels on the adjacent Capitol and K Street Mall and major improvements to Old Sacramento Historic Area (Old Town located west of Interstate 5).

The End of Redevelopment and a New Era for California

California's redevelopment agencies transformed local communities. Some of their efforts to eradicate blight produced fine examples of urban renewal in California, including economic development, infrastructure enhancement, and city beautification. Despite the many benefits, funding for these agencies and their programs became a problem.

Since the 1950s, the California Constitution gave redevelopment agencies 100% of the property tax growth inside the special redevelopment area project area, otherwise known as **property tax increment,** to assist the redevelopment agencies with their battle on blight.

Property tax increment was the primary source of revenue for redevelopment agencies. When a city or county activated a redevelopment agency and formed a project area, it froze the allocation of property tax revenues to local agencies. While the public agencies continue to receive the amount of property tax revenue they received in the redevelopment agency's base year, the agency got to keep any and all yearly increases in property tax revenues. As an example, after local property tax revenues had grown from $100,000 to $110,000, city, county, school, and special district allocations would remain flat, and the redevelopment agency would receive 100% of the additional $10,000. Absent redevelopment agency activity, revenues from these areas would have funded cities, counties, special districts, and most importantly, schools.

The state subsidized the revenue losses to schools, and in fiscal year 2009–2010, the annual state subsidy reached almost $3 billion. A major change was inevitable.

California's redevelopment agencies were officially dissolved as of February 1, 2012, as a result of the 2011 Budget Act despite numerous lawsuits by the agencies. The dissolution of these agencies would protect funding for cities, counties, schools, and public services.

SMART GROWTH

The Future of Real Estate Development

One of the latest and hottest trends in land use and real estate development in the United States, including California, is the development of ways of conserving natural resources, called **smart growth**.

Development decisions affect many of the things that touch our everyday lives, including our homes, health, schools, taxes, daily commute, the natural environment around us, economic growth in our communities, and the opportunities to achieve our dreams and goals. It can be best said that what, where, and how communities build will affect residents' lives for generations to come.

Communities across the country are using creative strategies to develop ways to preserve natural lands and critical environmental areas, protect water and air quality, and reuse already developed land. They attempt to conserve natural resources by reinvesting in existing infrastructure and reclaiming historic buildings. By designing neighborhoods that have shops, schools, churches, parks, and other amenities near homes, communities are giving their residents and visitors the option of walking, bicycling, taking public transit, or driving as they go about their business. A range of different types of homes makes it possible for senior citizens to stay in their homes as they age, young people to afford their first home, and families at all stages in between to find a safe, attractive home they can afford. Through smart growth approaches that enhance neighborhoods and involve local residents in development decisions, these communities are creating vibrant places to live, work, and play. The high quality of life in these communities makes them economically competitive, creates business opportunities, and improves the local tax base.

Smart growth is all about how we build our communities. Based on the experience of communities around the nation that have used smart growth approaches to create and maintain great neighborhoods, the Smart Growth Network developed a set of ten basic principles:

- Mix land uses

- Take advantage of compact building design

- Create a range of housing opportunities and choices

- Create walkable neighborhoods

- Foster distinctive, attractive communities with a strong sense of place

- Preserve open space, farmland, natural beauty, and critical environmental areas

- Strengthen and direct development towards existing communities

- Provide a variety of transportation choices

- Make development decisions predictable, fair, and cost effective

- Encourage community and stakeholder collaboration in development decisions

What Are the Environmental Benefits of Smart Growth?

Many studies show the environmental benefits of smart growth. Development guided by smart growth principles can minimize air and water pollution, encourage brownfields clean-up and reuse, and preserve natural lands. The built environment—the places where we live, work, shop, and play—has both direct and indirect effects on the natural environment. Where and how we develop directly affects natural areas and wildlife habitat and replaces natural cover with impervious surfaces such as concrete or asphalt. Development patterns and practices also indirectly affect environmental quality because they influence how people get around. Separating land uses, spreading development out, and providing little or no public transportation or safe walking and biking routes foster greater reliance on motor vehicles. As development grows more dispersed, people must drive further to reach their destinations, leading to more and longer vehicle trips. These increased trips create more air emissions and greenhouse gases that contribute to global climate change. Ultimately, air pollution and climate change can also harm water quality and wildlife habitats.

Smart growth practices can reduce the environmental impacts of development with techniques that include compact development, reduced impervious surfaces and improved water detention, safeguarding of environmentally sensitive areas, mixing of land uses (e.g., homes, offices, and shops), transit accessibility, and better pedestrian and bicycle amenities.

In practice, these techniques have created tangible environmental improvements. A 2000 study found that compact development in New Jersey would produce 40% less water pollution than more dispersed development patterns. A 2005 Seattle study found that residents of neighborhoods where land uses were mixed and streets were better connected (making non-auto travel easier and more convenient) traveled 26% fewer vehicle miles than residents of neighborhoods that were more dispersed and less connected.

Smart Growth Illustrated

Smart growth is all about how communities are built. The following examples are success stories that have been achieved throughout California utilizing several of the smart growth principles.

Hismen Hin-Nu Terrace, Oakland, California Hismen Hin-Nu Terrace, a 1.5-acre mixed-use development in the San Antonio district of Oakland, California, revitalized a distressed community and provided a variety of high-quality, affordable homes by redeveloping an abandoned retail site. In a joint venture, the San Antonio Community Development Corporation, East Bay Asian Local Development Corporation, and the Oakland Redevelopment Agency redeveloped an abandoned grocery store site. The result was a neighborhood with 92 affordable rental homes, a community center, three courtyards, and commercial space, including an early childhood education center, nonprofit offices, a convenience store, and a marketplace for street vendors.

The housing ranges from one- and two-bedroom apartments to three- and four-bedroom townhouses. Amenities include covered parking, wall-to-wall carpeting, dishwashers, and garbage disposals. The units provide high--quality homes for lower-income families and seniors, as 40% of the units will be available to households at 35% of median area income, with the remainder for those at 50 to 60% of median area income.

Michael Pyatok, the project architect, engaged community members in interactive design workshops. The workshop participants decided to step down the height of the building from four stories in front to three stories in back to create courtyard space for children's play while maintaining a relatively high residential density of 61 units per acre to keep the units affordable. In addition, the community chose a variety of finishing materials because they were considered to be more environmentally friendly. The resulting building reflects the Mission Revival style of older apartment buildings in the neighborhood. Balconies and windows on the street side allow residents to watch over the street, improving the community's security.

Also on the street front is a two-story market hall that houses local vendors and start-up businesses both inside and outside along the building's facade. This entrepreneurial activity contributes to the vibrancy of the street that, together with the landscaping, creates a comfortable, safe, walkable neighborhood. The building is on a major bus route that connects to the Fruitvale BART station two-thirds of a mile away. Hismen Hin-Nu Terrace also benefited from a National Endowment for the Arts grant that allowed it to create and display a variety of outdoor art that celebrates the cultural diversity of the residents and the neighborhood.

Hismen Hin-Nu Terrace's success was recognized with numerous awards, including the Rudy Bruner Silver Medal Award in 1997 for Excellence in Urban Environment, the Gold Nugget Award for Best Affordable Housing Development at the Pacific Coast Builders Conference in 1995, and the National Award for Merit from the National Association of Housing and Redevelopment Officials in 1995. It also spurred redevelopment in the surrounding neighborhood, including a new housing development across the street, a convenience store, and the renovation of two neighborhood restaurants.

Uptown District, San Diego, California   The Uptown District in San Diego, California, demonstrates how redeveloping abandoned retail centers, or **greyfields,** can help revive and reconnect communities. The project, a successful 14-acre mixed-use, high-density development in the city's Hillcrest neighborhood, was built on the site of an abandoned department store and its surrounding parking lot. The city of San Diego purchased the site in 1986 with the intent of building a new library but subsequently decided to keep the library downtown. The city conducted an intensive community planning process, including an early visual preference survey, to help formulate the design of the mixed-use development in 1987. The winning bidder, developer Oliver McMillan/Odmark and Thelan, then went back to the community to refine the design features.

The project combines a mix of uses, including 318 homes, 145,000 square feet of commercial and retail space, and a 3,000-square-foot community center. The residential density is over 20 units per acre, far more than the city average of less than three units per acre. The uses are mostly mixed horizontally, with most of the retail surrounding a central parking plaza anchored by a large grocery store in the rear. The housing is on an adjacent block with pedestrian courtyards connecting the units. There is some vertical mixing of uses in the housing block along with first-floor retail along Vermont Street and University Avenue.

Restoring old streets that had been removed to create the original store's parking lot helps create a pedestrian-friendly atmosphere. Smaller blocks, along with pedestrian pathways, make walking safer and easier. A pedestrian bridge over a busy street and a canyon connects the adjacent University Heights neighborhood with the project and University Avenue, giving University Heights residents access to shopping and transit. Underground parking for both the grocery store and the homes helps reduce the presence of automobiles in the project.

Most grocery retailers say that, to be successful, they need to be visible from a major arterial and have plenty of surface parking. Uptown's grocery store is located well off University Avenue and has only minimum street signage and mostly underground parking. Yet it is still one of the most successful stores in its chain.

Because the project was in an existing community adjacent to one of the city's busiest bus corridors, the developers could reduce parking below the requirements for conventional developments in the city. While the Hillcrest neighborhood averages 2.25 parking spaces per residential unit and one parking space per 250 square feet of commercial space, the uptown district offers two parking spaces per town house, 1.7 parking spaces per apartment, and one parking space per 270 square feet of commercial space.

Greyfield properties, like this one, offer many communities the opportunity to provide housing choices and new retail options without building over open space. They can also spur redevelopment of adjacent properties. By the time the Uptown District's construction was well underway, 15 other projects in the area had started or were in advanced stages of planning.

The Crossings, Mountain View, California   The Crossings, located in the city of Mountain View, 30 miles south of San Francisco, transformed a failing 1960s auto-oriented mall into a vibrant neighborhood that offers a variety of transportation choices. The 18-acre infill project, developed by

TPG Development, demolished the original shopping mall and replaced it with homes, retail shops, and a daycare center, all oriented toward the new San Antonio Avenue Caltrain commuter rail station. San Mateo Transit busses meet each train and connect to nearby communities. Narrow tree-lined streets and sidewalks and small pocket parks all combine to create a walkable and bikeable neighborhood. It takes residents less than five minutes to walk from any of the houses to the stores or to the commuter rail station, and two minutes or less to walk to a park. In order to meet fire department requirements, some of the narrowest streets are defined as private roads and owned by the neighborhood association.

Construction commenced in 1994 and was completed a few years later. The development features high-density housing averaging 30 units per net acre compared to an average overall density of seven to ten units per net acre in the rest of the city. Using on-street parking places to meet minimum parking requirements allowed more land to be used for homes, increasing overall density. The residences are diverse and include single-family bungalows, smaller cottages, townhouses, and condominium apartments. Although priced at market rates, the compact design makes the units relatively affordable in the high-cost Silicon Valley real estate market.

When the original mall failed, the city proposed reclassification of the site from retail to residential. Citizens asked for low densities with open space. Public education programs convinced the community that higher density was appropriate for a transit-oriented site. The developer's original proposal was for a more auto-oriented, mixed-use development. The city rejected the proposal, and the design firm of Calthorpe Associates was hired to conduct community design meetings, which resulted in their final plan.

Compact Development Endorsement Program, San Francisco Bay Area Communities, California Developers trying to build smart growth developments in the San Francisco Bay Area have an unusual ally: a conservation organization called the Greenbelt Alliance. "Smart" developers have found that a Greenbelt Alliance endorsement can help level the regulatory playing field that is tilted against smart growth in many communities.

In 1987, the Greenbelt Alliance realized that to conserve open space, communities would have to build more compactly to accommodate new growth and provide affordable housing. To address this concern, the alliance began endorsing affordable, compact housing developments as a complement to their open space conservation programs. Since then, the alliance has added mixed-use development projects that include affordable housing to the program.

The endorsement process begins when a developer submits an application that includes a description of the project, an environmental clearance, a description of the surrounding area, a description of the public hearing schedule, and a planning staff contact. One member of the endorsement team reviews the project against the following criteria: location, effect on automobile dependency, minimum density, affordability, design, size, and community input. The reviewer prepares a report for the whole committee, which then makes the endorsement decision. Endorsed projects get a letter of support and a news release that can be used to publicize and promote the project. The alliance also actively supports some projects at hearings and other public forums.

Completed projects endorsed by the Greenbelt Alliance include Ryland Mews, a high-density (56 units per acre) mews-style condominium apartment in San Jose. Completed in 1996, this project offered a moderately priced alternative to high housing prices in Silicon Valley during the dot-com boom. Because it is two blocks from a light rail transit stop and near shopping areas, the developer could keep the parking ratio to a relatively low 1.77 spaces per unit. This freed more space for housing, allowing 131 units to be built on less than 3.5 acres in a four-story building.

Another endorsed project, the Emeryville Warehouse Lofts, was one of the earliest housing developments in an old industrial and warehouse area in Emeryville. The old fruit-drying warehouse was converted into 157 loft-style condominiums, and two new buildings provided six live-work town houses, 15 studio lofts, and a parking garage. Twenty-one of the units were sold to moderate-income households, and five were sold to low-income households. This project proved the economic viability of housing in this area and helped balance the jobs–housing ratio in Emeryville. Built in the middle of an industrial and warehouse area, the Warehouse Lofts are now surrounded by a vibrant residential, retail, and office community.

Swan's Market is a mixed-use redevelopment of an abandoned historic market in downtown Oakland. Reopened in 1998, it includes 18 units of rental housing affordable to families with 20–60% of area median income, 20 market-rate co-housing condominiums, and one live-work space. The average residential density is 27 units per acre. In addition, a market hall houses the tenants of the historic Housewives Market, formerly located across the street. Restaurants and shops round out the commercial tenants. Civic presence is provided by a public courtyard, which is also home to a farmers market every Friday, and the Oakland Museum of Children's Art.

Like many of the projects endorsed by the Greenbelt Alliance, Swan's Market won several awards in 2001, including a Pacific Coast Builder's Golden Nugget award, a California Preservation Foundation Design Award, a California Redevelopment Association Award of Excellence, an AIA/HUD Secretary's Mixed-Use/Mixed Income award, and a Rudy Brunner Silver Medal for Urban Excellence.

From 1990 to 2004, the Greenbelt Alliance endorsed 95 development projects and 17 neighborhood plans that, if built, would create more than 48,000 residences within existing city limits. By endorsing these projects, the Greenbelt Alliance is making smart growth easier to build while simultaneously reducing pressure to build over green space.

The Present and the Future

Sprawling land development is gobbling up the American landscape at an alarming rate. As homebuyers become more environmentally conscious about where they choose to live and work, people are now beginning to turn to smart growth developments. Therefore, it becomes important for the real estate professional in the 21st century to understand the concepts of smart growth and green building programs such as **Leadership in Energy and Environmental Design (LEED)**.

Many of these programs not only promote developments that offer mixed-use, pedestrian-friendly neighborhoods that are environmentally friendly but also make the most of water and energy efficiency. In addition, today's homebuyers are seeking homes that provide healthier indoor environments and result in less stress on our natural resources.

What Is Green Building?

Green building is just applied common sense. The three fundamental objectives of green building involve

1. conserving natural resources;

2. increasing energy efficiency; and

3. improving indoor air quality.

Natural Resource Conservation Conventional building practices consume large quantities of wood, plastic, cardboard, paper, water, and other natural resources that will eventually lead to their depletion. For example, wood is the most common building material used in construction today. It is often used wastefully. Mankind has already harvested 95% of the nation's old-growth forests, a trend that cannot continue. Engineered lumber products such as wood I-Joists, wood fiber laminates, and oriented strand board utilize fast-growing farm trees as an alternative to old-growth forests. These products can use as little as 50% of the wood fiber to perform the same structural functions and are typically stronger, straighter, and lighter than solid sawn lumber. In today's market, builders have an ever increasing range of green building materials from which to choose from. This includes recycled content decking, insulation, reclaimed lumber, and other products that divert waste from landfills, while providing quality and durability.

Water conservation is another important issue in building green. Wise water usage reduces the strain on resources as well as lowers expenses. Today, many builders can take advantage of a new generation of high-efficiency washers, dishwashers, and landscape water management systems.

Energy Efficiency Energy efficiency is a cornerstone of any green building project. Generation and use of energy are major contributors to air pollution and global climate change. Improving energy efficiency and using renewable resources are effective ways to improve air quality and reduce the impacts of global warming.

Improving energy efficiency is also an economically effective choice for consumers. Lowering utility expenses allows residents and homeowners to enjoy the financial benefits year after year. The first step to increase energy efficiency is to add insulation and weather stripping wherever possible, install double-glazed/low-emission (low-E) windows, and upgrade to high efficiency appliances. Other energy upgrades/choices include installing solar water heaters, photovoltaic panels, and purchasing "green power" generated from renewable sources like the sun, wind, and biomass (when available).

Indoor Air Quality The U.S. Environmental Protection Agency (EPA) reports that the air in new homes can be 10 times more polluted than outdoor air. According to *The New England Journal of Medicine*, 40% of children will develop respiratory disease, in part due to the chemicals in their homes. Poor indoor air quality is caused by the off-gassing of chemicals found in many building materials as well as mold and mildew that build up in homes due to poorly designed and maintained heating and cooling systems.

One of the most common indoor air pollutants is **formaldehyde**, a suspected human carcinogen. Kitchen cabinets, countertops, shelving, and furniture are typically made from particleboard held together by formaldehyde-based adhesives. The formaldehyde is released into the home for years after these products have been installed in the home. Many paints and floor finishes also contain unhealthy **volatile organic compounds (VOCs)**. That "new house smell" is actually the odor off these volatile compounds off-gassing and is a telltale sign that there are harmful chemicals in the indoor environment.

The building products industry has responded to these indoor pollution problems by developing alternative paint, finish, and adhesive products. For example, solvent-free adhesives used in flooring and countertops can eliminate many of the suspected and known human carcinogens; paints, varnishes, and cleaners that do not utilize volatile compounds are now commonly available from most major manufacturers at costs comparable to conventional products.

In addition to the growing number of readily available and cost-effective green materials, an increasing number of builders and remodelers are also utilizing natural building materials such as straw-bale, rammed earth, adobe, and cob. While less common in their use, these natural building products have a positive impact on the environment as they are renewable and abundant, energy efficient in production and are non-polluting, and are durable and long lasting, which make economic sense.

What Are the Benefits of Building Green?

There are many reasons why many people are building green and why it is becoming an important factor for real estate professionals to understand the benefits of building green. These include a concern for the environment, an interest in building more efficiently, health considerations, a desire to create an environmentally friendly image for your business, and an ability to market your services as a real estate professional. By applying a sustainable perspective to design, construction, and remodeling, green building brings the benefits of resource conservation, energy savings, and healthy living.

The following is a list of green building features that convey the benefits of green building.

Higher Quality, Environmentally Sound Products   Most green building products and materials were developed to do something better than their conventional counterpart. These products usually perform better and are manufactured in an environmentally sound manner, thus protecting and restoring our natural resources. These products include the following:

- Recycled content decking

- FSC-certified wood

- Engineered lumber

- Interior steel studs

- Solvent-free adhesives

- Natural linoleum flooring

- Recycled content ceramic tile

- Fly ash in concrete

- Bamboo flooring

More Durable/Lower Maintenance Products   Next to quality, durability and reduced maintenance are very important. There is never enough time to do what needs to be done, and home maintenance is never high on the list of how to spend time away from work. For this reason, more and more builders are utilizing low maintenance materials, and homes are being marketed as having less maintenance costs associated with the use of the following materials:

- Fiber cement siding

- Recycled content decking

- Exposed concrete flooring

- Natural linoleum flooring

- Recycled content ceramic tile

- Resource-efficient landscapes and gardens

- 40-year roofing

Products and Practices That Provide Greater Comfort and Lower Utility Bills   Comfort is what drives high energy use. When it gets hot, people turn on the air conditioner. By increasing the amount of insulation and providing for natural cooling, the electricity demand can be reduced with no compromise in occupant comfort. Today "green homes" are incorporating the following features:

- Foundation/slab insulation
- Increased wall and ceiling insulation
- Spray cellulose insulation
- Advanced infiltration reduction practices
- Low-E windows
- Hydronic heating
- All ducts located in conditional spaces
- Ceiling fans
- Whole house fans
- Passive solar heating
- Natural cooling
- Energy Star appliances
- Attic ventilation systems

Healthier Products and Practices for Families   The public health community has identified homes as one of the most significant threats to children's health. The following is a list of products that are being incorporated into green homes today, so as to address health:

- Low/no VOC paints
- Natural linoleum in place of vinyl flooring
- Formaldehyde-free medium density fiber board (MDF)
- Solvent-free adhesives
- Water-borne wood finishes
- Clean ducts before occupancy
- Exhaust fan in attached garages
- Recycled-content fiberglass insulation with no added formaldehyde
- Seal all particleboard and MDF

Many communities, such as the city of Santa Barbara and Alameda County, have green building programs that provide assistance and guidance to builders and homeowners.

Market Appeal and Support   In many communities throughout California, developers are able to apply for a LEED rating from certified evaluators, which many call an "environmental stamp of approval" for good development. This has proven to be valuable in the marketplace as developers seek citizen goodwill and municipal approvals. Many forward-thinking developers have already enjoyed the benefits that come with LEED certification for green buildings. For example, in Santa Monica, California, the city allows expedited permitting for LEED-certified building projects, taking weeks off the approval and permitting process. Many municipalities have also been eager to adopt smart-growth zoning and tax incentives. For example, Baltimore County, Maryland, offers a 10-year property tax credit to new commercial buildings that qualify for a LEED silver level rating.

Monetary Incentives That Make Economic Sense   In addition to expedited permitting, mortgage money is available for buying green, through **Location Efficient Mortgages (LEMs)**. According to the National Resource Defense Council, a LEM increases the amount of money homebuyers in urban areas are able to borrow by taking into account the money they save by living in neighborhoods where they can shop at nearby stores and use public transit rather than driving to work and to the mall. The LEM program was developed to encourage the development of efficient, environmentally progressive communities and to reduce urban sprawl and dependence on the automobile.[15]

LEMs are not as prominent as they were a few years ago. Most LEMs are now handled through banks that work directly with developers. Generally they are only made in metropolitan centers (e.g., San Francisco, Los Angeles) as the idea was to get people out of their cars. Their use decreased drastically with the decrease overall in residential construction.

ENVIRONMENTAL ISSUES IN REAL ESTATE ECONOMICS

Climate Change

In California, two important pieces of legislation address climate change by reducing greenhouse gases: AB 32 and SB 375.

---

15. Natural Resources Defense Council, "Location Efficient Mortgage®," Natural Resources Defense Council, www.nrdc.org/cities/smartgrowth/qlem.asp (accessed April 2015).

AB 32   On September 27, 2006, California Governor Arnold Schwarzenegger signed into law Assembly Bill 32 (AB32), The California Global Warming Solutions Act of 2006, labeled as landmark legislation to reduce greenhouse gas emissions in the fight against global climate change. AB32 requires the California Air Resources Board (ARB) to develop regulations and market mechanisms that will ultimately reduce California's greenhouse gas emissions by 25% by the year 2020.

Prior to imposing any mandates or authorizing market mechanisms, the ARB is required to evaluate several factors, including, but not limited to, impacts on California's economy, the environment, and public health; equity between regulated entities; electricity reliability, conformance with other environmental laws, and ensuring the rules do not disproportionately impact low-income communities.

The initial scoping plan was developed and released by ARB in December 2008, which contained six key elements to address AB 32:

- Expanding and strengthening existing energy efficiency programs as well as building and appliance standards

- Achieving a statewide renewables energy mix of 33%

- Developing a California cap-and-trade program that links with other Western Climate Initiative partner programs to create a regional market system

- Establishing targets for transportation-related greenhouse gas emissions for regions throughout California, and pursuing policies and incentives to achieve those targets

- Adopting and implementing measure pursuant to existing state laws and policies, including California's clean car standards, goods movement measures, and the Low carbon Fuel Standards

- Creating targeted fees, including a public goods charge on water use, fees on high global warming potential gases, and a fee to fund the administrative costs of the state's long-term commitment to AB 32 implementation.[16]

According to ARB, AB 32 has been implemented with an array of strategies, and the state is on target for meeting the 2020 greenhouse gas emission

---

16. California Environmental Protection Agency Air Resources Board, "Executive Summary," Environmental Justice Advisory Committee, www.arb.ca.gov/cc/ejac/meetings/06_18_13/2008sp-exec-summary.pdf (accessed April 2015).

reduction goal. Many of the greenhouse gas reduction measures, such as Low Carbon Fuel Standards, Advance Clean Car Standards, and Cap-and-Trade have already been adopted; implementation is ongoing. However, all of the goals set forth in AB 32 have not yet been achieved to date and will be an ongoing effort. It should be noted that, at this time, there are no penalties for missing the agreed-upon targets. AB 32 requires the State of California to meet certain greenhouse gas reduction goals but has not yet mandated that local goals be achieved. It is likely that such requirements may become a requirement on local governments in the near future.

SB 375 **Senate Bill 375 (SB375)** authored by State Senator Darrell Steinberg was signed into law by Governor Schwarzenegger on September 30, 2008, and is intended to build on the existing regional transportation planning process (which is overseen by local elected officials with land-use responsibilities) to connect the reduction of greenhouse gas (GHG) emissions from cars and light trucks to land use and transportation policy.

SB375 has three goals:

- To use the regional transportation planning process to help achieve AB32 goals

- To use the California Environmental Quality Act (CEQA) streamlining as an incentive to encourage residential projects to achieve AB32 goals to reduce greenhouse gas emissions (GHGs)

- To coordinate the regional housing needs allocation process with the regional transportation planning process

How Does SB375 Stimulate the California Economy? SB375 not only works to implement AB32 in the reduction of greenhouse gas emissions but it also provides incentives for creating attractive, walkable, and sustainable communities and revitalizing existing communities. The bill allows homebuilders to obtain relief from certain environmental reviews under the California Environmental Quality Act if they build projects consistent with the new sustainable community strategies. Additionally, SB375 will encourage the development of more alternative transportation options, which will promote traffic congestion.

SB375 gives the state ARB authority to set targets for each of the 18 metropolitan regions in the state, working with local governments to do their fair share of reducing GHG emissions caused by land use and transportation policies. If SB375 is properly implemented, the following will result:

- Shorter commuting between home and work

- Less traffic congestion resulting in less air pollution

- Neighborhoods designed for shopping and other daily needs close to home

- Affordable housing for all income levels, which is closer to employment centers

- Protection of open space and agricultural lands

- Greater alternatives to automobile usage, including the creation of more pedestrian-friendly environments and greater access to public transportation

A CLOSER LOOK   What is happening in the San Francisco Bay Area, specifically in San Mateo County, to address climate change? Many local governments are making efforts to reduce carbon emissions. The following is what is currently occurring throughout San Mateo County:

- High-mileage, low-emission vehicles such as hybrids have been purchased for government operations in Redwood City, Burlingame, San Carlos, Foster City, Menlo Park, San Mateo, and South San Francisco.

- Renewable energy technologies have been installed in public facilities, such as solar panels in San Carlos, cogeneration systems at the Community College District and the Millbrae sewage plant, and solar heating in Brisbane and Menlo Park.

- Investments in energy efficiency have been made, such as the replacement of inefficient incandescent lighting with fluorescent lights in public facilities in many cities and the replacement of traditional traffic lights with long lasting light emitting diodes (LEDs) and low-power traffic lights in Foster City, San Carlos, and Millbrae.

- Alternative transportation schemes have been developed, such as bicycle lanes, shuttle services, housing and commercial developments near public transit, incentives for city employees to use public transit, and requirements that developers of commercial properties implement traffic reduction plans.

Call to Action   As a result of AB 32 and SB 375, what is occurring today is climate action planning at local levels in cities and counties. At an event at NASA's Ames Research Center, on May 23, 2013, California's governor joined more than 500 scientists and researchers to release a groundbreaking call to action on climate change and other global threats to humanity. What resulted was a message to policymakers, industry, and the general public at improving the nexus between scientific research and potential action on climate change. The call to action identified five key threats to the habitable environment that policymakers must address now to avoid the degradation of humanity's health. At the top of the list was climate change, followed by extinction, loss of ecosystems, pollution and population growth, and consumption. The impacts of climate change have already become evident in California and include changes to sea levels and temperature, which are affecting water supplies, growing conditions, and habitats.

As a result of the governor's call to action and to further implement AB 32 and SB 375, many local cities and counties are working on climate action plans that outline the specific activities that an agency will undertake to reduce greenhouse gas emissions. The first step communities began to take shortly after the passage of AB 32 was to go to the source of the problem and create inventories of those uses or activities in their communities that cause greenhouse gas emissions. Through local climate action plans, communities are looking for ways to reduce emissions from many sources (e.g., buildings, transportation, electrical grid, agriculture, forestry, solid waste, etc.).

The momentum started in California but has spread to the rest of the nation. On June 25, 2013, President Obama also released an action plan to address climate change. As a result, the president's 2014 fiscal year budget provided for increased funding for clean energy technology. Additionally, by 2020, goals have been set at the national level that commit to doubling wind and solar electricity generation and that the Department of the Interior permit enough renewable electricity generation to power more than 6 million homes. The president's plan also calls that by 2025, the Department of Defense, which is the single largest consumer of energy in the United States, is committed to deploying three gigawatts of renewable energy on military installations.

A CLOSER LOOK A result of efforts to reduce greenhouse gas emissions is the birth of new and innovative entrepreneurial approaches, which has included the expansion of Tesla Motors in the San Francisco Bay Area. Since 1984, Toyota and General Motors had operated NUMMI, a joint venture between the auto giants, producing as many as 450,00 automobiles a year from the 200-acre, 5½ million square foot facility in Fremont, California, until the plant was shuttered in April of 2010. With General Motors having declared bankruptcy the year before, and Toyota now looking for a new buyer for the plant facility, the City of Fremont was now going to be left with this massive vacant structure immediately east of Interstate I-880. Meanwhile, on the other side of the bay, Tesla Motors was producing a limited number of automobiles in a garage immediately behind its showroom in Menlo Park. In 2009, the U.S. government agreed to loan Tesla $465 million from an alternative vehicle fund and, in March of 2010, it acquired the former NUMMI facility in Fremont, which finally allowed Tesla a facility capable of mass producing its vehicles. Tesla Motors has come to be known for its design and manufacturing advances of electric vehicles and has been a large economic boost for the San Francisco Bay Area. On April 3, 2015, Tesla Motors announced that it had delivered 10,030 vehicles in the first quarter of 2015, which was a 55% increase over the previous first quarter of 2014.

Drought

The multi-year drought in California has affected virtually every part of the state and many industries and has created severe economic and environmental challenges. The drought was so severe that in January of 2015, the governor declared a drought state of emergency. The entire state is taking steps to reduce water consumption and eliminate water waste to prepare for a continued drought of unknown length.

How does the drought affect real estate? If a community is experiencing water shortages, the first issue typically raised by the community's existing residents is to look at new growth and its impact on the existing water supply. Many communities use moratoriums on development unless there is sufficient water. Many communities also limit the issuance of future water connections to new residential proposals. This impacts the future supply of housing units in many areas of California.

A CLOSER LOOK   The concept of desalination has once again been revived in California as the result of new stringent conservation measures, along with depleted reservoirs. Currently one of the largest and costly desalination plants in the Western Hemisphere is under construction on a coastal lagoon in Carlsbad, California, in Northern San Diego County, with an estimated price tag of $1 billion. This new desalination plant is scheduled to go into operation in November 2015. It is estimated that the plant will be capable of delivering up to 50 million gallons of water per day, providing water to approximately 112,000 households or 10% of the county's drinking water needs. Several hundred miles to the north, the City of Santa Barbara is taking steps to modernize and reactivate a smaller $34 million desalination plant built during the drought in the early 1990s but mothballed after a trial run in 1992. If approved by the Santa Barbara City Council in mid-2015, the plant could be in operation by the fall of 2016 and capable of producing three million gallons per day, or about 30% of the municipal demand. This will no doubt lead to other plants being constructed in California, which will not only address water availability, but bring back much needed construction jobs to the state.

Fracking

Hydraulic fracturing, or fracking, has become a concern for the public as well as for private landowners as it becomes more widespread in California and in the United States as a whole. According to the Center for Biological Diversity, fracking has been documented in 10 California counties: Colusa, Glenn, Kern, Los Angeles, Monterey, Sacramento, Santa Barbara, Sutter, Kings, and Ventura. Oil companies have also fracked offshore wells near California's coast from Seal Beach to Santa Barbara Channel. In Kern County, California's major oil-producing county, it is estimated that over 50% of new oil wells are subjected to hydraulic fracturing. According to environmental groups, hydraulic fracturing involves numerous types of toxic chemicals, including methanol, benzene, naphthalene, and trimethylbenzene. It has also been noted by the environmental groups that approximately 25% of chemicals used in fracking could cause cancer according to scientists with the Endocrine Disruption Exchange. Water quality can also be threatened by methane contamination tied to drilling and fracturing of rock formations.[17]

With the ever-changing disclosure laws associated with real estate, the high value of land in California, and with groundwater potentially being contaminated along with the continuation of the drought, fracking will continue to be in the forefront for many years to come.

A CLOSER LOOK In 2013, Senate Bill (SB) 4 (Pavely) was passed by the legislature and was signed by Governor Jerry Brown. The bill requires disclosure of well stimulation projects, advance notice to neighbors, and groundwater monitoring. It also required the State of California to establish standards/regulations by early 2015. However, many in California feel that SB4 did not go far enough. In 2014, two California counties (San Benito and Mendocino) banned fracking despite lobbying by oil and gas companies. Santa Barbara's efforts to ban fracking were unsuccessful.

THE NEXT ECONOMIC BOOST FOR CALIFORNIA

California's High Speed Rail Project

In November 2008, the voters of California approved the California High Speed Rail Project along with the issuance of up to $9.95 billion in bonds

---

17. Center for Biological Diversity, "Fracking in California: Nine Questions and Concerns," Center for Biological Diversity, www.biologicaldiversity.org/campaigns/california_fracking/faq.html (accessed April 2015).

for the project. The project calls for the high speed rail line to connect the San Francisco Bay Area with Los Angeles. It is projected that by 2029, the two regions will be connected by a rail system capable of reaching speeds of over 200 mph and making the trip within three hours. The system will eventually extend to Sacramento and San Diego, totaling 800 miles with up to 24 stations and will result in a statewide rail modernization effort that will invest billions of dollars in local and regional rail lines to meet the state's 21st century needs. [18]

Because the project is extensive and will run through a variety of geographical areas, it has been broken up into 10 sections:

1. San Francisco to San Jose

2. San Jose to Merced

3. Merced to Sacramento

4. Merced to Fresno

5. Fresno to Bakersfield

6. Bakersfield to Palmdale

7. Palmdale to Burbank

8. Burbank to Los Angeles

9. Los Angeles to Anaheim

10. Los Angeles to San Diego

When assessing the economic benefits of California's high speed rail program, the initial $2.6 billion investment from Proposition 1A bonds would result in a net economic benefit of $8.3 to $8.8 billion, or a 3 to 1 rate of return. The State of California is also forecasting that state and local governments would earn more than $600 million back in tax revenue, or 25% of what the State of California has estimated it will spend on initial construction of the system. The state estimates that approximately 20,000 construction and related jobs will be created in the initial stages of construction, connecting San Francisco with Los Angeles would result

---

18. California High-Speed Rail Authority, "Welcome," California High-Speed Rail Authority, www.hsr.ca.gov/(accessed April 2015).

in approximately 66,000 jobs annually for 15 years, and would ultimately result in 2,900 permanent operational jobs. Over the long term, approximately 320 billion fewer vehicle miles will be travelled over 40 years; 146 million hours in traffic saved annually; significant carbon monoxide emission reductions; 237 million gallons of automobile fuel will be saved annually; and 35 million gallons of aviation fuel will also be saved. These are just some of the economic, environmental, and quality-of-life benefits to be expected from the high speed rail system over the life of the project and beyond.

THE STATE OF THE REAL ESTATE MARKET

Trends Since the Recession

According to the California Association of REALTORS® (C.A.R.), home prices in California declined after peaking in mid 2007. By the 4th quarter of 2008, the median price of an existing detached single-family home in California had fallen by 41% from the same time one year earlier. The median price in the 4th quarter of 2008 was $281,800 compared to $492,490 for the 4th quarter of 2007. The significant decline in price was attributed largely to the dramatic change in the mix of sales since 2007 and the increase in the share of distressed sales. Prior to the beginning of the "Credit Crunch" in August 2007, the sub $500,000 price range accounted for 43% of sales, the middle segment ($500,000 to $1 million) made up 42%, and the over $1 million segment only captured 15% of the market.

The California drought website (http://ca.gov/drought/) provides information and resources regarding the drought and archives drought news.

What has been noted as unprecedented price declines had dramatically improved affordability in California. C.A.R.'s Housing Affordability Index for First-Time Buyers, which measures the share of all households that can afford the entry-level home, rose to 59% in the 4th quarter of 2008; thus, six in ten households in California were able to afford the entry-level home. Affordability of housing more than doubled between 2007 and 2009, when the Affordability Index was below 30%. Although we find that by 2012 and 2013, the real estate market in California made a turn-around, with prices on the rise since then.

Figure 16.1 provides a historical perspective of what has occurred in the market between 2007 and December 2014, including the dramatic change in the median price of a home in California and the sales of homes. As we can see from Figure 16.1, home sales in California continued to stay strong, with the price of residential housing beginning to recover and the median price of a single-family residence slowly increasing through December 2014.

FIGURE 16.1:   California Median Home Sales Price and Resale Activity (2007 to December 2014) Single-Family Detached Homes

	Median Home Sales Price	% Change Over Prev. Month		Median Home Sales Price	% Change Over Prev. Month
January 2007	$551,220	–3.2%	February 2010	$278,190	–1.4%
February 2007	$554,280	0.6%	March 2010	$300,900	–0.2%
March 2007	$582,930	5.2%	April 2010	$307,000	–4.0%
April 2007	$594,110	1.9%	May 2010	$327,460	14.7%
May 2007	$594,530	0.1%	June 2010	$313,890	–11.0%
June 2007	$591,280	–0.5%	July 2010	$318,550	–9.9%
July 2007	$587,560	–0.6%	August 2010	$320,860	2.1%
August 2007	$588,670	0.2%	September 2010	$309,720	1.8%
September 2007	$535,760	–0.9%	October 2010	$305,150	–2.3%
October 2007	$501,730	–6.4%	November 2010	$296,480	4.6%
November 2007	$490,511	–2.2%	December 2010	$304,770	2.4%
December 2007	$480,820	–2.0%	January 2011	$279,220	11.3%
January 2008	$427,200	–11.2%	February 2011	$271,370	–10.1%
February 2008	$418,260	–2.1%	March 2011	$286,550	1.0%
March 2008	$414,520	–0.6%	April 2011	$294,140	–1.0%
April 2008	$404,590	–2.4%	May 2011	$292,850	–4.7%
May 2008	$386,620	–4.4%	June 2011	$296,410	2.1%
June 2008	$373,100	–3.5%	July 2011	$297,660	0.6%
July 2008	$355,000	–4.9%	August 2011	$297,060	3.7%
August 2008	$353,240	–1.4%	September 2011	$288,700	–1.5%
September 2008	$317,900	–10.0%	October 2011	$277,450	0.8%
October 2008	$305,380	–3.9%	November 2011	$279,910	–0.2%
November 2008	$287,120	–6.0%	December 2011	$288,950	1.2%
December 2008	$282,930	–1.5%	January 2012	$271,490	2.2%
January 2009	$250,610	–11.4%	February 2012	$268,810	1.2%
February 2009	$245,170	–2.2%	March 2012	$291,330	–0.8%
March 2009	$250,190	2.0%	April 2012	$312,500	0.1%
April 2009	$253,390	1.3%	May 2012	$316,460	1.8%
May 2009	$263,600	4.0%	June 2012	$320,990	–3.7%
June 2009	$274,740	4.2%	July 2012	$334,220	1.4%
July 2009	$285,480	3.4%	August 2012	$343,800	1.4%
August 2009	$293,400	-0.8%	September 2012	$344,760	–4.3%
September 2009	$296,610	–0.9%	October 2012	$340,910	6.2%
October 2009	$297,500	5.4%	November 2012	$345,560	–2.5%
November 2009	$304,550	–2.0%	December 2012	$365,840	0.9%
December 2009	$306,860	–3.0%	January 2013	$336,650	–5.2%
January 2010	$284,600	–5.3%	February 2013	$333,180	–0.8%

FIGURE 16.1 (continued): **California Median Home Sales Price and Resale Activity (2007 to December 2014) Single-Family Detached Homes**

	Median Home Sales Price	% Change Over Prev. Month
March 2013	$379,000	–0.1%
April 2013	$402,830	1.3%
May 2013	$417,350	2.0%
June 2013	$428,700	–4.0%
July 2013	$433,910	6.9%
August 2013	$441,010	–1.9%
September 2013	$428,290	–4.8%
October 2013	$427,540	–3.1%
November 2013	$423,090	–2.8%
December 2013	$438,790	–6.6%
January 2014	$410,900	0.1%
February 2014	$404,250	–0.6%
March 2014	$435,580	1.4%
April 2014	$449,360	7.2%
May 2014	$466,320	–1.1%
June 2014	$457,160	1.3%
July 2014	$464,750	1.2%
August 2014	$480,280	–1.1%
September 2014	$461,370	0.4%
October 2014	$450,270	0.3%
November 2014	$444,830	–5.2%
December 2014	$452,570	–2.9%

Source: The California Association of REALTORS®

The Subprime Loan Market and the Implications on the Housing Market

Although subprime loans are not an active part of the lending market at this time, we should look back at the products that contributed to the downfall of many loan holders/homeowners in California. Looking back to the first quarter of 2007, the market was showing signs of stability, but attention turned towards potential problems subprime loans created and other alternative loan products that had increased in use. Simply stated, **subprime loans** generally are loans to qualified individuals with credit scores below 620. Indeed, the use of subprime loans in California had climbed dramatically in a short time, accounting for less than 5% of loans outstanding for several years before climbing to roughly 14% of the total by 2003, based on data from the Mortgage Bankers Association. Many concerns centered on how many subprime borrowers would face foreclosure in the coming years as their loans reset from lower teaser rates to fully indexed mortgage rates.

Delinquency rates provide an approximate measure of the potential down-side risk in the months and years ahead. The delinquency rate for all loans in California in the fourth quarter of 2007 stood at 3.25% compared to 5.31% for the United States as a whole. By 2007, as the recession was commencing, California had fared better than other states around the country because its economy had continued to grow and add jobs. Moreover, it experienced much larger price gains in the first half of the decade compared to many other parts of the country. However, according to the California Association of REALTORS®, the number of defaults in California escalated rapidly between 2007 and 2009, with 111,700 defaults by the third quarter of 2007, and a record high of 135,400 defaults being recorded in the first quarter of 2009.

According to the California Association of REALTORS®, many of the subprime borrowers were households who had subprime **adjustable-rate mortgages (ARMs)**. In the fourth quarter of 2006, subprime ARMs made up 8.6% of the total number of loans outstanding in California. Of all subprime ARMs in California, 12.1% were delinquent as of the fourth quarter and accounted for 1.04% of total loans outstanding. Only a fraction of all delinquent loans actually go into foreclosure because of measures taken by lenders to prevent costly foreclosures. For borrowers who face temporary problems, these include delaying payments for a short period of time or scheduling a lump-sum payment in the near future. For borrowers with more severe problems, alternatives include short sales or mortgage forgiveness.

The loans that posed the greatest risk of delinquency and/or foreclosure were underwritten in 2005 and 2006, with many of these loans reset in 2007 and 2008. Numerically, there were many more loans in 2005 (the record year for California home sales) than in 2006, so the 2005 cohort of loans was most worrisome. Given the timing of the resets, the greatest stress on the market and the economy occurred in 2007 and 2008.

The negative impact of subprime loans in California was limited to subprime borrowers—mainly those holding subprime ARMs—and to lenders who relied heavily on the subprime market segment for their business. Risks loom largest for marginally qualified households in newer developments with a concentration of borrowers holding subprime loans. The subprime mortgage crisis was considered a serious economic problem that manifested itself through liquidity deficits in the banking industry due to massive foreclosure rates that contributed to the financial industry crisis and government bailout occurring in October 2008.

What Were the Implications of Subprime Loans to the Economy?

Subprime borrowers/consumers with poor or questionable credit histories had been able to use a combination of rising home prices and easy credit to live beyond their means in recent years as wages stagnated. That spending helped to fuel the U.S. economy's growth.

In response to the beleaguered subprime loan market, Freddie Mac and Fannie Mae pledged to buy tens of billions of dollars of newly created subprime mortgage loans to help prop up the roughly $1.3 trillion subprime market as lenders tighten their credit standards or flee altogether. By 2007, Congress had become increasingly concerned with the rising number of defaults on subprime loans, which led to a wave of foreclosures and deprived hundreds of thousands of families of their homes. California saw the number of foreclosures at roughly 50,000 per quarter for 2008 and 2009. With government policies and lender practices instituted between late 2008 and the first part of 2009, home prices in much of the state held steady, aside from the normal fluctuations. Many policymakers and economists believed that the stabilization of home prices was necessary for discretionary sellers to return to the market and drive the supply side of the market to more normal conditions.

In order to deal with the mortgage crisis, the U.S. government embarked on a variety of programs. One such program was the Troubled Asset Relief Program (TARP). One purpose of TARP was to allow the U.S. government to purchase or insure assets and equity from financial institutions to strengthen the financial markets and provide for a recovery from the subprime mortgage crisis. The program allowed for the U.S. Treasury to purchase and insure up to $700 billion of troubled assets.

The major goal of TARP was to encourage banks to resume lending to businesses, consumers, and other lenders at levels previously seen prior to the mortgage crisis. The theory behind TARP is that if it can stabilize bank capital ratios, it should allow banks to increase lending instead of hoarding cash against future unforeseen losses from troubled investments and assets. Additionally through TARP, the goal was for banks to loosen credit through increased lending, which was to further bring order to the financial markets.

TARP operated as a revolving purchase facility, which purchased the assets of banks and sold them or held the assets and collected the coupons. The money received from sales and coupons went back into the pool, which facilitated the purchase of more assets. Congress initially authorized $350 billion for the program, which was released in October 2008. Congress subsequently voted to release an additional $350 billion on January 15, 2009, for the program. TARP allowed the Treasury to purchase both "troubled assets" and any other asset the purchase of which the Treasury Department determines necessary to further economic stability. As defined by the Treasury Department, troubled assets include real estate and mortgage-related assets and securities based on those assets, as well as the mortgages themselves, and foreclosed properties. TARP also helped to support the "Making Homes Affordable" program, which was implemented on March 4, 2009. TARP funds were authorized by the U.S. Treasury Department to also be used for the purchase of "at-risk mortgages," which were considered troubled assets. Further, the program allowed for mortgages held by Fannie Mae and Freddie Mac to be refinanced to a favorable loan modification.

The closest parallel action the federal government took to TARP was the government's investment in the Reconstruction Finance Corporation during the Hoover administration in 1932. The U.S. government made loans to distressed banks and bought stock in nearly 6,000 banks, which totaled $1.3 billion. When the economy commenced to stabilized, the U.S. government sold its bank stocks to private investors or the banks themselves.

Which Lenders Were Previously Responsible for the Majority of the Subprime Loans?

Among the top five home-mortgage lenders, Washington Mutual, Inc. made the highest percentage of loans to investors or second homebuyers in 2006. Many of those loans were generally considered riskier than those to owner occupants. Citigroup, Inc. and Washington Mutual had the highest concentrations of loans with higher interest rates, which are generally subprime mortgages or home loans made to those with weak credit records or high debt in relation to income. By the end of 2008, Washington Mutual had become insolvent and had been absorbed by Chase Bank.

According to the Wall Street Journal, 15% of the loans Washington Mutual originated in 2006 were backed by homes that were not the borrower's principal residence. That compares with 13% at Countrywide Financial

Corp., 11% at Wells Fargo & Company, 9% at J.P. Morgan Chase & Company, and 5% at Citigroup.

Historically, loans for investment properties carry more risk because borrowers are more likely to abandon an unsuccessful investment than stop meeting payments on their primary residence. Many of the loans to investors were option adjustable-rate mortgages, which gave borrowers the choice of payment levels each month, including one that covers only part of the interest and no principal. Such loans with minimal payments were fine for speculators who hoped to sell their homes quickly and were not concerned about paying down the loan balance. However, many of those speculators and investors did not foresee the slowdown in the housing market.

SUMMARY

California has become ground zero when it comes to developers' ability to accommodate changing market conditions and lay the groundwork for nationwide movements. Because of the high cost of housing, the traffic plaguing our communities, and our desire to become more environmentally conscious, it is believed that, in the future, we will see urban cores with greater housing density and more affordable units. The limited supply of land and stringent entitlement requirements in California will continue to push development costs upward. In response, developers will shift toward high-density projects so that such projects can be easily financed.

Young people in their 20s and 30s will choose more affordable urban core living in highrise developments that are close to their places of employment and cultural centers. It is anticipated that the pace of consumer spending will slow as the housing market recedes from its recent highs. Mortgage refinance activity has significantly dropped in recent years; thus, there is every expectation that it will continue to drop, heading to a downturn in consumer spending.

As the single-family market begins to rebound and investors continue to seek out different investment options, and with the trend among investors to rent rather than flip their investments, real estate such as apartments will become more attractive. Investors are shifting from buying and renting condominiums to investing in rental apartments as higher home prices are keeping potential buyers in the rental market. We saw that the recession had a significant impact on California's real estate market, with the median price of a single-family residence dropping by 59%, from the all-time high in May 2007 of $594,530 to a low of $245,170 in February 2009. By December 2014, the price of a median-priced, single-family residence had risen to $452,570. With job growth and solid economic expansion, household formation will experience a boost and demand will increase for rental and owner-occupied housing. As the economy continues to improve, there are promising signs for the housing industry because housing demand creates jobs and, in turn, fosters additional demand for construction. While prices continue to rise on average, they have done so at a slower rate over the course of 2014, and it is expected that the trend will continue through 2015.

Environmental issues such as fracking will continue to be in the forefront of California's residents, as oil and gas companies continue to explore the state for oil and gas resources.

REVIEW QUESTIONS

1. What are the 10 basic smart growth principles?

2. What types of incentives for affordable housing are in your community?

3. What is your city/community doing to foster affordable and sustainable housing projects?

4. In recent years, have there been in-fill developments in your community?

5. What efforts has your community undertaken to implement green building regulations?

6. What steps has your community done to implement AB32 and SB375 to reduce greenhouse gas emissions and address global warming?

7. What are the economic benefits of the proposed high speed rail project for California's Central Valley Region?

UNIT QUIZ

1. Retail development can be encouraged by
   a. traffic.
   b. high-density residential development.
   c. poor land-use planning.
   d. none of the above.

2. People who live in affordable residential developments
   a. drive less and own fewer cars.
   b. drive more and own more cars.
   c. cannot drive.
   d. do not want to drive.

3. Assembly Bill (AB32) was signed into law on September 27, 2006, with the intent of
   a. promoting smart growth.
   b. extending the redevelopment program.
   c. reducing California's greenhouse gas emissions.
   d. increasing aid to California's homeless population.

4. TARP stands for
   a. Troubled Asset Relief Program.
   b. Troubled Analytical Reset Program.
   c. Timed Asset Rotating Fund Program.
   d. none of these.

5. The construction of the state's high speed rail project is broken up into _____ sections.
   a. 12
   b. 100
   c. 10
   d. 22

6. In what year did the construction of second residential units become a ministerial act under state law?
    a. 1981
    b. 1982
    c. 2003
    d. None of these

7. Which state government agency's mission includes providing safe and affordable housing to all Californians?
    a. CalHFA
    b. Fannie Mae
    c. California Bureau of Real Estate
    d. Housing and Community Development

8. How many basic principles are there to smart growth?
    a. 11
    b. 10
    c. 5
    d. 15

9. Increased retail and commercial development and ease of walking and transit use are possible benefits of
    a. low-density housing.
    b. high-density housing.
    c. urban sprawl.
    d. none of these.

10. The primary purpose of LEMs is to
    a. fund apartments.
    b. increase monies to homebuyers in urban areas.
    c. refinance an existing high-rate subprime mortgage.
    d. construct a LEED-certified house.

UNDERSTANDING AND USING ECONOMIC DATA

KEY TERMS

Bureau of Labor
 Statistics (BLS)
Chained Consumer
 Price Index for All
 Urban Consumers
 (C-CPI-U)
cohort
cohort-component
 method
consumer expenditure
 surveys
Consumer Price Index
 (CPI)

Consumer Price
 Index for All Urban
 Consumers (CPI-U)
Consumer Price Index
 for Urban Wage
 Earners and Clerical
 Workers (CPI-W)
CPI market basket
economic assistants
economic indicator
employment cost
 index (ECI)
escalation

household projections
index
natural increase
net internal migration
net migration
owners' equivalent
 rent
point-of-purchase
 survey
population projection
producers price index
 (PPI)
U.S. Census Bureau

LEARNING OBJECTIVES

- List the major factors that are likely to contribute to population growth in the United States in the 21st century

- Describe what is meant by a "natural increase" in the populationy

■ Identify the categories of goods and services that contribute to the CPI

■ Distinguish the Consumer Price Index from the cost-of-living index

U.S. POPULATION PROJECTIONS TO 2060

The material in this section is adapted from information that can be found at the website of the **U.S. Census Bureau** *(www.census.gov).*

In addition to conducting the decennial (once a decade) census, the Census Bureau also prepares more frequent community population surveys and uses this ongoing stream of data to make population projections.

Creating a Population Projection

When demographers and statisticians refer to *births*, they mean the total number of live births occurring to residents of an area during a stated time period. When deaths are subtracted from births, the resulting number is the **natural increase** in the population. **Net internal migration** is the difference between internal in-migration to an area and internal out-migration from the same area during a stated time period. **Net migration** is the total of net internal migration plus net international migration.

A **population projection** is an estimate of the population at some future date. Projections illustrate plausible courses of future population change based on assumptions about future births, deaths, international migration, and domestic migration. Projected numbers are based on an estimated population consistent with the most recent decennial census with those figures being projected forward using a variant of what is termed the cohort-component method.

A **cohort** consists of the persons born in a given year. If you were born in 1986, your cohort consists of all of the people who were born in that year.

In the **cohort-component method**, the components of population change (fertility, mortality, and net migration) are projected separately for each birth cohort. The base population is advanced each year by using projected survival rates and net international migration by single year of age, sex, race, and Hispanic origin.

Each year, a new birth cohort is added to the population by applying the projected fertility rates by race and Hispanic origin to the female population as of January 1. The components of change are individually applied to each of the seven resulting race/ethnic groups to project the next year's population. The following are the groups that the United States is tracking by race and Hispanic origin:

1. White

2. Non-Hispanic White

3. Hispanic

4. Black or African American

5. American Indian and Alaska Native

6. Asian

7. Native Hawaiian and Pacific Islander

At the national level, a special procedure seeks to ensure that certain age-related biases, mainly underenumeration and age misstatement, do not advance in age.

Household projections also are made at the national level. These are future estimates of the number and composition of households and families. These projections are based on current household estimates and population projections and assumptions about future household structure and family composition. Household projections are not intended as forecasts but represent the results of assumptions about possible future trends in population change and household-type proportions.

To get household projections, household estimates are projected forward using alternative marital status and household-type proportions by age of householders. Three alternative series are used to illustrate alternative patterns of future household change:

1. The first series is based on a time series model and is the preferred projection in light of past and possible future trends in household change.

2. The second series reflects the consequences of projected change in the age/sex structure of the population only because it does not

assume any change in the proportion maintaining households for specific types by age and sex.

3. The third series assumes changes in both the age/sex structure and the race/origin composition of the population, but it also assumes no change in the proportions maintaining specific household types by these factors.

There are many more terms that are used in creating population and household projections, and the U.S. Census Bureau website allows further exploration of some of the fascinating data compiled there.

Interim Population Projections

Some interesting results were developed by applying the cohort-component method to data gathered shortly before and then confirmed by the 2010 census results.

Between 2014 and 2060, the U.S. population is projected to increase from 319 million to 417 million, reaching 400 million in 2051. According to the U.S. Census Bureau, the U.S. population is projected to grow more slowly in future decades than in the past. It is projected that by 2030 one in five Americans will be 65 and over, by 2044 more than half of all Americans will belong to a minority group (any group other than non-Hispanic White), and by 2060, nearly one in five of the nation's total population will be foreign born.

The mortality values used in the interim projections are identical to those used in the middle series of the projections published in December 2012. They assume that average life expectancy at birth will increase gradually from the 2015 value of 77.1 years for the male population and 81.8 years for the female population to 2060 values of 82.8 years for the male population and 86.8 years for the female population. (See Figure 17.1.)

FIGURE 17.1: Life Expectancy Projections

	Males	Females
2015	77.1	81.8
2060	82.8	86.8

Projected Trends in Population Size and Growth

The total U.S. population is projected to increase by 98.1 million between 2014 and 2060. The population is expected to increase from just under 319 million in 2014 to just under 417 million in 2060. This corresponds to an average increase of 2.1 million people per year. In 2014 the native population, or U.S. born, stood at 276 million. Between 2014 and 2060, the native population is expected to increase by 62 million (or 22%), reaching 339 million in 2060. At the same time, the foreign-born population is projected to grow from 42 million to 78 million, an increase of 36 million (or 85%). The foreign born, because of its rate of growth, is projected to outpace that of natives and is expected to account for an increasing share of the total population, reaching 19% in 2060, up from 13% in 2014. Of the 196.6 million births projected to occur between 2014 and 2060, 39.8 million (20.3%) are births to foreign-born women.

The population is projected to age over the coming decades, with a higher proportion of the nation's total population in the older ages (65 and over). Overall, the percentage of the total population that is under the age of 18 is projected to decrease from 23% to 20% between 2014 and 2060. Similarly, the working-age population is projected to decrease from 62% to 57% of the total population over the same interval. In contrast, the percentage of the population that is age 65 and over is expected to grow from 15% to 24%, an overall increase of 9%. The foreign-born population is projected to be concentrated in the adult ages, with fewer than 10% of its population age 17 and under, as compared to nearly a quarter of the native population. This youth population is predominately native because all children born in the United States (including children born to foreign mothers) are considered native, and also because rates of international migration are comparatively low in these ages. The youth population, defined as those under 18, is projected to experience the least amount of change, increasing slightly from 74 million in 2014 to 82 million in 2060. Conversely, the older population is projected to more than double in size from 46 million to 98 million over the same period. For the older population, the biggest increase is expected in the decade from 2020 to 2030, when the population age 65 and over is projected to increase by 18 million (from 56 million to 74 million). The timing of this increase is related to the aging of the baby boom generation. The baby boomers began turning 65 in 2011 and, by 2030, they all will be age 65 and older.

FIGURE 17.2: **United States Population Projections by Nativity and Age Group: 2014 to 2060 (Population in thousands)**

Nativity and age group	Population						Change 2014 to 2060	
	2014	2020	2030	2040	2050	2060	Number	Percent
Total all ages	**318,748**	**334,503**	**359,402**	**380,219**	**398,328**	**416,795**	**98,047**	**30.8**
Under 18	73,591	74,128	76,273	78,185	79,888	82,309	8,718	11.8
18 to 44	115,426	120,073	126,588	128,669	132,371	136,310	20,884	18.1
45 to 64	83,477	83,861	82,434	91,021	98,074	100,013	16,536	19.8
65 and older	46,255	56,441	74,107	82,344	87,996	98,164	51,909	112.2
Natives all ages	**276,398**	**286,611**	**302,545**	**315,103**	**326,030**	**338,564**	**62,166**	**87.5**
Under 18	71,083	71,683	73,486	75,189	76,735	79,055	7,972	8.4
18 to 44	95,441	99,369	105,145	106,053	108,433	111,141	15,699	22.5
45 to 64	69,717	67,196	62,302	68,986	74,761	75,493	5,776	14.4
65 and older	40,157	48,362	61,612	64,876	66,101	72,876	32,719	77.3
Foreign born all ages	**43,350**	**47,892**	**56,857**	**65,116**	**72,299**	**78,230**	**35,881**	**84.7**
Under 18	2,508	2,445	2,787	2,996	3,153	3,254	746	29.8
18 to 44	19,984	20,704	21,443	22,616	23,937	25,169	5,185	25.9
45 to 64	13,760	16,665	20,132	22,035	23,313	24,520	10,760	78.2
65 and older	6,098	8,079	12,495	17,469	21,895	25,288	19,190	314.7

Source: U.S. Census Bureau, 2014 National Projections

The United States is projected to become more racially and ethnically diverse in the coming years. Figure 17.3 represents projections of the size and distribution of the population by race and Hispanic origin in 2014 and 2060. The top panel illustrates the race of those reporting to have a single race (95.5% in 2014) as well as those reporting two or more races (2.5%). The middle panel illustrates all those reporting to have each race, either alone or in combination with others. The lower panel illustrates those who were Hispanic and non-Hispanic (17.4% and 82.6%, respectively) in 2014. The non-Hispanic White population is currently the majority group, as it is both the largest racial and ethnic group and accounts for greater than 50% share of the nation's total population. However, by 2060, the share of this group is projected to be just 44%, as its population falls from 198 million in 2014 to 182 million in 2060 as illustrated in Figure 17.3. The Two or More Races population is projected to be the fastest growing over the next 46 years, with its population expected to triple in size (an increase of 226%). This group is projected to increase from 8 million to 26 million between 2014 and 2060.

FIGURE 17.3:   United States Population Projections by Race and Hispanic Origin 2014 to 2060 (Population in thousands)

Race and Hispanic origin	2014		2060		Change 2014 to 2060	
	Number	Percent	Number	Percent	Number	Percent
Total Population	**318,748**	**100.0**	**416,795**	**100.0**	**98,047**	**30.8**
One Race	310,753	97.5	390,772	93.8	80,020	25.8
White	246,940	77.5	285,314	68.5	38,374	15.5
Non-Hispanic White	198,103	62.2	181,930	43.6	-16,174	-8.2
Black or African American	42,039	13.2	59,693	14.3	17,654	42.0
American Indian & Alaska Native	3,957	1.2	5,607	1.3	1,650	41.7
Asian	17,083	5.4	38,965	9.3	21,882	128.1
Native Hawaiian & Other Pacific Islander	734	0.2	1,134	0.3	460	62.6
Two or More Races	7,995	2.5	26,022	6.2	18,027	225.5
Race Alone or in Combination						
White	254,009	79.7	309,567	74.3	55,558	21.9
Black or African American	45,562	14.3	74,530	17.9	28,968	63.6
American Indian & Alaska Native	6,528	2.0	10,169	2.4	3,640	55.8
Asian	19,983	6.3	48,575	11.7	28,592	143.1
Native Hawaiian & Other Pacific Islander	1,458	0.5	2,929	0.7	1,470	100.8
Hispanic or Latino Origin						
Hispanic	55,410	17.4	119,044	28.6	63,635	114.8
Not-Hispanic	263,338	82.6	297,750	71.4	34,412	13.1

Source: U.S. Census Bureau, 2014 National Projections

The Asian population is projected to be the second fastest growing group, with an increase of 128%. The Hispanic population is projected to be the third fastest growing as illustrated in Figure 17.3. The Hispanic population is projected to increase from 55 million in 2014 to 119 million in 2060, an increase of 115%. In 2014, Hispanics accounted for 17% of the U.S. population. By 2060, approximately 29% of the U.S. population will be Hispanics, equal to 25% of the total population.

Between 2014 and 2060, the total population is projected to increase by approximately 31%, while the number of children is projected to increase by 12% as illustrated in Figure 17.2.

Figure 17.4 contains a breakdown of total population for California and each of the individual 58 counties from 2010 to 2060, in five-year increments. As we see from Figure 17.2 and 17.3, those projections are for the entire U.S. population and provide a general overview of where the nation is going as a whole. As it pertains to real estate, real estate professionals and demographers want to know what is happening in their communities today and what will happen in the future. As an example, we see that the state's population is at 38.8 million in 2015 and is projected to be approximately 51.6 million in 2060. Another example of where we see a significant change compared to other counties is in Humboldt County where, according to the state's projections, the county will encounter a growth spurt between 2010 through 2025 and then show a decline in population through 2060. Los Angeles County will also see a population decrease between 2055 and 2060 but will show steady growth between 2010 through 2050. However, many of the rural counties will continue to show steady growth but not as significant as their urban counterparts.

FIGURE 17.4:   Total Population Projections for California and Counties 2010 to 2060

	Estimates			Projections							
	2010	2015	2020	2025	2030	2035	2040	2045	2050	2055	2060
California	37,341,978	38,896,969	40,619,346	42,373,301	44,085,600	45,747,645	47,233,240	48,574,095	49,779,362	50,817,750	51,663,771
Alameda	1,513,005	1,599,888	1,682,348	1,763,028	1,835,340	1,905,482	1,978,656	2,052,285	2,115,824	2,165,023	2,195,999
Alpine	1,233	1,252	1,296	1,329	1,328	1,296	1,249	1,202	1,149	1,099	1,058
Amador	38,487	37,178	39,108	40,830	41,840	42,748	43,165	43,084	42,593	42,448	42,906
Butte	220,273	226,656	236,936	247,378	254,725	264,150	267,852	272,094	276,117	280,820	286,660
Calaveras	45,654	45,923	48,957	51,415	53,317	54,912	55,881	56,205	56,501	56,980	58,023
Colusa	21,642	22,555	24,291	25,821	27,258	28,558	29,688	30,578	31,327	31,983	32,581
Contra Costa	1,051,553	1,108,963	1,166,670	1,224,372	1,281,561	1,341,741	1,400,999	1,457,246	1,512,940	1,567,661	1,620,604
Del Norte	28,822	28,587	29,146	29,735	30,197	30,418	30,408	30,320	30,340	30,422	30,747
El Dorado	181,567	184,833	190,850	196,950	201,509	205,624	208,092	208,302	206,977	205,525	205,052
Fresno	932,969	981,681	1,055,106	1,130,406	1,200,666	1,269,714	1,332,913	1,396,837	1,464,413	1,528,444	1,587,852
Glenn	28,292	29,132	30,466	31,761	32,945	34,013	34,959	35,830	36,729	37,634	38,648
Humboldt	136,056	137,159	139,033	140,713	140,608	139,780	138,307	136,663	135,608	134,959	134,398
Imperial	175,520	187,689	211,973	233,610	252,300	270,331	286,336	300,907	314,346	326,184	336,492
Inyo	18,823	19,304	19,622	20,004	20,211	20,235	20,153	20,017	19,888	19,795	19,737
Kern	846,568	894,492	989,815	1,088,711	1,189,004	1,291,947	1,396,314	1,501,874	1,604,371	1,703,013	1,793,248
Kings	154,276	155,122	167,465	180,355	192,562	205,206	218,394	230,218	240,599	250,517	259,506
Lake	64,854	66,219	70,690	75,426	79,577	83,532	86,635	88,950	90,549	91,951	93,421
Lassen	35,030	35,190	36,386	37,490	38,224	38,719	39,073	39,495	39,891	40,429	40,941
Los Angeles	9,824,194	10,147,070	10,435,991	10,701,051	10,930,986	11,123,113	11,290,501	11,414,349	11,494,738	11,524,123	11,489,127
Madera	151,466	157,722	173,146	189,267	204,993	221,824	238,514	255,073	272,384	288,812	304,749
Marin	252,937	258,804	259,794	260,698	262,615	265,840	269,462	272,411	274,455	277,604	283,188
Mariposa	18,332	18,147	19,316	20,520	21,027	21,288	21,221	20,949	20,636	20,334	20,140
Mendocino	88,292	88,884	90,411	92,203	93,577	94,565	95,207	95,796	96,751	98,186	99,952
Merced	256,800	269,572	288,991	313,082	337,798	364,348	389,934	414,895	439,075	463,131	485,712
Modoc	9,802	9,410	9,691	9,866	9,852	9,812	9,770	9,632	9,343	9,113	8,875
Mono	14,338	14,525	15,147	15,750	16,252	16,671	16,823	16,828	16,834	16,767	16,626
Monterey	416,141	429,584	446,258	462,608	476,874	489,171	500,194	510,907	520,362	527,846	533,575
Napa	137,579	142,301	146,869	151,553	156,358	160,146	163,269	165,695	167,854	170,222	172,619
Nevada	98,938	98,633	101,767	105,389	108,111	110,224	111,885	113,469	115,350	118,071	121,517
Orange	3,014,996	3,150,934	3,243,261	3,305,644	3,361,556	3,410,509	3,449,498	3,471,003	3,481,613	3,480,392	3,464,374
Placer	350,230	373,503	396,203	421,002	447,625	478,196	509,936	539,147	566,954	593,084	620,037
Plumas	20,098	19,384	19,284	19,375	19,256	18,929	18,419	17,872	17,485	17,190	17,037

FIGURE 17.4 (continued): **Total Population Projections for California and Counties 2010 to 2060**

	Estimates	Projections									
	2010	2015	2020	2025	2030	2035	2040	2045	2050	2055	2060
California	37,341,978	38,896,969	40,619,346	42,373,301	44,085,600	45,747,645	47,233,240	48,574,095	49,779,362	50,817,750	51,663,771
Alameda	1,513,005	1,599,888	1,682,348	1,763,028	1,835,340	1,905,482	1,978,656	2,052,285	2,115,824	2,165,023	2,195,999
Riverside	2,194,933	2,323,527	2,478,059	2,662,235	2,862,915	3,053,812	3,215,291	3,353,445	3,480,980	3,587,525	3,678,439
Sacramento	1,421,236	1,475,381	1,554,022	1,639,613	1,730,276	1,823,985	1,912,838	1,989,722	2,047,662	2,100,788	2,153,833
San Benito	55,547	59,039	63,418	68,312	73,459	78,434	82,969	86,859	90,802	94,895	99,215
San Bernardino	2,039,040	2,116,461	2,227,066	2,366,662	2,515,972	2,658,556	2,783,746	2,892,353	2,997,446	3,096,772	3,190,566
San Diego	3,112,965	3,244,706	3,375,687	3,482,977	3,589,951	3,689,585	3,779,961	3,868,760	3,953,511	4,025,909	4,070,841
San Francisco	808,850	848,564	891,493	932,109	967,405	996,332	1,027,004	1,057,562	1,081,540	1,097,119	1,103,174
San Joaquin	687,095	723,506	766,644	822,755	893,354	966,889	1,037,761	1,104,903	1,171,439	1,239,301	1,306,271
San Luis Obispo	269,446	274,254	283,667	293,430	299,378	309,465	309,689	311,929	313,544	315,702	318,668
San Mateo	719,446	752,751	777,088	800,928	822,889	847,641	874,626	902,205	925,295	935,411	936,151
Santa Barbara	424,688	439,082	455,858	473,124	487,156	507,912	514,466	523,502	531,583	538,614	545,115
Santa Clara	1,785,089	1,890,424	1,970,828	2,059,786	2,151,165	2,243,474	2,331,887	2,411,116	2,482,347	2,539,090	2,585,318
Santa Cruz	263,709	273,695	281,870	290,674	295,538	303,626	303,512	305,289	307,606	311,054	314,875
Shasta	177,538	180,021	187,524	195,628	202,156	207,865	212,264	216,340	220,252	224,393	228,897
Sierra	3,319	3,257	3,174	3,091	3,008	2,918	2,830	2,757	2,697	2,675	2,677
Siskiyou	45,019	45,400	46,217	46,784	47,013	46,976	46,445	45,615	44,920	44,424	44,148
Solano	413,723	432,921	454,800	477,539	501,456	526,460	548,046	567,615	586,931	604,958	620,659
Sonoma	484,852	501,350	523,615	546,050	566,670	585,373	602,320	617,786	632,241	646,701	660,937
Stanislaus	515,459	538,689	573,794	611,376	648,076	681,703	714,910	748,324	783,005	819,598	856,717
Sutter	95,085	97,887	105,107	112,384	120,071	128,530	137,228	145,113	153,462	161,994	170,377
Tehama	63,710	65,193	67,336	69,326	71,118	72,504	73,196	73,553	73,975	74,599	75,460
Trinity	13,943	13,821	14,234	14,510	14,570	14,484	14,267	13,925	13,593	13,303	13,102
Tulare	443,487	467,170	498,559	537,015	578,858	616,547	650,819	683,533	715,722	747,912	779,772
Tuolumne	55,690	54,628	55,993	57,278	58,447	59,560	59,821	59,767	59,743	59,966	60,471
Ventura	825,193	850,206	876,124	902,722	927,304	949,765	966,084	977,890	987,568	996,303	1,004,070
Yolo	201,651	209,647	219,415	231,369	241,898	259,163	267,268	277,208	285,453	292,509	298,451
Yuba	72,498	75,093	81,467	88,282	95,445	103,044	110,285	116,891	122,049	126,473	130,166

Source: California Department of Finance

Between 2010 and 2060, California's total population is projected to increase approximately 38% as illustrated in Figure 17.5. Where we will see the most significant increases are in the older populations, specifically the 65 to 74 year olds at a 140% increase; 75 to 84 year olds at 203%; and the 85 and older age group at a 316% increase from 2010 to 2060. We will see a steady growth rate of preschool-aged children (ages 0–4 years) with an overall growth of 18%. We will see a 16% change in population in school-aged children (5–17 year olds), only a 10% change in the college-aged population (18–24 year olds); and, finally, a 23% change in the working-age population (25–64 year olds). We see two significant trends here: an overall increase in population between 2010 and 2060 (38% increase), and an aging population that will significantly increase over the next 45 years.

FIGURE 17.5:   State of California Population Projections by Major Age Group 2010 to 2060

California Year	Total All Ages	0–4 years	5–17 years	18–24 years	25–64 years	65–74 years	75–84 years	85 or Older
2010	37,341,978	2,526,568	6,747,186	3,938,575	19,848,598	2,296,157	1,374,454	610,440
2020	40,619,346	2,582,984	6,648,897	3,794,319	21,331,612	3,697,849	1,796,644	767,041
2030	44,085,600	2,654,422	6,967,489	3,871,223	21,964,706	4,642,204	2,937,737	1,047,819
2040	47,233,240	2,722,589	7,233,623	4,126,034	23,004,932	4,693,807	3,720,613	1,731,642
2050	49,779,362	2,895,153	7,461,555	4,260,081	23,960,477	5,078,477	3,814,038	2,309,379
2060	51,633,771	2,984,518	7,800,131	4,320,381	24,346,784	5,513,876	4,161,032	2,537,049

Source: California Department of Finance

A CLOSER LOOK   According to the U.S. Census Bureau, among the 50 largest counties with the most employees, Sacramento, California, had the highest rate of employment growth among all sectors between 2012 and 2013 (up 5.5% to 428,475). Sacramento was followed by two Texas counties: Travis County (up 4.9% to 514,749) and Harris County (up 4.7% to 2.0 million). The annual payroll in Sacramento rose 9.9% to $20.9 billion for the same period. Delaware led all states in rate of employment growth between 2012 and 2013 with employment levels climbing 5.1% to 382,128, followed by the State of Washington (up 3.5% to 2.4 million) and California (a 3.5% increase to 13.4 million). Payroll in Delaware increased 6.7% to $19.5 billion. The census also tells us that California had more establishments (874,243) and employees (13.4 million) and a larger annual payroll ($742.5 billion) than any other state in 2013. Texas followed in each measure (547,190 establishments, 9.7 million employees, and $468.4 billion in annual payroll). New York ranked third in all three measures with 532,669 establishments, 7.7 million employees, and $468.8 billion in annual payroll. Los Angeles, California, led all counties in the number of establishments (253,227) and employment (3.8 million) followed by Cook County, Illinois, in both measures (129,972 establishments and 2.3 million employees). New York, New York (Manhattan) topped all counties in annual payroll at $217.6 billion, while ranking third in establishments (105,439) and employees (2.1 million).[19]

These are just a few of the statistics that can tell real estate professionals how the housing market is likely to evolve in the next few decades. For example, with increases in the number of employees as a result of increased employment growth, we will begin to see a need for more housing to be constructed in a given area to accommodate the new employees coming into that particular market or region.

Figure 17.6 provides an overview or quick facts about certain population characteristics.

FIGURE 17.6: Population Quick Facts

	California	United States
Population 2014 estimate	38,802,500	318,857,056
Population, percent change April 1, 2010, to July 2014	4.2%	3.3%
Population estimate base (April 1) 2010	37,253,959	308,747,716
Persons under 5 years old, percent, 2013	6.5%	6.3%
Persons under 18 years old, percent, 2013	23.9%	23.3%
Persons 65 years old and over, percent, 2013	12.5%	14.1%
Female persons, percent, 2013	50.3%	50.8%
White persons, percent, 2013	73.5%	77.7%
Black persons, percent, 2013	6.6%	13.2%
American Indian & Alaskan Native persons, percent, 2013	1.7%	1.2%
Asian persons, percent, 2013	14.1%	5.3%
Native Hawaiian & other Pacific Islander, percent, 2013	0.5%	0.2%
Persons reporting two or more races, percent, 2013	3.7%	2.4%
Persons of Hispanic or Latino origin, percent, 2013	38.4%	17.1%
White persons not Hispanic, percent, 2013	39.0%	62.6%
Living in same house in 2009–2013, percent 1 yr old & over	84.2%	84.9%
Foreign-born persons, percent, 2009–2013	27.0%	12.9%
Language other than English spoken at home, percent, age 5 and over, 2009–2013	43.7%	20.7%

---

19. "Sacramento Tops Large Counties in Employment Growth Rate," April 23, 2015, United States Census Bureau, www.census.gov/newsroom/press-releases/2015/cb15-71.html.

FIGURE 17.6:   Population Quick Facts (cont.)

	California	United States
High school graduates, percent of persons age 25 and over, 2009–2013	81.2%	86.0%
Bachelor's degree or higher, percent of persons age 25 and over, 2009–2013	30.7%	28.8%
Persons with a disability, under age 65 yrs. old, 2009–2013	6.6%	8.4%
Mean travel time to work (minutes), workers age 16 and over, 2009–2013	27.2	25.5
Housing units, 2013	13,790,495	132,802,859
Owner-occupied housing unit rate 2009–2013	55.3%	64.9%
Median gross rent, 2009–2013	$1,224	$904
Median value of owner-occupied housing units, 2009–2013	$366,400	$176,700
Households, 2009–2013	12,542,460	115,610,216
Persons per household, 2009–2013	2.94	2.63
Median household income, 2009–2013	$61,094	$53,046
Per capita money income, 2009–2013	$29,527	$28,155
Persons below poverty, percent, 2013	16.8%	14.5%
Business Quick Facts		
Private non-farm employment, 2012	12,952,818	115,938,468
Private non-farm employment, percent change 2011–2012	2.0%	2.2%
Total number of firms, 2007	3,425,510	27,092,908
Manufacturer shipments, 2007 ($1,000)	491,372,092	5,319,456,312
Building permits, 2013	80,742	990,822
Retail sales, 2007 ($1,000)	455,032,270	3,917,633,456
Geography Quick Facts		
Land area, 2010 (square miles)	155,779.22	3,531,905.43
Persons per square mile	239.1	87.4

Source: U.S. Census Bureau

UNDERSTANDING THE CONSUMER PRICE INDEX

The material in this section is adapted from information that can be found at the website of the Bureau of Labor Statistics of the U.S. Department of Labor (www.bls.gov/cpi/cpifaq.htm).

The **Consumer Price Index (CPI)** is a measure of the average change over time in the prices paid by urban consumers for a market basket of consumer goods and services.

The **CPI market basket** is developed from detailed expenditure information provided by families and individuals on what they actually purchased. For the current CPI, this information was collected from the Consumer Expenditure Survey over the two years 2011 and 2012. In each of those years, about 7,000 families from around the country provided information on their spending habits in a series of quarterly interviews. To collect information on frequently purchased items such as food and personal care products, another 7,000 families in each of the two years kept diaries listing everything they bought during a two-week period.

Over the two-year period, 28,000 weekly diaries and 60,000 quarterly interviews were used in determining the importance, or weight, of the more than 200 categories in the CPI structure.

Buying Habits Reflected in the CPI

The CPI reflects spending patterns for each of two population groups: all urban consumers and urban wage earners and clerical workers. The all-urban consumer group represents about 87% of the total U.S. population. It is based on the expenditures of almost all residents of urban or metropolitan areas, including professionals, the self-employed, the poor, the unemployed, and retired persons, as well as urban wage earners and clerical workers.

Not included in the CPI are the spending patterns of persons living in rural nonmetropolitan areas, farm families, persons in the Armed Forces, and those in institutions, such as prisons and mental hospitals. The price change experience of the all-urban consumer group is measured by two indexes, namely, the traditional **Consumer Price Index for All Urban Consumers (CPI-U)** and the newer **Chained Consumer Price Index for All Urban Consumers (C-CPI-U)**.

A third measure, the **Consumer Price Index for Urban Wage Earners and Clerical Workers (CPI-W)**, is based on the expenditures of households included in the CPI-U definition that also meet two requirements: more than one-half of the household's income must come from clerical or wage occupations and at least one of the household's earners must have been employed for at least 37 weeks during the previous 12 months. The CPI-W's population represents about 32% of the total U.S. population and is a subset, or part, of the CPI-U's population.

The **Bureau of Labor Statistics (BLS)** bases the market baskets and pricing procedures for the CPI-U and CPI-W populations on the experience of the relevant average household, not on any specific family or individual. It is unlikely, therefore, that any household's experience will correspond precisely with either the national indexes or the indexes for specific cities or regions.

The CPI and the Cost of Living

The CPI frequently is called a cost-of-living index, but it differs in important ways from a complete cost-of-living measure. BLS has for some time used a cost-of-living framework in making practical decisions about questions that arise in constructing the CPI. A cost-of-living index is a conceptual measurement goal, however, and not a straightforward alternative to the CPI.

A cost-of-living index measures changes over time in the amount that consumers need to spend to reach a certain *utility level* or *standard of living*. Both the CPI and a cost-of-living index reflect changes in the prices of goods and services, such as food and clothing that are directly purchased in the marketplace, but a complete cost-of-living index would also take into account changes in governmental or environmental factors that affect consumers' well-being. It is very difficult to determine the proper treatment of public goods, such as safety and education, and other broad concerns, such as health, water quality, and crime, that would constitute a complete cost-of-living framework.

Goods and Services Included in the CPI

The CPI represents all goods and services purchased for consumption by the reference population (U or W), and BLS has classified all expenditure items into more than 200 categories in eight major groups. Major groups and examples of categories in each group are as follows:

1. Food and beverages (including breakfast cereal, milk, coffee, chicken, wine, service meals, and snacks)

2. Housing (including rent of primary residence, owners' equivalent rent, fuel oil, and bedroom furniture)

3. Apparel (including men's shirts and sweaters, women's dresses, and jewelry)

4. Transportation (including new vehicles, airline fares, gasoline, and motor vehicle insurance)

5. Medical care (prescription drugs, medical supplies, physicians' services, eyeglasses and eye care, and hospital services)

6. Recreation (including televisions, pets and pet products, sports equipment, and admissions fees)

7. Education and communication (including college tuition, postage, telephone services, and computer software and accessories)

8. Other goods and services (including tobacco and smoking products, haircuts and other personal services, and funeral expenses)

Using scientific statistical procedures for the more than 200 item categories, the BLS chooses samples of several hundred specific items within selected business establishments frequented by consumers to represent the thousands of varieties available in the marketplace. For example, in a given supermarket, the BLS may choose a plastic bag of golden delicious apples, U.S. extra fancy grade, weighing 4.4 pounds to represent the "apples" category.

Taxes Certain taxes are included in the CPI, namely, taxes that are directly associated with the purchase of specific goods and services (such as sales and excise taxes). Government user fees are also included in the CPI; for example, toll charges and parking fees are included in the transportation category, and an entry fee to a national park would be included as part of the admissions index.

In addition, property taxes should be reflected indirectly in the BLS's method of measuring the cost of the flow of services provided by housing shelter, called **owners' equivalent rent**, to the extent that these taxes influence rental values. Taxes not directly associated with specific purchases, such as income and Social Security taxes, are excluded, as are the government services paid for through those taxes.

For certain purposes, you might want to define price indexes to include rather than exclude income taxes. Such indexes would provide an answer to a question different from the one to which the present CPI is relevant and would be appropriate for different uses.

Investments The CPI does not include investment items, such as stocks, bonds, real estate, and life insurance. (These items relate to savings and not to day-to-day consumption expenses.)

Data Collection

The CPI is a product of a series of interrelated samples. First, using data from the 1990 census of population, the BLS selected the urban areas from which data on prices were collected and chose the housing units within each area that were eligible for use in the shelter component of the CPI.

The 1990 census also provided data on the number of consumers represented by each area selected as a CPI price collection area. Next, another sample (of about 16,800 families each year) served as the basis for a **point-of-purchase survey** that identified the places where households purchase various types of goods and services.

Each month, BLS data collectors called **economic assistants** visit or call thousands of retail stores, service establishments, rental units, and doctors' offices all over the United States to obtain information on the prices of the thousands of items used to track and measure price changes in the CPI. These economic assistants record the prices of about 80,000 items each month representing a scientifically selected sample of the prices paid by consumers for the goods and services purchased.

During each call or visit, the economic assistant collects price data on a specific good or service that was precisely defined during an earlier visit. If the selected item is available, the economic assistant records its price. If the selected item is no longer available, or if there have been changes in the quality or quantity (e.g., eggs sold in packages of eight when they previously had been sold by the dozen) of the good or service since the last time prices had been collected, the economic assistant selects a new item or records the quality change in the current item.

The recorded information is sent to the national office of the BLS, where commodity specialists who have detailed knowledge about the particular goods or services priced review the data. These specialists check the data for accuracy and consistency and make any necessary corrections or adjustments, which can range from an adjustment for a change in the size or quantity of a packaged item to more complex adjustments based on statistical analysis of the value of an item's features or quality. Thus, commodity specialists strive to prevent changes in the quality of items from affecting the CPI's measurement of price change.

How the CPI Is Used

An **index** is a tool that simplifies the measurement of movements in a numerical series. Most of the specific CPI indexes have a 1982–1984 reference base. That is, the BLS sets the average index level (representing the average price level) for the 36-month period covering the years 1982, 1983, and 1984 equal to 100. The BLS then measures changes in relation to that figure. An index of 110, for example, means there has been a 10% increase in price since the reference period; similarly, an index of 90 means a 10% decrease.

Movements of the index from one date to another can be expressed as changes in index points (simply, the difference between index levels), but it is more useful to express the movements as percentage changes. This is because index points are affected by the level of the index in relation to its base period while percentage changes are not.

Historically, the BLS has updated its reference periods every 10 years or so.

The CPI affects nearly all Americans because of the many ways it is used. The major uses of the CPI are as

- an economic indicator;

- a deflator of other economic series; and

- a means of adjusting dollar values.

Inflation has been defined as a process of continuously rising prices or, equivalently, of a continuously falling value of money.

Various indexes have been devised to measure different aspects of inflation. The CPI measures inflation as experienced by consumers in their day-to-day living expenses, the **producer price index (PPI)** measures inflation at earlier stages of the production and marketing process, and the **employment cost index (ECI)** measures inflation in the labor market. The BLS International Price Program measures inflation for imports and exports, and the gross domestic product deflator (GDP deflator) measures and combine the experience with inflation of governments (federal, state, and local), businesses, and consumers. Finally, there are specialized measures, such as measures of interest rates and measures of consumers' and business executives' expectations of inflation.

The best measure of inflation for a given application depends on the intended use of the data. The CPI is generally the best measure for adjusting payments to consumers when the intent is to allow consumers to purchase, at today's prices, a market basket of goods and services equivalent to one that they could purchase in an earlier period. The CPI also is the best measure to use to translate retail sales and hourly or weekly earnings into real or inflation-free dollars.

The CPI Reported in the Media

Each month, the BLS releases thousands of detailed CPI numbers to the media. However, the media usually focus on the broadest, most comprehensive CPI: *the CPI-U for the U.S. city average for all items, 1982–1984 = 100.* These data are reported on either a seasonally adjusted or an unadjusted basis. Often, the media will report some, or all, of the following:

■ Index level, not seasonally adjusted (e.g., May 2008 = 216.632)

■ 12-month percentage change, not seasonally adjusted (e.g., May 2007 to May 2008 = 4.2%)

■ 1-month percentage change on a seasonally adjusted basis (e.g., from April 2008 to May 2008 = 0.6%)

■ Annual rate of percentage change so far this year [e.g., from December 2007 to May 2008 (if the rate of increase over the first five months of the year continued for the full year, after the removal of seasonal influences, the rise would be 4.0%)]

■ Annual rate based on the latest seasonally adjusted one-month change (e.g., if the rate from April 2008 to May 2008 continued for a full 12 months, then the rise, compounded, would be 8.1%)

Accounting for Price Escalation   The decision to employ an **escalation** mechanism, as well as the choice of the most suitable index, is up to the user. When drafting the terms of an escalation provision for use in a contract to adjust future payments, both legal and statistical questions can arise. While the BLS cannot help in any matters relating to legal questions, it does provide basic technical and statistical assistance to users who are developing indexing procedures.

Seasonally Adjusted Data   By using seasonally adjusted data, economic analysts and the media find it easier to see the underlying trend in short-term price changes. It is often difficult to tell from raw (unadjusted) statistics whether developments between any two months reflect changing economic conditions or only normal seasonal patterns. Therefore, many economic series, including the CPI, are adjusted to remove the effect of seasonal influences—those that occur at the same time and in about the same magnitude every year. Among these influences are price movements resulting from changing climatic conditions, production cycles, change-overs of models, and holidays.

The BLS annually re-estimates the factors that are used to seasonally adjust CPI data, and seasonally adjusted indexes that have been published earlier are subject to revision for up to five years after their original release. There-fore, unadjusted data are more appropriate for escalation purposes.

Published Indexes

Beside the monthly publication of the national (or U.S. city average) CPI-U, C-CPI-U, and CPI-W, indexes are also published by area for the CPI-U and CPI-W. For the C-CPI-U, data for all items and 27 components are available at the national level only; for the CPI-U and CPI-W, 377-component series are published at the national level.

Monthly CPI-U and CPI-W indexes are published for the four census regions: Northeast, Midwest (formerly North Central), South, and West. Monthly indexes are also published for urban areas classified by population size—all metropolitan areas over 1.5 million, metropolitan areas smaller than 1.5 million, and all nonmetropolitan urban areas. Indexes are available as well within each region, cross-classified by area population size. For the Northeast and West, however, indexes for nonmetropolitan areas are not available.

The BLS also publishes indexes for 27 local areas. These indexes are by-products of the national CPI program. Each local index has a much smaller sample size than the national or regional indexes and is, therefore, subject to substantially more sampling and other measurement error. As a result, local area indexes are more volatile than the national or regional indexes, and the BLS strongly urges users to consider adopting the national or regional CPIs for use in escalator clauses. If used with caution, local area CPI data can illustrate and explain the impact of local economic conditions on consumers' experience with price change. Local area data are available according to the schedules that follow.

The BLS publishes data for three major metropolitan areas monthly:

- Chicago-Gary-Kenosha, IL-IN-WI

- Los Angeles-Riverside-Orange County, CA

- New York-Northern NJ-Long Island, NY-NJ-CT-PA

Data for the following additional 11 metropolitan areas are published every other month on an odd (January, March, etc.) or even (February, April, etc.) month schedule:

- Atlanta, GA (even)

- Boston-Brockton-Nashua, MA-NH-ME-CT (odd)

- Cleveland-Akron, OH (odd)

- Dallas-Fort Worth, TX (odd)

- Detroit-Ann Arbor-Flint, MI (even)

- Houston-Galveston-Brazoria, TX (even)

- Miami-Fort Lauderdale, FL (even)

- Philadelphia-Wilmington-Atlantic City, PA-NJ-DE-MD (even)

- San Francisco-Oakland-San Jose, CA (even)

- Seattle-Tacoma-Bremerton, WA (even)

- Washington-Baltimore, DC-MD-VA-WV (odd)

Note: The designation even or odd refers to the month during which the area's price change is measured. Because of the time needed for processing, data are released two to three weeks into the following month.

Data are published for of the following 13 metropolitan areas on a semiannual basis. These indexes, which refer to the arithmetic average for the six-month periods from January through June and July through December, are published with the release of the CPI for July and January, respectively, in August and February:

- Anchorage, AK
- Cincinnati-Hamilton, OH-KY-IN
- Denver-Boulder-Greeley, CO
- Honolulu, HI
- Kansas City, MO-KS
- Milwaukee-Racine, WI

- Minneapolis-St, Paul, MN-WI

- Pittsburgh, PA

- Portland-Salem, OR-WA

- St. Louis, MO-IL

- San Diego, CA

- Tampa-St. Petersburg-Clearwater, FL

For areas in which there is no CPI, the user can select the area most like the subject in terms of market conditions. Although the BLS can provide some guidance on this question, users must make the final decision.

The BLS strongly urges the use of the national or regional CPIs for use in escalator clauses. These indexes are more stable and subject to less sampling and other measurement error than are area indexes; therefore, they are more statistically reliable.

The CPI for individual areas should not be used to compare living costs among the areas. An individual area index measures how much prices have changed over a specific period in that particular area; it does not show whether prices or living costs are higher or lower in that area relative to another. In general, the composition of the market basket and relative prices of goods and services in the market basket during the expenditure base period varies substantially across areas.

Types of Data Published

Many types of data are published as outputs from the CPI program. The most popular are indexes and percentage changes. Requested less often are relative importance (or relative expenditure weight) data, base conversion factors (to convert from one CPI reference period to another), seasonal factors (the monthly factors used to convert unadjusted indexes into seasonally adjusted indexes), and average food and energy prices. Index and price change data are available for the U.S. city average (or national average), for various geographic areas (regions and metropolitan areas), for national population size classes of urban areas, and for cross-classifications of regions and size classes. Indexes for various groupings of items are available for all geographic areas and size classes.

Individual indexes are available for more than 200 items (e.g., apples, men's shirts, and airline fares) and more than 120 different combinations of items (e.g., fruits and vegetables, food at home, food and beverages, and all items) at the national or U.S. city average levels. The BLS classifies consumer items into eight major groups: food and beverages, housing, apparel, transportation, medical care, recreation, education and communication, and other goods and services. (Some indexes are available from as far back as 1913.)

Each month, indexes are published along with short-term percentage changes, the latest 12-month change and, at the national item and group level, unadjusted and (where appropriate) seasonally adjusted percentage changes (and seasonal factors), together with annualized rates of change. The annualized rates indicate what the rate of change would be for a 12-month period, if a price change measured for a shorter period continued for a full 12 months.

For areas, the BLS publishes less detailed groupings of items than it does for the national level. Annual average indexes and percentage changes for these groupings are published at the national and local levels. Semiannual average indexes and percentage changes for some of these groupings are also published.

Each month, the BLS publishes average price data for some food items (for the U.S. and four regions) and for some energy items (for the United States, 4 regions, 3 size classes, 10 cross-classifications of regions and size classes, and 14 metropolitan areas).

LIMITATIONS OF THE CPI

The CPI is subject to both limitations in application and limitations in measurement.

Limitations of Application

The CPI may not be applicable to all population groups. For example, the CPI-U is designed to measure the experience with price change of the U.S. urban population and, thus, may not accurately reflect the experience of people living in rural areas. Also, the CPI does not produce official estimates for the rate of inflation experienced by subgroups of the population, such as the elderly or the poor. (The BLS does produce and release an experimental index for the elderly population, but because of the significant limitations of this experimental index, it should be interpreted with caution.)

As noted earlier, the CPI cannot be used to measure differences in price levels or living costs between one place and another; it measures only time-to-time changes in each place. A higher index for one area does not necessarily mean that prices are higher there than in another area with a lower index, which merely means that prices have risen faster since the two areas' common reference period.

The CPI cannot be used as a measure of total change in living costs because changes in these costs are affected by such factors as social and environmental changes and changes in income taxes that are beyond the definitional scope of the index and so are excluded.

Limitations in Measurement

Limitations in measurement can be grouped into two basic types: sampling errors and nonsampling errors.

Sampling Errors Because the CPI measures price change based on a sample of items, the published indexes differ somewhat from what the results would be if actual records of all retail purchases by everyone in the index population could be used to compile the index. These estimating or sampling errors are limitations on the precise accuracy of the index, not mistakes in calculating the index. The CPI program has developed measurements of sampling error, which are updated and published annually in the CPI Detailed Report. An increased sample size would be expected to increase accuracy, but it would also increase CPI production costs. The CPI sample design allocates the sample in a way that maximizes the accuracy of the index given the funds available.

Nonsampling Errors These errors occur from a variety of sources. Unlike sampling errors, they can cause persistent bias in the measurement of the index. Nonsampling errors are caused by problems of price data collection, logistical lags in conducting surveys, difficulties in defining basic concepts and their operational implementation, and difficulties in handling the problems of quality change.

Nonsampling errors can be far more hazardous to the accuracy of a price index than sampling errors. The BLS expends much effort to minimize these errors. Highly trained personnel ensure the comparability of quality of items from period to period; collection procedures are extensively documented. The CPI program has an ongoing research and evaluation program to identify and implement improvements in the index.

UPDATES AND REVISIONS OF THE CPI

The CPI will need revisions as long as there are significant changes in consumer buying habits or shifts in population distribution or demographics. By developing annual **consumer expenditure surveys** and point-of-purchase surveys, the BLS has the flexibility to monitor changing buying habits in a timely and cost-efficient manner. In addition, the census conducted every 10 years by the Department of Commerce provides information that enables the BLS to reselect a new geographic sample that accurately reflects the current population distribution and other demographic factors.

Electronic Access to CPI Data

The BLS provides free, easy, and continuous online access to almost all published CPI data and press releases. The most recent month's CPI is made available immediately at the time of its release. In addition, a database called LABSTAT, which contains current and historical data on the CPI, is accessible. The BLS website at http://stats.bls.gov provides easy access to LABSTAT, as well as links to program-specific home pages.

In addition to furnishing data, the CPI home page at www.bls.gov/cpi/home.htm provides other CPI information, including a brief explanation of methodology, frequently asked questions and answers, a list of contacts for further information, and explanations of how the CPI handles special items, such as medical care and housing. Furthermore, CPI press releases and historical data for metropolitan areas can be accessed by linking to the regional office homepage from the main BLS website. This material also is accessible via the file transfer protocol (FTP). Send an e-mail to labstat.helpdesk@bls.gov for help on how to use any of these systems.

Subscriptions to CPI Publications

E-mail Subscription Service   The latest U.S. average and local CPIs can be delivered directly to a subscriber's e-mail address on the morning of their release. Just subscribe to one of the nine national and regional CPI subscriptions offered on the BLS News Service (www.bls.gov/bls/list.htm).

Summary Data   Summary data are available in a monthly two-page publication containing 1- and 12-month percentage changes for the U.S. city average CPI-U and CPI-W index series. The All Items index data for each local area are also included. To be added to the mailing list, write to: Office of Publications, Bureau of Labor Statistics, 2 Massachusetts Avenue, NE,

Room 2850, Washington, DC 20212-0001, or call 1-202-691-5200 or any of the BLS regional offices listed at the end of this document.

CPI Detailed Report This publication is the most comprehensive report of the CPI and may be ordered by writing to: New Orders, Superintendent of Documents, PO Box 371954, Pittsburgh, PA 15250-7954, or by calling 1-202-512-1800. Subscriptions cost $47 per year.

***Monthly Labor Review* (MLR)** The *MLR* provides selected CPI data included in a monthly summary of BLS data and occasional articles and methodological descriptions that are too extensive for inclusion in the *CPI Detailed Report*. The *MLR* costs $45 per year and may be ordered by writing to: New Orders, Superintendent of Documents, PO Box 371954, Pittsburgh, PA 15250-7954, or by calling 1-202-512-1800. The *MLR* home page iswww.bls.gov/mlr/.

Recorded CPI Data Summary CPI data are provided 24 hours a day on recorded messages. Detailed information on the CPI is available by calling 1-202-691-5200. Recorded summaries of CPI are also available by calling any of the metropolitan area CPI hotlines listed in the following section.

Area Hotline Numbers

Summaries typically include data for the U.S. city average, as well as the specified area. Recordings are approximately three minutes in length and are available 24 hours a day, seven days a week.

Anchorage	1-907-271-2770
Atlanta	1-404-331-3415
Baltimore	1-410-962-4898
Boston	1-617-565-2325
Chicago	1-312-353-1883
Cincinnati	1-513-684-2349
Cleveland	1-216-522-3852
Dallas	1-214-767-6970
Denver	1-303-844-1726
Detroit	1-313-226-7558
Honolulu	1-808-541-2808
Indianapolis	1-317-226-7885
Kansas City	1-816-285-7000
Los Angeles	1-310-235-6884
Miami	1-305-358-2305

Milwaukee	1-414-276-2579
Minneapolis-St. Paul	1-612-725-3580
New York	1-212-337-2400
Philadelphia	1-215-656-3948
Pittsburgh	1-412-644-2900
Portland	1-503-231-2045
St. Louis	1-314- 539-3581
San Diego	1-619-557-6538
San Francisco	1-415-625-2270
Seattle	1-206-553-0645
Washington, D.C.	1-202-691-6994

Other Sources of CPI Data

Technical information is available during normal working hours, Monday through Friday (ET), by calling 1-202-691-7000 or any of the regional offices.

Addresses and phone numbers for the nine regional offices are as follows:

Washington, D.C.
    Bureau of Labor Statistics
    Office of Prices and Living Conditions
    2 Massachusetts Avenue, NE
    Washington, DC 20212-0001
    1-202-691-7000

Atlanta
    Bureau of Labor Statistics
    Economic Analysis and Information
    61 Forsyth Street, SW, Room 7T50
    Atlanta, GA 30303
    1-404-331-3415

Boston
    Bureau of Labor Statistics
    Economic Analysis and Information
    JFK Federal Bldg., E-310
    Boston, MA 02203
    1-617-565-2327

Chicago
Bureau of Labor Statistics
Economic Analysis and Information
230 S. Dearborn Street, 9th Floor
Chicago, IL 60604
1-312-353-1880

Dallas
Bureau of Labor Statistics
Economic Analysis and Information
525 Griffin Street, Room 221
Dallas, TX 75202
1-214-767-6970

Kansas City
Bureau of Labor Statistics
Economic Analysis and Information
1100 Main Street, Suite 600
Kansas City, MO 64105-2112
1-816-285-7000

New York
Bureau of Labor Statistics
Economic Analysis and Information
201 Varick Street, Room 808
New York, NY 10014-4811
1-212-337-2400

Philadelphia
Bureau of Labor Statistics
Economic Analysis and Information
The Curtis Center Suite 610 East
170 South Independence Mall West
Philadelphia, PA 19106-3305
1-215-597-3282

San Francisco
Bureau of Labor Statistics
Economic Analysis and Information
PO Box 193766
San Francisco, CA 94119-3766
1-415-625-2270

Historical Tables   These include all published indexes for each of the detailed CPI components. They are available via the internet, by calling 1-202-691-7000 in the national office, or by contacting any of the regional offices.

Descriptive Publications   These publications describe the CPI and ways to use it. They include (1) simple fact sheets discussing specific topics about the CPI, (2) a broad, nontechnical overview of the CPI in a question-and-answer format, and (3) a quite technical and thorough description of the CPI and its methodology. These publications are available on request by calling 1-202-691-7000, and many are included on the CPI home page on the internet.

Special Publications   Also available are various special publications and materials describing the annual revisions of seasonally adjusted CPI data. For more information, call 1-202-691-7000.

SUMMARY

Real estate professionals can use demographic information to better understand the ever-changing needs of society, including identifying the communities that will experience growth and those that will experience declining population. One of the areas of concern for all is the aging population in the United States and California, which raises further questions as to the types of facilities and housing accommodations that will need to be planned for in the next decades to come. This also means that we should expect a continued increase in employment in the health care industry to address the aging population.

Housing demand, costs, and employment levels are all influenced by population changes. A healthy economy can translate into higher housing costs, however, as more people try to compete for the available housing in the market area.

The cost of a wide range of consumer goods and services must also be measured in order to project costs. The Consumer Price Index (CPI) is a measure of the average change over time in the prices paid by consumers for a fixed market of goods and services purchased for consumption by a referenced population. The major expense categories that are covered by the CPI are food, housing, apparel, transportation, medical care, recreation, and education. Over the years, new categories are added to keep pace with consumer lifestyles.

By understanding both how demographics are tracked and how we measure consumer prices, real estate professionals will have a better understanding of how to gauge the overall market and determine what consumers are able to spend on housing.

REVIEW QUESTIONS

1. What has been the change in population growth in your community, and how does it differ from the 1990s?

2. Using the 2010 census information, which age group shows the largest gain or decline in your area?

3. Which counties in California have shown the greatest changes in population increases and decreases?

4. Utilizing the CPI for your region, can you estimate the cost of labor for the building trades in your area?

5. What is the difference between the Consumer Price Index and the cost-of-living index?

6. In looking at the projected population statistics for California counties, what is the projected population for the county in which you reside in to be in 2060? Is that a significant change for the today's population?

UNIT QUIZ

1. Between 2014 and 2060, the total population is projected to
    a. increase by 98 million.
    b. increase by 40 million.
    c. increase by 34 million.
    d. remain stagnant.

2. Census household projections are made at what level?
    a. County
    b. City
    c. State
    d. National

3. If you were born in 1996, your cohort consists of all people born in what year?
    a. 2000
    b. 1996
    c. 1999
    d. None of these

4. Between 2014 and 2060, the U.S. population is projected to increase from
    a. 319 to 417 million.
    b. 98 to 400 million.
    c. 400 to 500 million.
    d. none of the above.

5. California is projected to have a total population of _____ by 2030.
    a. 44 million
    b. 47 million
    c. 38 million
    d. 217 million

6. One of the most significant trends to be experienced in the coming decades relative to population statistics is
   a. decline in 18-year-olds.
   b. increase in aging population.
   c. net migration.
   d. increase in birth rates.

7. The CPI takes into account the costs of all of the following *EXCEPT*
   a. food.
   b. stocks.
   c. housing.
   d. education.

8. What goods listed below are *NOT* measured by the Consumer Price Index?
   a. Fuel costs
   b. Housing
   c. Food
   d. Manufacturing

9. Who collects CPI prices for analysis and release by the government?
   a. California Bureau of Real Estate
   b. Bureau of Labor Statistics
   c. Census Bureau
   d. Housing and Community Development

10. Which CPI is the media mostly concerned with?
    a. CPI for all urban consumers
    b. CPI for all durable goods
    c. CPI for home mortgages
    d. CPI for cultural changes

I

CALIFORNIA FACTS

State Motto:	"Eureka" (I have found it)
State Bird:	California Valley Quail *(Lophortyx californica)*
State Flower:	California Golden Poppy *(Eschsholtzia)*
State Tree:	California Redwood—the coast redwood *(Sequoia sempervirens)*—and the giant sequoia *(Sequoia gigantea)*
State Reptile:	Desert Tortoise *(Gopherus agassizi)*
State Animal:	California Grizzly Bear *(Ursus californicus)*
State Folk Dance:	Square dance
State Amphibian:	Red legged frog *(Ranna draytonii)*
State Marine Fish:	Garibaldi *(Hypsypops rubicundus)*
State Colors:	Blue and Gold
State Marine Animal:	California Gray Whale
State Insect:	California Dogface Butterfly *(Zerene eurydice)*
State Mineral:	Gold
State Rock:	Serpentine
State Soil:	San Joaquin Soil
State Gemstone:	Benitoite
State Prehistoric Artifact:	Chipped Stone Bear
State Fossil:	Saber-Toothed Cat *(Smilodon californicus)*
State Fish:	Golden Trout *(Salmo agua-bonita)*
State Dance:	West Coast Swing Dancing
State Song:	"I Love You, California," written by F. B. Silverwood
State Theater:	Pasadena Playhouse
State Capital:	Sacramento

Size:	Third largest state, 158,706 square miles
Statehood:	31st state; admitted to the Union September 1850

State Geography

Land Area:	155,973 sq. mi.
Water Area:	7,734 sq. mi
Coastline:	840 miles
Highest Point:	Mt. Whitney—14,494 ft.
Lowest Point:	Death Valley—282 ft. below sea level
Geographic Center of State:	In Madera County, 35 mi. NE of City of Madera
Number of Counties:	58
Largest County by Population:	Los Angeles
Largest County by Area:	San Bernardino
Bordering States:	Nevada, Oregon, Arizona
Bordering Country:	Mexico
Bordering Body of Water:	Pacific Ocean
Principal Rivers in California:	Sacramento River; Colorado River; and San Joaquin River

Other Interesting Facts

State Nickname:	The Golden State
Origin of Name California:	The name California comes from a mythical Spanish Island ruled by the queen called Califia that was featured in a Spanish romance *(Las Sergas de Esplandian)* written by Garcia Ordonez de Montalvo in 1510. The Spanish explorers originally thought that California was an island.
State Flag:	The official state flag of California, called the Bear Flag, was first used on June 14, 1846, but was not officially adopted until 1911. The flag was designed by William Todd and pictures a grizzly bear and star.

CALIFORNIA'S COUNTIES

CALIFORNIA'S ORIGINAL 27 COUNTIES

On February 18, 1850, California's first governor, Peter Burnett, signed into law the creation of the state's original counties. They were as follows:

Butte
Calaveras
Colusa
Contra Costa
El Dorado
Los Angeles
Marin
Mariposa
Mendocino
Monterey
Napa
Sacramento
San Diego
San Francisco
San Joaquin
San Luis Obispo
Santa Barbara
Santa Clara
Santa Cruz
Shasta
Solano
Sonoma
Sutter
Trinity
Tuolumne
Yolo
Yuba

FIGURE II.a: The Original 27 Counties

FIGURE II.b: **California's 58 Counties Today**

FIGURE II.c: **County Square Mileage**

County	Miles	County	Miles
San Bernardino County	20,164	Stanislaus County	1,521
Inyo County	10,097	Placer County	1,507
Kern County	8,170	Mariposa County	1,461
Riverside County	7,243	Kings County	1,436
Siskiyou County	6,318	San Joaquin County	1,436
Fresno County	5,998	San Benito County	1,397
Tulare County	4,844	Lake County	1,327
Lassen County	4,690	Glenn County	1,319
Imperial County	4,598	Santa Clara County	1,316
Modoc County	4,340	Colusa County	1,156
San Diego County	4,281	Calaveras County	1,036
Los Angeles County	4,079	Yolo County	1,034
Shasta County	3,850	Sacramento County	1,015
Humboldt County	3,600	Del Norte County	1,003
Mendocino County	3,510	Nevada County	992
San Luis Obispo County	3,326	Sierra County	959
Monterey County	3,324	Solano County	872
Trinity County	3,223	Alameda County	825
Mono County	3,103	Contra Costa County	798
Tehama County	2,976	Napa County	797
Santa Barbara County	2,745	Orange County	785
Plumas County	2,618	Alpine County	727
Tuolumne County	2,293	Yuba County	639
Madera County	2,147	Sutter County	607
Merced County	2,008	Amador County	601
Ventura County	1,864	Marin County	588
El Dorado County	1,805	San Mateo County	531
Butte County	1,665	Santa Cruz County	440
Sonoma County	1,598	San Francisco County	91

APPENDIX THREE

WEBSITES

STATE OF CALIFORNIA

California Bureau of Real Estate
www.dre.ca.gov

STATE AND FEDERAL AGENCIES

California Department of Consumer Affairs/Bureau of Real Estate Appraisers
www.orea.ca.gov

California Department of Finance
www.dof.ca.gov

California Employment Development Department
www.edd.ca.gov

California Department of Housing and Community Development
www.hcd.ca.gov

California Department of Food and Agriculture
www.cdfa.ca.gov

California Department of Transportation (Caltrans)
www.dot.ca.gov

California Coastal Commission
www.coastal.ca.gov

California Department of Conservation
www.conservation.ca.gov

California Department of Veterans Affairs (Cal-Vet)
www.calvet.ca.gov

FEDERAL AGENCIES

United States Census Bureau
www.census.gov

American FactFinder
www.factfinder.census.gov/faces/nav/jsf/pages/index.xhtml

U.S. Department of Housing and Urban Development
www.hud.gov

U.S. National Archives and Records Administration
www.archives.gov

U.S. Department of Health & Human Services
www.hhs.gov

U.S. Department of Labor/Bureau of Labor Statistics
www.bls.gov

U.S. Department of the Treasury
www.ustreas.gov

U.S. Department of Veterans Affairs
www.va.gov

U.S. Small Business Administration
www.sba.gov

Office of the Comptroller of the Currency
www.occ.treas.gov

National Credit Union Administration
www.ncua.gov

Federal Deposit Insurance Corporation
www.fdic.gov

Federal Emergency Management Agency (FEMA)
www.fema.gov

FEMA in Spanish
www.fema.gov/spanish

ECONOMIC SITES

California Association of REALTORS®
www.car.org

Wall Street Journal
www.wsj.com

CNN Money
www.money.cnn.com

National Association of Home Builders (NAHB)
www.nahb.org

Real Estate Economics
www.realestateeconomics.com

The American Real Estate Economics and Urban Economics Association
http://areuea.org

California Governor's Office of Business and Economic Development
www.business.ca.gov

USDA Economics, Statistics and Market Information System
http://usda.mannlib.cornell.edu

Bureau of Economic Analysis
www.bea.gov

Federal Reserve
www.federalreserve.gov

Fannie Mae
www.fanniemae.com

APPRAISAL SITES

California Department of Consumer Affairs/Bureau of Real Estate Appraisers
www.orea.ca.gov

American Society of Appraisers
www.appraisers.org

Appraisal Institute
www.appraisalinstitute.org

The Appraisal Foundation
www.appraisalfoundation.org

HouseValues.com
www.housevalues.com

REAL ESTATE SERVICES

California Association of REALTORS®
www.car.org

National Association of REALTORS®
www.realtor.com

Inman (real estate news)
www.inman.com

The International Real Estate Directory
http://www.internationalrealestatedirectory.com/

Homes.com
www.homes.com

New Homes Online: Northern California
www.newhomesmag.com

Mortgage Calculator
www.mortgagecalculator.org

Coldwell Banker
www.coldwellbanker.com

Century 21
www.century21.com

RE/MAX
www.remax.com

First American Financial Corporation
www.firstam.com

Fidelity National Title Insurance Company
www.fntic.com

New Century Escrow, Inc.
www.newcenturyescrow.com

Yosemite Title Company
www.yotitle.com

For Sale By Owner
www.owners.com

Real Estate News and Advice
www.realtytimes.com

HomeAdvisor SM
www.homeadvisor.com

Urban Land Institute
www.uli.org

Mortgage Calculator
www.bankrate.com

Mortgage Rate Information
www.HSH.com

California Business Properties Association
www.cbpa.com

American Real Estate Society
www.aresnet.org

Old Republic Title Company
www.ortconline.com

AGRICULTURAL SITES

California Natural Resources Conservation Service
http://www.nrcs.usda.gov/wps/portal/nrcs/site/ca/home/

California Agricultural Statistics Service
http://www.nass.usda.gov/Statistics_by_State/California/index.asp

California Department of Food and Agriculture
www.cdfa.ca.gov

California Department of Conservation
www.conservation.ca.gov

LAND-USE PLANNING SITES

American Planning Association
www.planning.org

California Governor's Office of Planning and Research
www.opr.ca.gov

Los Angeles Forum for Architecture & Urban Design
www.laforum.org

Joint Venture Silicon Valley
www.jointventure.org

Urban Ecology
www.urbanecology.org

Transform (formerly TALC—Transportation and Land Use Coalition)
www.transformca.org

Los Angeles County Metropolitan Transportation Authority
www.metro.net/projects

Urban Land Institute
www.uli.org

U. S. Green Building Council
www.usgbc.org

GLOSSARY

absorption The measurement of the total square footage or units occupied over a given period of time such as monthly or annually. This approach of measuring absorption only applies to existing real estate as it serves as a baseline and would not take into account units under construction. In analyzing absorption, we examine the rate of which new homes are sold in a given geographical market area in comparison to the total units available for purchase. When absorption is high, this could lead to a depletion of the supply of homes in a given market area.

acceleration clause The clause in a mortgage or deed of trust that can be enforced to make the entire debt due immediately if the borrower defaults on an installment payment or other obligation.

accession rate The number of employees added to the payroll during a given period; an important leading indicator of future business conditions.

ad valorem A Latin term meaning "to value" or "in proportion to the value." Used to describe taxes where the amount of tax is based on the value of the thing taxed.

ADA Americans with Disabilities Act.

adaptive zoning The conversion of an existing building of historic, architectural, or cultural value from the use for which it was constructed to a new use compatible with neighborhood land uses by maintaining exterior integrity and adapting the interior to the new use.

added value The practice of processing a resource through additional steps in order to generate additional wealth/jobs within a community before the resource is sent outside the community.

adequate The threshold meeting minimum standards established by either regulation, ordinance, code, policy, or accepted standards.

adjustable-rate mortgage (ARM) A loan characterized by a fluctuating interest rate, usually one tied to a bank or savings and loan association cost-of-funds index.

adjusted cost basis The value on the books of a taxpayer, which is original cost plus improvements less depreciation.

advertising The public promotion of one's products and services.

affordability As applied to housing, a rent or price that does not severely strain the personal budget. Measures include (1) rent-to-income ratios, (2) percentage of households able to afford a median-price home, and (3) percentage of necessary income (what percentage of income necessary to qualify for a median-price house does a median-income family have?).

affordability index Measurement of the percentage of potential buyers who can afford a median-priced home.

agent One who acts or has the power to act for another. A fiduciary relationship is created under the *law of agency* when a property owner executes a listing agreement or management contract authorizing a licensed real estate broker to be his or her agent. A prospective property buyer may authorize a real estate broker to act as the buyer's agent to find a suitable property.

aggregate demand The sum of all expenditures within an economy, making up gross domestic product.

aggregate supply The total of all goods and services produced in an economy.

agribusiness Lands under contract with the provisions of the California Lands Conservation (Williamson) Act. These lands are primarily devoted to the production of food and fiber but may also include other lands.

agriculture The science and business of cultivating soil, producing crops, and raising livestock.

agricultural lands Lands devoted to the commercial growing of food and fiber.

agricultural preserve The sector of the economy concerned with the production, processing, and distributing of agricultural products.

allocation Allocation method or abstraction. A method of appraisal where land value is estimated by deducting the value of any site improvements from the overall sales price.

amenities Features that enhance the value of property.

amortization The liquidation of a financial obligation on an installment basis. The recovery of cost or value over a period of time. An amortized loan is one in which the principal, as well as interest, is payable in monthly or other periodic installments over the term of the loan.

amortize System of loan repayment through periodic installments of principal and interest over the entire term of the loan agreement.

annuity A guaranteed series of payments in the future purchased immediately for a lump sum.

annexation The legal steps and actions taken to attach a territory of land to an incorporated city or special district.

annual percentage rate (APR) The relationship of the total finance charges associated with a loan. This must be disclosed to borrowers by lenders under the Truth in Lending Act.

anticipation The appraisal principle holding that value can increase or decrease based on the expectation of some future benefit or detriment produced by the property.

amplitude The measure of highness and lowness of comparative points in the business cycle: the difference between a trough and a peak.

appraisal An estimate of the quantity, quality, or value of something. The process through which conclusions of property value are obtained; also refers to the report that sets forth the process of estimation and conclusion of value.

appreciation An increase in the worth or value of a property due to economic or related causes, which may prove to be either temporary or permanent; opposite of depreciation.

archaeology The scientific study of material remains of past cultures or human life and activities.

area plan A component of a General Plan that provides more precise planning information for an identified territory covered by the General Plan. The area plan must be internally consistent with the General Plan.

ARM *See* adjustable-rate mortgage.

asbestos A mineral once used in insulation and other materials that can cause respiratory diseases.

assessed value The value set on property for taxation purposes.

assessment The imposition of a tax, charge, or levy, usually according to established rates.

average A single number calculated to summarize and represent the values of items in a set (frequency distribution).

balance of trade The difference between a nation's exports and imports of merchandise to and from all other countries, usually covering a specific period.

balance sheet A financial statement showing assets, liabilities, and net worth as of a specific date.

balanced growth The state of an economy in which there is a constant relationship between the components of aggregate national income. Consumption expenditures, investment, and employment grow at the same rate as national income .

balloon frame A financial statement showing assets, liabilities, and net worth as of a specific date.

balloon payment Any payment on a note that is significantly greater than the other installment payments. California's Real Estate Law considers any payment that is twice the smallest installment payment as a balloon payment.

bank deposits The amount of money standing to the credit of a customer of a bank. Bank deposits are assets of its customers and liabilities of the bank.

banking The business of accepting deposits and lending money and also performing the function of safeguarding deposits and making loans, building societies, and financing houses.

bankruptcy A declaration by a court of law that an individual or company is insolvent; that is, it cannot meet its debts on the due dates.

barter A form of exchange in which goods or services are traded for goods or services. Before the invention of money, barter was the only basis for exchange. Money-based economies, however, have not eliminated the use of barter.

basis The financial interest that the Internal Revenue Service attributes to an owner of an investment property for the purpose of determining annual depreciation and gain or loss on the sale of the asset. If a property was acquired by purchase, the owner's basis is the cost of the property plus the value of any capital expenditures for improvements to the property, minus any depreciation allowable or actually taken. This new basis is called the *adjusted basis*.

bear A stock market speculator who sells stocks or shares that she may or not possess because she expects a fall in prices and expects to be able to buy them back later at a profit.

benchmark A statistical term for comprehensive data used as a basis for developing and adjusting interim estimates made from sample information.

birthrate The average number of live births occurring in a year for every 1,000 people.

blanket loan A mortgage covering more than one parcel of real estate, providing for each parcel's partial release from the mortgage lien upon repayment of a definite portion of the debt.

blighted area A declining area in which real property values are seriously affected by destructive economic forces, such as encroaching inharmonious property uses, poverty, and/or rapidly depreciating buildings.

blockbusting The illegal practice of inducing homeowners to sell their properties by making representations regarding the entry or prospective entry of persons of a particular race or national origin into the neighborhood.

board of supervisors Generally, the five elected officials governing a county.

boom A period of extraordinarily strong demand for goods and services and rapidly rising prices. Employment and use of productive capacity exceed normal levels.

boot Money or property given to make up any difference in value or equity between two properties in an *exchange*.

broker An intermediary between a buyer and seller in a highly organized market.

budget An estimate of income and expenditures for the future period as opposed to an account, which records financial transactions. Budgets are an essential element in the planning and control of the financial affairs of a nation or business and are made necessary essentially because income and expenditures do not occur simultaneously.

building A structure or a building, dwelling unit, or other physical development upon the land to house, protect, store, or cover persons or things.

building code An ordinance that specifies minimum standards of construction for buildings to protect public safety and health.

building permit Written governmental permission for the construction, alteration, or demolition of an improvement, showing compliance with building codes and zoning ordinances.

building coverage Also means "lot coverage," which means the percent of lot area covered by a building footprint. Building coverage can also mean "density" when related to nonresidential development.

bull A stock exchange speculator who purchases stocks and shares in the belief that prices will rise and that she will be able to sell them again later at a profit (speculation); the opposite of bear. The market is said to be bullish when it is generally anticipated that prices will rise.

bundle of legal rights The concept of land ownership that includes ownership of all legal rights to the land—possession, control within the law, enjoyment, exclusion, and disposition.

Burnham, Daniel H. Architect and city planner who was tremendously influential for his work on the 1893 World's Columbian Exposition and his development of The Plan for Chicago.

business cycle A type of fluctuation characterized by expansions occurring at about the same time in many economic activities, followed by similarly general contractions and then revivals. The sequence is recurrent but not of consistent length.

buydown A financing technique used to reduce the monthly payments for the first few years of a loan. Funds in the form of discount points are given to the lender by the builder or the seller to buy down or lower the effective interest rate paid by the buyer, thus reducing the monthly payments for a set time.

buyer's market Many properties for sale with few buyers; a supply and demand situation in which the buyer has the advantage in price negotiations due to a surplus of properties on the market at the same time.

California Association of REALTORS® (C.A.R.) The state organization of the National Association of REALTORS®. Founded in 1905, C.A.R. was originally titled the California State Realty Federation and was created to promote certain business standards in real estate dealings. In 1975, the association officially changed its name to the California Association of REALTORS®.

Cal-Vet California government loan program offering low interest rates for veterans.

capital One of the factors of production. Goods used for production of goods and services. Usually, but not always, refers to manmade goods such as machinery and structures. (Live animals would be part of the capital of a riding stable.)

capital, cost of (1) The rate of interest paid on the capital employed in a business. As capital will be usually drawn from a variety of sources, it will be an average cost derived from weighting the cost of each source, including equity capital, by its proportion of the total. A high cost of capital is considered detrimental to investment. (2) The cost of raising additional capital (i.e., the marginal cost). The marginal cost of capital on a discounted cash flow basis may be used as the minimum level of return in assessing investment projects.

capital expenditures Investments of cash or liability incurred for additions or betterments: usually land, buildings, machinery, and equipment.

capital formation Spending on fixed capital such as machinery and buildings. Public and private spending on capital formation is a measure of the extent to which an economy is socialized.

capital gain The gain received on the sale of real or personal property, other than property sold as stock-in-trade.

capital loss A reduction in the money value of an asset; opposite of capital gain.

capital market The market for long-term loanable funds as distinct from the money market, which deals in short-term funds. There is no clear-cut distinction between the two markets although, in principle, capital-market loans are used by industry and commerce mainly for fixed investment. The capital market is an increasingly international one. In any country, it is not one institution but all those institutions that match the supply and demand for long-term capital and claims on capital (e.g., the stock exchange, banks, and insurance companies). The capital market, of course, is not only concerned solely with the issue of new claims on capital in the primary or new issue market but also with dealings with existing claims in the secondary market. The marketability of securities is an important element in the efficient working of the capital market, as investors would be much more reluctant to make loans to industry if their claims could not easily be disposed of. All advanced countries have highly developed capital markets, but in developing countries, the absence of a capital market is often as much of an obstacle to the growth of investment as a shortage of savings. Governments and industrialists in these countries are obliged to raise capital in the international capital market (i.e., composed of the national capital markets in the advanced countries).

capital-output ratio The ratio derived by dividing the level of output into the stock of capital required to produce it. The incremental capital-output ratio is a change in output divided into a change in capital stock (i.e., investment). The relationship between incremental capital investment and output is described by the acceleration principle; the incremental capital-output ratio is the accelerator coefficient. The interdependence of capital and output play an important role in growth theory, in which various assumptions about the ratio are explored.

capital theory That part of economic theory concerned with analysis of the consequences of the fact that production generally involves inputs that have themselves been produced. The existence of these produced means of production, or capital, has profound implications for the nature of the economic system. A central element is the role of time and intertemporal planning. The production of capital requires the sacrifice of current consumption in exchange for future, possibly uncertain, consumption and the mechanisms by which this process is organized influence the growth and stability of the economy in important ways. The existence of capital is also central to the analysis of the income distribution. A major and controversial question has been what determines the income derived by the owners of capital relative to that of the suppliers of labor. Can their share be justified in terms of their contribution to the production of output? An understanding of the nature and implications of capital is fundamental to an understanding of our economic system and, indeed, as one leading contributor to the subject has remarked, the problem in attempting to define capital theory is to do it in such a way as to embrace something less than the whole of economics.

capitalism An economic system that emphasizes private ownership of the means of production and distribution, individual enterprise, profit as incentive, unfettered competition, and limited regulation of markets.

capitalization A mathematical process for estimating the value of a property using a proper rate of return on the investment and the annual net operating income expected to be produced by the property. The formula is expressed as follows: income ÷ rate = value.

capitalization rate The rate of return a property will produce on the owner's investment.

cartel An association of producers to regulate prices by restricting output and competition. Cartels are illegal in the United States, but cartels have been promoted by governments to achieve rationalization, as in Germany in the 1930s. They tend to be unstable because a single member can profit by undercutting the others, while price-fixing stimulates the development of substitutes. The most prominent example of an international cartel is the Organization of Petroleum Exporting Countries (OPEC).

cash (1) Coins and banknotes. (2) Legal tender in the settlement of debt.

cash flow The net spendable income from an investment, determined by deducting all operating and fixed expenses from the gross income. When expenses exceed income, a *negative cash flow* results.

cash ratio (1) The ratio of a banks' cash holdings to its total deposit liabilities. Liquidity ratio; banking. (2) For an individual firm, the proportion of its current liabilities that are accounted for by cash in hand, including bank deposits and sometimes payments due from customers.

caveat emptor A Latin phrase meaning "let the buyer beware."

census A count of population or some other characteristic, such as housing, and the statistical information derived from it. Every 10 years, the U.S. Bureau of the Census conducts a nationwide census of population and housing.

Census Bureau A bureau of the U.S. government that focuses on the administration and results of the decennial census and other surveys. Part of the U.S. Department of Commerce.

central bank A banker's bank. All developed and most developing countries have a central bank that is responsible for exercising control of the credit system, sometimes under instruction from government, and, increasingly often, under its own authority. Central banks typically execute policy through their lead role in setting short-term interest rates, rates of interest they control by establishing the rate at which loans of last resort will be made. Some central banks also use other devices to control money supply, such as special deposits. With an increasing consensus that monetary policy plays an important part in determining aggregate demand, the stability of the business cycle, and the rate of inflation, central banks have found themselves in an increasingly central role in economic management. *See* Federal Reserve System.

CEQA   California Environmental Quality Act.

CERCLA   The Comprehensive Environmental Response, Compensation, and Liability Act is a federal law that establishes a process for identifying parties responsible for creating hazardous waste sites, forcing liable parties to clean up toxic sites, bringing legal action against responsible parties, and funding the abatement of toxic sites. *See* Superfund.

certificate of deposit (CD)   A negotiable claim issued by a bank in return for a term deposit. CDs are securities that are purchased for less than their face value, which is the bank's promise to repay the deposit and, thus, offer a yield to maturity. The secondary market in CDs is made up by the discount houses and the banks in the interbank market. Where a depositor knows that he can, if necessary, sell his CD, the depositor will be willing to place funds with a bank for long periods. CDs were first issued in New York in the 1960s and, thus, denominated in dollars. Sterling CDs followed in 1968 .

change   The appraisal principle that holds that no physical or economic condition remains constant.

chattels   Items of personal property.

City Beautiful Movement   Late 19th/early 20th century philosophy that advocated beautifying cities for various social and economic reasons.

Civil Rights Act of 1866   An act that prohibits racial discrimination in the sale and rental of housing.

clustering   The grouping of home sites within a subdivision on smaller lots than normal, with the remaining land used as common areas.

CMA   *See* comparative market analysis.

coincident indicator   An indicator that experiences the peaks and troughs of the business cycle at approximately the same time as general economic activity.

COLAs   Cost-of-living adjustments, usually associated with wages.

collateral   Something having value that is given to secure repayment of a debt.

color of title   Condition in which a title appears to be good but is actually invalid because of a defect.

command economies   Economies that are largely government controlled. In general, the countries that are socialist are command-oriented but with some market activity permitted or even encouraged.

commercial banks   Privately owned banks operating check current accounts, receiving deposits, taking in and paying out notes and coins, and making loans.

commission Payment to a real estate professional for services rendered, such as in the sale or purchase of real property; usually a percentage of the selling price of the property.

commodity Any physical good or product, whether manufactured, agricultural, or mineral.

commodity exchange A market in which commodities are bought and sold. It is not necessary for the commodities to be physically exchanged; only rights to ownership need be.

comparables Properties used in an appraisal report that are substantially equivalent to the subject property.

comparative market analysis (CMA) A comparison of the prices of recently sold homes that are similar to a listing seller's home in terms of location, style, and amenities.

condemnation A judicial or administrative proceeding to exercise the power of eminent domain, through which a government agency takes private property for public use and compensates the owner.

conditional-use permit Written governmental permission allowing a use inconsistent with zoning but necessary for the common good, such as locating an emergency medical facility in a predominantly residential area.

conformity The appraisal principle holding that the greater the similarity among properties in an area, the better they will hold their value.

consumer An individual who purchases goods or services that are not for resale.

consumer good An economic good or commodity purchased by households for final consumption. Consumer goods include, for example, chocolate or draught beer consumed immediately, as well as durable goods that yield a flow of services over a period of time (e.g., a washing machine).

Consumer Price Index (CPI) Published by the Bureau of Labor Statistics, the CPI measures change in prices for a carefully defined market basket of goods and services, including food, rent, maintenance costs, medical and dental services, transportation, entertainment, clothing, and other items commonly purchased. The average prices of a base year are defined as 100, so an index of 200 means prices have doubled since that base year.

consumption The use of goods and services by consumer purchase or in the production of other goods.

contract A statement of the rights and obligations of each party to a transaction or transactions. A contract, as familiarly envisaged, is a formal written statement of the terms of a transaction or relationship.

contraction The segment of the business cycle curve that reflects a falling off of economic activity.

contribution The appraisal principle stating that the value of any component of a property is what it gives to the value of the whole or what its absence detracts from that value.

conventional loan A loan that requires no federally sponsored insurance or guarantee.

corporation An entity or organization, created by operation of law, whose rights of doing business are essentially the same as those of an individual. The entity has continuous existence until it is dissolved according to legal procedures.

correlation A statistical measure of the closeness of the variations in the values of one variable to the values of another.

cost As it applies to real estate, the amount expended (labor, material, and/or money) in acquiring or producing the commodity; the sum of money necessary to bring a property into existence.

cost approach The process of estimating the value of a property by adding to the estimated land value the appraiser's estimate of the reproduction or replacement cost of the building, less depreciation.

cost benefit analysis The appraisal of an investment project that includes all social and financial costs and benefits accruing to the project. The techniques adopted in order to evaluate and decide whether a proposed project should proceed—whether, that is, its benefits would exceed its cost—are the same as applied in investment (appraisal discounted cash flow, present value).

cost of living The money cost of maintaining a particular standard of living in terms of purchased goods and services.

cost of living index Retail prices index.

cost recovery An Internal Revenue Service term for *depreciation*.

CPI *See* Consumer Price Index.

credit The use or possession of goods and services without immediate payment.

credit card A plastic, personal magnetized card with the name and account number of the holder and the expiry date embossed. Purchases up to a prescribed limit may be credited on signature of a voucher franked by the card.

credit rating An evaluation of the financial trustworthiness of a company or individual, particularly with regard to meeting financial obligations.

credit union A nonprofit organization accepting deposits and making loans, operated as a cooperative. Credit unions are popular in the United States and some European countries. A mutual savings bank (mutual company).

creditor One to whom an amount of money is due. A firm's creditors are other firms, individuals, and perhaps the government to which the firm owes money in return for goods supplied, services rendered, and taxes for which it is liable.

cross-price elasticity of demand The proportionate change in the quantity demanded of one good divided by the proportionate change in the price of another good. If the two goods are substitutes (e.g., butter and margarine), this elasticity is positive. For instance, if the price of margarine increases, the demand for butter will increase. If the goods are complementary (complementary goods) (e.g., potted plants and flower pots), this elasticity is negative. If the price of potted plants rises, the demand for flower pots will fall.

curable or curable depreciation Depreciation that can be corrected at a reasonable economically feasible cost.

currency Notes and coin that are the "current" medium of exchange in a country (money supply). Gold, as well as national currencies, that act as reserve currencies—such as the dollar—are referred to as international currency because they are regarded as acceptable for the settlement of international debts. Banknote; exchange control; exchange rate; soft currency.

current prices Prices unadjusted for changes is the purchasing power of money. Whether prices are current or constant terms in a historical series of economic statistics is of great importance at times of inflation or deflation real terms.

cyclical industry An industry whose sales and profits reflect to a great extent the ups and downs of the business cycle.

cyclical unemployment Temporary unemployment resulting from lack of aggregate demand in a downswing in the business cycle.

data mining The practice of searching for correlations in data with the purpose of generating theoretical hypotheses.

dealer An Internal Revenue Service designation for a person who regularly buys and sells real property.

death rate The number of deaths occurring in any year for every 1,000 people (the crude death rate). It may be quoted for each sex and each age group.

debt A sum of money or other property owed to another by one person or organization. Debt comes into being through the granting of credit or through raising loan capital. Debt servicing consists of paying interest on a debt. Debt is an essential part of all modern, capitalist economies (capitalism).

debtor One who owes money to another. A firm's debtors, for example, are those to whom invoices have been sent for goods or services supplied that remain unpaid.

deed restrictions Clauses in a deed limiting the future uses of the property. Deed restrictions may impose a vast variety of limitations and conditions— for example, they may limit the density of buildings, dictate the types of structures that can be erected, or prevent buildings from being used for specific purposes or even from being used at all.

deficit An excess of an expenditure flow over income flow (e.g., budget deficit, balance of payments deficit, or an excess of liabilities over assets).

deflation A decrease in the general price level due to a decrease in total spending relative to the supply of goods on the market. The immediate effect is to increase purchasing power.

demand The amount of goods people are willing and able to buy at a given price; often coupled with *supply*.

demand curve A graphic display of demand for a particular product or service. The curve's slope is affected by the degree to which price affects demand. When price has a relatively small effect on demand, the line or curve will be close to the vertical. When price has a strong effect on demand, the line or curve will be closer to horizontal.

demographics The study and description of a population.

density Relative to residential development, density is the number of residential dwelling units per acre. This tends to be reflected on parcels of one acre or less as "X" units per acre of land area. For lands in which more than one acre is required for a residence, the density tends to be reflected as "X" acres per dwelling unit.

density zoning Zoning ordinances that restrict the maximum average number of housing units per acre that may be built within a particular area, generally a subdivision.

depletion theory The branch of economics concerned with the rate at which natural resources are consumed over time. For example, what determines the speed at which the world does (or ought to) use up its stock of oil? In general, economists view abstinence from using up a resource as a form of investment. By not using oil up now, we forgo some current consumption and leave ourselves more to consume in the future, just as we invest in machines today that will produce consumer goods tomorrow.

deposit Money placed in an account at a bank and constitution a claim on the bank. The term *bank deposit* includes deposits on all types of accounts, including current accounts.

deposit account An account with a bank, building society, or other financial institution in which deposits earn interest and withdrawals may require notice.

depreciation (1) In appraisal, a loss of value in property due to any cause, including *physical deterioration, functional obsolescence,* and *external obsolescence.* (2) In real estate investment, a deduction for tax purposes taken over the period of ownership of income property, based on the property's acquisition cost.

depression A period of very low use of productive capacity and very high unemployment.

deregulation The process of invigorating economic activity in a sector of the economy by reducing the burden of government controls, particularly those that have the effect of creating barriers to entry.

devaluation The reduction of the fixed official rate at which one currency is exchanged for another (currency depreciation) in a fixed exchange-rate regime.

developer One who attempts to put land to its most profitable use through the construction of improvements.

development The construction of improvements that benefit land.

diffusion The spreading of water from rain, snow, or underground springs over the surface of the ground.

discount Generally meaning a deduction from face value (i.e., the opposite of premium). Discount has a number of specific applications in economics and commerce: (1) A discount for cash is a percentage deductible from an invoice as an incentive for the debtor to pay within a defined period. (2) A deduction from the retail price of a good allowed to a wholesaler, retailer, or other agent. (3) A charge made for cashing a bill of exchange or other promissory note before its maturity date (discount house; factor). (4) The difference, where negative, between the present price of a security and its issue price. Discounting; present value.

discount points A loan fee charged by a lender to increase the lender's yield or effective interest rate. One discount point equals 1/8 percent of an interest rate.

discount rate The interest rate set by the Federal Reserve that member banks are charged when they borrow money through the Fed.

disguised unemployment A situation in which more people are available for work than is shown in the unemployment statistics. Married women, some students, or prematurely retired persons may register for work only if they believe opportunities are available to them. Also referred to as "concealed unemployment" and the "discouraged worker effect." Disguised unemployment will be revealed in an unusually low participation rate.

disinflation The reduction or elimination of inflation. *See* deflation.

disintermediation (1) Flows of funds between borrowers and lenders avoiding the direct use of financial intermediaries. Companies, for example, may lend surplus funds to each other without the use of the banking system or may issue bills guaranteed (accepted) by the banks but sold to nonbanks. Disintermediation may make it more difficult to measure and control the money supply as the authorities' measures to do so are focused upon financial intermediaries, which can avoid controls based upon deposits by lending through parallel money markets (special deposits). The use of financial intermediaries for lending and borrowing activities previously carried out outside them (i.e., the opposite of disintermediation, is called "re-intermediation"). (2) Disintermediation is the sudden withdrawal of funds from a financial intermediary in order to seek a higher yield (i.e., savings to stocks, bonds, mutual funds, money markets, treasuries, or real estate).

disinvestment Negative investment that results in the destruction of part of the capital stock. Negative investment in which gross investment is less than capital consumption (i.e., capital equipment is not replaced as it wears out). Antonym for investment.

disposable income Total income of households less income tax and employee national insurance contributions.

diversification Extending the range of goods and services in a firm or geographic region. The motives for diversification include declining profitability or growth in traditional markets, surplus capital, or management resources and a desire to spread risks and reduce dependence upon cyclical activities.

division of labor The allocation of labor so that each worker specializes in one or a few functions in the production process. Adam Smith illustrated the principle in the different stages of pin-making: drawing the wire, cutting, head-fitting, and sharpening. The division improved labor productivity (1) by more efficiently acquiring specialist skills and (2) saving time because workers did not have to move from one operation to another. Through the division of labor, economies of scale could be achieved. The exchange economy was essential to its operation. Each worker could specialize as long as he was assured that he could exchange his output for others to satisfy his needs. The principle applies to firms and countries also; similar benefits may be achieved by specialization in those activities in which the firm or country has a comparative advantage.

Dow-Jones Industrial Average An economic indicator that measures prices paid for 30 representative companies in the stock market.

downsizing Large-scale shedding of employees by major corporations, sometimes also used to refer to the disposal of subsidiaries and other unwanted activities. Downsizing is generally a response to pressures from competition, or investors, to reduce costs. It may, in some cases, reflect a long-delayed reaction to technological change, which allows output to be maintained with fewer employees.

due diligence A fair, proper, and due degree of care and activity. An expressed or implied requirement in certain real estate contracts stating that a person use good-faith efforts to perform the obligations of the contract.

durable goods Consumer goods, such as washing machines, motor cars, and TV sets that yield services or utility over time rather than being completely used up at the moment of consumption. Most consumer goods are, in fact, durable to some degree, and the term is often used in a more restricted sense to denote relatively expensive, technologically sophisticated goods—"consumer durables"—such as the examples given. The significance of the durability of these goods is that the conventional apparatus of demand analysis must be supplemented by the modes of analysis developed in capital theory.

duration In a business cycle, the length of a contraction, an expansion, or the period from trough to trough or from peak to peak.

dwelling unit A single dwelling for habitation by individuals or families.

earnings The return for human effort, as in the earnings of labor and the earnings of management. In labor economics, wage earnings are distinguished from wage rates; the former include overtime, the latter relate only to earnings per hour or standard working week. Earnings may be quoted as pretax or post-tax and other deductions (gross or net) and in real terms or money terms.

easement A right to use the land of another for a specific purpose, such as for a right-of-way or utilities; an incorporeal interest in land because it does not include a right of possession.

econometrics The setting up of mathematical models describing economics relationships (such as that the quantity demanded of a good is dependent positively on income and negatively on price); testing the validity of such hypotheses (statistical inference); and estimating the parameters in order to obtain a measure of the strengths of the influences of the different independent variables. Econometricians most commonly use the techniques of regression analysis (least squares regression), in which the relationship between a dependent variable and an independent variable is analyzed, based on the correlation in the variation of the two.

economic base The sector of an economy that sells products and services to customers from outside the community, bringing external dollars into the community. Customers need not literally be outside the community at the time of the transaction; they may be business visitors or tourists. The important thing is that their money is outside money.

economic development The growth of national per capita income of developing countries. Such countries need to generate sufficient savings and investment in order to diversify their economies from agriculture to industry, with the necessary supporting infrastructure such as roads and seaports.

economic efficiency The state of an economy in which no one can be made better off without someone being made worse off.

economic good Any service rendered or any physical object, natural or man-made, that could command a price in a market.

economic growth The increase in a country's national income or, sometimes, its per capita national income. Growth is taken as the basis of advancing human welfare although, in fact, there are problems in the measurement of national income (some activities—such as employing do-it-yourself car maintenance rather than the services of a garage mechanic, or transacting in the black economy—may not take place in a market, or not in a market for which statistics are collected).

economic history The study of the subject matter of economics in a historical context. Economic history was originally part of political economy, the antecedent of modern economics, and was taught in the faculties of history and moral philosophy. In the late 19th century, economic history began to separate from history and economics and is now a distinct discipline.

economic indicators Measures of the economy's performance. The Commerce Department's Bureau of Economic Analysis (BEA) uses 300 indicators, classified as leading, coinciding, or lagging. Leading indicators warn in advance of changes in business activity. Coinciding indicators reflect the present state of the economy. Lagging indicators trail the business cycle, rising for several months after a downturn has started.

economic life The number of years during which an improvement will add value to land.

economic rent The difference between the return made by a factor of production and the return necessary to keep the factor in its current occupation. In general, economic rents accrue where changes in supply of this sort are not possible.

economics The social science that studies, describes, and analyzes an economy.

economy Any system designed for the production, distribution, and consumption of necessary and desired goods and services.

EIR *See* Environmental Impact Report.

EIS *See* Environment Impact Statement.

elasticity of demand The responsiveness of demand to price. Demand is defined as elastic if a 1% price reduction results in a 1% (or more) increase in demand. It is defined as inelastic if a 1% price reduction results in less than a 1% increase in demand.

elasticity of supply The responsiveness of quantity supplied to price. If a 1% increase in price prompts at least a 1% increase in offerings on the market, then supply is said to be elastic.

eminent domain The right of a government or municipal quasi-public body to acquire property for public use through a court action called *condemnation*, in which the court decides that the use is a public use and determines the compensation to be paid to the owner.

employee Someone who works as a direct employee of an employer and has employee status. The employer is obligated to withhold income taxes and Social Security taxes from the compensation of employees.

enabling acts State legislation that confers zoning and other powers on municipal governments.

encapsulation A method of controlling environmental contamination by sealing off a dangerous substance, such as asbestos.

encumbrance Anything—such as a mortgage, tax, or judgment lien; an easement; a restriction on the use of the land; or an outstanding dower right—that may diminish the value or use and enjoyment of a property.

enterprise One or more firms under common ownership or control. A term used in the census of production to distinguish the reporting unit (establishment) from the firm or unit of control.

enterprise zone A designated zone in a depressed, generally inner-urban area, in which firms located in the zone are given favorable taxation concessions and freedom from a number of planning constraints.

entrepreneur Someone who personally starts a business and undertakes its risks.

Environmental Impact Report (EIR) A detailed informational document prepared by a public agency responsible for evaluating a project as part of the environmental review (CEQA) process. It describes and analyzes a project's significant environmental effects and discusses ways and means to mitigate such impacts or avoid those effects.

Environmental Impact Statement (EIS) A statement that details the impact a project will have on the environment.

Equal Credit Opportunity Act (ECOA) The federal law that prohibits discrimination in the extension of credit because of race, color, religion, national origin, sex, age, marital status, or receipt of public assistance.

equalization The raising or lowering of assessed values for tax purposes in a particular county or taxing district to make them equal to assessments in other counties or districts.

equalization factor A factor (number) by which the assessed value of a property is multiplied to arrive at a value for the property that is in line with statewide tax assessments. The *ad valorem tax* would be based on this adjusted value.

equilibrium point The middle stage of the life cycle of property value; the static point at the peak of its value; the point at which supply and demand are in harmonious balance.

equilibrium price The price at which supply and demand are in balance. The price on the vertical axis opposite the point of intersection of demand and supply curves.

equity The interest or value that an owner has in property over and above any indebtedness.

escalator clause A clause in a lease providing for an increase or decrease in rent to cover specific contingencies. Some leases have escalator clauses based upon the cost of living index and are referred to as index-leases.

Euro European Monetary Union currency adopted in 2002 as standard currency.

exchange A transaction in which all or part of the consideration is the transfer of *like-kind* property (e.g., real estate for real estate).

excess demand The state of a market for a commodity in which consumers would choose to buy more of the commodity than is available at the prevailing price.

excess supply The state of the market for a commodity in which more of the commodity is available for purchase than consumers choose to buy at the prevailing price.

exchange rate The price (rate) at which one currency is exchanged for another currency.

expansion The segment of the business cycle curve that reflects a rise in economic activity.

exports The goods and services produced by one country that are sold to another country in exchange for the second country's own goods and services.

externalities The principle that economic or noneconomic factors outside a property may have positive or negative effects on its value.

Fair Housing Act The federal law that prohibits discrimination in housing based on race, color, religion, sex, disability, familial status, and national origin.

fair market value The most probable price a willing, fully informed buyer will pay to a willing, fully informed seller in an arm's-length transaction.

familial status One or more individuals under age 18 living with a parent or guardian; also includes a woman who is pregnant and anyone who is in the process of assuming custody of a child under age 18.

Fannie Mae A government-supervised enterprise established to purchase any kind of mortgage loans in the secondary mortgage market from the primary lenders.

Federal Home Loan Mortgage Corporation (Freddie Mac) A federally chartered corporation established in 1970 for the purpose of purchasing mortgages in the secondary mortgage market. Freddie Mac was created as a part of the savings association system and, while it is not so limited, its loan purchase policies are designed to accommodate savings association needs.

Federal Open Market Committee (FOMC) U.S. government body responsible for making monetary policy; composed of the governors and directors of the Federal Reserve banks.

Federal Reserve System (Fed) The country's central banking system, which establishes the nation's monetary policy by regulating the supply of money and interest rates.

feudal system A system of ownership usually associated with precolonial England, in which the king or other sovereign is the source of all rights. The right to possess real property was granted by the sovereign to an individual as a life estate only. Upon the death of the individual, title passed back to the sovereign, not to the decedent's heirs.

FHA-insured loan A loan insured by the Federal Housing Administration and made by an approved lender in accordance with FHA regulations.

FHLMC *See* Freddie Mac.

finance The provision of money when and where required. Finance may be short term (usually up to one year); medium term (usually more than one year and up to five to seven years); and long term.

financial intermediaries Institutions that hold money balances of, or that borrow from, individuals and other institutions to make loans or other investments. Hence, they serve the purpose of channeling funds from lenders to borrowers. Intermediaries provide services to each, often at little or no cost compared to direct investment.

Financial Institutions Reform, Recovery, and Enforcement Act (FIRREA) This act restructured the savings and loan association regulatory system; enacted in response to the savings and loan crisis of the 1980s.

fiscal policy The government's policy in regard to taxation and spending programs. The balance between these two areas determines the amount of money the government will withdraw from or feed into the economy, which can counter economic peaks and slumps.

fixed costs Costs that do not vary with output (e.g., the rent on a factory lease).

fixture An item of personal property that has been converted to real property by being permanently affixed to the realty.

forecast An estimate of future events, stated as probabilities. A forecast may be implicit or explicit.

forecasting In appraisal, taking the past as a guide to the future together with present conditions and tempering this with the appraiser's judgment for the projection of the future.

foreign investment The acquisition by governments, institutions, or individuals in one country of assets in another.

Freddie Mac *See* Federal Home Loan Mortgage Corporation.

free market A market uncontrolled by government, free of regulations. Producers in such a market are free to produce what they want in quantities and at prices that they choose. Production restraints or incentives come from responses of potential buyers.

free trade The condition in which the free flow of goods (economic goods) and services in international exchange is neither restricted nor encouraged by direct government intervention.

free trade zones A customs-defined area in which goods or services may be processed or transacted without attracting taxes or duties or being subjected to certain government regulations.

friable Used in reference to asbestos, it means brittle or easily crumbled.

Friedman, Milton Nobel Prize-winning economist and proponent of monetarist and free-market economics.

function A description of the relationship that governs the behavior of two or more related variables.

functional obsolescence A loss of value to an improvement to real estate arising from problems of design or utility.

game theory The branch of economics concerned with representing economic interactions in a highly stylized form, with players, pay-offs, and strategies.

Gantt chart A bar-style chart commonly used in scheduling construction projects, in which project activities are shown on a horizontal time scale.

general partnership *See* partnership.

General Plan A long-range comprehensive document required to be prepared for every city and county under state law. It addresses the broad range of issues associated with a city or county's development. The role of the General Plan is to act as a "constitution," a basis for rational decisions regarding a city's or county's long-term physical development.

gift tax A levy on the value of certain property given away to others and paid by the donor, often referred to as an inheritance tax.

Ginnie Mae *See* Government National Mortgage Association.

globalization Geographical shifts in domestic economic activity around the world and away from nation states.

GNMA *See* Ginnie Mae.

gold standard A system of valuing a nation's currency based on the amount of gold in the National Treasury (the "gold standard").

goods Material things perceived to have monetary or exchange value.

Government National Mortgage Association (GNMA) Ginnie Mae is a government agency that plays an important role in the secondary mortgage market. It sells mortgage-backed securities that are backed by pools of FHA and VA loans.

gross annual multiplier Appraises an income property based on a multiple of the gross annual income.

gross domestic product (GDP) The measure of the total flow of goods and services produced by the economy over a specified time period, normally a year or a quarter. It is obtained by valuing outputs of goods and services at market prices and then aggregating.

gross income multiplier (GIM) "Rule of thumb" method of appraising income-producing (commercial or industrial) property. price ÷ gross annual income.

gross monthly multiplier Appraises a rental residence based upon a multiple of the gross monthly income.

gross national product (GNP) The dollar value of all goods and services produced by a nation's economy in a year. Technically, this means the market value of newly produced final goods and services. The value of intermediate goods and services is assumed to be incorporated in the final value.

gross rent multiplier (GRM) The figure used as a multiplier of the gross monthly income of a property to produce an estimate of the property's value; usually used for single-family residential property.

ground rent Earnings of improved property credited to earnings of the ground itself after allowance is made for earnings of improvements.

groundwater Water that exists under the earth's surface within the tiny spaces or crevices in geological formations.

growth control Limits placed upon the amount of land that is allowed to be developed.

growth cycles A cyclic pattern in rates of economic growth rather than in the general level of economic activity reflected in business cycles.

growth theory The area of economics concerned with the development of models that explains the rate of economic growth in an economy.

handicap A person who suffers from a physical or mental impairment that substantially limits one or more major life activities.

hedge Action taken by a buyer or seller to protect her business or assets against a change in prices.

hidden unemployment Describes those individuals who are no longer counted in the unemployment statistics compiled by both the federal and state government. These individuals include those who are no longer seeking employment or are working in a different or unrelated industry or trade that does not utilize the skills of the individuals, and no longer are these individuals counted by the government's official unemployment figures, thereby becoming hidden or uncounted.

highest and best use The legally permitted and physically possible use of a property that would produce the greatest net income and, thereby, develop the highest value.

hoarding The accumulation of idle money balances, inactive money. Liquidity preference.

home equity loan A loan under which a property owner uses the property as collateral and can then draw funds up to a prearranged amount against the property. Also called a *home equity line of credit*, or *HELOC*.

homogeneous products Goods and services purchased by consumers in which the latter consider perfect substitutes (perfect competition).

Hotelling's Law The observation by Hotelling that in many markets, it is rational for all the producers to make their products similar as possible. Suppose, for example, there are two newsagents in a street, each of which wanted to maximize its share of local business by locating its shop so that it is the nearest newsagent for as much of the trade visiting the street as possible. In this situation, both newsagents will position themselves in the middle of the street guaranteeing themselves half the market. It would be socially more desirable for them to separate themselves and sit a third of the way along the street from different ends. Unfortunately, if one newsagent did this, the other could position himself so as to capture more than half the total market. Too little variety results from the process. Hotelling's Law manifests itself in numerous markets (e.g., competing bus operators scheduling their buses to run at the same time).

household All the persons who live in a housing unit.

housing A cluster of rights to the occupancy of permanent structures built for long-term occupation and designed to support personal living, not the production of goods or services. When we buy or rent housing, we are purchasing those rights. Housing refers to the physical stock of dwelling units in a community, state, or nation.

housing starts Beginning construction of new housing. Housing starts are an index of construction activity and, thus, an important economic indicator.

housing stock The total dwelling units in a community or state or the nation as a whole.

housing unit A physical structure with a full range of living facilities in one or more rooms, within which an individual, group, or family may live privately, separated from people in other units.

HUD Acronym for the U.S. Department of Housing and Urban Development.

human capital The skills and knowledge embodied in the labor force. A metallurgist can expect to earn more than a laboratory assistant because of investing more in education and training. These higher earnings are a return on the investment the metallurgist (or the parents, or the state) has made in school fees and forgone earnings.

hypothecation To pledge property as security for an obligation or loan without giving up possession of it.

hypothesis A theoretical explanation of the behavior of phenomena that can be tested against the facts.

immobility The fact that property cannot be relocated to satisfy demand where supply is low, nor can buyers always relocate to areas with greater supply.

imperfect market A market in which the forces that tend to endure productive and allocative efficiency are thwarted (economic efficiency).

import restrictions Restrictions on the importation of products into a country may be affected by means of tariffs, quotas, or imports deposits, and are generally imposed to correct a balance-of-payments deficit.

imports The flow of goods and services that enter for sale into one country and are the products of another country.

improvement (1) Any structure, usually privately owned, erected on a site to enhance the value of the property (e.g., a building, fence, or driveway). (2) A publicly owned structure added to or benefiting land (e.g., a curb, sidewalk, street, or sewer).

income approach The process of estimating the value of an income-producing property through capitalization of the annual net income expected to be produced by the property during its remaining useful life.

income tax A tax on income.

incorporation The action of forming a company by carrying out the necessary legal formalities.

incurable obsolescence The functional obsolescence of an improvement that is not economically feasible to repair or correct.

index method The appraisal method of estimating building costs by multiplying the original cost of the property by a percentage factor to adjust for current construction costs.

indicators Certain characteristics or facets of an economy relied on by economists as symptoms of the relative health of the whole. Indicators may be coincident (reflecting the economy's present state), lagging (trailing the business cycle), or leading (providing advance notice of change).

industrial park An area laid out with streets and plots to provide a landscaped setting for light industry, warehouses, and other businesses. Today these are often called business parks, reflecting the shift to service firms.

Industrial Revolution The profound transformation of the means of production that first occurred in England between 1750 and 1850. In that century, England changed from a country of farming villages and cottage industries to a country of factory towns. New machinery, new energy sources, and new ways of organizing labor were at the core of this revolution: the steam engine, improved textile machines, the use of coal rather than wood as fuel, and the rise of the factory system.

industrialization The process of developing industry in a location.

inferior good A good the demand for which falls as income rises; that is, its income elasticity of demand is negative. An example would be the demand of married couples for small apartments. A good that is not inferior is called a normal good.

inflation The gradual reduction of the purchasing power of the dollar, usually related directly to increases in the money supply by the federal government.

inflation target The adoption of an explicit level of inflation to which monetary policy is geared towards steering the economy.

infrastructure Basic physical and social facilities: roads, dredged harbors, airports, bridges, electrical power generation and transmission, schools and universities, mail and telephone systems, radio, television and newspapers, water supply, and waste disposal.

innovation Putting new products and services—or new means for producing them—into the market. Innovation is preceded by research that may lead to an invention, which is then developed for the market (research and development). Innovation is an important source of economic expansion and productivity.

insolvency The state of a firm when its liabilities, excluding equity capital, exceed its total assets (bankruptcy). A less stringent definition is that a firm is insolvent if it is unable to meet its obligations when due for payment.

institutional economics A type of economic analysis that emphasizes the role of social, political, and economic organizations in determining economic events.

institutional lender A financial intermediary or depository, such as a savings and loan association, commercial bank, or life insurance company, that pools money of its depositors and then invests funds in various ways, including real estate loans.

interest A charge made by a lender for the use of money.

interest rate A rate of return on capital. The percentage of a sum of money charged for its use.

interim financing A short-term loan usually made during the construction phase of a building project (often referred to as a *construction loan*).

internal rate of return (IRR) A measurement that compares the value of different types of investments objectively. Usually expressed as an annual return on the original investment.

International Monetary Fund (IMF) The organization set up by the Bretton Woods Agreement of 1944 that came in to operation in March 1947. The fund was established to encourage international operation in the monetary field and the removal of foreign exchange restrictions; to stabilize exchange rates; and to facilitate a multilateral (multilaterism) payment system between member countries. In 1995 the fund had 181 members.

Interstate Land Sales Full Disclosure Act (ILSA) A federal law that regulates the sale of certain real estate in interstate commerce.

intrinsic value An appraisal term referring to the value of a property unaffected by a person's personal preferences.

inventories Terms for stocks of raw materials, work in progress, and finished goods. Inventories represent capital tied up in unsold goods and require storage space, insurance, and other incurred costs but are an inevitable part of the process of production and distribution.

investment Money directed toward the purchase, improvement, and development of an asset in expectation of income or profits.

IRS Internal Revenue Service. Section of the U.S. Department of the Treasury responsible for collecting taxes.

joint venture The joining of two or more people to conduct a specific business enterprise. A joint venture is similar to a partnership in that it must be created by agreement between the parties to share in the losses and profits of the venture. It is unlike a partnership in that the venture is for one specific project only rather than a continuing business relationship.

just compensation Payment due to a land owner when the government seizes his property in exercising its police power.

Keynes, John Maynard Author of the *General Theory of Employment, Interest and Money* (1936). Argued in favor of government intervention in the free market in order to stimulate full employment.

labor A factor of production. The term not only includes the number of people available for or engaged in the production of goods or services but also their physical and intellectual skills and effort. Employment, full; human capital; labor force; sow's ear effect; unemployment.

labor force The total number of people in a country who are either working or unemployed but looking for work.

labor market The market in which wages, salaries, and conditions of employment are determined in the context of the supply of labor (labor force) and the demand for labor.

laissez faire A free market system with little or no governmental control.

land The earth's surface, extending downward to the center of the earth and upward infinitely into space, including things permanently attached by nature, such as trees.

lead Used as a pigment and drying agent in alkyd oil-based paint in about 75% of housing built before 1978. An elevated level of lead in the body can cause serious damage to the brain, kidneys, nervous system, and red blood cells. Children younger than six are most vulnerable.

lease A written or oral contract between a landlord (the lessor) and a tenant (the lessee) that transfers the right to exclusive possession and use of the landlord's real property to the lessee for a specified period of time and for a stated consideration (rent). By state law, leases for longer than a certain period of time (generally one year) must be in writing to be enforceable.

leaseback An agreement in which the owner of property sells that property to a person or institution and then leases it back again for an agreed period and rental. Leaseback is often used by companies that want to free capital tied up in buildings for other uses.

legal tender A form of money that, by law, must be accepted in payment for all debts. Currency and coins are legal tender; checks are not.

letter of credit A nonnegotiable order from a bank to a bank abroad authorizing payments of a particular sum of money or up to a limit of a certain sum to a person named in the letter.

leverage The use of borrowed money to finance an investment.

liabilities Claims of creditors; debts.

lien A right given by law to certain creditors to have their debts paid out of the property of a defaulting debtor, usually by means of a court sale.

limited partnership A business arrangement in which the operation is administered by one or more general partners and funded, by and large, by limited or silent partners, who are, by law, responsible for losses only to the extent of their investments.

liquidity The ability to sell an asset and convert it into cash, at a price close to its true value, in a short period of time.

loan The borrowing of a sum of money by one person, company, government, or other organization from another. Loans may be secured or unsecured (securities); interest bearing or interest free; long term, redeemable, or irredeemable. Loans may be made by individuals and companies, building societies and other financial intermediaries, pawnbrokers, or by the issuing of securities.

loan-to-value (LTV) ratio The relationship between the amount of the mortgage loan and the value of the real estate being pledged as collateral.

local tax Taxation levied by (or for) local rather than central government.

long-term unemployment Joblessness for a period in excess of six months, a year, or two years.

M1 The Federal Reserve's basic measure of the nation's money supply.

macroeconomics The study of whole economic systems aggregating over the functioning of individual economic units. It is primarily concerned with variables that follow systematic and predictable paths of behavior and can be analyzed independent of the decisions of the many agents who determine their level. More specifically, it is a study of national economies and the determination of national income.

manufactured home A structure transportable in one or more sections, designed for dwelling. Includes mobile homes but is not the same as factory-built (prefabricated or modular) housing.

market A place where goods can be bought and sold and a price established.

market economy Free-market economy.

market price The price actually paid for property.

market rent The rental income that a property would probably bring in the open market, based on market data.

market value The most probable price that a property would bring in an arm's-length transaction under normal conditions on the open market.

marketing All the activities that contribute to the sale of a product or service.

Marx, Karl Author of the *Communist Manifesto* (1848) and *Das Kapital* (1867). Exponent of worker control of the means of production and the historical inevitability of a socialist revolution to attain economic equality.

master plan A comprehensive government plan to guide the long-term physical development of a particular area.

median The middle number in a series. If there are five numbers ranging from low to high, the third number is the median: 126, 128, 130, 145, 158. The median is not the same as the average: here, the average is 137.4.

median home price Refers to the middle figure in a set of numbers, in this case the purchase price of homes in a given area.

mercantilism An economic policy of European trading states during the 16th, 17th, and 18th centuries when, through exploration and colonization, they extended European power to other parts of the globe. The policy emphasized strong state control over imports and exports with a view to importing only raw materials, exporting finished goods, and accumulating precious metals that could be used to pay mercenary armies.

merchant banks Institutions that carry out a variety of financial services, including the acceptance of bills of exchange, the issue and placing of loans and securities, portfolio and unit trust management, and some banking services.

microeconomics The study of economics at the level of individual consumers, groups of consumers, or firms. No very sharp boundary can be drawn between microeconomics and the other main area of the subject, macroeconomics, but its broad distinguishing feature is to focus on the choices facing, and the reasoning behind, individual economic decision making.

minimum wage Legislation prohibiting the paying of wages below some specified level.

mixed economies Contemporary economies in which economic decisions and actions are undertaken in both private and public spheres.

mode A measure of the central tendency of a variable. The mode (or modal range) of a sample of observations is that value (or range of values) that occurs with greatest frequency.

mold A form of fungus that can be found almost anywhere and can grow on almost any organic substance, so long as moisture and oxygen are present. Mold growth can gradually destroy what it is growing on, as well as cause serious health problems.

monetarist Monetarists are economists who believe that control of the economy is best accomplished through control of the money supply. A monetarist policy is one that uses control of the money supply to accomplish particular goals. Noted monetarists include Nobel Prize-winning economist Milton Friedman.

monetary policy Governmental regulation of the amount of money in circulation through such institutions as the Federal Reserve Board.

money Any object or commodity that people in a given society or group commonly accept and use in payment for goods or services.

money market The financial institutions that deal in short-term securities and loans, gold, and foreign exchange.

money supply The stock of liquid assets in an economy that can freely be exchanged for goods or services. Money supply is a phrase that can describe anything from notes and coins alone (monetary base) to the sum of all cash plus bank deposits because by writing checks, individuals exchange bank deposits for goods or services

monopoly A market in which there is only one supplier. Three features characterize a monopoly market: (1) the firm in it is motivated by profits, (2) it stands alone and barriers prevent new firms from entering the industry (barriers to entry); and (3) the actions of the monopolist itself affect the market price of its output (marginal revenue)—it is not a price taker.

mortgage A conditional transfer or pledge of real estate as security for the payment of a debt. Also, the document creating a mortgage lien.

mortgage banker A mortgage loan company that originates, services, and sell loans to investors.

mortgage broker An agent of a lender who brings the lender and the borrower together. The broker receives a fee for this service.

mortgagee A lender in a mortgage loan transaction.

mortgage lien A lien or charge on the property of a mortgagor that secures the underlying debt obligation.

mortgagor A borrower in a mortgage loan transaction.

Nasdaq National Association of Securities Dealers Automated Quotation System.

Nasdaq 100 Index A common stock market indicator representing the 100 largest nonfinancial domestic companies on the Nasdaq market.

National Association of REALTORS® (NAR) The largest real estate organization in the world; NAR members subscribe to a strict code of ethics. Active members are allowed to use the trademarked designation, REALTOR®.

natural increase In a population, excess of births over deaths.

natural resources Commodities or assets with some economic value that exists without any effort of mankind. The value they have is usually only realized, however, when they are exploited, that is, dug out of the ground, processed, or refined. Natural resources are necessary ingredients of all economic activity.

needs Certain resources are absolutely needed for biological survival (e.g., water, food, and protection from the elements). For the most part, "needs" are defined by the group within which one lives, and the group's definitions of need are influenced by capability. An unattainable condition will seldom be defined as a need.

negotiable instrument A written promise or order to pay a specific sum of money that may be transferred by endorsement or delivery. The transferee then has the original payee's right to payment.

neighborhood An identifiable grouping of individuals, buildings, or business enterprises within, or as part of, a larger community. An area within a town or city that may or may not have formal boundaries. Inside the neighborhood, residents and/or merchants often have a sense of common identity or at the very least shared locality.

net absorption As applied to real estate markets, net absorption is the measurement of the total square footage or units in a specific market area defined by geography (city or region) and by type of properties (i.e. retail, office, and residential) that is occupied minus (–) the total space vacated in a given period of time, typically a monthly or annual basis.

net income Net profit on earnings after tax and, where appropriate, after minority interest.

net lease A lease requiring the tenant to pay not only rent but also costs incurred in maintaining the property, including taxes, insurance, utilities, and repairs.

net migration Characteristic of a population study in which the number of people coming into an area is divided by the number of people who leave during the same period.

net operating income (NOI) The income projected for an income-producing property after deducting anticipated vacancy and collection losses and operating expenses.

New Deal The U.S. federal government under President Roosevelt began, in 1933, a number of projects designed to give financial assistance and work to the large number of people thrown out of employment by the Great Depression that followed the stock market collapse on Wall Street in 1929. This change of policy was called the New Deal. It met with a certain amount of opposition because it led to budget deficits (balanced budget).

New York Stock Exchange (NYSE) The leading New York stock exchange and largest in the world in terms of market capitalization. The second U.S. exchange, also in New York, is the American Stock Exchange, Inc. (AMEX). The NYSE is also referred to as the "Big Board" and as "Wall Street."

NIMBY "Not In My Backyard": a term that describes the tendency for some communities to resist affordable housing projects and other development that might lessen the value of a local property.

North American Free Trade Agreement (NAFTA) A free-trade area set up beginning in 1994 comprised of Canada, the United States, and Mexico. Import tariffs, quotas, and other trade barriers (nontariff barriers) between the member countries are to be phased out over a period of up to 15 years. The agreement also includes environmental provisions relating to the use of renewable resources, health, and pollution.

NYSE *See* New York Stock Exchange.

nonconforming use A use of property that is permitted to continue after a zoning ordinance prohibiting it has been established for the area.

nonhomogeneity A lack of uniformity; dissimilarity. Because no two parcels of land are exactly alike, real estate is said to be nonhomogeneous.

obsolescence The loss of value due to property features that are outmoded or less useful. Obsolescence may be functional or external.

open-end loan A mortgage loan that is expandable by increments up to a maximum dollar amount, with the full loan being secured by the same original mortgage.

option An agreement to keep open for a set period an offer to sell or purchase property.

overdraft A loan facility on a customer's current at a bank permitting the customer to overdraw up to a certain agreed limit for an agreed period. Interest is payable on the amount of the loan facility actually taken up, and it may, therefore, be a relatively inexpensive way of financing a fluctuating requirement. The terms of the loan are normally that it is repayable on demand, or at the expiration of the agreement, and it is, thus, distinct from a term loan.

ownership Having title to a piece of property.

package loan A real estate loan used to finance the purchase of both real property and personal property, such as in the purchase of a new home that includes carpeting, window coverings, and major appliances.

participation loan As a concession for making a loan on commercial property, the lender is given a portion of ownership, which allows him to participate in the profits.

partnership An association of two or more individuals who carry on a continuing business for profit as co-owners. Under the law, a partnership is regarded as a group of individuals rather than as a single entity separate from the individual owners. A *general partnership* is a typical form of joint venture in which each general partner shares in the administration, profits, and losses of the operation. A *limited partnership* is a business arrangement whereby the operation is administered by one or more general partners and funded, by and large, by limited or silent partners, who are by law responsible for losses only to the extent of their investments.

passive activity income Income from real estate or other business in which an owner does not actively participate in management. An IRS classification.

payment cap The limit on the amount the monthly payment can be increased on an adjustable-rate mortgage when the interest rate is adjusted.

peak The top segment of the business cycle curve, a period during which productivity and employment are higher than in the preceding and succeeding periods.

pension funds Sums of money laid aside and normally invested to provide a regular income on retirement, or in compensation for disablement, for the remainder of a person's life.

per capita income Income per head, normally defined as the national income divided by the total population. International comparisons of per capita income at current exchange rates need to be interpreted with caution. Purchasing-power parity; real exchange rate.

percentage lease A lease, commonly used for commercial property, whose rental is based on the tenant's gross sales at the premises; it usually stipulates a base monthly rental plus a percentage of any gross sales above a certain amount.

personal loan A bank loan made without collateral security to a private customer for specific purposes.

physical deterioration A reduction in a property's value resulting from a decline in physical condition; can be caused by action of the elements or by ordinary wear and tear.

planned unit development (PUD) A planned combination of diverse land uses, such as housing, recreation, and shopping, in one contained development or subdivision.

planning commission A local government body that plans the physical growth of a community and recommends zoning ordinances and other laws for that purpose.

plottage The increase in value or utility resulting from the consolidation (*assemblage*) of two or more adjacent lots into one larger lot.

point A term used for a percentage of the principal loan amount charged by the lender. Each point is equal to 1% of the loan amount.

police power The government's right to impose laws, statutes, and ordinances, including zoning ordinances and building codes, to protect the public health, safety, and welfare.

population (1) The number of people living in any defined area, such as New York or India. (2) In statistics, a term applied to any class of data of which counts are made or samples are taken (e.g., a car population). The study of the characteristics of human population is called demography.

poverty Government agencies use a technical definition based entirely on money income. It changes every year to reflect the Consumer Price Index.

poverty guidelines An annual measure established by the federal government based on an annual income for a family of four. The federal guidelines also take into consideration different income levels for the 48 continental states, Alaska, and Hawaii based on the cost of living and the number of people within a household. The guidelines are updated each year and serve as the basis for establishing the federal poverty level, which are utilized to determine the amount of financial assistance granted to families based on their annual incomes.

predatory pricing Setting prices at very low levels with the objective of weakening or eliminating competitors or keeping out new entrants to a market. Because prices will be raised again once these objectives have been achieved, there is no permanent benefit to the consumer. Predatory pricing is a means of establishing or maintaining monopoly power.

prepayment penalty A charge imposed on a borrower who pays off the loan principal early. This penalty compensates the lender for interest and other charges that would otherwise be lost.

present value The discounted value of a financial sum arising at some future period.

price What must be given in exchange for something. Prices are usually expressed in terms of a quantity of money per unit of a commodity (a good or service), but in barter, the price of a good is what other good or goods it can be exchanged for. Price changes are the means by which the competitive process determines the allocation of resources in the free-market economy.

prime rate The rate of interest charged by commercial banks to first-class-risk corporate borrowers for short-term loans. The prime rate is the basis of the whole structure of commercial interest in the United States.

primary mortgage market The mortgage market in which loans are originated, consisting of lenders such as commercial banks, savings associations, and mutual savings banks.

principal (1) A sum loaned or employed as a fund or an investment, as distinguished from its income or profits. (2) The original amount (as in a loan) of the total due and payable at a certain date. (3) A main party to a transaction; the person for whom an agent works.

private enterprise In economics, the term "private" is used to identify an activity that is not owned or operated by government. A private enterprise is a business not owned or operated by government.

profit Making a gain from an investment after subtracting expenses.

progression An appraisal principle that the value of a lesser-quality property is favorably affected by the presence of a better-quality property.

progressive tax A tax that takes an increasing proportion of income as income rises.

promissory note A financing instrument that states the terms of the underlying obligation, is signed by its maker, and is negotiable (transferable to a third party).

prosperity In the business cycle, the ideal state of a healthy economy: high employment, productivity, and income combining to create a general sense of stability.

public utility An industry supplying basic public services to the market and possibly enjoying monopoly power. Usually, electricity, gas, telephones, postal services, water supply, and rail, and often other forms of transport, are regarded as public utilities. These services all require specialized capital equipment and elaborate organization.

purchase money mortgage (PMM) A note secured by a mortgage or deed of trust given by a buyer, as borrower, to a seller, as lender, as part of the purchase price of the real estate.

pyramiding The process of acquiring additional property by refinancing property already owned and investing the loan proceeds in additional properties.

quantitative easing A monetary policy whereby the U.S. Central Bank of the United States directly influences the economy by increasing the amount of cash in circulation in order to stimulate the economy. This is done by purchasing securities and lowering interest rates significantly where traditional methods employed by the Fed are ineffective.

quantity-survey method The appraisal method of estimating building costs by calculating the cost of all the physical components in the improvements, adding the cost to assemble them, and then including the indirect costs associated with such construction.

quantity theory of money The theory that changes in the money supply have a direct influence on prices and nothing else. The theory is derived from the identity $MV = PT$ (called the Fisher equation), where M is the stock of money; V is the velocity with which the money circulates (velocity of circulation); P is the average price level; and T is the number of transactions.

quasi-money Near money.

quit rate Measures the percentage of individuals who leave or "quit" their employment each year. This statistic is utilized to determine if individuals are content with their employment, including compensation and benefits received. A high quit rate indicates individuals are discontent with their employment; a lower quit rate, on the other hand, indicates contentedness.

radon A naturally occurring gas that is suspected of causing lung cancer.

rate cap The limit on the amount the interest rate can be increased at each adjustment period in an adjustable rate loan. The cap may also set the maximum interest rate that can be charged during the life of the loan.

rate of interest The proportion of a sum of money that is paid over a specified period of time in payments for its loan. It is the price a borrower has to pay to enjoy the use of cash she does not own, and the return a lender enjoys for deferring her consumption or parting with liquidity. The rate of interest is a price that can be analyzed in the normal framework of demand and supply analysis.

rate of return Usually, net profit after depreciation as a percentage of average capital employed in a business. The rate of return may be calculated using profit before or after tax, and there are a number of other variations of the concept.

real estate Land; a portion of the earth's surface extending downward to the center of the earth and upward infinitely into space, including all things permanently attached to it, whether naturally or artificially.

Real Estate Investment Trust (REIT) Trust ownership of real estate by a group of individuals who purchase certificates of ownership in the trust, which in turn invests the money in real property and distributes the profits back to the investors free of corporate income tax.

real estate market Consists of properties for sale and buyers in search of properties. The market is most often local, but modern information systems facilitate national offerings and searching, and the market for very expensive properties is often international.

Real Estate Mortgage Investment Conduit (REMIC) A tax entity that issues multiple classes of investor interests (securities) backed by a pool of mortgages.

Real Estate Settlement Procedures Act (RESPA) The federal law that requires certain disclosures to consumers about mortgage loan settlements. The law also prohibits the payment or receipt of kickbacks and certain kinds of referral fees.

real property Land, things fixed to the land (e.g., buildings, roads, walls, natural and planted vegetation), and appurtenances including incidental rights such as easements. The interests, benefits, and rights inherent in the ownership of real estate.

recession At least two successive quarters of economic contraction.

reclamation Any method for bringing waste natural resources into productive use.

reconciliation The final step in the appraisal process, in which the appraiser considers the estimates of value received from the sales comparison, cost, and income approaches to arrive at a final opinion of market value for the subject property.

recovery In the business cycle, the process of an economy recovering from a depression.

redevelopment Rehabilitation of a blighted area, such as clearing slum housing and erecting new buildings.

redlining The illegal practice by a lending institution of denying loans or restricting their number for certain areas of a community.

regional analysis Examination of a region's population and economy.

regression An appraisal principle that the value of a better-quality property is affected adversely by the presence of a lesser-quality property.

Regulation Z Implements the Truth in Lending Act, requiring credit institutions to inform borrowers of the true cost of obtaining credit.

rehabilitation Restoration to a former or improved condition.

rent control Ordinances that limit the amount of rent a lessor may charge.

replacement cost The construction cost at current prices of a property that is not necessarily an exact duplicate of the subject property but serves the same purpose or function as the original.

reproduction cost The construction cost at current prices of an exact duplicate of the subject property.

reserve funds Monies a lender requires a borrower to set aside as a cushion for future payment of various items.

reserve requirements Percentage of deposits the Federal Reserve requires member banks to set aside as a safety measure.

resource allocation The assignment of a role to scarce resources (factors of production) in the economy to the production of outputs. The fact of scarcity leads to the need for allocation.

resources Scarce inputs that can yield utility through production or provision of goods and services (depletion theory, factors of production, natural resources, production function, resource allocation).

restrictive covenant A clause in a deed that limits the way the real estate ownership may be used.

return on investment Net annual income divided by cash investment equals a percentage of return on investment.

reverse annuity mortgage (RAM) A loan under which the homeowner receives monthly payments based on her accumulated equity rather than a lump sum. The loan must be repaid at a prearranged date or upon the death of the owner or the sale of the property.

risk assessment A measure of the risks of a course of action and the costs and benefits of reducing those risks. Risk assessment has been promoted as a means of preventing economic activity that creates more dangers than are reasonable.

sales comparison approach The process of estimating the value of a property by examining and comparing sales and listings of comparable properties.

sales tax A tax levied as a proportion of the retail price of a commodity at the point of sale.

sample The study of a few members of a population for the purpose of identifying attributes applicable to the population as a whole.

saturation point A level beyond which the relative absorption of a product or service is not expected to increase. It is defined in terms of a ratio (e.g., ownership of videos per household or per hundred persons). Once the saturation point is reached, the growth of demand slows down to levels determined by population growth and replacement, although in some cases, predictions of saturation points have been falsified by the emergence of multiple ownership (e.g., cars and television sets).

savings bank A bank that accepts interest-bearing deposits of small amounts. The earliest savings banks were established in the private sector but later were set up or supported by governments to encourage individual savings. In the United States, savings banks are also called thrift institutions or savings and loans (S&L) associations, many of which are mutual companies.

scarcity A situation in which the needs and wants of an individual or group of individuals exceed the resources available to satisfy them.

seasonal adjustment The elimination from a time series of fluctuations that exhibit regular patterns at a particular time during the course of a year that are similar from one year to another. For instance, unemployment rises in the winter months because of the interruption of work by winter weather conditions.

secondary mortgage market A market for the purchase and sale of existing mortgages, designed to provide greater liquidity for mortgages. Mortgages are first originated in the *primary mortgage market.*

sector Specialized area of economic activity, as the agricultural sector, manufacturing sector, or trade sector.

securities (1) In the widest sense, documents giving title to property or claims on income that may be lodged (e.g., as security for a bank loan). (2) Income yielding and other paper traded on the stock exchange or in secondary markets. Usually a synonym for stocks and shares.

self-employed Working on her own account.

seigniorage The difference between the cost of minting coins and a coin's face value.

service-producing sector A major category of employment that includes wholesale and retail trade, services, transportation, real estate, finance, and insurance. In the terminology of agencies that collect and report data on employment, "services" is a subcategory of service-producing.

services Activities perceived to have monetary or exchange value, such as legal advice, health care, repair work, entertainment, transportation, and business services.

Sherman Antitrust Act Federal law that makes it illegal for competitors to agree that they will all charge the same fees for products and services.

shopping center A group of buildings or spaces leased to commercial establishments, planned, developed, owned, and managed as an operating unit.

site Land improved to the extent that it is ready to be used for a specific, planned purpose.

site analysis An evaluation of the site itself, including zoning, title, CC&Rs (conditions, covenants, and restrictions), soil analysis, and utilities.

small business A firm managed in a personalized way by its owners or part owners that has only a small share of its market and is not sufficiently large to have access to the stock exchange in raising capital.

Smith, Adam Author of *The Wealth of Nations* (1776). Written as a reaction against mercantilism, Smith's book marks the foundation of modern capitalist theory.

social benefits The total increase in the welfare of society from an economic action. In effect, it is the sum of two benefits: (1) the benefit to the agent performing the action (e.g., the producer's surplus or profit made) and (2) the benefit accruing to society as a result of the action (e.g., an increase in tax revenues—externalities). The phrase is sometimes used to describe the second of these on its own. Social welfare.

socialism Economic system under which the ownership, management, and control of the means of production and distribution are held by the community; a command economy.

socially defined needs Those things not biologically necessary but deemed necessary for adequate life by a particular group or society.

special assessment A tax or levy customarily imposed against only those specific parcels of real estate that will benefit from a proposed public improvement like a street or sewer.

special purpose Property that has only one highest and best use because of the special design of the land and improvements.

specialization Concentration on a particular sphere of activities. Not the same as division of labor, which involves splitting a process into very small steps and assigning individual workers to each step. A specialist goes beyond general knowledge with special knowledge and skills. Typically, the specialist is highly skilled and highly paid, while the divided-task worker is low skilled and low paid.

specie A form of money; minted metal coinage.

speculation Buying and selling with a view to buying and selling at a profit later when prices have changed.

square-foot cost The cost of one square foot of an improvement.

square-foot method The appraisal method of estimating building costs by multiplying the number of square feet in the improvement being appraised by the cost per square foot for recently constructed similar improvements.

stagflation The simultaneous existence of unemployment and inflation.

standard of living A society's definition of the resources and facilities required to provide minimally acceptable material comfort and well-being.

static equilibrium Equilibrium in which the relevant variables do not change over time (in contrast to dynamic equilibrium in which the variables change over time). Balanced growth.

steady-state growth In growth theory, a dynamic condition of an economy where all real variables are growing at a constant proportional rate.

steering The illegal practice of channeling home seekers to particular areas based on their race, national origin, religion, or other protected classification.

stock broker A member of the stock exchange who buys and sells shares on his own account, or for nonmembers, in return for a commission on the price of the shares. Broker, market maker.

stock exchange A market in which securities are bought and sold.

straight-line method A method of calculating depreciation for tax purposes, computed by dividing the adjusted basis of a property by the estimated number of years of remaining useful life.

straight loan A loan in which only interest is paid during the term of the loan, with the entire principal amount due with the final interest payment.

subdivider One who buys undeveloped land, divides it into smaller, usable lots and sells the lots to potential users.

subdivision A tract of land divided by the owner, known as the *subdivider*, into blocks, building lots, and streets according to a recorded subdivision plat, which must comply with local ordinances and regulations.

subsidy Government grants to suppliers of goods and services. A subsidy may be intended to keep prices down (i.e., to raise real income of buyers), to maintain incomes of producers (e.g., farmers), or to maintain a service or employment.

substitution An appraisal principle that the maximum value of a property tends to be set by the cost of purchasing an equally desirable and valuable substitute property, assuming that no costly delay is encountered in making the substitution.

Superfund Popular name of the hazardous-waste cleanup fund established by the Comprehensive Environmental Response, Compensation, and Liability Act (CERCLA).

supply The amount of goods available for sale in the market. The term is often coupled with *demand*.

supply curve A graphical representation of the quantity of a good or service supplied at different price levels. With price on the vertical axis and quantity supplied on the horizontal axis, supply curves normally slope upwards for two reasons: (1) higher prices allow profits to be made at higher levels of production for firms already in the market and (2) if profits are made, new entrants are attracted into a market.

supply and demand The appraisal principle that follows the interrelationship of the supply of and demand for real estate. Because appraising is based on economic concepts, this principle recognizes that real property is subject to the influences of the marketplace as with any other commodity.

supply-side theory Focuses on how government can encourage supply to fight inflation. The favored tool is the tax cut. The theory holds that low taxes stimulate production, supply outruns demand, and the excess supply dampens inflationary pressures. The high level of business activity stimulated by tax cuts results in a higher national income, which, in turn, provides additional tax revenues to the government. Contrasts with the Keynesian emphasis on stimulation of demand to reenergize a weak, high-unemployment economy.

syndicate A combination of people or firms formed to accomplish a business venture of mutual interest by pooling resources. In a *real estate investment syndicate*, the parties own and/or develop property, with the main profit generally arising from the sale of the property.

taking The act of a government body seizing privately owned property for a public purpose through its police power. The owner is entitled to just compensation for the property seized. The term derives from the Fifth Amendment to the U.S. Constitution: "nor shall private property be taken for public use, without just compensation."

takeover The acquisition of one company by another. Takeovers are sometimes financed by paying cash at an offer price in excess of the market price of the shares, but, more frequently for large acquisitions, by the exchange of shares or loan stock, possibly with some cash adjustment, issued by the acquiring company for the shares of the acquired company. The term *takeover* is normally used to imply that the acquisition is made on the initiative of the acquirer and often without the full agreement of the acquired company; distinct from a merger.

TARP Troubled Asset Relief Program

tax A compulsory payment of a percentage of income, property value, or sales price for the support of services provided by a government.

taxation The process by which a government body raises monies to fund its operation.

tax avoidance Arranging one's financial affairs within the law to minimize taxation liabilities, as opposed to tax evasion, which is failing to meet actual tax liabilities through (e.g., not declaring income or profit).

tax base The quantity or coverage of what is taxed. The tax base for income tax is the assessed incomes of the whole population. The tax base for value-added tax does not include sales of most foods, books, and financial services.

technology The sum of knowledge of the means and methods of producing goods and services. Technology is not merely applied science because it often runs ahead of science—things are often done without precise knowledge of how or why they are done, except that they are effective.

tenant improvements Alterations to the interior of a building to meet the functional demands of the tenant. Also known as *build-outs*.

term loan A bank advance for a specific period (normally three to ten years) repaid, with interest, usually by regular periodic payments. Term loans are common practice in the U.S. commercial banking system for business finance and, for larger borrowing, the loan may be syndicated (i.e., the provision of funds and the interest earned are shared between several banks).

third world A synonym for developing countries.

tight money A market condition in which loan funds are scarce and interest rates and discount points are high.

time deposit Money in a (U.S.) bank account for which the bank may require notice of withdrawal, usually of up three months.

topography Nature of the surface of the land.

trade barrier A general term covering any government limitation on the free international exchange of merchandise. These barriers may take the form of, for instance, tariffs, quotas, import deposits, restrictions on the issue of import licenses, or stringent regulations relating to health or safety standards.

trade gap The excess of the value of imports of goods and services over the value of exports of goods and services.

transfer payments Grants or other payments not made in return for a productive service (e.g., pensions), unemployment benefits (jobseeker's allowance), and other forms of income support, including charitable donations by companies. Transfer payments are a form of income redistribution, not a return to the factors of production.

transferability One of the four essential elements of value. A commodity must be transferable as to use or title in order to be marketable.

Treasury, U.S. Department of In the United States, the government department that administers most revenue collections, the manufacture of coin and currency, and some law enforcement. It is involved in estimating revenue and monitoring changes in the tax system.

Treasury bill Instruments for short-term borrowing by the government.

trend Changes that have a long-term, consistent direction. In appraisal, a series of related changes brought about by a chain of causes and effects.

trough The bottom segment of the business cycle curve.

Truth in Lending Act (TILA) Federal government regulates the lending practices of mortgage lenders through this act.

unavoidable costs Opportunity costs that have to be borne, even if no output is produced.

uncertainty The state in which the number of possible outcomes exceeds the number of actual outcomes, and when no probabilities can be attached to each possible outcome. It differs from risk, which is defined as having measurable probabilities.

underground economy Unofficial market in which individuals trade goods and services while avoiding income taxation or as a means of using barter to obtain goods and services not otherwise affordable.

unearned increment The business of insuring against risk. An underwriter, in return for a commission or premium, agrees to bear a risk or a proportion of a risk.

underwriting An increase in the value of property, not anticipated by the owner, due primarily to the operation of social forces, such as an increase in population.

unemployment The existence of a section of the labor force able and willing to work but unable to find gainful employment. Unemployment is measured as the percentage of the total labor force out of work.

unit-in-place method The appraisal method of estimating building costs by calculating the costs of all of the physical components in the structure, with the cost of each item including its proper installation or connection.

upper turning point The point on the business cycle curve at which contraction of the economy begins.

USPAP *Uniform Standards of Professional Appraisal Practice.*

utility The ability of a product to create desire in consumers. One of the four essential elements of value.

VA-guaranteed loan A mortgage loan on approved property made to a qualified veteran by an authorized lender and guaranteed by the U.S. Department of Veterans Affairs in order to limit the lender's possible loss.

valuation The act or process of assigning value; an appraisal.

value The power of a good or service to command other goods in exchange for the present worth of future rights to its income or amenities.

variable The number that may take different values in different situations. For instance, quantity of a good demanded will vary according to its price.

variance (1) In economic terms, it is a measure of the degree of dispersion of a series of numbers around their mean (average). The larger the variance, the greater the spread of the series around its mean. (2) Relative to land use, a variance is a deviation from an established development standard, usually specified in the zoning ordinance; an exception granted to a property owner, relieving her from obeying certain aspects of a zoning ordinance. Its granting is discretionary with the zoning authorities and is based on undue hardship suffered by the property owner because of unique circumstances affecting the property, such as size, shape, and topography.

venture capital Medium long-term funds invested in enterprises particularly subject to risk, as in new ventures.

Wall Street New York Stock Exchange.

wants People are taught to want many of the goods and services they purchase. Wants are socially defined. These wanted goods and services may be viewed either as intrinsically desirable or as effective means to an end.

warrants Securities giving the holder a right to a share or a bond at a given price and from a certain date. Warrants, which are commonly issued "free" alongside the shares of new investment trusts when launched, and carry no income or other rights to equity, immediately trade separately on the stock exchange but at a price lower than the associated share or bond.

wealth Anything valued by more than one person and "in hand" (controlled by humans). Anything potentially subject to exchange. Something that is perceived by others as having value.

weighted average An average in which each item in the series being averaged is multiplied by a "weight'" relevant to its importance, the result summed, and the total divided by the sum of the weights.

welfare economies The study of the social desirability of alternative arrangements of economic activities and allocations of resources. It is, in effect, the analysis of the optimal behavior of individual consumers at the level of society as a whole.

wholesale banking The making of loans or acceptance of deposits on a large scale between banks and other financial institutions, especially in the interbank market. As distinct from retail banking, a term for the business of the commercial banks carried out with customers of their branches.

wholesale markets Generally a market in which goods or services are bought and sold on a large scale among professionals. The financial wholesale markets ("the financial markets") include the money market, the foreign-exchange market, and the stock exchange.

Williamson Act A procedure authorized by California state law to preserve agricultural lands.

withholding tax Taxation deducted from payments to nonresidents. Withholding taxes are usually in the form of a standard rate of income tax applied to dividends or other payments by companies and are often reclaimable against tax liabilities in the country of residence of the recipient under a double-taxation agreement.

working capital That part of current assets financed from long-term funds.

World Trade Organization (WTO) The World Trade Organization was set up in Geneva in 1995. The WTO is charged with the further development of and the policing of the multilateral trading system along the principles followed by the eight rounds of trade negotiations concluded under its predecessor. It provides the resources and the legal status for the resolution of trade disputes through independent dispute panels.

wraparound loan A method of refinancing in which the new mortgage is placed in a secondary, or subordinate, position; the new mortgage includes both the unpaid principal balance of the first mortgage and whatever additional sums are advanced by the lender. In essence, it is an additional mortgage in which another lender refinances a borrower by lending an amount over the existing first mortgage amount without disturbing the existence of the first mortgage.

yield The ratio of annual net income from the property to its cost. The ratio of the annual interest and dividends from an investment to its cost.

yield curve A graphical representation of the relationship between the annual return on an asset and the number of years the asset has before expiring.

zoning A regulatory tool that helps communities regulate and control how land is used.

zoning ordinance An exercise of police power by a municipality to regulate and control the character and use of property.

ANSWERS TO UNIT
QUIZ QUESTIONS

Unit 1
1. b   (2)
2. d   (4)
3. c   (8)
4. b   (8)
5. a   (17)
6. c   (14)
7. d   (9)
8. b   (15)
9. d   (16)
10. c   (17)

Unit 2
1. d   (21)
2. a   (22)
3. b   (22)
4. d   (26)
5. c   (29)
6. b   (30)
7. d   (30)
8. b   (31)
9. b   (33)
10. a   (37)

Unit 3
1. c   (42)
2. c   (43)
3. b   (46)
4. d   (45)
5. d   (46)
6. a   (50)

7. b   (54)
8. a   (67)
9. a   (65)
10. b   (72)

Unit 4
1. d   (81)
2. c   (84)
3. c   (84–85)
4. d   (86)
5. b   (87)
6. a   (90)
7. b   (91)
8. d   (95)
9. a   (96)
10. b   (98–99)

Unit 5
1. c   (108)
2. d   (114)
3. c   (109)
4. d   (110)
5. b   (112)
6. d   (117)
7. b   (121)
8. a   (117)
9. c   (117)
10. c   (114)

Unit 6
1. b   (142)
2. a   (146)
3. c   (133)
4. d   (134)
5. d   (135)
6. a   (137)
7. b   (138)
8. a   (139)
9. a   (143)
10. b   (144)

Unit 7
1. c   (156)
2. a   (169)
3. a   (157)
4. d   (169)
5. a   (173)
6. c   (164)
7. b   (165)
8. c   (171–172)
9. b   (166)
10. d   (174)

Unit 8

1. b (185)
2. c (198)
3. a (183)
4. a (194)
5. d (183–184)
6. c (186)
7. c (200)
8. b (194)
9. c (196)
10. a (207)

Unit 9

1. b (220)
2. d (221)
3. b (225)
4. a (227)
5. a (228)
6. d (225, 229–230, 233)
7. d (234)
8. c (234)
9. b (239)
10. b (243)

Unit 10

1. c (250)
2. d (256–257)
3. d (251)
4. b (253)
5. a (254)
6. d (261)
7. c (265)
8. d (265)
9. c (266)
10. b (265)

Unit 11

1. d (285–286)
2. c (286)
3. b (287)

4. d (287–288)
5. a (291)
6. b (293)
7. c (295)
8. c (296–297)
9. d (303–304)
10. c (311–312)

Unit 12

1. a (327)
2. b (328)
3. d (330)
4. c (331)
5. c (332)
6. c (332)
7. d (334)
8. b (334)
9. c (335)
10. b (335)

Unit 13

1. b (344)
2. c (345)
3. c (349–350)
4. b (350)
5. c (350)
6. c (352)
7. d (352)
8. b (353)
9. d (356)
10. d (358–359)

Unit 14

1. d (368–369)
2. d (369–370)
3. c (372–373)
4. d (376)
5. b (376)
6. d (377)
7. c (378)

8. a (379)
9. c (379–380)
10. b (380)

Unit 15

1. c (387)
2. c (387)
3. b (388)
4. d (389)
5. d (388–389)
6. b (391)
7. b (391–392)
8. b (392)
9. b (394)
10. d (390–392)

Unit 16

1. b (413)
2. a (413)
3. c (437)
4. a (448)
5. c (443)
6. c (420)
7. d (416)
8. b (425)
9. b (413–414)
10. b (436)

Unit 17

1. a (458)
2. d (457)
3. b (456)
4. a (458)
5. a (463)
6. b (459)
7. b (469–470)
8. d (469–470)
9. b (471)
10. a (473)

INDEX

Notes